Modern Critical Views

Chinua Achebe
Henry Adams
Aeschylus
S. Y. Agnon
Edward Albee
Raphael Alberti
Louisa May Alcott
A. R. Ammons
Sherwood Anderson
Aristophanes
Matthew Arnold
Antonin Artaud
John Ashbery
Margaret Atwood
W. H. Auden
Jane Austen
Isaac Babel
Sir Francis Bacon
James Baldwin
Honoré de Balzac
John Barth
Donald Barthelme
Charles Baudelaire
Simone de Beauvoir
Samuel Beckett
Saul Bellow
Thomas Berger
John Berryman
The Bible
Elizabeth Bishop
William Blake
Giovanni Boccaccio
Heinrich Böll
Jorge Luis Borges
Elizabeth Bowen
Bertolt Brecht
The Brontës
Charles Brockden Brown
Sterling Brown
Robert Browning
Martin Buber
John Bunyan
Anthony Burgess
Kenneth Burke
Robert Burns
William Burroughs
George Gordon, Lord
  Byron
Pedro Calderón de la Barca
Italo Calvino
Albert Camus
Canadian Poetry: Modern
  and Contemporary
Canadian Poetry through
  E. J. Pratt
Thomas Carlyle
Alejo Carpentier
Lewis Carroll
Willa Cather
Louis-Ferdinand Céline
Miguel de Cervantes

Geoffrey Chaucer
John Cheever
Anton Chekhov
Kate Chopin
Chrétien de Troyes
Agatha Christie
Samuel Taylor Coleridge
Colette
William Congreve & the
  Restoration Dramatists
Joseph Conrad
Contemporary Poets
James Fenimore Cooper
Pierre Corneille
Julio Cortázar
Hart Crane
Stephen Crane
e. e. cummings
Dante
Robertson Davies
Daniel Defoe
Philip K. Dick
Charles Dickens
James Dickey
Emily Dickinson
Denis Diderot
Isak Dinesen
E. L. Doctorow
John Donne & the
  Seventeenth-Century
  Metaphysical Poets
John Dos Passos
Fyodor Dostoevsky
Frederick Douglass
Theodore Dreiser
John Dryden
W. E. B. Du Bois
Lawrence Durrell
George Eliot
T. S. Eliot
Elizabethan Dramatists
Ralph Ellison
Ralph Waldo Emerson
Euripides
William Faulkner
Henry Fielding
F. Scott Fitzgerald
Gustave Flaubert
E. M. Forster
John Fowles
Sigmund Freud
Robert Frost
Northrop Frye
Carlos Fuentes
William Gaddis
Federico García Lorca
Gabriel García Márquez
André Gide
W. S. Gilbert
Allen Ginsberg
J. W. von Goethe

Nikolai Gogol
William Golding
Oliver Goldsmith
Mary Gordon
Günther Grass
Robert Graves
Graham Greene
Thomas Hardy
Nathaniel Hawthorne
William Hazlitt
H. D.
Seamus Heaney
Lillian Hellman
Ernest Hemingway
Hermann Hesse
Geoffrey Hill
Friedrich Hölderlin
Homer
A. D. Hope
Gerard Manley Hopkins
Horace
A. E. Housman
William Dean Howells
Langston Hughes
Ted Hughes
Victor Hugo
Zora Neale Hurston
Aldous Huxley
Henrik Ibsen
Eugène Ionesco
Washington Irving
Henry James
Dr. Samuel Johnson and
  James Boswell
Ben Jonson
James Joyce
Carl Gustav Jung
Franz Kafka
Yasonari Kawabata
John Keats
Søren Kierkegaard
Rudyard Kipling
Melanie Klein
Heinrich von Kleist
Philip Larkin
D. H. Lawrence
John le Carré
Ursula K. Le Guin
Giacomo Leopardi
Doris Lessing
Sinclair Lewis
Jack London
Robert Lowell
Malcolm Lowry
Carson McCullers
Norman Mailer
Bernard Malamud
Stéphane Mallarmé
Sir Thomas Malory
André Malraux
Thomas Mann

Modern Critical Views

Katherine Mansfield
Christopher Marlowe
Andrew Marvell
Herman Melville
George Meredith
James Merrill
John Stuart Mill
Arthur Miller
Henry Miller
John Milton
Yukio Mishima
Molière
Michel de Montaigne
Eugenio Montale
Marianne Moore
Alberto Moravia
Toni Morrison
Alice Munro
Iris Murdoch
Robert Musil
Vladimir Nabokov
V. S. Naipaul
R. K. Narayan
Pablo Neruda
John Henry Newman
Friedrich Nietzsche
Frank Norris
Joyce Carol Oates
Sean O'Casey
Flannery O'Connor
Christopher Okigbo
Charles Olson
Eugene O'Neill
José Ortega y Gasset
Joe Orton
George Orwell
Ovid
Wilfred Owen
Amos Oz
Cynthia Ozick
Grace Paley
Blaise Pascal
Walter Pater
Octavio Paz
Walker Percy
Petrarch
Pindar
Harold Pinter
Luigi Pirandello
Sylvia Plath
Plato

Plautus
Edgar Allan Poe
Poets of Sensibility & the
    Sublime
Poets of the Nineties
Alexander Pope
Katherine Anne Porter
Ezra Pound
Anthony Powell
Pre-Raphaelite Poets
Marcel Proust
Manuel Puig
Alexander Pushkin
Thomas Pynchon
Francisco de Quevedo
François Rabelais
Jean Racine
Ishmael Reed
Adrienne Rich
Samuel Richardson
Mordecai Richler
Rainer Maria Rilke
Arthur Rimbaud
Edwin Arlington Robinson
Theodore Roethke
Philip Roth
Jean-Jacques Rousseau
John Ruskin
J. D. Salinger
Jean-Paul Sartre
Gershom Scholem
Sir Walter Scott
William Shakespeare
    Histories & Poems
    Comedies & Romances
    Tragedies
George Bernard Shaw
Mary Wollstonecraft
    Shelley
Percy Bysshe Shelley
Sam Shepard
Richard Brinsley Sheridan
Sir Philip Sidney
Isaac Bashevis Singer
Tobias Smollett
Alexander Solzhenitsyn
Sophocles
Wole Soyinka
Edmund Spenser
Gertrude Stein
John Steinbeck

Stendhal
Laurence Sterne
Wallace Stevens
Robert Louis Stevenson
Tom Stoppard
August Strindberg
Jonathan Swift
John Millington Synge
Alfred, Lord Tennyson
William Makepeace Thackeray
Dylan Thomas
Henry David Thoreau
James Thurber and S. J.
    Perelman
J. R. R. Tolkien
Leo Tolstoy
Jean Toomer
Lionel Trilling
Anthony Trollope
Ivan Turgenev
Mark Twain
Miguel de Unamuno
John Updike
Paul Valéry
Cesar Vallejo
Lope de Vega
Gore Vidal
Virgil
Voltaire
Kurt Vonnegut
Derek Walcott
Alice Walker
Robert Penn Warren
Evelyn Waugh
H. G. Wells
Eudora Welty
Nathanael West
Edith Wharton
Patrick White
Walt Whitman
Oscar Wilde
Tennessee Williams
William Carlos Williams
Thomas Wolfe
Virginia Woolf
William Wordsworth
Jay Wright
Richard Wright
William Butler Yeats
A. B. Yehoshua
Emile Zola

Modern Critical Views

CONTEMPORARY POETS

Edited and with an introduction by
Harold Bloom
Sterling Professor of the Humanities
Yale University

CHELSEA HOUSE PUBLISHERS
New York ◊ Philadelphia

Copyright © 1986 by Chelsea House Publishers, a division of
Main Line Book Co.

Printed and bound in the United States of America

10   9   8   7   6

∞ The paper used in this publication meets the minimum
requirements of the American National Standard for Permanence
of Paper for Printed Library Materials, Z39.48–1984.

Library of Congress Cataloging-in-Publication Data
Contemporary poets.
    (Modern critical views)
    Includes bibliographies and index.
    Summary: Critical essays on the works of twenty-eight
modern American poets.
    1. American poetry—20th century—History and criticism.
[1. American poetry—20th century—History and
criticism] I. Bloom, Harold. II. Series.
PS325.C66 1986   811'.5'09   86–8306
ISBN 0–87754–709–2

Contents

Editor's Note   ix

Introduction   1
    Harold Bloom and David Bromwich

ROBERT PENN WARREN
Modes and Ranges of a Long Dawn   9
    John Hollander

ROBERT FITZGERALD
The Poetry of Robert Fitzgerald   19
    Harold Bloom

ELIZABETH BISHOP
Elizabeth Bishop's Dream-Houses   27
    David Bromwich

GWENDOLYN BROOKS
A Street in Bronzeville, The Harlem Renaissance
and the Mythologies of Black Women   43
    Gary Smith

ROBERT DUNCAN
A Memoir and a Critical Tribute   57
    Denise Levertov

MAY SWENSON
"Turned Back to the Wild by Love"   85
    Richard Howard

RICHARD WILBUR
Richard Wilbur's World   103
    Robert B. Shaw

ANTHONY HECHT
The Poetry of Anthony Hecht   113
    Ashley Brown

JAMES DICKEY
From "The Other" through *The Early Motion*   127
    Harold Bloom

DENISE LEVERTOV
Inside and Outside in the Poetry
of Denise Levertov   143
    Diana Collecott

KENNETH KOCH
Kenneth Koch   157
    John Hollander

A. R. AMMONS
"When You Consider the Radiance"   165
    Harold Bloom

JAMES MERRILL
Lost Paradises   199
    J. D. McClatchy

ALLEN GINSBERG
Bound Each to Each   213
    Diane Middlebrook

GALWAY KINNELL
"The Rank Flavor of Blood"   221
    Charles Molesworth

JOHN ASHBERY
A Magma of Interiors   235
    Alfred Corn

W. S. MERWIN
The New Transcendentalism: The Visionary
Strain in Merwin   245
    Harold Bloom

JAMES WRIGHT
"The Body Wakes to Burial"   251
    Richard Howard

IRVING FELDMAN
"Who Will Call These Things His Own?"   269
  Richard Howard

ADRIENNE RICH
Ghostlier Demarcations, Keener Sounds   281
  Helen Vendler

ROBERT PACK
Robert Pack   309
  Paul Mariani

JOHN HOLLANDER
The Sound and Sense of the Sleight-of-Hand Man   327
  David Lehman

ALVIN FEINMAN
Preambles to What Was Possible   347
  Harold Bloom

GARY SNYDER
The Work of Gary Snyder   357
  Crunk

MARK STRAND
Negative Capability   371
  Linda Gregerson

AMIRI BARAKA
The Changing Same: Black Music in the Poetry
of Amiri Baraka   395
  Nate Mackey

JAY WRIGHT
"The Aching Prodigal": Jay Wright's
Dutiful Poet   411
  Robert B. Stepto

DARYL HINE
Fabulous Traveler   421
  John Hollander

Biographical Notes   433

Contributors   449

Bibliography   451

Acknowledgments   467

Index   471

Editor's Note

Contemporary American poetry, in this book, is taken to extend from the work of our greatest living poet, Robert Penn Warren, through the achievement of the poets of my own generation. Some of the poets studied in this volume are now lost to us: Elizabeth Bishop, Robert Fitzgerald, James Wright, but they are still very much part of the poetry of the contemporary scene, as Robert Lowell, John Berryman, Randall Jarrell perhaps no longer are.

I would not be prepared to assert that all of the twenty-five living poets examined here are likely to prove canonical. But Ashbery, Ammons, and Merrill are of the eminence of Warren and Bishop, and there are books, sequences, and separate poems by several of the others that should be permanent also. I do not believe that canonization is an arbitrary process, and I am aware that many readers will regret some of the prominent omissions from this volume. But the same readers are unlikely to welcome the presence both of Daryl Hine and of Gary Snyder. Admirers of Robert Duncan and of Anthony Hecht tend to be separate individuals. I myself am not much moved by the work of Allen Ginsberg, or of Amiri Baraka, or of the recent phase of Adrienne Rich, but they all have their informed admirers. With some poets, such as Dorn and Creeley, the right critical essays just did not seem to suggest themselves. Finally, there are poets only recently come to prominence, like Amy Clampitt, Vicki Hearne, Douglas Crase, and Alfred Corn, where there has been little time as yet for critical reception to mature.

The essayists, like the poets, are not necessarily inevitable choices, but all of them know the extreme difficulties that are involved when contemporary poetry is analyzed. I am aware that eleven of these twenty-eight essays are by Richard Howard, John Hollander, and myself, but I did not set out to achieve such a result. Howard on Swenson, James Wright, and Feldman; Hollander on Warren, Koch, and Hine; Bloom on Fitzgerald, Dickey, Ammons, Merwin, and Feinman, seemed the most appropriate I could find, particularly in regard to considerations that balanced length and range.

That there is some diminishment in the course of American poetry since the death of Wallace Stevens in 1955 is a sadness, but the arts, as Hazlitt observed, are not progressive. Warren and Bishop, Ashbery and Merrill, are not of the eminence of their precursors, Eliot and Stevens, Frost and Hart Crane, but then Stevens and Frost, in the longest perspective, are shadowed by Whitman and Dickinson, the greatest of our poets. I have been accused by some of being a contemporary Thomas Love Peacock, writing another version of *The Four Ages of Poetry*. But, like Peacock himself, we come after Wordsworth, and to follow the only authentic inventor of a modernist poetry is necessarily to be haunted by a permanent sense of belatedness. Wordsworth, in relation to the European tradition from Homer through Goethe, was a true original. No one since Wordsworth, in any language, has been able to achieve such discontinuity again. Himself shadowed by Shakespeare and Milton, Wordsworth nevertheless triumphantly made it new. In comparison, Pound and Eliot stand under the mingled long shadows of Browning and Whitman, and Tennyson and Whitman, respectively. As the discoverer of a poetry that had no subject but subjectivity, Wordsworth permanently both saved and ruined poetry.

But originality itself becomes different after Wordsworth, and so remains different in the Age of Ashbery. It is fascinating though sad to see Ashbery omitting from his recent *Selected Poems* so many of the poems one loves best: "Evening in the Country," "Fragment," "The One Thing That Can Save America" among them. Evidently he does not regard them as original enough, or perhaps they are exquisitely painful to him. But, together with "Soonest Mended" and "Wet Casements" and "Tapestry" and perhaps a dozen more, they remain his best poems and will not be discarded by anyone except himself. Poets and critics alike seem compelled to regard literary survival as ever more problematical, and the shadows are longest in the evening-land that is America.

Whitman and Dickinson had Emerson, the Bible, and the British High Romantics as both hindrances and resources, but only Emerson was American, and his essays were far superior to his poems. After Whitman and Dickinson, Frost and Stevens, Eliot and Pound, W. C. Williams and Hart Crane, the American tradition in poetry becomes so strong as both to inspire and inhibit fresh creation.

This volume opens with an introduction written by the editor in collaboration with David Bromwich. It is reprinted here as a guide to American poetic schools and techniques, as relevant now as it was in 1974.

Essays on the individual poets are arranged here according to the age of the poets, starting with Robert Penn Warren. John Hollander offers an appreciation of Warren's poetry, setting it in the broad contexts of poetic form, upon which Hollander is an acknowledged authority. My own appreciation of the work of the late Robert Fitzgerald sets that superb classical poet in the line of Virgil and of Landor. The late Elizabeth Bishop is analyzed by David Bromwich in terms of her "dream-houses," remarkable and ramshackle structures that are metaphors for her poems themselves.

Gwendolyn Brooks, the foremost living black woman poet, is discussed by Gary Smith in the double context of the Harlem Renaissance and of male myths about black women. Denise Levertov, in a tribute to Robert Duncan, both frees him from false myths and restores the poet to his own mythic concerns. A neglected and highly original writer, May Swenson is acutely surveyed by Richard Howard. Then two distinguished poets of high civilization, Richard Wilbur and Anthony Hecht, are sketched in the large by Robert B. Shaw and Ashley Brown, respectively.

My essay on the demonic bard James Dickey considers only what he himself calls his "early motion," culminating in the volume *Helmets*. Denise Levertov returns, this time as the subject of Diana Collecott's meditation on dualism and its healing in Levertov's work. John Hollander then makes a reentry with his exuberant appreciation of Kenneth Koch, the most exuberant of all contemporary poets.

I have chosen my own essay on the Transcendental, earlier A. R. Ammons, certainly the legitimate living representative of the American Sublime. J. D. McClatchy, poetic disciple of James Merrill, ponders the elegant dialectics of the lesson of the master, after which, in a violent juxtaposition, Diane Middlebrook follows with Allen Ginsberg, who is for many the legitimate bardic figure at this time, but for others (myself included) a bard too much resembling James Macpherson's "Ossian."

Four authentic descendants of Whitman—Galway Kinnell, John Ashbery, W. S. Merwin, and the late James Wright—are analyzed in their characteristic strengths by Charles Molesworth, Alfred Corn, myself, and Richard Howard, respectively. Howard returns immediately with his rich meditation upon Irving Feldman, a poet whose disciplined development begins to establish real importance. Adrienne Rich, an important poet for many current readers, receives a generous tribute from Helen Vendler, who nevertheless shrewdly notes echoes and overtones that I would say sort oddly with Rich's fiercely feminist stance.

Robert Pack, a distinguished poet of the middle way, is described by Paul Mariani as an instance of rare experiential maturity in contemporary poetry. David Lehman eloquently studies John Hollander's diverse works, astonishingly neglected in proportion to their achievement, after which I analyze a very difficult and esoteric poet, Alvin Feinman.

Crunk (Robert Bly) follows with an apt tribute to the originality of Gary Snyder, admirable laureate of ecology and a humane anthropology.

Mark Strand, a lyric artist of superb finish, whose metaphysical darknesses are constant, is discussed by Linda Gregerson as the contemporary instance of a Keatsian "negative capability." Two very different black poets, the polemical Amiri Baraka and a subtle quietist, the splendid Jay Wright, are then depicted by Nate Mackey and Robert B. Stepto, respectively. Finally, John Hollander concludes this book with an erudite appreciation of the erudite Daryl Hine, a great and greatly neglected artist.

HAROLD BLOOM and DAVID BROMWICH

Introduction

"Ask the fact for the form," Emerson said, but the history of American poetry has tended to illustrate a rival quest, which is to beg the form for the fact. Emerson urged the American bards to emulate his Merlin, who mounted to paradise by the stairway of surprise, but even the greatest among Emerson's immediate progeny, Whitman and Dickinson, chose to present their poetic selves through repetitive modes of continuous and overwhelming formal innovation. American poetry since the end of World War II is an epitome of this reverse Emersonianism: no other poets in Western history have so self-deceivingly organized themselves along the supposed lines of formal divisions. The mimic wars of "closed" against "open" formers have masqueraded as conflicts between spiritual stances and ideological commitments: closed form, governed by metric and stanza, could thus be writ large as a settled insulation from experience, whereas open form, free-style and full of vatic self-confidence, reduced all experience to a chaos. And yet if we stand back now, after a quarter-century, we behold mostly a welter of wholly shared anxieties that unite the feuding camps.

The poets who were gathered together at their first full strength circa 1945 would include Robert Penn Warren, Richard Eberhart, Theodore Roethke, Elizabeth Bishop, Robert Lowell, John Berryman, Delmore Schwartz, J. V. Cunningham, Randall Jarrell, Richard Wilbur, Charles Olson, and Robert Duncan. They had as predecessors the most formidable group of poets in the American tradition, one that began with Edwin Arlington Robinson and Frost and proceeded through Pound, Eliot, Moore, Williams, Stevens, Ransom, and Jeffers down to a somewhat younger trio of e. e. cum-

1

mings, Hart Crane, and Allen Tate. Almost all the poets born in the first
two decades of the twentieth century seem diminished today when juxta-
posed very closely with those born in the last two or three decades of the
nineteenth. Great achievement by the fathers sometimes exacts a price from
the children, and something of the current strength of American poets born
during the 1920s may derive from the sorrows and sacrifice of the middle
generation of Roethke, Berryman, Jarrell, Lowell, and others.

We can distinguish two formal strains in the important American poets
born during the closing decades of the nineteenth century. If we examine
American poetic practice as opposed to theory in the nineteenth century, we
see that the main British line of Spenserian-Miltonic poetry, which emerges
as the romantic tradition, was carried on through Bryant, Poe, Longfellow,
Timrod, and Lanier, while native strains were invented most plainly by Whit-
man, and more subtly by a gnomic group that includes Emerson, Thoreau,
Melville, and, most grandly, Dickinson. The two strains, those of the English
Romantic and the Emersonian gnomic, met and mingled in Robinson and
Frost.

A third strain of Whitmanian innovation ended in the major outburst
of 1915 and afterwards. The immediate influence of Whitman here—on
Edgar Lee Masters, Vachel Lindsay, Carl Sandburg—was not fructifying,
though these poets continue to be popular and their simplified idiom has
much to do with the recent development of a quasi-folk music. However, a
Whitmanian element in Pound, Williams, and even Eliot today seems far
more central and vitalizing than the European influences so directly exalted
by Eliot and Pound themselves and by their followers. An even more elusive
Whitmanian influence, wholly divorced from formal considerations, was crucial for Stevens, whose major formal inheritance is as close to Wordsworth,
Keats, and Tennyson as ever Bryant, Poe, and Longfellow were.

Despite its enormous range and power, Stevens's poetry has waited until
the late 1960s and early 1970s to find a strong disciple in John Ashbery,
whose own work took a turn away from surrealism and automatic writing
in *The Double Dream of Spring, Three Poems,* and a number of uncollected
lyrics. In Ashbery's best poems we look back through Stevens to Whitman
in the employment of a long line, and in a rather oblique use of the cata-
loguing effect. There is a similar background for poets whose middle range
of ancestry and poetic temperament appears to be occupied by Eliot. For
instance, W. S. Merwin began during the mid-1960s to experiment with a
celebratory kind of neoprimitivism: in *The Moving Target* and *The Lice,*
broken syntax is making the dissociation Eliot saw as historically unfortunate
but necessary. Yet Merwin has recovered the consolatory strain that belonged

to Whitman and decisively affected *The Waste Land* and *Four Quartets,* though Eliot in his own quite ambivalent public pronouncements had tried to eliminate Whitman from the acceptable "tradition" of poetry in the English language.

These cases illustrate the emergence during the past few years of a transcendentalism that has always been essential to American poetry but was for a time anxiously rejected by its surest descendants. The poets of the generation of Roethke-Lowell-Wilbur began with the sober admonition of Eliot and Auden; they were to return to closed forms, and forsake metrical innovation. They, together with their younger followers in the 1950s—Ashbery, Merwin, James Dickey, James Merrill, Anthony Hecht, James Wright, Louis Simpson, Richard Howard, John Hollander—discovered in their various ways that neither closed nor open forms could be anything but an evasion. Poets who came into their force somewhat later, such as Gary Snyder, A. R. Ammons, Galway Kinnell, and Mark Strand, were less troubled by constraints of form and so could start more comfortably from the fact. In short, never having labored under the illusion that there was some cross-cultural modern idiom to which they ought to aspire, they declared themselves from the first to be successors of Emerson and Whitman.

Among the closed formers it is Auden rather than Eliot who has been the steadiest influence. His idiom is still going strong in the most recent work of Merrill, Howard Moss, and Wilbur, had a determining effect on the early efforts of Hollander and Howard, and never left Jarrell. What separates the American disciples of Auden from many of their British counterparts is a revision of Auden's characteristic irony, which (as Donald Davie has remarked in a slightly different context) begins to realize in it the attitude that nature strikes in confronting man: not merely a man's own pose in confronting himself. This shift is evident also in matters of detail. Wilbur can be representative: his early and late poems look very nearly the same, but their technical evenness covers a progress away from the metaphysical conceits which used to lie thick on his pages. Similarly, Jarrell in his last work moved to the Wordsworthian pathos that had been his theme all along, and wrote increasingly in a loose iambic that allowed for much of the "inclusiveness" he had explicitly admired in Whitman. Howard in his most recent volumes has written dramatic monologues after the manner of Browning, while Hollander has tended to favor syllabics or else a highly enjambed accentual verse. Such a list might go on: the point is that poets who had their beginning in Auden, and whose early work can often be mistaken for Auden's, have by whatever route found a resting place in the native tradition.

Our emphasis ought to fall on a Wordsworthian-Whitmanian *subjec-*

O'Hara's *Second Avenue* can be considered an exemplum of the new mode thereby brought into being, which might be described as comic phantasmagoria. Such a poetics is in the last degree an urban phenomenon, and will be found irrevocably at odds with the school of pre-Wordsworthian, or indeed—as it likes to be thought—prehistorical clarity which we connect with the names of James Wright and Robert Bly.

Sooner or later, as has been noted, the proliferation of schools and methods must be understood as an impediment, not an aid to appreciation. There are two innovations that have some importance: first, the definitive sloughing off of the Georgian diction by Pound, Frost, and a few others. That the advance took place at a certain time and place has come to seem a truism, yet it holds within it an essential truth. There is also, a bit later, Williams's reassertion in free verse of the full range of ambiguity made possible by enjambment, when, as John Hollander has indicated, the rhetorical flexibility of that particular feature of English poetry had been allowed to lapse after Milton in the poetry of the late romantics and the Victorians. But, once we have taken these into account, the arguments within and between self-proclaiming schools are at best misleading. In the strongest and most characteristic poetry of the late 1960s and early 1970s, a transcendental synthesis of the various native strains seems to be developing, and what is emerging is clearly an expressionistic and severe version of American romanticism. At any rate, that is our safest generalization as we trace the continuity of individual careers. Thus Simpson, who was once allied with Bly and the Midwest clarifiers, appears in his liveliest work to have been relatively free of their defining impulse. Ashbery, sometimes categorized quite simply as one of the New York poets, instead moves together with Schuyler in an enormous ambience that includes the otherwise very diverse Merrill, Wright, Hecht, Ammons, Merwin, Hollander, Alvin Feinman, Kinnell, Strand, and many others, who are visionary, as Emerson prophesied they must be. The *stance* of all these poets makes impossible an expression in either closed- or open-phrased fields, and each has been compelled, in order to escape the fall into the confessional, to perform a deliberate curtailment of the revisionary impulse toward an endlessly journalistic scrutiny of himself, while simultaneously asking the fact for the form.

For what, finally, can poetic form mean to an American? Every American poet who aspires to strength knows that he starts in the evening-land, realizes he is a latecomer, fears to be only a secondary man.

> Solitary,
> Patient for the last voices of the dusk to die down, and the dusk

To die down,
Listeners waiting for courteous rivers
To rise and be known

                      but in the large view, no
lines or changeless shapes: the working in
    and out, together
      and against, of millions of events: this,
          so that I make
          no form of
          formlessness

Suspended somewhere in summer between the ceremonies
Remembered from childhood and the historical conflagrations
Imagined in sad, learned youth—somewhere there always hangs
The American moment.
          Burning, restless, between the deed
And the dream is the life remembered

    In new rocks new insects are sitting
    With the lights off
    And once more I remember that the beginning

    Is broken
    No wonder the addresses are torn

Glad of the changes already and if there are more
    it will never be you that minds
Since it will not be you to be changed, but in the evening in the
    severe lamplight
    doubts come
From many scattered distances, and do not come too near.
As it falls along the house, your treasure
Cries to the other men; the darkness will have none of you, and
    you are folded into it
    like mint into the sound of haying.

    These are five representative poets of their generation; the excerpts have
been taken at random from a recent anthology. Every passage, whether in

tone, in cognitive aim, or in human stance, shows the same anxiety: to ask the fact for the form, while being fearful that the fact no longer has a form. This is what Geoffrey Hartman has called "the anxiety of demand": that which can be used can be used up. The generation of poets who stand together now, mature and ready to write the major American verse of the 1980s, may yet be seen as what Stevens called "a great shadow's last embellishment," the shadow being Emerson's.

JOHN HOLLANDER

Modes and Ranges of a Long Dawn

If old statesmen make us sneer, old athletes and teachers make us applaud condescendingly, and old soldiers make us nervous, who is to be wise? Only old painters and poets, perhaps, those who can with profit and pleasure become their own grandfathers. (We all become our fathers, but not knowing what to do about all that becomes part of our continuing domestic tragicomedy.) The problem of wisdom in America was in heroic crisis prophetically earlier than our nation itself appeared to be. But, our imaginations being our best part, and the decline of the best always dragging down behind it the inert worst, this should hardly surprise. Poetry, observed Stevens in a revision of Pareto, is a cemetery of nobilities, but the grass growing around the monuments, we might add, is wisdom.

Robert Penn Warren is our wisest man of letters, and has become not only part of the literary landscape of America but, more significantly, part of the way in which we view the landscape. As the coauthor, with Cleanth Brooks, of perhaps the most influential textbook for the study of poetry in our time in America—great-great grandsons of *Understanding Poetry* are still being spawned—he helped generations of students learn that creating a reading of a poetic text can be as much an act of intensity and joy as composing one. In novels like *At Heaven's Gate, All the King's Men, World Enough and Time*, and that remarkable meta-southern novel, *Flood* (I list only my personal canon) he represented the more than complex fate of southern America—the non-Emersonian, old new world—as an emblem of uni-

Published for the first time in this volume. © 1986 by John Hollander.

9

versal, rather than of sectional, human conditions. Many of the themes handled in his novels, and occasionally embodied in their inset philosophical lyric sections, have reappeared in and among his poetry. The ruined and haunted pastoral of the American field, the deaths of fathers and mothers, the nightmare ever knocking at the child's door in the mind of the man, the failure of the American West as a measure of our more general failures, the saving shreds of affirmation: we see these becoming, in Robert Penn Warren's later poetry, not so much subjects, as regions of poetic experience.

It is his poetry, rather than his telling of tales, upon which I wish to comment, and if not to treat him specifically as what Spenser called a poet historical, then nevertheless as one who "thrusteth into the middest, even where it most concerneth him . . . there recoursing to the things forepast, and divining of things to come." The paradoxes of American history, and the profundities of some of its violences, have served his vision of the enduringness of promise—even unto the breakers of promises—even under the most stained and faded of rainbows. "Such a subject"—Warren once wrote this of the Civil War "bloodily certified by actuality" for Herman Melville's poetry—"such a subject would serve his need only if the centrifugal whirl toward violent action was perfectly balanced by the centripetal pull toward an inwardness of apparently unresolvable mystery, or tormenting ambiguity." In many ways this describes the uses to which Warren's own poetry has put the historical anecdote, the tale of which he is always in some way the teller. Throughout the growth of his oeuvre, the expansions of narrative—parable, oblique anecdote, text for meditation—have marked his originations of form and new lyric genres. From *The Ballad of Billie Potts* and the internalized horrors of "Original Sin," he moved to the form of the historical episode reconstituted and redeemed in that remarkable extended eclogue, *Brother to Dragons*. There, the novelist Robert Penn Warren becomes one of the governing presences in a poem whose end is, among other things, to teach some of the meanings of history to its other major presence, Thomas Jefferson.

In his poems since *Promises* (1957), the created moments of personal and public history grew more passionate and complex. The unreeling of story or of account became more a matter of what mythographers call the unfolding of myth. These newer, long suites of poems—chains of questionings, revisions of meditative position—constitute some of the most original poetry written in English today. In form, too, they are quite unique; original structures of free verse, they rework and recall, but never trivially imitate, complex odelike rhyming schemes. They allow both narrative and an increasingly frequent mode of self-catechism (this surfaced first, I should imagine, in the remarkable "Ballad of a Sweet Dream of Peace" in *Promises*) to transform the programs of modern lyric. It is instructive, perhaps, to glance for a moment at the ways in which they evolved.

In Warren's early poems one finds the tight metrical and epigrammatic homages to seventeenth-century lyric that are epitomized in the allusive version of Marvell's garden of verses (a garden in which one would not dwell forever, but wherein, fifteen years later, my own generation played as poetic children). Warren's version of this was a garden

> Where all who came might stand to prove
> The grace of this imperial grove,
> Now jay and cardinal debate,
> Like twin usurpers, the ruined state.

(The touches of archaism here extend even to the older meaning of "prove" as "test.") But even in these earlier poems, the allusiveness is no mere stylistic or tonal marker. In the famous "Bearded Oaks," under the trees that are "subtle and marine,"

> Upon the floor of light, and time,
> Unmurmuring, of poly made,
> We rest; we are, as light withdraws
> Twin atolls on a shelf of shade

the Shakespearean sea-change from *The Tempest* extends to the Marvellian sea of grass from "Upon Appleton House," revised on the forest floor. But the very mode of wit is itself being self-consciously revised, and its light filtered through the poem's own meditative leaves, until the inevitable conclusion about time has moved far beyond a mere *carpe diem*. Indeed, the poem's last quatrain is proleptically thematic for much of Warren's recent poetry:

> We live in time so little time
> And we learn all so painfully
> That we may spare this hour's term
> To practice for eternity.

Later on in his work, the "hour's term" collapses to a far more intense moment, Hardy's moments of vision and beyond these; at the same time, the poems embodying them expand rhetorically into quasi narratives. Back in these same years in which he was still working with seventeenth-century echoes, Warren was engaging with certain lyrical-narrative forms developed by Hardy and, in particular, writing onrushing, run-on long lines that flooded the banks even of purely rhythmic scansion.

He himself has written of how important an early poem called "The Return: An Elegy" (1930) was for him, how uncannily it seemed to know more about his life—and his mother's nearing death—than he did as he wrote it. Formally, it does indeed look ahead to the strange, irregular odes of the past two decades; rhetorically, it prefigures them in its way of arguing with itself, of interjecting mysterious bits of broken refrain. But like the poems in tight quatrains or more expanded balladry, it is still something of an echo-chamber, whether half-consciously recalling Eliot, on the one hand

> the old bitch is dead
> what have I said!
> I have only said what the wind said
> wind shakes a bell the hollow head
>
> By dawn, the wind, the blown rain
> Will cease their antique concitation.
> It is the hour when old ladies cough and wake,
> The chair, the table, take their form again
> And earth begins the matinal exhalation

or, on the other, ironically quoting—and demolishing with an Eliotic device—Elizabeth Akers Allen's celebrated parlor-piece:

> turn backward turn backward O time in your flight
> and make me a child again just for tonight
> good lord he's wet the bed come bring a light.

There are moments of what might be called in at least two senses a middle style in *Brother to Dragons* that approach prophetic cadence. Of its memorable set pieces one is the song of chill, of the encroachment of winter:

> And the year drove on. Winter. And from the Dakotas
> The wind veers, gathers itself in ice-glitter
> And star-gleam of dark, and finds the long sweep of the valley.
> A thousand miles and the fabulous river is ice in the starlight
> The ice is a foot thick, and beneath, the water slides back like
>   a dream.
> And in the interior of that pulsing blackness and thrilled zero,
> The big channel-cat sleeps with eyes lidless, and the brute face
> Is the face of the last torturer, and the white belly
> Brushes the delicious and icy blackness of mud.
> But there is no sensation. How can there be
> Sensation when there is perfect adjustment? The blood

Of the creature is but the temperature of the sustaining flow:
The catfish is in the Mississippi and
The Mississippi is in the catfish and
Under the ice both are at one with God.
Would that we were!

This is the time of the literally and figuratively cold-blooded for whom violence and rage will not be heat. The language of the narration (the speech of Robert Penn Warren in the poem) rises to a more overtly prophetic strain a few pages after:

And now is a new year: 1811.
This is the *annus mirabilis.* Signs will be seen.
The gates of the earth shall shake, the locked gate
Of the heart be stricken in might by the spear-butt.
Men shall speak in sleep, and the darkling utterance
Shall wither the bride's love, and her passion become
But itch like a disease: scab of desire.
Hoarfrost shall lie thick in bright sun, past season, and twitch
    like fur.
The call of the owl shall discover a new register.
When ice breaks, the rivers shall flood effortlessly,
And the dog-fox, stranded on the last hillock,
Shall bark in hysteria among the hazel stems.
Then the bark shall assume a metronomic precision.
Toward the end, silence. The first water coldly fingers
The beast's belly. Then silence, He shudders, lets
The hind quarters droop beneath the icy encroachment.
But the head holds high. The creature shivers again,
And the rigid muzzle triangulates the imperial moon.
Until the spasm, the creature stares at the moon
With the aggrieved perplexity of a philosopher.

Here, though, as the prophecy gives way to a kind of moralized narration, we find another sort of anticipation of the structures of the later poetry. It is interesting to observe the way in which the more regular cadences of this passage give way, in Warren's 1979 revision of *Brother to Dragons,* to a muting of both the meter and the grammar of the prophetic mode, and how the whole passage with its powerful but problematic transition, is broken into two after "fur." Other characteristic devices of the mixed modality of the recent poetry have included that puzzling, article-less form of title, sometimes mocking a newspaper headline (an early occurrence, in *Promises,* is "School Lesson Based on Word of Tragic Death of Entire Gillum Family"; another, from the same book and resonant more of a picture-title, is "Mad Young Aristocrat on Beach"). In Warren's early poetry, the kind of irony this allusiveness would generate would be rather easier to pin down; in these later poems, from *Promises* on, the strange grammar is no longer a matter of establishing a distanced tone, but rather comes to invoke a whole range of tones: bitter, Olympian, sympathetic, detached.

So, too, the increasingly common formal scheme of isolating a cadential line from a strophelike structure as if to make it a stanza of its own, or have it stand in for a closing couplet in a sonnet, or a longer, more pastoral fade-out conclusion. He uses it in "Fall Comes in Back-Country Vermont" and throughout, to conclude sections in the Emerson poem, also from *Tale of Time.* This later, characteristic device of closure, the separated, single final line, neither purely epigrammatic nor partaking of lyrical coda, is deployed in a rich variety of situations. A typically complex instance of this occurs at the end of a poem I have always particularly liked, perhaps as much for the way in which it makes romance of a central epistemological moment, as for what has seemed to me to be its mode of invoking another, very different modern American poem. William Carlos Williams's ode to the spring wind, beginning "By the road to the contagious hospital" (from *Spring and All),* celebrates in a strange, problematically modernist way the birth of a moment of realization: the cold wind felt at the beginning of the poem yields up its true identity as the breath of spring, in what is half-likened to a birth-process. Buds that look at first like gnarled, perhaps even diseased, protuberances of bare stalk release the green shoots that "enter the new workd naked, / cold, uncertain of all / save that they enter." Williams's usual undersong, the suppression of conceptualization in favor of the trope he calls "things," itself struggles against this poem's own metaphor of focusing an optical device (either miscroscope or field glass), as "One by one objects are defined— / It quickens: clarity, outline of leaf."

Warren's remarkable "Brotherhood in Pain" (from *Can I see Arcturus from Where I Stand* and closely related to many of the poems in the "Speculative" section of *Now and Then,* which followed it in 1978) is far less reticent about its trope for that central act of consciousness so important to poets and so played down by philosophers, the act of *noticing.* The birth of an element of the external world is a painful one, but the pain is, inevitably, shared by subject and object; perhaps the grammar of "in pain" of the title is a revision of that of "[conceived] in sin," or "[conceived] in liberty":

Fix your eyes on any chance object. For instance,
The leaf, prematurely crimson, of the swamp maple

That dawdles down gold air to the velvet-black water
Of the moribund beaver-pond. Or the hunk

Of dead chewing gum in the gutter with the mark of a molar
Yet distinct on it, like the most delicate Hellenistic chisel-work.

Or a black sock you took off last night and by mistake
Left lying, to be found in the morning, on the bathroom tiles.

Or pick up a single stone from the brookside, inspect it
Most carefully, then throw it back in. You will never

See it again. By the next spring flood, it may have been hurled
A mile downstream. Fix your gaze on any of these objects,

Of if you think me disingenuous in my suggestions,
Whirl around three times like a child, or a dervish, with eyes
    shut,

Then fix on the first thing seen when they open.
In any case, you will suddenly observe an object in the obscene
    moment of birth.

It does not know what it is. It has no name. The matrix from
    which it is torn
Bleeds profusely. It has not yet begun to breathe. Its experience

Is too terrible to recount. Only when it has completely
    forgotten
Everything, will it smile shyly, and try to love you,

For somehow it knows that you are lonely, too.
It pityingly knows that you are more lonely than it is, for

You exist only in the delirious illusion of language.

To begin with, the objects of contemplation are by no means "chance," for they are all emblems of death, traditional or modern instances of what has been sloughed off, what time has caused, like bodies and life itself, to be cast aside. With the end of the sixth couplet, however, the poem's attention turns ironically aside ("if you think me disingenuous in my suggestions") to deal with a true "chance object," perhaps as if the latent memento mori in any monumental emblem, in any powerful figure from nature, had somehow to be purged before the ultimate matter of the relation of world and knowledge could be approached. As it is, this is no "spousal hymn," as Wordsworth called it, of that relationship, but the celebration of the birth of a sibling.

The "matrix" from which bits of reality are always being most timely ripped is, in its original sense a womb, and in its derived one, a conceptual paradigm, and the two meanings themselves seem both conjoined and torn apart in the figure that embodies them. Whose womb it is—just *who* gives birth to any object (and who, implicitly, to the observer)—may be too terrible for the poem to contemplate. The repression of the nature of that mother may have something to do with the powerful further turnabout of the final line (a turnabout emphasized by the enjambed conjunction "for" at the end of the preceding couplet). Ordinarily, we should feel for the contingency of the external world, of the recently born observable piece of reality. But with something like metaphysical condescension, the object pities the subject, who cannot ever know its own birth, notice itself, or—and again, only implicitly—observe of its own death. The subject's existence "in the delirious illusion of language" is the inferential quality of that existence, no matter how much pain it may be sharing with the world. And yet "language" has never been a primary issue in the poem until now (save for the fact that the "it" has, at birth, no name—only the subject, living and breathing the air of the realm of language, will have one for it). The powerful closing line reflects also the original and unique mixture of genres in the poem itself: meditative lyric, spiritual exercise, very brief narrative. All of these modes "end" differently, and the operations of all three of those endings are effected in this one, which seems as well to close out all the issues of the poem itself.

In the past twenty years, then, Warren's formal invention has grown to meet the demands of new and varied forms of fabling. From the modernist dogma about tight form holding in check the violence of passion and revelation, he began to roam through old and new woods, like the John James Audubon of his own poem, a quester crashing through prosodic brush and drawing the blood of rhetoric in pursuit of greater precision and wider views. In that marvelous book *Incarnations* (1968), a poem like "The Leaf" could announce a period of late greatness in the work of a poet who knew, like Yeats, that old embroideries had to be shed. Yet this was a true poet, who knew that, after Yeats, "walking naked" could only be a literary enterprise, and not a poetic one. He knew that the far-from-barren leaves of the reclaimed image of the fig tree in "The Leaf" could alone authenticate the trope of late poverty in order that there be late fruition. This was to be the

major poet of nature, one who could recall—as no wandering botanizer
could catalog, or pursuing hunter could overlook—

> All day, I had meandered in the glittering metaphor
> For which I could find no referent.

Nature in these late poems yields up its parables of delicacy and violence in
subtle interrelations. Warren's hawk, the creature of range, high vision, and
the power of lightning descent upon particulars, wings through time as well
as across space. His long poem *Or Else* (1974) extended the questing of the
Audubon figure to new structures, modes, and ranges of voice. These continued to evolve in *Now and Then* (1978), in which the struggle with present
phenomena kept yielding the vision of new twists in the troublesome riddle
of time. Beyond narative, beyond the forms of meditative lyric, Warren's
poetry of the last decade suggests the deep story-telling of biblical commentary—tales told us in elucidation of the true story we all know but cannot
comprehend. Robert Penn Warren's poetry has emerged now as perhaps the
grandest part of his writing. His poems have become parts of our world. He
now astonishes us—as Cocteau said we had to be astonished—but no longer
with the amazement of youthful fireworks (or as the French say, *feux d'artifice*), but with the deep and continuing astonishingness of a long dawn.

HAROLD BLOOM

The Poetry of Robert Fitzgerald

Fitzgerald is widely known and esteemed for the magnificence of his versions of Homer and Virgil, and for other superb translations, some done in collaboration with Dudley Fitts. His own poems, gathered in *Spring Shade* (New Directions, 1971), have had many discerning admirers through the decades, but are not well enough known to younger readers. A rereading of Fitzgerald, at this time, reveals that he occupies among modern poets a place precisely similar to that of Walter Savage Landor among the Romantics. Landor and Fitzgerald were elegiac poets, lyric masters who invested classic forms and stances with their own highly individual passions. Both studied the nostalgias, in a Virgilian mode, and with a cognitive edge of Christian stoicism.

Landor is the best poet in the world, for some things, and so in his way is Fitzgerald. Both excel in meditative lyrics that appear to be marmoreal reveries, yet are replete with Yeatsian passionate intensity. The phenomenon, in both poets, is not an effect of repression, whether of drives, or of the language and stances of precursor poets. Landor and Fitzgerald choose a different contest, which tends to separate them from Romantic tradition, with its violent and sometimes glorious Oedipal struggles for strength. The place of the agon is taken up by an acceptance of Western traditions of restraint, Roman and Christian. Neither Landor nor Fitzgerald escapes some of the negative consequences of refusing the Romantic tradition of the crisis-lyric. The creative turbulences of catastrophe and the compensatory sudden

Published for the first time in this volume. © 1986 by Harold Bloom.

uprushes of rhetorical power are thus excluded from their poetry. Yet Landor
and Fitzgerald are not weak poets, even if they will not compete for Miltonic
or Wordsworthian strength. Their mode, Virgilian in its origins, is best
represented in English by one strain in Tennyson, where he is closest to
Virgil.

Fitzgerald's finest poem, in my experience of reading him across more
than two decades, is the Virgilian elegy "Souls Lake," comparable to Landor's exquisite "Memory." Fitzgerald subtly celebrates the joy of coming into
his own poetic power, but in measures that intimate the intricate cost of a
heightened consciousness. "Souls Lake" is clearly in the tradition of the poem
of barely secularized epiphany, of Browning's "good moment" and Pater's
"privileged hour." But Fitzgerald refuses the crisis-element that tends to be
associated with the tradition. Alone with his friends (who may be the hushed
trees) he yields his art "to the pure mind of night," even though he initially
writes his poem in a contest against the night:

> The evergreen shadow and the pale magnolia
> Stripping slowly to the air of May
> Stood still in the night of the honey trees.
> At rest above a star pool with my friends,
> Beside that grove most fit for elegies,
> I made my phrase to out-enchant the night.

The beautiful phrase "the pure mind of night" catches up all of the Emersonian Not-Me, embracing nature and history (and thus precursor poets)
but also other selves and one's own body. So Fitzgerald speaks of the natural
hush as being both due to him and also befitting to an unexpected marriage-
song for his union with night's pure mind:

> The epithalamion, the hush were due,
> For I had fasted and gone blind to see
> What night might be beyond our passages;
> Those stars so chevalier in fearful heaven
> Could not but lay their steel aside and come
> With a grave glitter into my low room.

Dominating the poem is its masterful central trope, the "star pool" of
Souls Lake, which becomes one with the poet's body and eyes:

> Vague though the population of the earth
> Lay stretched and dry below the cypresses,
> It was not round-about but in my night,

> Bone of my bone, as an old man would say;
> And all its stone weighed my mortality;
> The pool would be my body and eyes.

This allows the achieved majesty of the fourth stanza, where nature yields utterly to the poet's makings, and becomes a "colorable, meek and limpid world":

> The air my garment and material
> Whereof that wateriness and mirror lived—
> The colorable, meek and limpid world.
> Though I had sworn my element alien
> To the pure mind of night, the cold princes,
> Behold them there, and both worlds were the same.

Yet a felt menace is preserved in the stoic phrase "the cold princes," who personify night's pure and only momentarily surrendered otherness of mind.

Few modern poems end as inevitably as this, perhaps because so much otherness returns in the last stanza:

> The heart's planet seemed not so lonely then,
> Seeing what kin it found in that reclining.
> And ah, though sweet the catch of your chorales,
> I heard no singing there among my friends;
> But still were the great waves, the lions shining,
> And infinite still the discourse of the night.

The trees remain in the chorale of their hush, kindred but distinct from the poet's singing. A pure irreality enters with the imagery of the penultimate line, as ancient emblems of poetic power, ocean and the lions, are manifest but subdued in response to the poet's power. The last line is rich with an ambiguity that the poem's argument requires: we cannot know if the ongoing discourse of the night is a return to its infinite, pure mind, excluding the poet, or whether the epithalamion aspect of the poem, marrying poet's to night's mind, still continues. Either way, there has been and remains a measured triumph.

One would expect the poet of "Souls Lake" to be an effective elegist of other poets, and Fitzgerald is. Two of his most moving achievements are his "Portraits," an extended and disjunctive elegy for his friend the extraordinary poet John Brooks Wheelwright, and the somber meditative sonnet "Dudley Fitts," mourning his former teacher, collaborator, and friend. "Portraits" uncannily delineates the perpetual surprises of Wheelwright's poetry and personality, at once highest in true moral seriousness, and endlessly outrageous in evading or sabotaging both literary and social convention. Whether Wheelwright, who himself wrote the best of the elegies for Hart Crane, can be said to have written a sterner myth than Crane's, as Fitzgerald avers, is disputable, but within the nervously adroit rhetoric of "Portraits" the assertion acquires a singular authority.

It is part of the authentic tribute to Wheelwright that no other poem by Fitzgerald is so extravagant in its diction, as in the Joycean language of the poem's second section:

> Morphine more fines they cried within
> And just to be precisely more
> Redactuate of tit and tin
> Convexed a junior editor
>
> To keep the Pentateuch unpent
> Or pig it on the whizzy door
> His tag was up, his kilter sent
> To be a junior editor
>
> Wherries of unwhiggish light
> Seasang from the fusty hoar
> But Lubgub tub his rubbers tight
> And was a junior editor
>
> Figgy and transleafy ching
> O summer sobwith freckle o'er
> Erotic him; but Lubgubbing
> Was still a junior editor.

But the satirical intensity suits Wheelwright, and contrasts with the noble, Landorian quatrains of the poem's first section. So powerful and incisive are the last four quatrains of that section, that an attentive reader may be moved to regret our poetry's loss in Fitzgerald's refusal to write more often in this hard, driving, specifically judgmental mode:

> Yet upward in LaFarge's flame
> His savior twisted, and does still;
> The true line comes as once it came
> To masculine Homer's steady will;
>
> Control and charity of the just,
> And their wild laughter flung at night,

> Commemorate his death, his dust,
> His gaiety. John Wheelwright.

The gentler strains of the third and final section are more characteristic of Fitzgerald:

> The brutal present and the soft past
> His constants are; all else is variable;
> Through waking weather and the climates of dream
> That mathematic shapes his character;
>
> As one love-lost, bemused by memory,
> He smiles, moves sunny hands, goes out
> To April's shadowing air or to machine guns
> Punching in dust their rows of periods.

This elegiac intensity in Fitzgerald's verse achieves a culmination in the "Dudley Fitts" sonnet, which Landor would have cherished. Few brief poems of mourning have combined as inextricably the accents of a sincere grief and an accurate account of the departed friend's special ethos and talents. Landor's poem "On the Death of Southey" finds here a worthy companion:

> The organist has closed his instrument
> After recessional, and closed his book;
> Counterpoint that his fingers undertook
> Into the world of light has made ascent.
> Airy agilities for perfection spent
> Have quieted at last, but not the look
> From the musician's eyes that will not brook
> A blundering word upon a great event.
> Far from New England's leafiness I write
> In that land of the old latinity
> And golden air to which at length he came,
> My master and friend, as to his own birthright.
> What farther land he found I hope to see
> When by my change our evenings are the same.

I have space to comment upon only two more poems, and choose "Solstitium Saeculare" as Fitzgerald's own self-portrait, and "Metaphysical," to give just one instance of his achievement as a devotional poet. Indeed, the first poem is devotional also, and both lyrics show the new severity and even greater elegance of Fitzgerald's later work. Devotional poetry is very difficult to write, perhaps now all but impossible, yet Fitzgerald's achievement is to succeed in these poems precisely where I think Auden failed, in justly conveying that good and evil of eternity which, according to Dr. Johnson, were too ponderous for the wings of wit. They are not ponderous in Fitzgerald, who writes "Solstitium Saeculare" in the refreshing persona of a kind of Roman Catholic Odysseus, perhaps only possible for the translator whose *Odyssey* is unsurpassed:

> I hold my peace at home
> And call to my wondering mind
> The chaos I came from—
>
> Waste sea and ancient wind
> That sailing long I fought,
> Unshriven and thin-skinned.
>
> God knows why I perished not,
> But made it here by grace
> To harbor beyond my thought,
>
> To the stillness of this place.
> Here while I live I hold
> Young hope in one embrace
>
> With all the ruin of old,
> And bless God's will in each;
> And bless His word of gold
>
> As far as heart can reach,
> Turning the Apostle's page
> Or Thomas, who would teach
>
> Peace to the heart's rage.

It is the Virgilian Fitzgerald (who gave us our best version of the *Aeneid*) who writes the logocentric and firm "Metaphysical." Virgilian patience, restraint and resignation combine here in the noble pathos of understanding that all "the downward longitudes are dark":

> Winter blows on my eaves,
> And tall stalks nod in the snow
> Pitted by dripping trees.
>
> The strong sun, brought low,
> Gives but an evening glare
> Through black twigs' to-and-fro

> At noon in the cold air.
> A rusty windmill grates.
> I sit in a Roman chair.

I have read only a few of the poems that Fitzgerald wrote in the 1970s and 1980s, since they have not yet appeared as a book. I would expect that they, like Landor's in his later phases, attained to an even more austere lyric eloquence. They too will compel us to speak of a canon that leads from Virgil through Landor and Tennyson on to Robert Fitzgerald.

DAVID BROMWICH

Elizabeth Bishop's Dream-Houses

In a very striking passage of "Roosters," Elizabeth Bishop turns to address the shiny, gloating, and definitively male creatures whose cries disturb her sleep:

> each one an active
> displacement in perspective;
> each screaming, "This is where I live!"
>
> Each screaming
> "Get up! Stop dreaming!"
> Roosters, what are you projecting?

The sleeper, as she tells us in another poem, eventually recovers from these assaults and continues to inhabit "my proto-dream-house, / my crypto-dream-house, that crooked box / set up on pilings." She has taken in enough of the roosters' admonitions to concede, "Many things about this place are dubious." But the force of her rhetorical question—"What are *you* projecting?"—suggests a reserve of personal strength. Bishop's own poems are active displacements of perspective. They too project a warning about where she lives, and they have the authority of dreams rather than awakenings.

That she was praised throughout her career for a humbler kind of success is doubtless just as well: charitable misunderstandings help an artist to go on working quietly. Yet it is worth recalling the standard terms of this praise, for they reveal how little had changed in the years that separate

From *Raritan* 4, no. 1 (Summer 1984). © 1984 by *Raritan*.

Bishop's first appearance from that of Emily Dickinson. Admirers of "Success
is counted sweetest" (who thought it probably the work of Emerson) were
replaced by encouragers of the best woman poet in English. And a sure
ground of appreciation for so special a performer was taken to be her "accuracy." What did that mean? Not, evidently, that she adapted the same style
to different situations, and not that she changed all the time, with a relentless
originality. It was an aesthetic compliment, difficult to translate into English.
Similarly, Bishop was prized for her "charm." In the sense of a warm socia-
bility, she certainly was not charming, least of all when she meant to be, as
in her poems about the poor. In any other sense, charm is a tedious virtue
for a poet, just as accuracy is an impracticable vice. And yet, in spite of their
evasiveness, both words converge on a trait which all of Bishop's readers
have felt in her poems: the presence of an irresistible self-trust. To her, art
is a kind of home. She makes her accommodations with an assurance that
is full of risk, and, for her as for Dickinson, the domestic tenor of some
poems implies a good-natured defiance of the readers she does not want.
The readers she cares for, on the other hand, are not so much confided in
as asked to witness her self-recoveries, which have the quality of a shared
premise. Her work is a conversation which never quite takes place but whose
possibility always beckons.

My point of departure in testing what this feels like in practice is an
early poem, "The Monument." Bishop appears to have conceived it as an
oblique eulogy for herself, and she frames it deferentially enough to suit a
posthumous occasion. The poem's authority and weight have less in common
with modern inventions like Joseph Cornell's boxes than they do with an
older tradition of immortality—"Not marble, nor the gilded monuments /
Of princes, shall outlast this pow'rful rhyme." We are well-advised at the
start not to measure a sure distance between those lines and these:

> Now can you see the monument? It is of wood
> built somewhat like a box. No. Built
> like several boxes in descending sizes
> one above the other.
> Each is turned half-way round so that
> its corners point toward the sides
> of the one below and the angles alternate.
> Then on the topmost cube is set
> a sort of fleur-de-lys of weathered wood,
> long petals of board, pierced with odd holes,
> four-sided, stiff, ecclesiastical.

Irony, in one of its meanings, is a pretense of concern in a speaker, for the sake of revising a listener's whole structure of concerns; the pretense here is that Bishop's listener, in order to cherish the monument, need only hear it described just so. She patiently adjusts the description ("It is X. No. Like several X's . . .") to anticipate any complaint, as later in the poem she will give the listener a more official embodiment by composing speeches for him. All this self-qualification is a gravely enacted farce. When it is over we will find ourselves still staring at the monument and rehearsing what she has said about it, until we see that the object of the poem was to compel our attention without giving reasons.

In the course of the one-woman narration, with its imagined interruptions, we listeners are permitted exactly four objections to the monument. These may be summarized abstractly: I don't understand what this thing is trying to be; I've never seen anything hang together like this; It's just too makeshift to succeed; and, What are you trying to prove, anyway? In short, it is museum-boredom ("Big deal; take me somewhere else"), which the poet meets at first with a curatorial delicacy. But her final speech, which takes up almost a third of the poem, overcomes all defensiveness and simply expands the categorical authority of her earlier statement, "It is the monument."

> It is an artifact
> of wood. Wood holds together better
> than sea or cloud or sand could by itself,
> much better than real sea or sand or cloud.
> It chose that way to grow and not to move.
> The monument's an object, yet those decorations,
> carelessly nailed, looking like nothing at all,
> give it away as having life, and wishing;
> wanting to be a monument, to cherish something.
> The crudest scroll-work says "commemorate,"
> while once each day the light goes around it
> like a prowling animal,
> or the rain falls on it, or the wind blows into it.
> It may be solid, may be hollow.
> The bones of the artist prince may be inside
> or far away on even drier soil.
> But roughly but adequately it can shelter
> what is within (which after all
> cannot have been intended to be seen).
> It is the beginning of a painting,

> a piece of sculpture, or poem, or monument,
> and all of wood. Watch it closely.

This ending allies "The Monument" with other American appeals to the
power of metaphor to shape a life, particularly Frost's "A Star in a Stone-
Boat" and Stevens's "Someone Puts a Pineapple Together." Even in their
company, Bishop's poem keeps on growing as one thinks of it. It has perhaps
less invention than they have; but then, it presumes a questioner suspicious
of all that is new; and its persistent skepticism is a grace equal to any
exuberance.

Earlier in the poem, still explaining the look of the monument itself,
Bishop had composed a diagram of the viewer's relation to what he sees,
which may also be read as a geometric proof of her own power over her
readers.

> The monument is one-third set against
> a sea; two-thirds against a sky.
> The view is geared
> (that is, the view's perspective)
> so low there is no "far away,"
> and we are far away within the view.

I take the first five lines to mean that our eye is placed just above horizon-
level, so that the whole sky and sea appear as a flat vertical backdrop, without
depth and therefore without any far or near. But in what sense can we be
said to be "far away within the view"? It must be that the view looks out
at us too, as through the wrong end of a telescope, from a perspective capable
of absorbing everything: it takes us in as it pleases. Indeed, the monument
can contain the world, by implication. That is the sense of the listener's
disturbed question, "Are we in Asia Minor, / or in Mongolia?"—site of
"Kubla Khan," where a kindred monument was decreed by imaginative fiat.
So the poem says here, with the metaphor of perspective, what it says at the
end by the rhetoric of conjecture: an active mind alone makes the world
cohere, as "Wood holds together better / than sea or cloud or sand could by
itself, / much better than real sea or sand or cloud." The flat declaration "It
chose that way to grow and not to move" only seems to announce a faith
in the autonomy of art objects; Bishop returns us to the human bias of the
thing, by her emphasis on those features of the monument which "give it
away as having life, and wishing; / wanting to be a monument, to cherish
something." Before it can be, it must want to be something. And we read it
for whatever spirit it communicates; we cannot do more than watch. But we

are accompanied by the prowling sun which also keeps watch—a casual sublimity, the reward of the poet's discovery of a shelter uniquely right for herself. It is an image to which Bishop will return in "The End of March," where "the lion sun ... who perhaps had batted a kite out of the sky to play with," is mysteriously connected with the wire leading out from her dream-house "to something off behind the dunes."

The monument will do for a figure of a poem, which turns out to be an allegory of what it is to *make* anything in the optative mood. A figure of a poet appears in the more straightforward allegory called "The Man-Moth." In a brief note, Bishop traces the title to a newspaper misprint for "mammoth," but the reason for its appeal to her is plain when one remembers the man-moth of Shelley's "Epipsychidion":

> Then, from the caverns of my dreamy youth
> I sprang, as one sandalled with plumes of fire,
> And towards the lodestar of my one desire,
> I flitted, like a dizzy moth, whose flight
> Is as a dead leaf's in the owlet light,
> When it would seek in Hesper's setting sphere
> A radiant death, a fiery sepulchre.

Part of Bishop's aim is to translate this image of the poet to a less radiant climate—that of the modern city—where his quest can take on the shape of an almost biological compulsion.

> Up the façades,
> his shadow dragging like a photographer's cloth behind him,
> he climbs fearfully, thinking that this time he will manage
> to push his small head through that round clean opening
> and be forced through, as from a tube, in black scrolls on the light.
> (Man, standing below him, has no such illusions.)
> But what the Man-Moth fears most he must do, although
> he fails, of course, and falls back scared but quite unhurt.

Where the monument chose a certain way to be, the Man-Moth acts without a will: his quest is merely a condition of existence. It is as if he were born knowing, *there is a creature (and you are he) who does all of this*—climbs skyscrapers because he "thinks the moon is a small hole at the top of the sky"; travels backward in underground trains, where he dreams recurrent dreams; and through all his risks, looks on mortality as "a disease he has inherited the susceptibility to." He is defined not by his activity but by the contrast he makes with man, who

does not see the moon; he observes her vast properties,
feeling the queer light on his hands, neither warm nor cold,
of a temperature impossible to record in thermometers.

Man's shadow is no bigger than his hat; the Man-Moth's is almost palpable, trailing "like a photographer's cloth behind him"; and one is reminded that "shadow" is still our best English word for *figura* and *typus*. In a way that can be shown but not said, the Man-Moth, by being what he is, interprets man to himself. But the poem makes a lighter fable of this. Like any other second-story artist, the Man-Moth abstracts a few choice possessions from his victim and flees the scene.

How his theft may be retrieved is the subject of Bishop's final stanza, which is addressed to man, still "observing" and coldly pragmatic.

If you catch him,
hold up a flashlight to his eye. It's all dark pupil,
an entire night itself, whose haired horizon tightens
as he stares back, and closes up the eye. Then from the lids
one tear, his only possession, like the bee's sting, slips.
Slyly he palms it, and if you're not paying attention
he'll swallow it. However, if you watch, he'll hand it over,
cool as from underground springs and pure enough to drink.

The Man-Moth's eye is "an entire night itself," a complete image of that world of the earth's surface in which he seeks what is most different from himself. The object of his quest he calls a tiny hole of light; man, less interestingly, calls it the moon. To reach it would mean suffusion by the light and hence, to an eye all pupil, destruction. The Man-Moth, however, is sustained by the fantasy of an ascent through "that round clean opening," and of being forced "in black scrolls on the light." In this dream of consummation he would become his writing.

One may interpret the dream as at once expressing and concealing a hope that some principle of self will survive the dissolution of the body. Of course, the fallacy is easy to expose: immortality is not a form of health to which one can inherit a susceptibility. Yet this analysis gives no comfort to man, about whom we have heard it said that "Man, standing below, has no such illusions"; for the compliment holds in reserve a fierce irony: "Man, standing below, has no such ambitions." Nor does Bishop herself want to unbuild our illusions. She is interested in the use we make of everything the illusion-bound creature brings back from his journeyings. This is figured in the poem as hardly calculable refreshment, with the character almost of bodily secretion. The Man-Moth's "one tear, his only possession, like the bee's sting," may be his gift to us. The image comes close to a hackneyed sentiment about perfection and pain, and hovers near an allusion to Keats's "Melancholy," but slips free of both. It is hard not to read it poignantly—the reader, like the map-printer in another of Bishop's poems, "here experiencing the same excitement / as when emotion too far exceeds its cause." But the tear is not really a possession, the light that produced it after all was man's, and both parties seem amenable to the exchange. Our acceptance of every curiosity in the poem owes something to its conscious urbanity: the opening line even gives us the "battered moonlight" of a cityscape—battered by too much jingling in the pockets of too many songwriters, but still salvageable by one poet. Elsewhere, the same word appears to evoke a larger freedom with imagery that looks worn or already found: the fish that is "battered and venerable / and homely"; the big tin basin, "battered and shiny like the moon." "The Man-Moth" and "The Monument" go beyond the dignity of statement—the somewhat ponderous naturalism—that such diction has usually aimed to license and keep honest. They stand apart from the poems of Bishop's generation in the stubbornness with which they try ingenuity by the test of prosaic heft.

To an exceptional degree in modern poetry, Bishop's work offers resistance to any surmise about the personality of the author. One reason is that the poems themselves have been so carefully furnished with eccentric details or gestures. These may seem tokens of companionability, yet a certain way into a poem the atmosphere grows a little chill; farther in, as the conversation strolls on, one senses the force field of a protective ease. Some day, a brief chapter in a history of poetry will describe Lowell's misreading of Bishop as a voice of resonant sincerity, and his appropriation for journalistic ends of her more marked traits of syntax, punctuation, and anomalous cadence. But to the reader who returns to these poems for their own sake, the question likeliest to recur is: what are they concealing? It helps, I think, to frame this as a question about a difficult passage—for example, about the pathos of some lines near the end of "Crusoe in England," in which Crusoe describes the objects that recall his years of solitude.

> The knife there on the shelf—
> it reeked of meaning, like a crucifix.
> It lived. How many years did I
> beg it, implore it, not to break?
> I knew each nick and scratch by heart,
> the bluish blade, the broken tip,

>the lines of wood-grain on the handle . . .
>Now it won't look at me at all.

Like many comparable passages of her work, the description is weirdly circumstantial. What does it mean for a poet who is a woman to write, as a man, of an object so nearly linked with masculine assertion, with this mingling of tenderness, pity, and regret?

The poetic answer, which has to do with the cost of art to life, does not exclude the sexual one, which has to do with an ambivalent femininity. The poet's own weapons in art as in life have been more dear to her than she can easily confess. The punishment for deserting them is that they refuse to return her gaze; they lose their aura, and she ceases to be a poet. A similar recognition is implied in other poems, where a wish to conquer or dominate—resisted at first, then acted on—darkens the celebration of having come through every challenge. Thus, "The Armadillo" moves from horror of a creature, quite distinct from the poet, to wonder at the same creature, which in the meantime has been implicitly identified with her. She devotes a poem to the armadillo because it is a survivor, forearmed against any catastrophe. Like her, it watches in safety a dangerous and beautiful spectacle, the drifting of the "frail, illegal fire balloons" which at any moment may splatter "like an egg of fire / against the cliff." As for the poet herself, the poem is proof of her armor. In the same way, in "Roosters" she is a second and unmentioned crier of the morning; the poem, with its "horrible insistence" three notes at a time, announces exactly where she lives.

These identifications go deep. Such poems are not, in fact, animal-morality pieces, in the vein of Marianne Moore. They more nearly resemble Lawrence's "Fish," "The Ass," "Tortoise Shell," and "Tortoise Family Connections"—protestant inquests concerning the powers of the self, which have the incidental form of free-verse chants about animals. Bishop writes without Lawrence's spontaneous humor, and without his weakness for quick vindications. Indeed, there is something like self-reproach in a line that begins the final movement of "Roosters": "how could the night have come to grief?" By a trick of context, this phrase opens up an ambiguity in the cliché. It warns us that there has been matter for grieving during the night, before the first rooster crowed, at a scene of passion which was also a betrayal. "The Armadillo" too reveals the complicity of love with strife, in its italicized last stanza; here the last line and a half is a chiasmus, in which strength is surrounded by a yielding vulnerability.

>*Too pretty, dreamlike mimicry!*
>*O falling fire and piercing cry*

> *and panic, and a weak mailed fist*
> *clenched ignorant against the sky!*

"Weak" and "ignorant" are meant to temper the surprise of the "mailed fist clenched," and they cast doubt on those three central words: the fist, emblem of contest, is defended by weakness and ignorance, its only outward fortifications. The gesture of defiance, however, becomes all the more persuasive with this glimpse of a possible defeat. The way "The Armadillo" comes to rest has felt tentative to some readers, and yet the only question it asks is rhetorical: "See how adequately I shelter my victory?" In other poems, just as surely, an elaborate craft gives away the poet as always present, at a scene she has painted as uninhabitable. The repeated line in a very late poem, "One Art," will declare her control by rhyming "disaster" with "The art of losing isn't hard to master"; as if we could expect her endurance to be taxing of course, but no more doubtful than her ability to pair the words for a villanelle.

Sexuality is the most elusive feature of Bishop's temperament—before writing any of the poems in *North & South*, she had learned to allegorize it subtly—and the reticence of her critics alone makes its existence worth noting. Like other habitual concerns, it interests her as it joins a care for what she sometimes calls the soul. This is an argument carried on from poem to poem, but its first appearance, in "The Imaginary Iceberg," is startling.

> Icebergs behoove the soul
> (both being self-made from elements least visible)
> to see them so: fleshed, fair, erected indivisible.

Until these concluding lines the poem has been a light entertainment, a "Convergence of the Twain" told from the iceberg's point of view. The lines shift our perspective on everything that came before—in effect, they translate a poem which did not seem to need translation. "Fleshed, fair, erected indivisible": the words, we see at once, belong to the human body rather than the soul. They are monstrously beautiful because they are a lie. For in the metaphor about the soul which has been perfectly built up, the comparison rightly demands instead: cold, white, immense, indestructible. This yields a pleasant description of an iceberg which, when we ponder it, is replaced by a sublime representation of the soul.

It is characteristic of Bishop's wit that she should have begun the same poem fancifully: "We'd rather have the iceberg than the ship, / although it meant the end of travel." Translating, as the poem suggests we do, this becomes: "We'd rather have the soul than the body, / although it meant the

    wealth plus a brand-new pleasure.
    Directly after Mass, humming perhaps
    L'Homme armé or some such tune,
    they ripped away into the hanging fabric,
    each out to catch an Indian for himself—
    those maddening little women who kept calling,
    calling to each other (or had the birds waked up?)
    and retreating, always retreating behind it.

In the light of this ending, the poem may be read as a colonial dream of all that seems infinitely disposable in the colonized.

But it is also about something that evades our grasp in every object that appeals to the human love of conquest. The Indian women, "those maddening little women who kept calling, calling to each other"—but not to their pursuers—only repeat the attraction of the female lizard, "her wicked tail straight up and over, / red as a red-hot wire." Both alike appear to beckon from behind the tapestry of the jungle fabric. They entice, and bind their spell. Another retreat will always be possible to them, since the jungle has gone opaque to the men hunting them, who believe at every point that it is transparent. This is another way of saying that the invaders have become victims of their own conquering perspective. They recreate here "an old dream of wealth and luxury"; yet the dream was "already out of style when they left home"; and the new place, as disclosed to other eyes, has seemed far from homelike. In the end their crossing of this threshold, "hard as nails, / tiny as nails," says most about their sense of home, which was equally marked by a failure of knowledge. What they take to be an act of possession is not, therefore, even a successful repossession, but the enactment of a familiar ritual of self-seduction.

This poem shows Bishop moving well outside the limits of the travel sketch. By itself, it is almost enough to persuade us that she exploits the genre elsewhere chiefly to break with it, from an impulse comparable to Dickinson's in revising the poem of "home thoughts." At any rate, the sketch that goes furthest to appease the worldly taste of her readers carries a suspicious title, "Over 2,000 Illustrations and a Complete Concordance," and the steady mystification of its narrative seems bent on protracting our suspicion. The poem, with an unsettling confidence, treats worldliness as a form of literal reading that is death—but the title is worth pausing over. What is a concordance? A system of reference to all the uses of every important word in the Bible, or for that matter in any sacred book, including the work of a great poet. The illustrations accompanying it may be pictures—the picture-postcard atmosphere of much of the poem will toy with this—yet they are as likely to be passages longer than a phrase, which give a fuller context for the entries. When reading a concordance, we do not look at individual words to be sure of their reference, but to satisfy ourselves of a fateful pattern of choice. From the sum of an author's repetitions, we may learn a tact for whatever is irreducible in his character. "Over 2000 Illustrations" owes its force to the propriety with which one can substitute both "reader" and "traveller" for "author," and view a place in the world as denoting a locus in a text.

The thought that troubles Bishop at the start is that the book of nature and history may not be either a clean text or an already canonical one, whether Bible or secular fiction, but something more like just such a concordance, with occasional glimpses into its depths coming from the illustrations alone.

> Thus should have been our travels:
> serious, engravable.
> The Seven Wonders of the World are tired
> and a touch familiar, but the other scenes,
> innumerable, though equally sad and still,
> are foreign. Often the squatting Arab,
> or group of Arabs, plotting, probably,
> against our Christian Empire,
> while one apart, with outstretched arm and hand
> points to the Tomb, the Pit, the Sepulcher.
> The branches of the date-palms look like files.
> The cobbled courtyard, where the Well is dry,
> is like a diagram, the brickwork conduits
> are vast and obvious, the human figure
> far gone in history or theology,
> gone with its camel or its faithful horse.
> Always the silence, the gesture, the specks of birds
> suspended on invisible threads above the Site,
> or the smoke rising solemnly, pulled by threads.

The broken, randomly spliced rhythm of this opening, the discreteness of its sentences, as well as the words "often" and "always," suggest the episodic quality of the moments chronicled in the illustrations. They tell a story, apparently senseless, and in no particular order, which the poem later names the story of "God's spreading fingerprint." Only the Christians in the illustrations make a connection from place to place; and in the margin, everywhere, are faintly sinister Arabs, plotting or "looking on amused": together, these figures give it the unity it has. But as the account moves on, it grows still more oddly inconsequential: "In Mexico the dead man lay / in the blue arcade; the dead volcanoes / glistened like Easter lilies. / The jukebox went on playing 'Ay, Jalisco!'" The blare of the jukebox comes in when the story's meaning appears to have been surely lost, and it signals a transition. Now, the tone of the illustrations (which somehow have become cheap guidebook images) drifts toward the hallucinatory:

> And in the brothels of Marrakesh
> the little pockmarked prostitutes
> balanced their tea-trays on their heads
> and did their belly dances; flung themselves
> naked and giggling against our knees,
> asking for cigarettes. It was somewhere near there
> I saw what frightened me most of all:
> A holy grave, not looking particularly holy,
> one of a group under a keyhole-arched stone baldaquin
> open to every wind from the pink desert.

By the first five lines of this passage, every worldly fact has been rendered exchangeable with every other, and the loss is of nothing less than the history and the pathos of the things one may come to know.

Bishop is frightened "most of all" by the suddenly exposed grave in the desert because it reminds her of a life emptied of causes and consequences, with "Everything only connected by 'and' and 'and.'" The conclusion of the poem brings together author, reader, and traveller a last time, and envisions a sort of text that would return attention to something beyond it.

> Everything only connected by "and" and "and."
> Open the book. (The gilt rubs off the edges
> of the pages and pollinates the fingertips.)
> Open the heavy book. Why couldn't we have seen
> this old Nativity while we were at it?
> —the dark ajar, the rocks breaking with light,
> an undisturbed, unbreathing flame,
> colorless, sparkless, freely fed on straw,
> and, lulled within, a family with pets,
> —and looked and looked our infant sight away.

Much less than everything is restored by this ending. Though the holy book, once opened, confronts us with an ideal representation of our origins, we have to read it uninnocently. We know how thoroughly we have revised it already by our later imaginings, by every arrangement which makes the end of a life or work distort its beginning. To deny our remoteness from the scene would be to cancel the very experience which permits us to pass through "the dark ajar." Thus, we stand with the poet, both in the scene and outside it, uncertain whether pleasure is the name for what we feel. Her wishfully innocent question—"Why couldn't we have seen / this old Nativity while we were at it?"—has the tone of a child's pleading, "Why couldn't we *stay* there?"—said of a home, or a place that has grown sufficiently like home. Some time or other we say that about childhood itself. The book, then, is hard to open because it is hard to admit the strength of such a plea; harder still, to hear it for what it says about our relationship to ourselves. Any place we live in, savage or homely, dream-house or rough shelter, we ourselves have been the making of. And yet, once made, it is to be inherited forever. Everything may be connected by "because" and "therefore," and every connection will be provisional. The last line accordingly yields an ambiguous truth about nostalgia: to look our sight away is to gaze our fill, but also to look until we see differently—until, in our original terms, we do not see at all. The line, however, warrants a more general remark about Bishop's interest in the eye. In common with Wordsworth, she takes the metaphor of sight to imply the activity of all the senses, and these in turn to represent every possibility of conscious being. Sight is reliable because it can give no account of itself. We make it mean only when we look again, with "that inward eye / Which is the bliss of solitude" (words, incidentally, which the hero of "Crusoe in England" tries reciting to himself on the island, but can remember only after his rescue). It is in the same poem that Wordsworth says of the daffodils, "I gazed—and gazed"; and the action of "The Fish" turns on this single concentrated act: "I stared and stared," and the colors of the boat changed to "rainbow, rainbow, rainbow," and she let the fish go.

In passing from sight to vision, or to "what is within (which after all / cannot have been intended to be seen)," Bishop always respects the claims of unbelievers different from herself. Her mood is almost always optative, in its readiness to inquire into not-yet-habitable truths; and I want to conclude with an especially full expression of that mood, from "Love Lies Sleeping." She writes there of a dawn in a city, with eleven lines of a soft introductory cadence, good enough for the opening bars of a Gershwin tune; with a memory of the waning night and its "neon shapes / that float and swell and glare"; with a panoramic view and a long tracking view that ends in the window of one dwelling, where the poet asks the "queer cupids of all persons getting up" to be mild with their captives:

> for always to one, or several, morning comes
> whose head has fallen over the edge of his bed,
>> whose face is turned
>> so that the image of
>
> the city grows down into his open eyes
> inverted and distorted. No. I mean
>> distorted and revealed,
>> if he sees it at all.

The words are as serious and engravable as an epitaph. At the same time, with a doubt exactly the size of a comma, they point to a revelation that may have occurred, and, for the sake of its distortion as well as its truth, keep it living in surmise.

GARY SMITH

A Street in Bronzeville,
The Harlem Renaissance and the
Mythologies of Black Women

When Gwendolyn Brooks published her first collection of poetry, *A Street in Bronzeville* (1945), with Harper and Brothers, she already enjoyed a substantial reputation in the literary circles of Chicago. Nearly a decade earlier her mother, Keziah Brooks, had arranged meetings between her daughter and James Weldon Johnson and Langston Hughes, two of the most distinguished black writers of America's Harlem Renaissance. Determined to mold Gwendolyn into a *lady* Paul Laurence Dunbar, Mrs. Brooks proffered poems for the famous writers to read. While Johnson's advice to the young poet was abrupt, eventually he exerted an incisive influence on her later work. In a letter and a marginal note included on the returned poems, addressed to her on 30 August 1937, Johnson praised Brooks's obvious talent and pointed her in the direction of Modernist poetry:

> My dear Miss Brooks: I have read the poems you sent me last. Of them I especially liked *Reunion* and *Myself*. *Reunion* is very good, and *Myself* is good. You should, by all means, continue you[r] study and work. I shall always be glad to give you any assistance that I can. Sincerely yours. James Weldon Johnson.

> Dear Miss Brooks—You have an unquestionable talent and feeling for poetry. Continue to write—at the same time, study carefully

From *MELUS* 10, no. 3 (Fall 1983). © 1983 by the University of Cincinnati. Originally entitled "Gwendolyn Brooks's *A Street in Bronzeville*, The Harlem Renaissance and the Mythologies of Black Women."

43

the work of the best modern poets—not to imitate them, but to help cultivate the highest possible standards of self-criticism. Sincerely, James Weldon Johnson.

Of course, the irony in Johnson's advice, addressed as it is to the future *lady* Dunbar, is that he actually began his own career by conspicuously imitating Dunbar's dialect poems, *Lyrics of a Lowly Life*; yet he encourages Brooks to study the work of the "best Modern poets." He was, perhaps, reacting to the latent elements of modernism already found in her poetry; but the effect was to turn Brooks momentarily away from the black aesthetic of Hughes's *Weary Blues* (1926) and Countee Cullen's *Color* (1925) toward the Modernist aesthetics of T. S. Eliot, Ezra Pound, and e. e. cummings. It is interesting to note, however, that, even though Johnson's second letter admonishes Brooks to study the Modernist poets, he cautions her "not to imitate them," but to read them with the intent of cultivating the "highest possible standards of self-criticism." Flattered by the older poet's attention and advice, Brooks embarked upon a serious attempt to absorb as much Modernist poetry as she could carry from the public library.

If Johnson played the part of literary mentor, Brooks's relationship with Hughes was more personal, warmer, and longer lasting. She was already on familiar terms with *Weary Blues,* so their first meeting was particularly inspirational. Brooks showed Hughes a packet of her poems, and he praised her talent and encouraged her to continue to write. Years later, after Brooks's reputation was firmly established by a Pulitzer prize for *Annie Allen* (1949), her relationship with Hughes blossomed into mutual admiration. Hughes dedicated his collection of short stories, *Something in Common* (1963), to her. While Hughes's poetic style had an immeasurable influence on Brooks's poetry, she also respected his personal values and lifestyle. As she noted in her autobiography, Hughes was her idol:

> Langston Hughes! The words and deeds of Langston Hughes were rooted in kindness, and in pride. His point of departure was always a clear pride in his race. Race pride may be craft, art, or a music that combines the best of jazz and hymn. Langston frolicked and chanted to the measure of his own race-reverence.
>
> He was an easy man. You could rest in his company. No one possessed a more serious understanding of life's immensities. No one was firmer in recognition of the horrors man imposes upon man, in hardy insistence on reckonings. But when those who knew him remember him the memory inevitably will include

laughter of an unusually warm and tender kind. The wise man, he knew, will take some juice out of this one life that is his gift.

Mightily did he use the street. He found its multiple heart, its tastes, smells, alarms, formulas, flowers, garbage and convulsions. He brought them all to his table-top. He crushed them to a writing paste. He himself became the pen.

In other words, while Johnson encouraged Brooks to find "standards for self-criticism" in Modernism, Hughes underscored the value of cultivating the ground upon which she stood. In Hughes, in both the poet and man, Brooks found standards for living: he was a model of witty candor and friendly unpretentiousness and, most importantly, a literary success. Hughes convinced Brooks that a black poet need not travel outside the realm of his own experiences to create a poetic vision and write successful poetry. Unlike the Modernist Eliot who gathered much of his poetic material from the drawingrooms and salons of London, Hughes found his material in the cold-water flats and backstreets of Harlem. And Brooks, as is self-evident in nearly all her poetry, learned Hughes's example by heart.

II

The critical reception of *A Street in Bronzeville* contained, in embryo, many of the central issues in the scholarly debate that continues to engage Brooks's poetry. As in the following quotation from *The New York Times Book Review,* most reviewers were able to recognize Brooks's versatility and craft as a poet:

If the idiom is colloquial, the language is universal. Brooks commands both the colloquial and more austere rhythms. She can vary manner and tone. In form, she demonstrates a wide range: quatrains, free verse, ballads, and sonnets—all appropriately controlled. The longer line suits her better than the short, but she is not verbose. In some of the sonnets, she uses an abruptness of address that is highly individual.

Yet, while noting her stylistic successes, not many critics fully understood her achievement in her first book. This difficulty was not only characteristic of critics who examined the formal aspects of prosody in her work, but also of critics who addressed themselves to the social realism in her poetry. Moreover, what Brooks gained at the hands of critics who focused on her tech-

nique, she lost to critics who chose to emphasize the exotic, Negro features
of the book, as the following quote illustrates:

> *A Street in Bronzeville* ranges from blues ballads and funeral
> chants to verse in high humor. With both clarity and insight, it
> mirrors the impressions of life in an urban Negro community.
> The best poem is "The Sundays of Satin-Legs Smith," a poignant
> and hour-by-hour page out of a zoot-suiter's life. A subtle change
> of pace proves Brooks' facility in a variety of poetic forms.

The poems in *A Street in Bronzeville* actually served notice that Brooks
had learned her craft well enough to combine successfully themes and styles
from both the Harlem Renaissance and Modernist poetry. She even achieves
some of her more interesting effects in the book by parodying the two traditions. She juggles the pessimism of Modernist poetry with the general
optimism of the Harlem Renaissance. Three of her more notable achievements, "kitchenette building," "the mother," and "Sundays of Satin-Legs
Smith," are parodic challenges to T. S. Eliot's dispirited anti-hero J. Alfred
Prufrock. "[K]itchenette building" begins with Eliot-like emphasis on the
dry infertility of modern life: "We are things of dry hours and the involuntary
plan." The poem concludes with the humored optimism that "Since
Number 5 is out of the bathroom / we think of lukewarm water, we hope to
get in it." Another example is the alienated, seemingly disaffected narrator
of "the mother" who laments the loss of her children but with the resurgent,
hopeful voice that closes the poem: "Believe me, I loved you all." Finally a
comparison could be made between the elaborate, self-assertive manner with
which Satin-legs Smith dresses himself for his largely purposeless Sunday
outing and the tentative efforts of his counterpart, J. Alfred Prufrock.

Because of the affinities *A Street in Bronzeville* shares with Modernist
poetry and the Harlem Renaissance, Brooks was initiated not only into the
vanguard of American literature, but also into what had been the inner circle
of Harlem writers. Two of the Renaissance's leading poets, Claude McKay
and Countee Cullen, addressed letters to her to mark the publication of *A
Street in Bronzeville*. McKay welcomed her into a dubious but potentially
rewarding career:

> I want to congratulate you again on the publication of 'A Street
> in Bronzeville' and welcome you among the band of hard working
> poets who do have something to say. It is a pretty rough road we
> have to travel, but I suppose much compensation is derived from

the joy of being able to sing. Yours sincerely, Claude McKay. (October 10, 1945)

Cullen pinpointed her dual place in American literature:

> I have just finished reading 'A Street in Bronzeville' and want you to know that I enjoyed it thoroughly. There can be no doubt that you are a poet, a good one, with every indication of becoming a better. I am glad to be able to say 'welcome' to you to that too small group of Negro poets, and to the larger group of American ones. No one can deny you your place there. (August 24, 1945)

The immediate interest in these letters is how both poets touch upon the nerve ends of the critical debate that surrounded *A Street in Bronzeville*. For McKay, while Brooks has "something to say," she can also "sing"; and for Cullen, she belongs not only to the minority of Negro poets, but also to the majority of American ones. Nonetheless, the critical question for both poets might well have been Brooks's relationship to the Harlem Renaissance. What had she absorbed of the important tenets of the Black aesthetic as expressed during the New Negro Movement? And how had she addressed herself, as a poet, to the literary movement's assertion of the folk and African culture, and its promotion of the arts as the agent to define racial integrity and to fuse racial harmony?

Aside from its historical importance, the Harlem Renaissance—as a literary movement—is rather difficult to define. There is, for example, no fixed or generally agreed upon date or event that serves as a point of origin for the movement. One might easily assign this date to the publication of McKay's poems *Harlem Shadows* (1922), Alaine Locke's anthology *The New Negro* (1925), or Cullen's anthology *Caroling Dusk* (1927). Likewise, the general description of the movement as a Harlem Renaissance is often questioned, since most of the major writers, with the notable exceptions of Hughes and Cullen, actually did not live and work in Harlem. Finally, many of the themes and literary conventions defy definition in terms of what was and what was not a New Negro poet. Nonetheless, there was a common ground of purpose and meaning in the works of the individual writers that permits a broad definition of the spirit and intent of the Harlem Renaissance. Indeed, the New Negro poets expressed a deep pride in being black; they found reasons for this pride in ethnic identity and heritage; and they shared a common faith in the fine arts as a means of defining and reinforcing racial pride. But in the literal expression of these artistic impulses, the poets were either romantics or realists and, quite often within a single poem, both. The

realistic impulse, as defined best in the poems of McKay's *Harlem Shadows,*
was a sober reflection upon blacks as second-class citizens, segregated from
the mainstream of American socioeconomic life, and largely unable to realize
the wealth and opportunity that America promised. The romantic impulse,
on the other hand, as defined in the poems of Sterling Brown's *Southern
Road* (1932), often found these unrealized dreams in the collective strength
and will of the folk masses. In comparing the poems in *A Street in Bronzeville*
with various poems from the Renaissance, it becomes apparent that Brooks
agrees, for the most part, with their prescriptions for the New Negro. Yet
the unique contributions she brings to bear upon this tradition are extensive:
1) the biting ironies of intraracial discrimination, 2) the devaluation of love
in heterosexual relationships between blacks, and 3) the primacy of suffering
in the lives of poor black women.

III

The first clue that *A Street in Bronzeville* was, at the time of its publication, unlike any other book of poems by a black American is its insistent
emphasis on demystifying romantic love between black men and women. The
"old marrieds," the first couple encountered on the walking tour of Bronzeville, are nothing like the youthful archetype that the Renaissance poets often
portrayed:

> But in the crowding darkness not a word did they say.
> Though the pretty-coated birds had piped so lightly all the day.
> And he had seen the lovers in the little side-streets.
> And she had heard the morning stories clogged with sweets.
> It was quite a time for loving. It was midnight. It was May.
> But in the crowding darkness not a word did they say.

In this short, introductory poem, Brooks, in a manner reminiscent of Eliot's
alienated *Waste Land* characters, looks not toward a glorified African past
or limitless future, but rather at a stifled present. Her old lovers ponder not
an image of their racial past or some symbolized possibility of self-renewal,
but rather the overwhelming question of what to do in the here-and-now.
Moreover, their world, circumscribed by the incantatory line that opens and
closes the poem, "But in the crowding darkness not a word did they say,"
is one that is distinctly at odds with their lives. They move timidly through
the crowded darkness of their neighborhood largely ignorant of the season,
"May," the lateness of the hour, "midnight," and a particular raison d'être,
"a time for loving." Their attention, we infer, centers upon the implicit need

to escape any peril that might consume what remains of their lives. The tempered optimism in the poem, as the title indicates, is the fact that they are "old-marrieds": a social designation that suggests the longevity of their lives and the solidity of their marital bond in what is, otherwise, an ephemeral world of change. Indeed, as the prefatory poem in *A Street in Bronzeville,* the "old marrieds," on the whole, debunks one of the prevalent motifs of Harlem Renaissance poetry: its general optimism about the future.

As much as the Harlem Renaissance was noted for its optimism, an important corollary motif was that of ethnic or racial pride. This pride—often thought a reaction to the minstrel stereotypes in the Dunbar tradition—usually focused with romantic idealization upon the black woman. A casual streetwalker in Hughes's poem, "When Sue Wears Red," for example, is magically transformed into an Egyptian queen:

> When Susanna Jones wears red
> Her face is like an ancient cameo
> Turned brown by the ages.
> Come with a blast of trumpets,
>   Jesus!
>
> When Susanna Jones wears red
> A queen from some time-dead Egyptian night
> Walks once again.

Similarly, six of the first seven poems in Cullen's first published work, *Color* (1925), celebrate the romanticized virtues of black women. The second poem in the volume, "A Song of Praise," is particularly noteworthy in its treatment of the theme:

> You have not heard my love's dark throat,
>   Slow-fluting like a reed,
> Release the perfect golden note
>   She caged there for my need.
> Her walk is like the replica
>   Of some barbaric dance
> Wherein the soul of Africa
>   Is winged with arrogance.

In the same manner, McKay's sonnet "The Harlem Dancer" extolls the misunderstood virtue of a cabaret dancer:

> Applauding youths laughed with young prostitutes
> And watched her perfect, half-clothed body sway;

> Her voice was like the sound of blended flutes
> Blown by black players upon a picnic day.
> She sang and danced on gracefully and calm,
> The light gauze hanging loose about her form;
> To me she seemed a proudly-swaying palm
> Grown lovelier for passing through a storm.

In *A Street in Bronzeville,* this romantic impulse for idealizing the black woman runs headlong into the biting ironies of intraracial discrimination. In poem after poem in *A Street in Bronzeville,* within the well-observed caste lines of skin color, the consequences of dark pigmentation are revealed in drastic terms. One of the more popular of these poems, "The Ballad of Chocolate Mabbie," explores the tragic ordeal of Mabbie, the black female heroine, who is victimized by her dark skin and her "saucily bold" lover, Willie Boone:

> It was Mabbie without the grammar school gates.
> And Mabbie was all of seven.
> And Mabbie was cut from a chocolate bar.
> And Mabbie thought life was heaven.

Mabbie's life, of course, is one of unrelieved monotony; her social contacts are limited to those who, like her, are dark skinned, rather than "lemon-hued" or light skinned. But as Brooks makes clear, the larger tragedy of Mabbie's life is the human potential that is squandered:

> Oh, warm is the waiting for joys, my dears!
> And it cannot be too long.
> O, pity the little poor chocolate lips
> That carry the bubble of song!

But if Mabbie is Brooks's parodic victim of romantic love, her counterpart in "Ballad of Pearl May Lee" realizes a measure of sweet revenge. In outline, Brooks's poem is reminiscent of Cullen's *The Ballad of the Brown Girl* (1927). There are, however, several important differences. The first is the poem's narrative structure: Pearl May Lee is betrayed in her love for a black man who "couldn't abide dark meat," who subsequently makes love to a white girl and is lynched for his crime of passion, whereas Cullen's "Brown Girl" is betrayed in her love for a white man, Lord Thomas, who violates explicit social taboo by marrying her rather than Fair London, a white girl. Moreover, Cullen's poem, "a ballad retold," is traditional in its approach to the ballad form:

> Oh, this is the tale the grandams tell
> In the land where the grass is blue,
> And some there are who say 'tis false,
> And some that hold it true.

Brooks's ballad, on the other hand, dispenses with the rhetorical invocation of the traditional ballad and begins in medias res:

> Then off they took you, off to the jail,
> A hundred hooting after.
> And you should have heard me at my house.
> I cut my lungs with my laughter,
>   Laughter,
>   Laughter.
> I cut my lungs with my laughter.

This mocking tone is sustained throughout the poem, even as Sammy, Pearl May Lee's lover, is lynched:

> You paid for your dinner, Sammy boy,
> And you didn't pay with money.
> You paid with your hide and my heart, Sammy boy,
> For your taste of pink and white honey,
>   Honey,
>   Honey,
> For your taste of pink and white honey.

Here, one possible motif in the poem is the price that Pearl May Lee pays for her measure of sweet revenge: the diminution of her own capacity to express love and compassion for another—however ill-fated—human being. But the element of realism that Brooks injects into her ballad by showing Pearl May Lee's mocking detachment from her lover's fate is a conscious effort to devalue the romantic idealization of black love. Furthermore, Pearl May Lee's macabre humor undermines the racial pride and harmony that was an important tenet in the Renaissance prescription for the New Negro. And, lastly, Pearl May Lee's predicament belies the social myth of the black woman as *objective correlative* of the Renaissance's romanticism.

   In another poem that uses the Blues tradition as its thematic structure, Brooks takes the reader backstage, inside the dressing room of Mame, "The Queen of the Blues." As the central figure in the poem, Mame is similar to Sterling Brown's Ma Rainey, "Mother of the Blues":

> Would the lads who walked with her in dusk-cooled byways
>   Know Bessie now should they meet her again?
> Would knowing men of Fifth St. think that Bessie ever
>   Was happy-hearted, brave-eyed as she was then?

For Hughes, too, the black woman in "Young Prostitute" is described not as an Egyptian cameo, but rather as a "withered flower":

> Her dark brown face
> Is like a withered flower
> On a broken stem.
> Those kind come cheap in Harlem
> So they say.

In each of the above poems, the impulse toward romantic idealism of black women gives way to critical realism; the mythic disguises that mask the harsh realities of social and economic deprivations are stripped away, and poor black women are revealed as the most likely victims of racism within American society.

For Brooks, unlike the Renaissance poets, the victimization of poor black women becomes not simply a minor chord but a predominant theme of *A Street in Bronzeville*. Few, if any, of her female characters are able to free themselves from the web of poverty and racism that threatens to strangle their lives. The black heroine in "obituary for a living lady" was "decently wild / As a child," but as a victim of society's hypocritical, puritan standards, she "fell in love with a man who didn't know / That even if she wouldn't let him touch her breasts she / was still worth his hours." In another example of the complex life-choices confronting Brooks's women, the two sisters of "Sadie and Maude" must choose between death-in-life and life-in-death. Maude, who went to college, becomes a "thin brown mouse," presumably resigned to spinsterhood, "living all alone / In this old house," while Sadie who "scraped life / With a fine-tooth comb" bears two illegitimate children and dies, leaving as a heritage for her children her "fine-tooth comb." What is noticeable in the lives of these black women is a mutual identity that is inextricably linked with race and poverty.

For Hattie Scott, Brooks's protagonist in a series of vignettes that chronicle the life of a black domestic worker, the struggle to assert a female identity begins with the first poem, "the end of day." Hattie's life, measured by the sun's rising and setting, is described as a ceaseless cycle of menial tasks. The second poem in the series, "the date," details Hattie's attempt to free herself from the drudgery of domestic work:

> Whatcha mean talkin' about cleanin' silver?
> It's eight o'clock now, you fool.
> I'm leavin'. Got somethin' interestin' on my mind.
> Don't mean night school.

Hattie's "date'" in the third poem, an appointment "at the hairdresser's,'" turns out to be a rather farcical attempt to have her hair done in an "up-sweep" with "humpteen baby curls." Like Sadie's comb, Hattie's "upsweep" becomes symbolic of her persistent efforts to assert a positive identity. The reader senses, though, that her cosmetic changes, like her previous efforts with "Madame C. J. Walker" and "Poro Grower" (two hairdressers that promise instant beauty), will end in marginal success. Indeed, in the poem that follows, "when I die," Hattie imagines her funeral as a solitary affair attended by "one lone short man / Dressed all shabbily."

The final poem in the series, "the battle," ends not on a note of personal triumph for Hattie, but rather resignation and defeat. Hattie's neighbor and spiritual counterpart, Moe Belle Jackson, is routinely beaten by her husband:

> Moe Belle Jackson's husband
> Whipped her good last night.
> Her landlady told my ma they had
> A knock-down-drag-out fight.

Hattie's perception of the beating is charged with the anger and indignation of a *secret sharer* who, perhaps, realizes her own life in Moe Belle's predicament:

> I like to think
> Of how I'd of took a knife
> And slashed all the quickenin'
> Out of his lowly life.

Nonetheless, in what is surely one of the finest examples of macabre humor in Brooks's poetry, Hattie combines psychological insight and laconic understatement in her final musings about Moe Belle's fate:

> But if I know Moe Belle,
> Most like, she shed a tear,
> And this mornin' it was probably,
> "More grits, dear?"

Brooks's relationship with the Harlem Renaissance poets, as *A Street in Bronzeville* ably demonstrates, was hardly imitative. As one of the important links with the black poetic tradition of the 1920s and 1930s, she enlarged the element of realism that was an important part of the Renaissance worldview. Although her poetry is often conditioned by the optimism that was also a legacy of the period, Brooks rejects outright their romantic pre-scriptions for the lives of black women. And in this regard, she serves as a vital link with the Black Arts Movement of the 1960s that, while it witnessed the flowering of black women as poets and social activists as well as the rise of black feminist aesthetics in the 1970s, brought about a curious revival of romanticism in the Renaissance mode.

However, since the publication of *A Street in Bronzeville*, Brooks has not eschewed the traditional roles and values of black women in American society; on the contrary, in her subsequent works, *Annie Allen* (1949), *The Bean Eaters* (1960), and *In the Mecca* (1968), she has been remarkably consistent in identifying the root cause of intraracial problems with the black community as white racism and its pervasive socioeconomic effects. Fur-thermore, as one of the chief voices of the Black Arts Movement, she has developed a social vision, in such works as *Riot* (1969), *Family Pictures* (1970), and *Beckonings* (1975), that describes black women and men as equally integral parts of the struggle for social and economic justice.

DENISE LEVERTOV

A Memoir and a Critical Tribute

In the early spring of 1948 I was living in Florence, a bride of a few months, having married American literature, it seemed, as well as an American husband. Both of us haunted the U.S.I.S. library on the via Tornabuoni—Mitch to begin rereading at leisure the classics of fiction he had been obliged to gallop through meaninglessly at Harvard, I to discover, as a young writer of the British "New Romantic" phase of the 1940s, the poetry of what was to be my adopted country. I had read at that time a minimal amount of Pound (anthologized in a Faber anthology) and Stevens ("discovered" in Paris a few months before when Lynne Baker lent me a copy of *The Man with the Blue Guitar*). William Carlos Williams I had found for myself in the American bookstore on the Rue Soufflot, near the Sorbonne, but though I knew with mysterious certainty that his work would become an essential part of my life, I had not yet heard enough American speech to be able to hear his rhythms properly; his poems were a part of the future, recognized but held in reserve. The rest of American poetry was terra incognita, except for Whitman (in the William Michael Rossetti edition of 1868) and a few poems by Emily Dickinson, Robert Frost, and Carl Sandburg—again, anthology pieces only. I had read Eliot; but like most English readers at that time, I thought of him as an *English* poet (and of course, the fact that it was possible to do so was precisely what made Williams so angry with him, as I later understood). Also I had read and loved, at George Woodcock's house in London

From *Insight,* edited by R. J. Berthoff. © 1979 by New Directions Publishing Corp. Originally entitled "Some Duncan Letters—A Memoir and a Critical Tribute."

a year or so before, a few poems from Rexroth's *Signature of All Things*.
Those were the limits of my acquaintance with U.S. poetry.

The American library was not, to my recollection, rich in poetry; but
among my findings were some issues of *Poetry*, Chicago; and in one of these,
a review by Muriel Rukeyser of Robert Duncan's *Heavenly City, Earthly
City*. Both these people, then just names to me, were to become, in varying
ways, close friends who influenced my history—as did Dr. Williams. Thinking back from the present (1975) I realize how destiny was sounding the
first notes, in that cold Florentine spring, of motifs that would recur as
dominant themes in the fifties and sixties (and in the case of Muriel Rukeyser,
with whom I visited Hanoi in 1972, into the seventies) and which, indeed,
are so intervowen in my life that whatever changes befall me they must be
forever a part of its essential music.

In Muriel's review of *Heavenly City, Earthly City*, she quoted:

> There is an innocence in women
> that asks me, asks me;
> it is some hidden thing they are
> before which I am innocent.
> It is some knowledge of innocence.
> Their breasts lie undercover.
> Like deer in the shade of foliage,
> they breathe deeply and wait;
> and the hunter, innocent and terrible,
> enters love's forest.

These lines, and the whole review, so stirred me that I convinced myself no
one in Florence needed that particular issue of *Poetry* more than I did, and
I not only kept it out for months but, when we left for Paris, took it with
me. It is the only such rip-off I have ever committed.

Retrospectively, I see that I was drawn to Duncan's poems of that period
not only by their intrinsic beauty but because they must have formed for me
a kind of transatlantic stepping-stone. The poems of my own first book (*The
Double Image*, 1946) and those that Rexroth included in *The New British
Poets* (New Directions, 1949) belonged to that wave of Romanticism which
Rexroth documented, an episode of English poetry that was no doubt in
part a reaction against the fear, the drabness, and the constant danger of
death in the daily experience of civilians as well as of soldiers in World
War II. While the subject matter of the poems of the "New Romantic" movement may often have been melancholy and indeed morbid, the formal impulse
was towards a richly sensuous, image-filled music. When the war ended,

English poetry quickly changed again and became reactively dry, as if embarrassed by the lush, juicy emotionalism of the forties. But though not many individual poems of the New Romantics stand up very well to time and scrutiny, they still seem preferable to the dull and constipated attempts at a poetry of wit and intellect that immediately succeeded them, for their dynamic connected them with a deeper, older tradition, the tradition of magic and prophecy and song, rather than of ironic statement. And it was to that old, incantatory tradition that Duncan, then and always, emphatically (and, as I did not then know, consciously) belonged. So here, I must have intuited, was an *American* poet whose musical line, and whose diction, were accessible to me. It must have made my emigration, which I knew was not far distant, seem more possible, more real. Lines of my own (from a poem in *The Double Image* which Duncan—years later—read and admired) may serve to show some of the affinity I felt:

To Death

Enter with riches. Let your image wear
brocade of fantasy, and bear your part
with all the actor's art and arrogance.
Your eager bride, the flickering moth that burns
upon your mouth, brings to your dark reserve
a glittering dowry of desire and dreams.

These leaves of lightness and these weighty boughs
that move alive to every living wind,
dews, flowers, fruit, and bitter rind of life,
the savour of the sea, all sentient gifts
you will receive, deserve due ritual;
eloquent, just, and mighty one, adorn
your look at last with sorrow and with fire.
Enter with riches, enviable prince.

In a 1964 letter, after talking about a then new poem of mine called "Earth Psalm," Duncan tells how after rereading it that day he had read, or reread, "To Death" and, "I began to conjure the Tudor, no Stuart (something between King James's Bible and Bunyan) dimension (a fourth dimensional of you) with figures from a masque. . . . Haven't we, where we have found a source, or some expression of what we love in human kind, to give it a place to live today, in our own gesture (which may then speak of nobility or ardour)—Well, if Orpheus can come forward, so, by the work of the poem, Death and His Bride in brocade—

"How many correspondences there are," he goes on to say, "between your *Double Image,* 1946, and my *Medieval Scenes* written in 1947. In this poem 'To Death'—'brocade of fantasy': in 'The Banners' where the 'bright jerkins of a rich brocade' is part of the fabric of the spell; or in 'The Conquerors' compare 'The Kingdom of Jerusalem.' . . ." And after a few more lines of comment he begins, right *in* the letter, the poem "Bending the Bow"

> We've our business to attend Day's
> duties, bend back the bow in dreams as we may,
> til the end rimes in the taut string
> with the sending . . .
>
> I'd been
>
> in the course of a letter—I am still
> in the course of a letter—to a friend,
> who comes close in to my thought so that
> the day is hers. My hand writing here
> there shakes in the currents of . . . of air?
> of an inner anticipation of . . . ? reaching to touch
> ghostly exhilarations in the thought of her.

But here, noting the life-loom caught in the very act of its weaving, I anticipate. In 1948 I had nothing of Duncan's but those quotations in *Poetry,* fragments congenial and yet mysterious; and when I arrived in New York for the first time in the fall of that year I was too passive, disorganized, and overwhelmed by unrecognized "culture shock" (the term had not yet been invented) to do anything so methodical as to try and find his book or books: so that when I did happen upon *Heavenly City, Earthly City* on the sale table outside the Phoenix Bookshop on Cornelia Street, just a few blocks from where I was living, it seemed an astonishing, fateful coincidence—as in a sense it was.

The book enlarged and confirmed my sense of affinity and brought me, too, a further dim sense of the California of fog, ocean, seals, and cliffs I was by then reading about in Robinson Jeffers.

> Turbulent Pacific! the sea-lions bark
> in ghostly conversations and sun themselves
> upon the sea-conditiond rocks.
> Insistent questioner of our shores!
> Somnambulist, old comforter!

Duncan wrote in the title poem; and:

> Sea leopards cough in the halls of our sleep.
> swim in the wastes of salt and wreck of ships,

and:

> The sea reflects, reflects in her evening tides
> upon a lavender recall of some past glory,
> some dazzle of a noon magnificence.

Much, much later—in 1966, it must have been, when I visited Carmel and Monterey—there was possibly some recall of those lines in a poem of mine, "Liebestodt": "Where there is violet in the green of the sea. . . ."

But the impact of Duncan's rich romanticism was perhaps less powerful by the time I found the book, for I was also beginning to get a grip on William Carlos Williams's sound by then, able to "scan" it better now that I was surrounded by American speech, no longer baffled by details like "R.R." (railroad—in England it is railway) or obstructed in reading by the difference in stresses (e.g., the first American menu I saw announced "Hot Cakes" which I ordered as "hot *cakes*").

Now I was quickly, eagerly, adapting to the new mode of speaking, because instinct told me that to survive and develop as a poet I had to; and Williams showed me the way, made me listen, made me begin to appreciate the vivid and figurative language sometimes heard from ordinary present-day people, and the fact that even when vocabulary was impoverished there was some energy to be found in the here and now. What I connected to, originally, in Duncan, was a music based in dream and legend and literature; and though my love of that music has proved to be enduring, it was not uppermost in my needs and pleasures just then when I was seeking a foothold in the realities of marriage, of keeping house in a tenement flat, raising a strenuous baby, buying groceries at the Bleecker Street Safeway.

Meanwhile Duncan, unknown to me still, was changing too, on the other side of the continent. There was of course this big difference in us, a thread of another texture in among those that we held in common: he had a sophistication in which I was quite lacking, which gave to his romanticism an edge, not of the type of wit academics of the period cultivated anxiously—like a young man's first whiskers—but of an *erotic irony* such as Thomas Mann adumbrates in his essays on Goethe and elsewhere. He was not only a few years older than I; he had already an almost encyclopedic range of knowledge, he had studied history with Kantorowitz, he had read Freud, and he lived in a literary and sexual ambience I didn't even know existed. Whatever he wrote was bound to include an element of complex consciousness; indeed, I can see now that while my task was to develop a greater degree of conscious intelligence to balance my instincts and intuitions, *his* was, necessarily, to keep his consciousness, his diamond needle intellect, from becoming overweening, violating the delicate feelings-out of the Imagination; and it was just because his awareness of every nuance of style, of every double meaning, was so keen, that he has, through the years, been almost obsessively protective of the gifts of chance, of whatever the unconscious casts upon on his shore, of "mistakes" which he has cherished like love-children.

My first direct contact with Duncan came in the early fifties and was almost a disaster. By this time I had become friends with Bob Creeley and *Origin* had begun to appear. Mitch and I had gone back to Europe on the G.I. Bill in 1950, when our son was just over a year old, and in 1951 the Creeleys came to live a mile or two away from us in the Provençal countryside. Sitting on the ground near our cottage, by the edge of a closely pruned vineyard under the slope of the Alpilles, Creeley and Mitch would talk about prose, and Creeley and I about poetry: Williams, Pound, Olson's "Projective Verse" which had just come out, how to cut down a poem to its sinewy essence—pruning it like the vines. I learned a lot; and am not sure what, if anything, I gave in exchange, though I know I was not merely a silent listener. Duncan had not yet met or been acknowledged by either Olson (with whom Creeley was corresponding) or Creeley, and though he had not been dislodged from my mind I don't recall mentioning him. After I was back in New York, and just about the time Cid Corman included some poems of Duncan's in *Origin* (1952) I received a communication from a San Francisco address signed only "R. D." It was a poem-letter that (I thought) attacked my work, apparently accusing it of brewing poems like "stinking coffee" in a "staind pot." When the letter spoke of "a great effort, straining, breaking up all the melodic line," I supposed the writer was complaining. How I could have misread what was, as Duncan readers will recognize, "Letters for Denise Levertov: an A muse ment"—how I could have so misinterpreted his tribute, it is difficult now to imagine. I've never been given to paranoia; perhaps it was simply that the mode of the poem, with its puns, lists, juxtapositions (more Cubist than Surreal) was too sophisticated for me to comprehend without initiation. I had at the time not even read half the people he mentions in the poem as sources, or at any rate as forming an eclectic tradition from which I thought he was saying I had unwarrantably borrowed (but to which, in fact, he was joyfully proclaiming that I belonged): Marianne Moore, Pound, Williams, H. D., Stein, Zukofsky, Bunting, St.-J. Perse. Of these, I had by then read only Williams, Marianne Moore and Perse in any quantity; I knew Pound's *ABC of Reading* pretty well but had not tackled the *Cantos*. Of H. D. I knew only the anthologized Imagist poems of her youth, and of Stein only "Melanctha"; of Zukofsky and Bunting, nothing. Duncan also speaks in the poem of Surrealism and Dada: and I was at least somewhat acquainted with French Surrealism (and the English poet, David Gascoyne's book about it) but with Dada not at all. So much of the corresponding intellectual background, in the simplest sense, was lacking in me as a recipient of the letter.

I wrote to "R. D." inquiring plaintively why he had seen fit to attack me for a lack of originality for I took phrases like

> Better to stumb-
> ll to it,

and

> better awake to it. For one
> eyes-wide-open vision
> or fotograph
> than ritual

as stern admonitions, when, of all the names he cited, only Williams was to me a master, and from him I believed myself to be learning to discover my own voice. I concluded my letter by saying, in all innocence, "Is it possible that the initials you signed with, R. D., stand for Robert Duncan? You don't sound like him!—But in case that's who you are, I'd like to tell you I loved *Heavenly City, Earthly City,* and therefore hope it's not Robert Duncan who dislikes my poems so much." I quote from memory, but that's a pretty close approximation. It is a wonder that Duncan was not furious at my stupidity; especially at my saying he did not sound like himself. If he had been, I wonder if our friendship would ever have begun? Certainly if it had not, my life would have been different. But luckily he responded not with anger (or worse, not at all) but with a patient explanation (on the envelope he added the words, "It is as it was in admiration") of his intent, including his sense— central to an understanding of his own poetry—that "borrowings" and "imitations" were in no way to be deplored, but were on the contrary tributes, acts of faith, and the building-stones of a living tradition of "the communion of poets." This concept runs through all of Duncan's books. It is most obvious in the Stein imitations, or in his titling books *Derivations,* or *A Book of Resemblances,* but is implicit in every collection, though not in every poem; and it is closely tied to his recognition of poetry (and of all true art) as being a "power, not a set of counters" as he put it in a section of "The H. D. Book" that deals with H. D.'s detractors, the smart, "bright" critics.

If Poetry, the Art of Poetry, is a Mystery, and poets the servers of that
Mystery, they are bound together in fellowship under its Laws, obedient to
Its power. Those who do not recognize the Mystery suppose themselves
Masters, not servants, and manipulate Poetry's power, splitting it into little
counters, as gold is split into coins, and gaming with it; each must accu-
mulate his own little heap of manipulative power-counters—thus so-called
"originality" is at a premium. But within the Fellowship of the Mystery there
is no hoarding of that Power of Poetry—and so-called borrowings are simply
sharings of what poetry gives to Its faithful servants. By the light of this
concept we can also understand Duncan's often criticized "literariness," that
is, his frequent allusions to works of literary and other art and his many
poems that not only take poetry itself as theme but overtly incorporate the
"languaging" process into their essential structure—as he does even in this
very first "Letter" in the sections subtitled "Song of the Languagers," and
later in such poems as "Keeping the Rhyme," "Proofs," "Poetry, a Natural
Thing" or "The Structure of Rime" series, and so many others.

Some readers—even deep and subtle ones—object to poems about
poems (or about the experiencing of any works of art) and about writing
and language, on the grounds that they are too inverted; I have never agreed
(except in regard to conventional set pieces "about" works of art, those
which seem written in fulfillment of commissions or in the bankrupt manner
of British poets laureate celebrating Royal weddings). If much of a poet's
most passionate and affective experiences are of poetry itself (or literature
more generally, or painting, etc.) why should it not be considered wholly
natural and right for him to celebrate those experiences on an equal basis
with those given him by nature, people, animals, history, philosophy, or
current events? Poetry also is a current event. The poet whose range is
confined to any single theme for most of a working life may give off less
energy than one who follows many themes, it is true—and if any single thing
characterizes those whom we think of as world poets, those of the rank of
Homer, Shakespeare, Dante, it is surely breadth of range. But Duncan, although in tribute to the Mystery he is avowedly and proudly "literary,"
cannot be accused of narrow range, of writing *nothing but* poems about
poetry.

It was in 1955 that I first met Duncan. He spent a few days in New
York on his way, with Jess, to spend a year in Europe—chiefly in Majorca,
near to Robert Creeley with whom he had by this time entered into correspondence but still not met. I am not able to locate the letters that preceded
this joyful meeting, nor do I remember our conversation. But the tentative
friendship that had begun so awkwardly was cemented by his visit, and I

recall with what a pang I watched him go down the stairs, he looking back up the stairwell to wave farewell, I leaning over the landing banister. I gave him a notebook for his journey; he used it as a drawing book and gave it back to me full of pictures a year later; and still later I wrote captions for them.

Whatever had passed between us before that time—and Duncan years later claimed that "we must have been in full correspondence by fall of '54"—it was now that the exchange of letters which continued into the early seventies began in earnest. Somehow, in the course of a busy life and many changes of dwelling, a few of the letters Duncan wrote to me have been mislaid, though I am confident that they are not irretrievably lost, for I always treasured them. I have a stack of letters for every year from 1955 to 1972. The written word was not the only dimension of our friendship: from time to time Duncan would come East; in 1963 he and I were both at the Vancouver Poetry Conference; and three times I was in the San Francisco Bay area (in 1969 for six months). At these times we would have the opportunity to "talk out loud" rather than on paper and I have happy memories of visits to museums and galleries, to the Bronx Zoo and the Washington Zoo, and of walks in the Berkeley Hills. Over the years we acquired many mutual friends; and during my son's childhood Duncan and Jess befriended him too, sending him wonderful old Oz books they would find in thrift shops. But it was the correspondence, with its accompaniment of poems, newly finished or in progress, that sustained the friendship most constantly and importantly.

Looking through these letters from Robert I am confirmed in my sense of their having been for me, especially in the first ten years, an extremely important factor in the development of my consciousness as a poet. Pondering what I gave Duncan in exchange, besides responding in kind to his admiration and love, I recall his speaking of how writing to me and to Creeley gave him "a field to range in," and in a 1958 letter he writes of me as serving as a "kind of artistic conscience" (not that he needed one). I had, certainly, the great advantage of not being connected to any "literary world" in particular, and being quite free from the factionalism so prevalent in San Francisco.

Both Duncan and I are essentially autodidacts, though he did have a high school and some college education while I had no instruction after the age of twelve, and the education I received before that was unconventional. I had a good background in English literature, a strong sense of the European past, and had read widely but unmethodically. Duncan read deeply in many fields I was ignorant of—the occult, psychoanalysis, certain areas of science. He did not teach me about these matters, which were not what I was really interested in—but he did give me at least some awareness of them as fields of energy. Because of my family background I knew a little about Jewish and Christian mysticism, so that when Duncan mentioned the Shekinah or Vladimir Soloviev I recognized what he was talking about. The Andrew Lang *Fairy Books* and the fairytales of George MacDonald (and some of his grownup stories too) were common ground, along with much, much else—many loves in literature and art. It was in those areas of twentieth-century literature, American poetry in particular, of which at the time of that first "Letter" I had been ignorant, and—more importantly—in the formation of what I think of as "aesthetic ethics," that Duncan became my mentor. Throughout the correspondence there run certain threads of fundamental disagreement; but a mentor is not necessarily an absolute authority, and though Duncan's erudition, his being older than I, his often authoritative manner, and an element of awe in my affection for him combined to make me take, much of the time, a pupil role, he was all the more a mentor when my own convictions were clarified for me by some conflict with his. Perhaps there was but one essential conflict—and it had to do with the role of a cluster of sources and impulses for which I will use "convictions" as a convenient collective term (though no such term can be quite satisfactory). Although, having written poetry since childhood (beginning, in fact, several years before Duncan wrote *his* first poems), I had experienced "lucky accidents" and the coming of poems "out of nowhere," yet I needed, and was glad to get from him, an aesthetic rationale for such occurrences—reassurances to counter the "Protestant ethic" that makes one afraid to admit, even to oneself, the value of anything one accomplishes without labor. Nevertheless, then and now (and I fully expect to so continue) my deepest personal commitment was to what I believed Rilke (whose letters I'd been reading and rereading since 1946) meant in his famous admonition to Herr Kappus, the "Young Poet," when he told him to search his heart for its *need*. The "need to write" does not provide academic poem-blueprints, so there was no conflict on that level; but such "inner need" *is* related to "having something" (at heart) "to say," and so to a high valuation of "honesty"—and our argument would arise over Duncan's sense that what I called honesty, he (as a passionate anarchist or "libertarian") sometimes regarded as a form of self-coercion, resulting in a misuse of the art we served. He saw a cluster, or alignment, that linked *convictions* with *preconceptions* and *honesty* with *"ought,"* while the cluster I saw linked *convictions* with *integrity* and *honesty* with *precision*. Related to this was my distrust of Robert's habit of attributing (deeply influenced as he was by Freud) to every slip of the tongue or unconscious pun not merely the revelation of some hidden attitude but, it appeared to me—and it seemed and still seems perverse of him—*more validity* than that of what the speaker meant to say, thought he or she said, and indeed (in the case of poems of homonyms noticed only by Duncan) *did* say. To discount the earnest intention because of some hinted, unrecognized, contradictory coexisting factor has never seemed to me just; and to automatically suppose that the unrecognized is necessarily *more* authentic than what has been brought into consciousness strikes me as absurd. Jung (whom I was reading throughout the sixties—Duncan disliked his style and for a long time refused to read him) had made the existence of the "dark side," and the imperative need to respect it, very clear to me; it was Duncan's apparent belief that the dark side was "more equal," as the jest puts it, that I could not stomach.

However, the first time I find this matter touched upon in one of Robert's letters it was not in a way that affronted or antagonized me but one which, on the contrary, belongs with the many ways in which he opened my mind to new realizations. I had been puzzled by some ballads of his, inspired, in part, by Helen Adam (to whose fascinating work he soon introduced me). I found them, I suppose, a curious retrogression from the exciting pioneering into the "open field" in which we and a few others were engaged. What was the Duncan of *Letters,* the Duncan who in a letter of that same summer (1955) was excited by my poem "The Way Through" (printed in *Origin*) and who shared my love of Williams, what was he doing being so "literary"?—I must have asked. For I myself was engaged in "de-literaryfying" myself, in developing a base in common speech, contemporary speech-rhythms. "I don't really understand your ballads," I wrote (I quote now from Duncan's transcription of part of my letter in his preface for a projected volume to be called *Homage to Coleridge*), "why you are writing that way. It seems wasteful both of yourself and in general . . . when I remember what else you have written, even long since, as well as of late especially, I can't quite believe they aren't like something you might have written very long ago." My hesitations about questioning anything he did are evident in the circuitous syntax and its qualifiers—"I don't really"—"I don't quite"—"it seems." And in his reply he wrote,

> it is the interest in, not the faith, that I wld take as my clue. Ideally that we might be as readers or spectators of poetry like botanists—who need not tell themselves they will accept no matter what a plant is or becomes; or biologists—who must pursue the evidence of what life is, haunted by the spectre of what it ought to be [though] they might be. As *makaris* we make as we

are, o.k., and how else? it all however poor must smack of our
very poorness or if fine of our very fineness. Well, let me sweep
out the old validities: and readdress them. They are inventions of
an order within and out of nonorders. And it's as much our life
not to become warriors of these orders as it is our life to realize
what belongs to our order in its when and who we are and what
does not. I can well remember the day when Chagall and Max
Ernst seemed bad to me, I was so the protagonist of the formal
(like Arp or Mondrian) against the Illusionary. The paintings have
not changed. Nor is it that I have *progressed,* or gone in a direction. But my spiritual appetite has been deranged from old
convictions.

This openness was something I was happy in; and indeed, in such passages
Duncan often sounded for me a note of "permission" to my native eclecticism
that some shyness in me, some lack of self-confidence, longed for. Yet even
this liberation was in some degree a source of conflict—not between us, but
within me. For years no praise and approval from anyone else, however
pleasant, could have reassured me until I had Robert's approval of a poem;
and if I had that—as I almost always did—no blame from others could bother
me. "The permission liberates," wrote Duncan in 1963 (about a procedure
of his own, relating to a habit of "reading too much the way some people
eat too much" as he put it elsewhere) "but then how the newly freed possibility can insidiously take over and tyrannize over our alternatives."

Duncan's wit is not a dominant note in the letters but it does flash forth,
whether in jest or in epigram. In September 1959 for example, he complains
that Soloviev had been, alas, "a Professor of Philosophy—that hints or sparks
of a life of Wonder can show up in such a ground is a miracle in itself. What
if Christ's disciples had not been simple fishermen and a whore, and he the
son of a carpenter, but the whole lot been the faculty of some college?" Of
a highly cultured friend he wrote in 1957, "he has enthusiasms but not
passions. . . . He collects experience [but he doesn't] undergo the world."
He described San Francisco audiences for poetry readings (preparing me for
my first public reading anywhere, in December 1957, which he had gone to
considerable trouble to arrange): "The audiences here are avid and tough-
ened—they've survived top poetry read badly; ghastly poetry read ghastly;
the mediocre read with theatrical flourish; poets in advanced stages of discomfort, ego-mania, mumbling, grand style, relentless insistence, professorial
down-the-nosism, charm, calm, schizophrenic disorder, pious agony, auto-
erotic hypnosis, bellowing, hatred, pity, snarl and snub."

Among recurring topics are friendships and feuds among fellow writers: his publishing difficulties (due in part to his very high standards of what a book should look like and in what spirit its printing and publication should be undertaken); and—more importantly—his current reading and its relationship to his work; as well as his work itself. Sometimes poems would have their first beginnings right there on the page, as "Bending the Bow" did; or if not their beginning, the origins of poems enclosed are often recounted. (These, however, I do not feel inclined to quote; they are, as they occur in letters, a part of the intimacy of communion, not to be broadcast—not because they say anything Robert might not say to someone else or to the world in general, but because in their context they are said in an expectation of privacy.)

It is not easy to isolate from the fabric some threads of the essential, the truly dominant theme I have already named—clumsily but not inaccurately—the "ethics of aesthetics"; for the pattern of the whole is complex: negatives and positives entwined and knotted. Everywhere I discover, or rediscover, traces both of the riches Duncan's friendship gave me and of the flaws in mutual confidence which in the 1970s impoverished that friendship.

Perhaps a point at which to begin this drawing-out of one thread is what he says about revision. I had read the notebook excerpts, printed in a S.F. broadside, in which the beautiful phrase occurs, "My revisions are my re-visions." In the beginning I supposed it to mean it was best never to work over a poem, but instead to move on to the next poem—the renewed vision. But taking it to myself as the years passed, I have come to know its meaning as being the necessity of constant re-visioning *in the very act* of refining: that is, that changes made from outside the poem, applied as a reader would apply (supply) them, cannot partake of the poem's vitality; the valid, viable *re*working of a poem must be as much from within, as seamlessly internal to the process, as the primary working. Duncan himself in May '58 explicated:

> I revise (a) when there is an inaccuracy, then I must re-see, as e.g. in the Pindar poem—now that I found the reproduction we had someplace of the Goya painting, I find Cupid is not wingd: in the poem I saw wings. I've to summon up my attention and go at it. (b) when I see an adjustment—it's not polishing for me, but a "correction" of tone, etc., as in the same poem "hear the anvils of human misery clanging" in the Whitman section bothered me, it was at once the measure of the language and the content—Blake! not Whitman (with them *anvils*) and I wanted a

long line pushed to the unwieldy with (Spicer and I had been talking about returning to Marx to find certain correctives—as, the ideas of *work*) Marxist flicker of *commodities*. (c) and even upon what I'd call decorative impulse: I changed

> "follow
> ~~obey~~ to the letter
> freakish instructions"

to gain the pleasurable transitions of l- to l-r and f to f-r.

The idea in back of no revisions as doctrine was that I must force myself to abandon all fillers, to come to correct focus *in the original act*; in part there's the veracity of experience (. . . the poem "comes" as I write it; I seem—that is—to follow a dictate), but it's exactly in respect to that veracity that I don't find myself sufficient. . . . I had nothing like "I write as I please" in mind, certainly not carelessness but the extreme of care kept in the moment of a passionate feeling. . . . My "no revisions" was never divorced from a concept of the work. Concentration. . . . I've got to have the roots of words, the way the language works, at my fingertips, learned in the nerves from whatever studies, in addition to the thing drawn from—the sea, a painting, the face of Marianne Moore—before there's even the beginning of discipline. And decide, on the instant, that's the excitement, between the word that's surrounded by possible meanings, and the word that limits direction.

Copying this out in December 1975 I find the dialogue continuing, for I feel I want to respond to that last sentence: ah, yes, and here I see a source of the difference in tendency between your poetry and mine (though there is a large area in which our practices overlap): you *most often* choose the word that is "surrounded by possible meanings," and willingly drift upon the currents of those possibilities (as you had spoken in "The Venice Poem" of wishing to drift; and I *most often* choose the word that "limits direction"—because to me such "zeroing in" is not limiting but revelatory.

In August of the same year (1958) Duncan resumes the theme:

> I've found myself sweating over extensive rehaulings of the opening poem of the field and right now am at the 12th poem of the book which I want to keep but have almost to reimagine in order to establish it. . . . It's a job of eliminating what doesn't belong to the course of the book, and in the first poem of reshaping so

that the course of the book is anticipated. I mistrust the rationalizing mind that comes to the fore, and must suffer through—like I did when I was just beginning twenty years ago—draft after draft to exhaust the likely and reach the tone in myself where intuition begins to move. It comes sure enuf then, the hand's feel that "this" is what must be done.

He quotes Ezra Pound saying in a 1948 manifesto, "You must understand what is happening"; and makes it clear the significant emphasis is on "what is happening," the presentness, the process. "Most verse," Duncan comments, "is something being made up to communicate a thing already present in the mind—or a lot of it is. And don't pay the attention it shld to what the poet don't know—and won't [know] until the process speaks." He quotes the passage from T. S. Eliot's *Three Voices of Poetry* in which Eliot incorporated a line from Beddoes: "bodiless childful of life in the gloom / crying with frog voice, 'What shall I be?'" and noted that there is "first . . . an inert embryo or 'creative germ' and, on the other hand, the language. . . . [The poet] cannot identify this embryo until it has been transformed into an arrangement of the right words in the right order." And from Eliot he passes directly to a recent poem by Ebbe Borregard—"What Ebbe's got to do is to trust and obey the voice of *The Wapitis*. Where obedience means certainly your 'not to pretend to know more than he does.' But the poem is not a pretention to knowing; it is not, damn it, to be held back to our knowing, as if we could take credit for the poem as if it were a self-assertion. We have in order to obey the inspired voice to come to understand, to let the directives of the poem govern our life and to give our minds over entirely to know[ing] what is happening."

Most of this rang out for me in confirmation of what I believed and practiced. But I question one phrase—that in which he *opposes,* to the trusting of a poem's own directives, the communication of "a thing already present in the mind"; for unless one qualifies the phrase to specify a fully formed, intellectualized, *conscious* "presence in the mind" I see no true opposition here. The "veracity of experience" does not come into being only in the course of the poem, but provides the ground from which the poem grows, or from which it leaps (and to which it fails to return at its peril). "The sea, a painting, the face of Marianne Moore," *are* indeed the "things drawn from." What the writing of the poem, the process of poetry, the following-through of the *radiant gists* In W. C. Williams's phrase) of language itself, does for the writer (and so for the reader, by a process of transference which is indeed communication, communion) is to *reveal the potential* of what is "present in the mind" so that writer and reader *come to know what it is they know,* explore it and realize, real-ize, it. In the fall of '65, commenting anew on my "Notes on Organic Form" which he had read in an earlier, "lecture" form, he quotes with enthusiasm: "whether an experience is a linear sequence or a constellation raying out from and in to a central focus or axis . . . discoverable only in the work, not before it"— but in that phrase I meant "discoverable" quite precisely—that is, not "that which *comes into being* only in the work" but that which, though present in a dim unrecognized or *ungrasped* way, is only *experienced in any degree of fullness* in art's concreteness: The Word made Flesh, Concept given body in Language. One cannot "discover" what is not there. Yet the poem is not merely a representation of the thing discovered—a depiction of an inscape seen; it is itself a new inscape, the seen and the seer conjoined. And it is in the action of synthesizing, of process in language, that the poet is voyager, sailing far beyond that lesser communication, the conveyance of information, to explore the unknown. Duncan seems always on the brink of saying one does not even *start off* from the known.

At times it seems as if it were his own brilliant intellect he is struggling to keep from domination of his art—beating not a dead horse but a horse that does not exist in me, or in others about whose poetry he wrote. In 1956, writing from a small village in Majorca, wondering if he and Jess can afford to travel to London at Christmas time (their budget was $100 a month) he spoke of

> craving the society of English speech. My notebooks are becoming deformed by the "ideas" which ordinarily I throw away into talk, invaluable talk for a head like mine that no waste basket could keep clean for a poem. I can more than understand dear old Coleridge who grew up to be a boring machine of talk; I can fear for my own poor soul. And, isolated from the city of idle chatter, here my head fills up, painfully, with insistent IMPORTANT things-to-say. I toss at night, spring out of bed to sit for hours, crouched over a candle, writing out—ideas, ideas, ideas. Solutions for the universe, or metaphysics of poetry, or poetics of living. Nor does my reading matter help—I have deserted Cocteau for a while because his ratiocination was perhaps the contagion; and the Zohar which irritates the cerebral automatism. Calling up, too, conflicts of poetry's—impulses toward extravagant fantasy, my attempt to reawaken the "romantic" allegiances in myself, to Poe, or Coleridge, or Blake, are inhibited by a "modern" consciousness; I grow appalled at the diffusion of the concrete.

And in 1958, "Sometimes when I am most disconsolate about what I am working at, and most uneasy about the particular 'exaltations' that may not be free outflowings of imagination and desire but excited compulsions instead . . . I feel guilty before the ever-*present* substantial mode of your work." But of course, it was more than an overactive intellect that he had to contend with; the struggle was often with the sheer complexity of vision. His cross-eyes saw deep and far—and it is part of the artist's honor not to reduce the intricate, the multitudinous, multifarious, to a neat simplicity. In 1961 he wrote,

> It's the most disheartening thing I find myself doing in this H. D. study, trying to win her her just literary place—and what I find (when I reflect on it) is that I lose heart (I mean I get that sinking feeling in my heart and lungs, I guess it is, as if I had played it false). I know I can't just avoid this playing it false—you know, direct sentences like sound bridges from good solid island to good solid island; and contrive thought lines like pipe lines to conduct those few clear streams—because the bog is the bog" (he has previously written of "the bog I get into with prose") "*and I really want to discover it on its own terms.*" (my italics) "which must be the naturalist's terms. . . . that damned bog would have to be drained and filled in to be worth a thing, but it is a paradise for the happy frog-lover, or swamp-grass enthusiast—and in its most rank and treacherous backwaters a teeming world of life for the biologist.

Instances of particular changes made in poems in progress (and here I return to the interwoven theme of revision) occur in many letters, following poems sent earlier. The mind's bog was fully inhabited by very exact, green, jewel-eyed frogs. Here are two typical examples:

Nov. 29, 1960

Dear Denny, That *Risk!*—how hard it seems for me to come down to cases there. This time it is not the wording (tho I did alter "simple" to "domestic" in "turning the mind from domestic pleasure") but what necessitated my redoing the whole 3 pages was just the annoying fact that I had phrased certain lines wrong—against my ear. I never did read it "not luck but the way it falls choose / for her, lots" etc., which would mean either an odd stress of the phrase on "for" or a stress I didn't mean on "her." I was reading it from the first "choose for her" with the

stress of the phrase on "choose"; and that terminal pitch height-
ening "falls" in the line before. And again: What did I think I
was hearing when I divided "I had not the means / to buy the
vase" or whatever—was it?—worse! "I had not the means to
buy / the vase" etc.? Anyway, here I was going on like any hack
academic of the automatic line-breaking school . . . not listening
to the cadence of the thing. My cadence, my care, is changing
perhaps too—and I was notating this from old habits contrary
to the actual music.

Or in March 1963 he gives the following revisions for "Structure of
Rime XXI":

> "solitude" for "loneliness" . . . "A depresst key" for "a touched
> string"—a depresst key is what it actually is (when the sympa-
> thetic sound rings) and also because both "depresst" and "key"
> refer to the substrata of the poem.

> "steps of wood" = notes of the scale on a xylophone.

There are also the occasional suggestions for revision—or for more
comprehensive change—of my own work (for until the late sixties we probably exchanged manuscripts of most of what we wrote). Sometimes his criticism was deeply instructive; of this the most telling instance concerns a
1962 poem in which I had *overextended my feelings*. Hearing that a painter
we both knew (but who was not a close friend of mine, rather a friendly
acquaintance whose work had given me great pleasure) had leukemia or some
form of cancer, I plunged, as it were, into an ode that was almost a premature
elegy. An image from one of his paintings had already appeared in another
poem of mine—"Clouds"—which Duncan particularly liked. In his criticism
of this new poem he showed me how the emotional measure of the first
(which dealt with matters "proved upon my pulses," among which the remembrance of clouds he had painted "as I see them—/rising / urgently, ro-
seate in the / mounting of somber power"—"surging / in evening haste over
hermetic grim walls" entered naturally, although the painter as a person
played no part in the poem) was just; whereas in the new poem, focusing
with emotional intensity upon an individual who was not in fact anywhere
close to the center of my life, however much his paintings had moved me,
the measure was false. Although I thought (and looking it over now, still
think) the poem has some good parts, I was thoroughly convinced, and shall
never publish it. It was a lesson which, like all valuable lessons, had appli-
cability not only to the particular occasion; and one which has intimately to

do with the ideogram Ezra Pound has made familiar to us—the concept of integrity embodied in the sign-picture of "a man standing by his word."

There were other occasions, though, when I paid no attention to Robert's criticism because he was misreading. For example, reading my prose "Note on the Imagination" in 1959, he speaks of

> distrusting its discrimination (that just this is imagination and that—"the feared Hoffmanesque blank—the possible monster or stranger"—was Fancy), but wholly going along with the heart of the matter: the seed pearls of summer fog in Tess's hair, and the network of mist diamonds in your hair. But the actual distinction between the expected and the surprising real thing here (and taking as another term the factor of your "usual face-in-the-mirror") is the contrived (the work of Fancy) the remembered (how you rightly [say] "at no time is it hard to call up scenes to the mind's eye"—where I take it these are remembered) and the presented. But you see, if the horrible, the ugly, the very feard commonplace of Hoffman and Poe had been the "presented thing" it would have been "of the imagination" as much as the delightful image. . . .
>
> . . . The evaluation of Fancy and Imagination gets mixed up with the description. All these terms of seeing: vision, insight, phantasm, epiphany, it "looks-like," image, perception, sight, "second-sight," illusion, appearance, it "appears-to-be," mere show, showing forth . . . where trust and mistrust of our eyes varies. However we trust or mistrust the truth, necessity, intent etc. of what is seen (and what manifests itself out of the depths through us): we can't make the choice between monster as fancy and the crown-of-dew as imagination.

Here the disagreement is substantial, for the very point I was trying to make concerned the way in which the active imagination illuminates common experience, and not by mere memory but by supplying new detail we recognize as authentic. By common experience I mean that which conforms to or expresses what we share as "laws of Nature." Hoffman's fantasies, known to me since childhood, had given me pleasure because they were "romantic" in the vernacular sense (and my edition had attractive illustrations) but they did not illumine experience, did not "increase the sense of living, of being alive," to use Wallace Stevens's phrase. In the "Adagia" Stevens says that "To be at the end of reality is not to be at the beginning of imagination, but to be at the end of both." To me—then and now—any kind of "sci fi," any

presentation of what does not partake of natural laws we all experience, such
as gravity and mortality, is only a work of imagination if it is dealing symbolically with psychic truth, with soul-story, as myth, fairytales, and sometimes allegory, do. Duncan continues,

> Jess suggests it's not a matter or either/or (in which Fancy rep-
> resented a lesser order and Imagination a higher order . . .) but
> of two operations or faculties. Shakespeare is rich in both imag-
> ination and fancy . . . where Ezra Pound totally excludes or lacks
> fancy. . . . George MacDonald [spoke] of "works of Fancy and
> Imagination." But I think he means playful and serious. Some-
> times we use the word "fancy" to mean the trivial; but that surely
> does injustice to Shelley's landscapes or Beddoes' Skeleton's Songs
> or the description of Cleopatra's barge that gives speech to Shake-
> speare's sensual fancy

and here I think the difference of views is semantic; for I indeed would attach
the words "playful" and sometimes "trivial" and frequently "contrived,"
"thought-up," to the term fancy, and for the instances cited in Shelley or
Beddoes, would employ the term *fantasy*. The description of Cleopatra's
barge is neither fancy nor fantasy but the rhetoric of enthusiasm accurately
evolving intense sensuous experience; an act of imagination. Fantasy does
seem to me one of the functions of the imagination, subordinate to the greater
faculty's deeper needs—so that "In a cowslip's bell I lie" and other evocations of faery in the *Midsummer Night's Dream,* for example, are delicate
specifics supplied by the power of fantasizing for the more precise presentation of an *imagined,* not fancied or fantasied, world that we can apprehend
as "serious"—having symbolic reality—even while we are entertained by its
delightfulness and fun. The more significant divergence of opinion concerns
"the presented thing," as Duncan called it—for there he seems to claim a
value for the very fact of presentation, as if every image summoned up into
some form of art had thereby its justification; a point of view he certainly
did not, does not, adhere to, and yet—perhaps, again, just because he has
had always so to contend with his own contentiousness and tendency to be
extremely judgmental—which he does seem sometimes to propound, almost
reflexively. "What I do," he wrote in January 1961, "—in that letter regarding your essay on Imagination, or yesterday in response to your letter
and the reply to ———'s piece . . . is to contend. And it obscures perhaps
just the fact that I am contending my own agreements often. . . . Aie! . . . I
shall never be without and must work from those 'irritable reachings after
fact and reason' that must have haunted Keats too—" One of the ways in

which what Duncan says here seems, unfortunately, to be true is manifest in this very statement, which assumes without due warrant (I think) that just because Keats saw in Coleridge that restless, irritable reaching, he himself was subject to it. Yet, however contentious, Duncan is often self-critical in these letters—as above, or as when he speaks (September 1964) of "my . . . 'moralizing,' which makes writing critically such a chore, for I must vomit up my strong puritanical attacking drive . . . this attacking in others what one fears to attack in oneself." And in the midst of arguments he was often generous enough to combine self-criticism, or at least an objective self-definition, with beautiful examples of his opponent's point of view—for instance, in the October 1959 letter already referred to, discussing Fancy and Imagination, he says,

> Jess said an image he particularly remembers from Tess is stars reflected in puddles of water where cows have left hoof tracks— But, you know, I think I am so eager for "concept" that I lose those details. Or, more exactly—that my "concept" lacks details often. For, where you or Jess bring my attention back to the "little fog" intenser "amid the prevailing one" or the star in the cow-tracked puddle: the presence of Tess and Angel leaps up. . . . But for me it's not the perceived verity (your seed pearls of summer fog from Tess; or Madeline Gleason years ago to demonstrate the genius of imagination chose a perceived verity from Dante where the eyes of the sodomites turn and:
>
> > e si ver noi aguzzavan le ciglia,
> > come vecchio sartor fa nella cruna
>
> "towards us sharpened their vision, as an aged tailor does at the eye of his needle"). I am drawn by the conceptual imagination rather than by the perceptual imagination.

There were other times when Robert objected to some particular word in a poem of mine not in a way that instructed me but rather seemed due to his having *missed* a meaning. He himself was aware of that. In October 1966 he writes:

> And especially with you, I have made free to worry poems when there would arise some feeling of a possible form wanted as I read. Sometimes, as in your questionings of the pendent of Passages 2, such queries are most pertinent to the actual intent of the poem. And I think that even seemingly pointless dissents

from the realized poem arise because along the line of reasoning
a formal apprehension, vague but demanding, has arisen that dif-
fers from the author's form. In a mistaken reading, this will arise
because I want to use the matter of the poem to write my own
"Denise Levertov" poem. Crucially astray.

He wanted me to change an image of grief denied, dismissed, and ignored,
in which I spoke of "Always denial. Grief in the morning, washed away / in
coffee, crumbled to a dozen errands between / busy fingers" to "dunked" or
"soaked" in coffee, not understanding that I meant it was washed *away,*
obliterated; the "errands," the "busy fingers" and whatever other images of
the poem all being manifestations of a turning away, a refusal to confront
grief.

   The attribution to others of his own intentions, concerns, or hauntings,
an unfortunate spin-off of his inner contentions, occasioned another type of
misreading—a reading—into, a suspicion of nonexistent complex motives
that obstructs his full comprehension of what *does* exist. "What is going
on," he writes in July 1966, "in your:

> still turns without surprise, with mere regret
> to the scheduled breaking open of breasts whose milk
> runs out over the entrails of still-alive babies,
> transformation of witnessing eyes to pulp-fragments,
> implosion of skinned penises into carcass-gulleys

—the words in their lines are the clotted mass of some operation . . . having
what root in you I wonder? Striving to find place in a story beyond the
immediate." In this comment of his I find, sadly, that the "irritable reaching"
stretches beyond "fact and reason" to search out complications for which
there is no evidence. He misses the obvious. Having listed the lovely attributes
of humankind, I proceeded, anguished at the thought of the war, to list the
destruction of those very attributes—the violence perpetrated by humans
upon each other. Because I believed that "we are members one of another"
I considered myself morally obliged to attempt to contemplate, however
much it hurt to do so, just what that violence can be. I forced myself to
envision, in the process of writing, instances of it (drawing in part on material
supplied by the Medical Committee for Human Rights or similar accounts;
and elaborating from that into harsh language-sounds). There was no need
to look for "what was going on" in me, "from what root" such images
came—one had only to look at the violation of Viet Nam. And from the
misreading of this very poem stemmed, ultimately, the loss of mutual con-

fidence that caused our correspondence to end—or to lapse at least—in the early seventies. But Duncan had conscious justification for such misreadings. In a 1967 interview of which he sent me a transcript he expounded it in terms of what the writer himself must do as reader of his own poem-in-process—but it is clearly what he was doing as a reader of my (and others') poems also:

> The poet must search and research, wonder about, consult the meaning of [the poem's] event. Here, to read means to dig, to let the forces of the poem work in us. Many poets don't read. For instance, take an awfully good poet like Robert Frost; while he writes a poem, he takes it as an expression of something he has felt and thought. He does not read further. It does not seem to be *happening to him,* but coming out of him. Readers too who want to be entertained by [or] to entertain the ideas of a writer will resent taking such writing as evidence of the Real and protest against our "reading into" poems, even as many protest the Freudians reading meanings into life that are not there. The writer, following images and meanings which arise along lines of a melody or along lines of rhythms and impulses, experiences the poem as an immediate reality. . . . I am consciously and attentively at work in writing—here I am like any reader. But I ask further, what is this saying? What does it mean that this is happening here like this?

This statement, as always with Duncan, contains, it seems to me, a valuable reminder of how closely writers must see what they do, to be responsible for it; and of how readers, similarly, should not be content with the superficial, the face value of a poem. But unfortunately, though his "digging for meanings" results in many felicities and resonances of his own work, the method often makes him a poor reader of others, a reader so intent upon shadow that he rejects, or fails to see, substance.

Meanwhile, if Duncan did not see what was obvious in that poem of mine, he certainly did see the war. Increasingly, from the mid-sixties on, its dark, dirty, oppressive cloud pervades his letters. In 1965, responding to a form letter I sent out to gather money and signatures for a full page ad in the *New York Times*—"Writers and Artists Protest the War in Viet Nam"— he had written, "We feel as we know you and Mitch must feel—a helpless outrage at the lies upon which the American policy is run, and at the death and suffering 'our' armaments, troops, and bombers have inflicted upon Viet Nam. Count on us for all protests and write if the protest needs more money.

We will tell you if we can't make it; but we want to do whatever we can."
And along with his sense of helplessness in face of the outrage—where for
all of us the horror itself was compounded by being committed *in our name,*
as Americans—he began to worry about my increasing involvement in the
anti-war movement.

> Denny, the last poem (it was *Advent 1966*) brings with it an
> agonizing sense of how the monstrosity of this nation's War is
> taking over your life, and I wish that I could advance some—not
> consolation, there is none—wisdom of how we are to at once
> bear constant (faithful and ever-present) testimony to our grief
> for those suffering in the War and our knowledge that the gov-
> ernment of the U.S. is so immediately the agent of death and
> destruction of human and natural goods, and at the same time
> as constantly in our work (which must face and contain somehow
> this appalling and would-be spiritually destroying evidence of
> what human kind will do—for it has to do with the imagination
> of what is going on in Man) now, more than ever, to keep alive
> the immediacy of the ideal and of the eternal. Jess and I have
> decided that we will wear black armbands (as the Spanish do
> when some member of their immediate family has died) *always*
> and keep a period of mourning until certainly the last American
> soldier or "consultant" is gone from Viet Nam—but may it not
> be the rest of our lives? until "we" are no longer immediately
> active in bringing grief to members of the family of man. I started
> to wear a Peace button for the first time during the Poetry festival
> in Houston, and I found that it brought me to bear witness at
> surprising times—a waitress, a San Salvador millionaire, a Texas
> school teacher asked me what it meant. And I rejoiced in being
> called to my responsibility. Just at times when I was most for-
> getting myself and living it up.

Just over a year later, again, February 1967—"I have thought often how,
if the outrage and grief of this war preoccupy my mind and heart as it does,
the full burden of it must come upon you and Mitch with Nik so immediately
involved." (Our son Nikolai was by now of draft age.) "And I was fearful
in January that you were having a bad time compounded with that other
constant claim upon one's life the whole literary structure would make, and
where you have a greater exposure in New York. . . . I think also of how
much [anti-]war groups and other organizations would lay claim. . . . It

seems to me too that whatever is not volunteered from the heart, even goodness and demonstrations against the war, when it is conscripted is grievous."

There is, I feel, a confusion here. Certainly, as that poem *Advent 1966*
and others attest, the ever-present consciousness of the war darkened my life
as it darkened the lives of us all. Yet Duncan's affectionate anxiety about
me and Mitch was in a sense misplaced. Duncan himself suffered, surely, a
greater degree of frustration than we did, because we lightened that burden
for ourselves by taking on the other burden of action. Duncan did bear
testimony with his peace button and black armband; he attended a number
of demonstrations, including the rally of writers, artists, and intellectuals at
the Justice Department (which led to the conspiracy trial of Dr. Spock and
four others, of whom Mitch Goodman was one) and the huge march on the
Pentagon the following day, in fall of 1967; and he participated in group
poetry readings given as benefits for the Resistance movement. But he did
not join with others on a day-to-day basis in organizing anti-war activities.
Meanwhile, even though grief, rage, shame and frustration inevitably continued, and indeed even grew as my political awareness grew and I began to
see how this war was only one facet of a complex of oppression, I nevertheless
was experiencing unforeseen blessings. Not only was ongoing action a relief,
an outlet for frustration, however small a drop in the bucket of resistance
to that oppression one knew it to be; but—much more importantly—there
was the experience of a new sense of community as one worked, or picketed,
or even merely "milled around" with comrades. As a good Anarchist from
his youth up, Duncan mistrusted group action; and he was just enough older
than I to have a ready suspicion of "Stalinism" every time he confronted
some action planned or carried out in a way that did not strike him as entirely
"voluntarist." This habit of distrust had shown itself to me as far back as
1959, when he expressed hesitations concerning a magazine he otherwise
liked (and which in fact was quite nonpolitical in its concerns) merely because
of its "exaggerated estimate of Neruda . . . plus the poem by Celan where I
suspected the reference to Madrid as standing for Spain in the Civil War"
and added that he had sent "a prodding letter" to the editor, "to see if there
was any neo-Stalinism going on there." This fear in him, by being a large
factor in keeping him out of more involvement in the Movement during the
sixties and early seventies had two effects: one was that his political awareness, formed in the forties and early fifties, remained static; and the other,
that he did not experience the comradeship, the recognition of apparent
strangers as brothers and sisters, that so warmed the hearts of those who
did feel it, giving us in the difficult present some immediate token of hope
for a truly changed future—a comradeship which depended precisely upon

a political awareness that was *not* static, but *in process of becoming*. Had he but realized it, the spirit of those days was (except in certain factions not central to the movement) not Stalinist, coercive, and regimented at all, but essentially as voluntarist as he could have desired. But we did gather together, and we did shout slogans—and it was perhaps due not only to ideological difference, but to temperamental distaste, that Duncan did not and could not do so. He was, therefore, isolated in his very real anguish; his blood pressure soared; and he could not see that there was nothing I was engaged in that was not "volunteered from the heart."

But the wedge driven between us by his supposition that I was acting coercively, toward myself and—possibly—toward others (a supposition which had, as I see it, no foundations in truth) had not yet gone very deep. In December 1968, a time of private troubles for me as well as of shared political ones, he wrote,

> to reassure you my thoughts are with you. And a prayer . . . not to something I know, yet "to," but *from* something I know very well—the deep resources I have had in our friendship, the so much we have shared and share in what we hold good and dear for human life, and the service we would dedicate our art to. My own thought has been dark this year and in some part of it I have been apprehensive of how much more vulnerable and involved you are: I mean here about the crisis of the war and then the coming-to-roost of the American furies. What we begin to see are the ravening furies of Western civilization. And it corresponds with our own creative generation's arriving at the phase when the furies of our own art come-home-to-roost. Denny, just as I have been carried in my own work to a deeper, grander sense of the ground, I have begun to be aware of gaps and emptinesses— in my being? in the ground?—and I have now to turn next to work again on the H. D. book where I had begun to dread having to do with the inner conflicts I sensed at work there. The *World Order* essay, as I wrote, was written in phases of inertia, dread and breakthrus.
>
> Does it help at all to consider that in part your affliction is the artist's? The personal pain is compounded in it.
>
> Well I couldn't speed this off. My sense that I was doing no more than identifying a brooding center in my own feeling with your inner pain halted me in my tracks. Only, this morning, to find that my thought as I woke turning to you still revolved

around or turned to the concept of inner trials belonging to the
testing of the creative artist, which we as poets and artists come
to, as surely as the fairytale hero or heroine comes to some imprisonment or isolation—to dwell in the reality of how the loved
thing is to be despaired of. I am thinking of the story of the
forgotten bride and groom dwelling close to her or his beloved
in despised form.

Only, in this fumbling, to try to say that your dread, pain, and
being at a loss—personal as it must be, is also the share of each
of us who seeks to deepen feeling. Not an affliction in and of
itself but belonging to the psychic metamorphosis—we cannot
direct it, or, it is directed by inner orders that our crude and
unwilling conscious self dreads. Eros and his Other, Thanatos,
work there.

That beautiful letter, in which the feeling-tone of an earlier time in our
friendship resounds at a deeper, darker pitch, and which sums up, or rather,
is representative of, the rich, the immeasurable gift given me by this association, seems almost valedictory. Yet it was not yet so, in fact, for a month
later Mitch and I arrived on the West Coast to spend six months at Berkeley.
During this period, though my teaching job and participation in current
events (this was 1969, the spring of the Third World strike and of People's
Park) prevented me from seeing Robert as often as I had hoped, there were
some quiet times of reading current poems to one another (and to Mitch
and Jess) and at least one or two walks in the mimosa- and eucalyptus-
scented lanes above Berkeley, a terrain he knew intimately and seemed curiously at rest in.

It was not until after that, in the early seventies, that our correspondence
faltered and jarred to a halt. I will not deal here with the way every negative
element that had ever arisen between us, but especially the false interpretation
begun in his questioning of "Life at War," began to take over in our letters,
each of us taking fierce, static, antagonist "positions," he of attack, I of
defense. It is a conflict still unresolved—if this is in some sense a narrative,
the end of the story has perhaps not yet been reached. But I think of my
Duncan letters as a constellation rather than as a linear sequence. And in
that constellation the major stars are without question the messages of instruction by means of which my intelligence grew keener, my artistic conscience more acute; messages of love, support, and solidarity in the fellowship
of poetry. None of my many poet friends has given me more; and when I
look back to Florence, 1948, I know I came then upon what was for two
decades a primary current of my life.

RICHARD HOWARD

"Turned Back to the Wild by Love"

When May Swenson, speaking in her thaumaturgical fashion of poetry, says that "attention to the silence in between is the amulet that makes it work," we are reminded, while on other occasions in her work we are reassured, that there is a kind of poetry, as there used to be a kind of love, which dares not speak its name. Indeed, it was in the latter's heyday (1891, when Mallarmé thanked Oscar Wilde for *The Picture of Dorian Gray,* "one of the only books that can move me, for its commotion proceeds from an essential reverie, and from the strangest silences of the soul"), that the former's program was devised, by the thanker: "to *name* an object is to suppress three-quarters of our pleasure in the poem, a pleasure which consists in gradually divining . . . ; to *suggest,* that is the ideal. That is making perfect use of the kind of mystery which constitutes the symbol." Of course, there is a complementary impulse to *identify* in this reluctance to call a spade a spade; it is an impulse implicit in the very paradox supported by the word *identification,* which we use both to select an object in all its singularity, and to dissolve that "identical" object into its likeness with another. The refusal, or the reluctance, to *name* in order that she may the more truly *identify* is what we notice first about May Swenson's poetry—though she does not proceed so strictly with the enterprise as Mallarmé, for whom the designation of a flower enforced its *absence* from any bouquet. When Miss Swenson says:

From *Alone with America.* © 1980 by Richard Howard. Atheneum, 1980. Originally entitled "May Swenson: 'Turned Back to the Wild by Love.'"

> beautiful each Shape
> to see
> wonderful each Thing
> to name

she means the kind of ascertaining of Existence Hölderlin meant when he
said that poetry was a naming of the Gods—and for such an appeal (such
an appellation), the ordinary labels do not suffice. Miss Swenson would not
be so extreme about her magic as the symbolists, but she is plainly aware of
the numbing power of proper names; as the story of Rumpelstiltskin demonstrates, there is an awful mastery in knowing what a being is called, and
in so calling him—indeed such mastery suggests, to May Swenson at least,
a corresponding lack of attention to the quality of being itself, a failure, by
the wielding of nomination's "mace petrific," to encounter, to espouse form
as it *becomes* what it is.

It is an old kind of poetry, then, that this poet resumes in her quest for
"my face in the rock, my name on the wildest tree," a poetry that goes back
to Orpheus, probably, and moves forward through Blake and Emily Dickinson, whom May Swenson specifically echoes, I think, in her eagerness to
see Being wherever she looks:

> Any Object before the Eye
> can fill the space can occupy
> the supple frame of eternity
>
> my Hand before me such
> tangents reaches into Much
> root and twig extremes can touch
>
> any Hour can be the all
> expanding like a cunning Ball
> to a Vast from very small
>
> any Single becomes the More
> multiples sprout from alpha's core
> from Vase of legend vessels of lore.

It is the poetry which comes into existence whenever the need is felt (as by
Valéry most recently, most magisterially) to *charm,* to *enchant,* to *bind by
spells* an existence otherwise apprehended as inaccessibly other. For as Valéry
says of Orpheus, it was only by his songs that trees knew the full horror of
dancing. Similarly, in May Swenson's kennings, their method "a parliament
of overlappings" and their goal "an assuaging singleness," we find that the

hand in her lap, the cat on the sill, the cloud in the sky become, before we
have a chance to adjust our sights and to enslave our other senses as well to
what we *know*, fables of unlabelled Being:

> For each path leads both out and in
> I come while going   No to and from
> There is only here   And here
> is as well as there   Wherever
> I am led I move within the care
> of the season
> hidden in the creases of her skirts
> of green or brown or beaded red
> And when they are white
> I am not lost   I am not lost then
> only covered for the night.

Evidently, Miss Swenson's effort has been to discover runes, the conjurations
by which she can not only apostrophize the hand, the cat and the cloud in
their innominate otherness, but by which she can, in some essential and
relieving way, *become them,* leave her own impinging selfhood in the para-
lyzed region where names are assigned, and assume instead the energies of
natural process.

From the first—in 1954 came *her* first collection, the significantly titled
Another Animal—May Swenson has practiced, in riddles, chants, hex-signs
and a whole panoply of invented sortilège unwonted in Western poetry since
the Witch of Endor brought up Samuel, the ways not only of summoning
Being into her grasp, but of getting herself out of that grasp and into alien
shapes, into those emblems of power most often identified with the sexual:

> on this ball   oh to Endure
> half dark   like the stone
> half light   sufficient
> i walk Upright   to itself alone
> i lie Prone
> within the night   or Reincarnate
>   like the tree
> the longing   be born each spring
> that i know   to greenery
> is in the Stone also
> it must be   or like the lion
> the same that rises   without law

in the Tree   to roam the Wild
the longing   on velvet paw.
in the Lion's call
speaks for all

Consider the array of instruments in this fragment of the first poem from
that first book, "Evolution": the incantatory use of rhyme; the rhythms of
the spell; the typography that lines up the first column to stand not only pat
but put, as it were, against the outer verticality of the second column, so
that the poem on the page articulates, by the space it leaves as by the form
it takes, a regular *passage* through which the forces can move to their completion; the lower-casing of the first-person pronoun, and the capitalization
of the three Entities addressed, then their relegation to lower-case too, and
the assumption of capital status by the two crucial verbs, "Reincarnate" and
"Endure," and by the hypostatized adjective "Wild"; the irregular little stanzas content to exhibit, in loving complacency, a single word as an entire line;
the rejection of punctuation as an unnecessary artifice in this organum of
being. Evidently, this poet is engaged, and more than engaged, is elated, by
the responsibilities of form. In subsequent poems in *Another Animal,* as in
her other books, Miss Swenson exhibits a very determined attitude toward
contrivance; aware, I suppose, of the danger inherent in her own siren-songs,
with their obsessive reliance on the devices of incantation, she is more than
eager to cast off the blasphemies of "Satanic Form":

Things metallic or glass
frozen twisted flattened
stretched to agonized bubbles
bricks beams receptacles vehicles
forced through fire hatched to unwilling form

—and to assume in their place the "blessed" and organic avatars it is her
art to invoke, not so much to counterfeit as to conjure:

flower and stone not cursed with symmetry
cloud and shadow not doomed to shape and fixity
the intricate body of man without rivet or nail
O love the juice in the green stem growing.

Contraption, like naming, is seen as the wrong version of experience. The
paradox of the riddling poet is that she must identify without naming, make
without artifice, "a model of time, a map of space." Miss Swenson is engaged
in the Higher Fabrication, that *poesis* which is the true baptism; when she

fails to devise charms that capture Being in their toils, she becomes, like Dickinson, again, merely charming; the appeal is no more, at times, than appealing, when it needed to be a summons:

> I lived by magic
> A little bag in my chest held a whirling stone
> so hot it was past burning
> so radiant it was blinding
>
> When the moon rose worn and broken
> her face like a coin endlessly exchanged
> in the hands of the sea
> her ray fell upon the doors which opened
> and I walked in the living wood.

Throughout this book, as the title itself suggests, and in the course of the collections to come, May Swenson has found a figure which allows her to escape the difficulties of both nomination and mechanism; it is the figure of the centaur, which cannot be merely named for it is imaginary, and which cannot be merely artificial for it is alive. She begins, in the title poem:

> Another animal imagine moving
>   in his rippling hide
>   down the track of the centaur

the shaped verses undulate down the page in a first presentment of "dappled animals with hooves and human knees"; in "To Confirm a Thing," the figure is moralized a little:

> In the equal Night where oracular beasts
>   the planets depose
> and our Selves assume their orbits . . .
> My thighs made marble-hard
>   uncouple only to the Archer
> with his diametrical bow
>   who prances in the South
> himself a part of his horse . . .
> Then let me by these signs
>   maintain my magnitude
> as the candid Centaur his dynasty upholds
>   And in the Ecliptic Year
> our sweet rebellions

                            shall not be occulted but remain
     coronals in heaven's Wheel.

And finally, in "Question," the same figure, which has become perhaps too cosmic, too "mechanical" in its astronomic implications, is returned to its erotic energies, the self addressed in that animal form where, by a certain incantation, Miss Swenson best finds her being in its highest range:

           Body my house
           my horse my hound
           what will I do
           when you are fallen

           Where will I sleep
           How will I ride
           What will I hunt
           Where can I go
           without my mount
           all eager and quick . . .

           With cloud for shift
           how will I hide?

    May Swenson's second book was published in 1958; *A Cage of Spines*, garlanded with praise by Elizabeth Bishop, Richard Wilbur and Robert Lowell, among others; of these, only Howard Moss seems taken with the notion that in Swenson's "world," Being is illuminated so that "whatever she describes is not only more itself but more than itself." The strategies and devices, the shamanism and sorcery this poet deploys have become, in this larger, luminous collection, more elaborate, more convinced, and deserve further attention; their accommodation of the mystery that only when a thing is apprehended as something else can it be known as itself is fierce and full in *A Cage of Spines*. But we must note, first, an interesting development, from implication to statement, of the Centaur theme, the projection of energies and erotics into animal form, so that the poet may ask, "to what beast's intent / are we the fodder and nourishment?" The new note sounded occurs at the very start of the book, in a poem explicit enough to be called "The Centaur." For the first time, Swenson evokes life—her life—in the chatty, novelistic mode previously judged "too effusive in design for our analyses":

The summer that I was ten—
Can it be there was only one
summer that I was ten? It must

have been a long one then—

Looking down the prospect of her imagination, the poet reports how she would ride her willow branch all morning:

I was the horse and the rider,
and the leather I slapped to his rump
spanked my own behind

and come inside, after an exhausting morning's riding (and being ridden):

Where have you been? said my mother.
Been riding, I said from the sink,
and filled me a glass of water . . .

Go tie back your hair, said my mother,
and *Why is your mouth all green?*
*Rob Roy, he pulled some clover
as we crossed the field,* I told her.

Here not by incantation but by exactitude in narrative, Miss Swenson gets across the doubleness in being she strives for throughout. It is a method she will resume in the book after this one, but the rest of *A Cage of Spines* is dedicated to the means of witchcraft. By riddles and charms, the poet aspires to a more resonant being than the life grudgingly acknowledged in her own body:

I would be inheritor
of the lamb's way and the deer's,
my thrust take from the ground
I tread or lie on. In thighs of trees,
in recumbent stones, in the loins
of beasts is found
that line my own nakedness carried.
Here, in an Eden of the mind,
I would remain among my kind,
to lake and hill, to tree and beast married.

Not only the shaped poems, the compulsive rhymes and puns ("what seams is only art"), the riddles and agnominations ("the shape of this box keels me oval / Heels feel its bottom / Nape knocks its top"—from the conundrum about eggs), but the discovery of the secret messages hidden within ordinary speech, as Being is concealed by Labels, excite Miss Swenson to poems of an almost frantic hermeticism: in two homages to writers, she extends her method to a kind of esoteric dalliance. First in "Frontispiece," which appears to describe a picture of Virginia Woolf in terms of the circumstances that led her to suicide, we realize from an odd, ominous resonance the lines have, that not only the names of the writer herself ("your chaste-fierce name") but the titles of all her books have been braided into the verse; thus the "frontispiece" is a compendium of names indeed, only disguised, worked back into the texture of Being and used not as nominations but proof:

> The waves carve your hearse and tomb
> and toll your voyage out again again.

The second poem of dedication is even more curious, for in it not merely names but all words are susceptible of disintegration into their secret content; what we are offered is ostensibly a description of Frost ("R. F., His Hand Against a Tree") but the account is continually breaking down as Miss Swenson discovers, like Nabokov (whose English is so often a matter of perpetual inside jokes), that she can say more about her subject by letting the language speak for itself, merely doing a little pruning and spacing to let the sense in:

> Lots of trees in the fo
> rest but this one's an O
> a K that's plan
> ted hims elf and nob
> oddy has k nots of that hand
> some polish or the knarl
> edge of ear th or the obs
> tiny ate servation his blueyes
> make or the tr easures his sent
> ient t humb les find.

These are, as she calls them, "glyphs of a daring alphabet" indeed, and "hide what they depend on." There are other diableries in this book likely to exasperate as well as to exalt; chiefly a poem called "Parade of Painters" in which thirty-six painters are "assigned" first a characteristic color, then a texture ("Manet porcelain, Matisse thistles," etc.), then a shape. Then the whole thing is assembled in a litany of thirty-six lines which reads something like a dada catalogue, save that Swenson has shown us her method and its underlying logic: we cannot fault it, but we may fail to be *charmed* by the procession, as it passes, of painter, shape, texture and color:

> Delacroix mouth viscera iris
> Degas witchmoth birch clay
> Pissaro dhow privet marble
> Seurat hourglass linen popular
> Dufy glove pearl azure
> Rouault mummy serge blood.

Much more characteristic of Swenson's excellence, I think, is "News from the Cabin," in which all her impulses congregate joyously around a less arbitrary theme: visits from four creatures, none named but all identified by the characteristic textures, rhythms, and vocabulary we should associate with a woodpecker, a squirrel, a jay, and a snake, if we were to *become* them by the power of our *recital* (rather like the interludes young Arthur experiences, in T. H. White's books, as he serves his apprenticeship to fish, hawks, even hedgehogs in order to learn how to be a man). Consider the sound of this from "Hairy":

> Cried *peek!* Beaked it—chiselled the drupe.
> His nostril I saw, slit in a slate whistle,
> White-black dominoes clicked in his wings.
> Bunched beneath the dangle he heckled with holes,
>   bellysack soft, eye a brad, a red-flecked
>   mallet his ball-peen head, his neck its haft.

and the movement of the end of "Scurry":

> Sat put, pert, neat, in his suit and his seat, for a minute,
>   a frown between snub ears, bulb-eyed head
>   toward me sideways, chewed.
> Rocked, squeaked. Stored the stone in his cheek.
> Finished, fell to all fours, a little roan couch;
>   flurried paws loped him off, prone-bodied,
>   tail turned torch, sail, scarf.

In these extraordinary poems, animal life is invoked, is actually *acquired* for the conjurer's purposes (extended energy, a generalized erotic awareness) by the haptic qualities of language itself, even more than by the riddling process so programmatically set up in the other pieces. The generosity, the abundance of Swenson's means may allow her, on the one hand, to speak somewhat sentimentally in "East River" of Brooklyn seen across the water as "a shelf

of old shoes, needing repair, but clean knots of smoke are being tied and
untied," and thereby we see, though both are patronized, Brooklyn *and* the
shoes; but in "News from the Cabin," on the other, she also commands, as
in the last section, "Supple," an utterance whose imagery is assimilated
without condescension to its very movement, a diction so wedded to appearances that the speaker "leaves the spot" enriched with an access of being,
an increment which comes only when life has been enchanted to its own
understanding:

> I followed that elastic: loose
>   unicolored knot, a noose he made as if unconscious.
> Until my shadow touched him; half his curd
>   shuddered, the rest lay chill.
> I stirred: the ribbon raised a loop;
>   its end stretched, then cringed like an udder;
>   a bifid tongue, his only rapid, whirred
>   in the vent; vertical pupils lit his hood.
> That part, a groping finger, hinged, stayed upright.
> Indicated what? That I stood
>   in his light? I left the spot.

In 1963, a large group of poems from Miss Swenson's first two volumes,
with some fifty new poems, was published under the general title *To Mix
with Time*, a phrase which in its own context reiterates her project: "One
must work a magic to mix with time / in order to become old." Here the
very compression, the proliferation *inward* of the new abracadabras seem to
have enabled the poet to be elsewhere quite explicit about her undertaking:

> There unraveled
> from a file in my mind a magic motion
> I, too, used to play with: from chosen words a potion
> could be wrung; pickings of them, eaten, could make
>   you fly, walk
> on water, be somebody else, do or undo anything, go back
> or forward on belts of time.

It is good to have it spelled out, for there are here many poems of a specifically esoteric quality, whose organization on the page, as in the ear, suggests
the location of a mystery in Being which the poet would attain to only by a
ritual, a litany of participles and lattices of space:

> There is a   Swaddled Thing
> *There is a   Swaddled Thing*

There is a	Rocking Box
There is a	*Covered Box*
The	Unwrapping
the	Ripening
Then the	Loosening
the	Spoiling
The	Stiffening
then the	Wrapping
The	Softening
but the long long	Drying
The	Wrapping
the	Wrapping
the	Straightening
and	Wrapping
The rigid	Rolling
the gilded	Scrolling
The	Wrapping
and	Wrapping
and careful	Rewrapping
The	Thinning
and	Drying
but the	Wrapping
and	Fattening
There is the worm	Coiled
and the straw	Straightened
There is the	Plank
and the glaucous	Bundle
the paper	Skull
and the charred	Hair
the linen	Lip
and the leather	Eyelid
There is a	Person
of flesh that is *a rocking*	*Box*
There is a	Box
of wood that is *a painted*	*Person*

to which the poet, her own exegete, adds this "Note from a diary: I remembered Giotto's fresco, 'Birth of the Virgin' in a cloister in Florence: the

'Mother of God' was a swaddled infant held upright, like a board or plaque, by her nurse . . . and I remembered a mummy in the Vatican Museum in Rome: in her sarcophagus shaped and painted like herself, an Egyptian girl 2000 years old lay unwrapped to the waist." The notation, in the poem, of identities between the infant and the mummy, and the enactment of vital, or mortal, differences that reaches the climax of the last four lines, with their paradoxical reversals, dramatizes the kind of formal extremes May Swenson is ready to risk. "The idea," she says in "Out of my Head," the first poem in this book, "is to make a vehicle out of it." To employ, that is, the spell in order to be taken somewhere; or as she says in another place, and in her most orphic cadences:

> we weave asleep
> a body
> and awake unravel
> the same veins
> we travel.

The unravelling of those travelled veins is undertaken, of course, in other ways besides such necromantic ones. There is a group of poems, in *To Mix with Time,* written in France, Italy, and Spain and concerned with the re- porting of surfaces, not the casting of spells. As in the earlier "The Centaur," the poet appears sufficiently possessed of her identity to feel no need of commanding her surround by voodoo. She can trust her sensibility, in these new old places, to do its work, and oblige the genius loci to give up its own ghost:

> Gondola-slim
> above the bridge, a new moon held a dim
> circle of charcoal between its points.
> Bats played in the greenish air,
> their wing-joints
> soft as moths' against the bone-gray palazzi where
> not a window was alight.

These are secular poems, then, rarely moralized or magicked, but left to speak for themselves, in the descriptive mode of Elizabeth Bishop, though there are exceptions, occurring (as we might expect) in the case of the "Foun- tains of Aix," where the word "water" is disjoined fifteen times from the lines and made to slide down the side of a stanza:

> A goddess is driving a chariot through   water.
> Her reins and whips are tight white   water.

Bronze hooves of horses wrangle with   water.
Faces with mossy lips unlocked
                always uttering   water
                              Water
        wearing their features blank,
        their ears deaf, their eyes mad
        or patient or blind or astonished at   water
        always uttered out of their mouths.

and again in a poem about death, "The Alyscamps at Arles," in which the
words "bodies," "bones," "died," "stones" and "flesh" are isolated in a
central column, set off like tombs in each line, and recurring some two dozen
times. Europe, we take it, is sacred ground, and the mere fact of treading it
is enough, almost, for Miss Swenson's genius to speak low to her. The con-
jugation, in this book, of a temporal response to earth and a runic riddling
of it is indeed "to mix with time"; there is a relaxation of need, somehow,
as if the poet had come to find things enthralling enough in themselves:

        In any random, sprawling, decomposing thing
        is the charming string
        of its history—and what it will be next.

Like "Evolution," her first poem in her first book, her last one here, "The
Exchange," recapitulates her enterprise—to get out of herself and into those
larger, warmer energies of earth, and to do so by liturgical means ("Words?
Let their / mutations work / toward the escape / of object into the nearest
next / shape, motion, assembly, temporal context"):

        Populous and mixed is mind.
        Earth take thought,
        my mouth be moss . . .

        Wind be motion,
        birds be passion,
        water invite me to your bed.

   Things Taking Place was the working title May Swenson had originally
given *To Mix with Time,* and its suggestion of a larger interest in a secular
world where events occur, where life "happens," and a lessening concern
with the cosmic energies of "mere" Being, is even more applicable to the
poet's latest work, published in 1967 in a long book called *Half Sun Half
Sleep.* Not that Miss Swenson is any less interested in the energies, the powers
that drive the stars in their courses, or in the measurements and movements

responsible for that formal echo of dune and wave, beach and tide—rather, the largest impulses which often she could *handle,* precisely, as abstractions only, are now accommodated into the observed intercourse of her body and its environment, her life and its limits. There are charms here too, but they are *secular* charms, and the fact that so many of the rhyme words are tucked away in the "wrong" parts of the line suggests the profane intentions of these cunning incantations—if Miss Swenson has designs on life, they are subordinated to a surface she prefers unruly:

> Well, do they sing? If so, I *expect* their
> note is extreme. Not something one *hears,*
> but must watch the cat's *ears* to *detect*
>   (emphasis mine)

she furthers, too, her old mistrust, even her outright distaste for the exemplars of "Satanic Form," which she finds in most of our modern enclosures, elevator cages, Pullman cars and airplane bellies, and specifically in our satellites and space missiles. One of the most brilliant pieces in the new book is "August 19, Pad 19," a jeering, nerve-end journal of an astronaut "positioned for either breach birth / or urn burial." Reminiscent of her other entrapped forms—the mummy and the swaddled infant—the astronaut is prepared:

> Never so helpless, so choked with power.
> Never so impotent, so important.
> So naked, wrapped, equipped, and immobile,
> cared for by 5000 nurses.
> Let them siphon my urine to the nearest star.
> Let it flare and spin like a Catherine.
>
> . . . T minus 10 . . . The click of countdown stops.
> My pram and mummy case, this trap's
> tumescent tube's still locked to wet,
> magnetic, unpredictable earth.
> All my system's go, but oh,
> an anger of the air won't let me go.
> On the screen the blip is MISSION SCRUBBED

and the poem's ultimate irony is to oblige this sequestered consciousness, furious in its failure, to feel "out on the dome some innocent drops of rain." The titles suggest the poet's preferences: "On Handling Some Small Shells from the Windward Islands," "A Basin of Eggs," "Drawing the Cat," "On

Seeing Rocks Cropping out of a Hill in Central Park" and—quintessen-
tially—"Things in Common." There is of course a certain trust in her old
ways of working, call them weapons even, the sharp-edged, riddling means
of tricking us into the poem; the book itself is arranged with the titles in
alphabetical order, and there are a number of shaped poems, of spells and
counting-rhymes, for as she says in "The Truth," a poem about a snake that
is snake-shaped,

> Speculation about shape amount to a counting
> of the coils.

But there is a moving away from the kind of hermetic indication that cannot
show loss as well as gain. There is the sense, recorded in a poem about two
trees leaning together, "All That Time," that our interpretations of phenomena may be cruelly aberrant:

> And where their tops tangled
> it looked like he was crying
> on her shoulder.
> On the other hand, maybe he
>
> had been trying to weaken her,
> break her, or at least
> make her bend
> over backwards for him

and that we must devise a form that will account for "strange abrasions /
zodiacal wounds." The important thing, she says, is

> To be the instrument
> and the wound of feeling.

As the book's title suggests, the balance between sacred and profane, ritual
and report, with its implication of the balance between seeing and dreaming,
speech and somnambulism, is carefully tended:

> The tug of the void
> the will of the world
> together.

These poems are exuberant in their hocus-pocus, surely, but they are also a
little rueful about the facility to which one can trust in the hope of getting
out of the self ("One must be a cloud to occupy a house of cloud . . . refusing
the fixture of a solid soul"); also they are not so explicit in exploring "the

suck of the sea's dark mind": if Swenson still asks, in a poem called "The Lightning" through which a diagonal gutter of space jabs through her twenty lines to the word "entrails," "When will I grope my way clear of the entrails of intellect?" she is nonetheless prepared to use the mementos of that gutted intellect to deal with the sea's dark mind, referring to the "ancient diary the waves are murmuring" and accounting in terms of gains as well as losses for her existence as a rational animal:

> When I was a sea worm
> I never saw the sun,
>
> but flowed, a salty germ,
> in the bloodstream of the sea.
> There I left an alphabet
>
> but it grew dim to me.
> Something caught me in its net,
> took me from the deep
>
> book of the ocean, weaned me,
> put fin and wing to sleep,
> made me stand and made me
>
> face the sun's dry eye.
> On the shore of intellect
> I forgot how to fly . . .
>
> In brightness I lost track
> of my underworld
> of ultraviolet wisdom.
>
> My fiery head furled
> up its cool kingdom
> and put night away.

These are no longer nor even want to be the poems of a small furry animal ("the page my acre") nor of a selfless demiurge ("They founded the sun. / When the sun found them / it undertook its path and aim . . . / The air first heard itself / called glory in their lungs"); they are the witty resigned poems of a woman "hunting clarities of Being," asking

> Have I arrived from
> left or
> right to hover here

> in the clear permission of my
>   temperature? Is my
>   flow a fading
>   up or
>   down—my glow
>   going? Or is my flush
>   rushing to a rose of ripe
>   explosion?

a woman eager still to manipulate the phenomenal world by magic, but so possessed, now, of the means of her identity that the ritual, spellbinding, litaneutical elements of her art have grown consistent, even coincident, with her temporal, conditioned, suffering experience and seem—to pay her the highest compliment May Swenson could care to receive—no more than natural.

ROBERT B. SHAW

Richard Wilbur's World

A poet whose work has been widely acclaimed for thirty years is bound
to encounter critical reassessment in the later phases of his career. To judge
from some early reviews of *The Mind-Reader,* Richard Wilbur's sixth collection and his first to appear in seven years, he is presently under the revisionist guns. Wilbur's poems are well-made enough to be their own best
defense. But a consideration of the charges urged against them is a convenient
way of examining their style and meaning, both of which are more pertinent
to our condition than the poet's detractors have lately been willing to allow.

Three overlapping complaints seem largely to be shared among Wilbur's
antagonists. First, that the formal properties of Wilbur's poems—meter,
rhyme, and a diction more literary than colloquial—effectively prevent them
from exploring areas of experience which are of interest to contemporary
minds. Wilbur's metrical strategies are seen as self-complacent games, isolating him from readers who favor directness of communication and who
feel, in regard to style, that less is more. Second, and more narrowly, Wilbur
is criticized for remaining obdurately within the boundaries defined by his
earliest successes. The degree of stylistic similarity in early and recent poems
is sufficiently high to set him apart from many of the poets of his generation
whose careers have featured deliberate departures from their own earlier
ways of writing. The continuum of virtuosity extending from *The Beautiful
Changes* (1947) to *The Mind-Reader* (1976) is perceived by the hostile critic
as evidence of arrested development, lack of dynamism, daring, self-

From *Parnassus* 5, no. 2 (Spring 1977). © 1977 by the Poetry in Review Foundation.

questioning, what you will. Third, Wilbur's themes and attitudes have come
in for attack among critics looking for something to dismiss besides his style.
He is said to be platitudinous, or unimaginatively orthodox, or unreflectively
esthetic, or inconsequentially flippant. He is by turns a prim reactionary or
a fuzzy liberal. However they may be phrased, these characterizations stem
from an obscure intimation that the poet who wrote these poems has not
suffered enough: he is too happy. So runs the indictment.

A fully adequate answer to the first of these objections would extend
beyond the bounds of this discussion to become a defense of traditional
poetic form. Limiting discussion strictly to Wilbur's use of the traditional,
we may say that for him form is something more than a game—though he
would never deny the presence of a ludic element that enlivens composition—
and that it is not pursued as an escape from the pressures of reality. It is,
rather, a calculated means of confronting those pressures. *Ceremony* is the
title of Wilbur's second book; and the attempt in his work to harness the
power inherent in ceremony is unremitting. Wilbur may in this title have
been thinking of Yeats's "Ceremony's a name for the rich horn, / And custom
for the spreading laurel tree." We misunderstand the lines if we start thinking
of drawing rooms. Yeats, like Wilbur later, is referring not so much to polite
society as to the creative sources in ritual which make any kind of society
possible. As John Crowe Ransom and others have pointed out, it is the formal
aspects of poetry, such as meter and rhyme, that are its most primitive. The
poem enters us as sound before we construe its sense. The arrangements of
sound address the roots of our being; the poem whose formal effects are
most conspicuous is thus the most radical in its aim and method. Form in
poetry takes its rise from form in primitive religious ritual, the aim of which
is not to estrange men from nature, but to integrate them anew into the
patterned fabric of the cosmos. (The root-meaning of "religion"—a binding
or tying back—suggests this much.) Only by viewing Wilbur's urbanity apart
from his argument can one fail to notice the seriousness with which he insists
on form as a means of relating us to the natural:

> But ceremony never did conceal,
> Save to the silly eye, which all allows,
> How much we are the woods we wander in.

I shall need to deal further with this idea of form as a realization of natural
vitality when I come to talk of Wilbur's themes; here, it is sufficient to note
that the structures created by his expertise have functions far different from
those of the ivory tower. If he seems an isolated figure, it is not because he

holds himself aloof, but because there is a refusal on the part of some readers to enter the circle of ritual into which his art invites them.

Wilbur's supposed "lack of development" can be dealt with even more briefly. Numerous contemporary examples to the contrary notwithstanding, it remains a fact that not every poet is impelled to violent transformations of style. There are poets, of course, whose every major work is attended by a sense of stylistic experiment—Eliot and, more recently, Lowell come to mind. But there are poets as well who, having mastered their idiom, are content to spend a lifetime in its continued refinement, and in applying it to a handful of themes whose fascination never wanes for them. Poets as seemingly diverse as Emily Dickinson and Edwin Muir supply instances of such deliberately confined intensity. Wilbur is a poet of this, rather than of the former sort. His attention to his chosen subjects deepens without yielding often to passing distractions. This continuous deepening is more deservedly termed development, one might feel, than is a series of stylistic departures whose genealogical relations to one another are not easily to be traced.

Wilbur's chief recurrent theme is implicit in his approach to style. His intricately patterned poems reflect the discovery of patterns of natural beauty; and the poet's art thus strives to be an adequate analogy to the surrounding creation. The art of man mirrors the art of God. Creative energy finding its expression in natural and esthetic form is what Wilbur continually contemplates, praises, and seeks to realize in his own writing. Such a concern, and Wilbur's treatment of it, may broadly be described as Catholic. I say this without reference to Wilbur's religious affiliation, of which I have no knowledge. Perhaps a better word is "sacramental": the poems at their deepest level are acts of sacramental perception, with similarities in thought (though few in style) to the lyrics of Hopkins, which also treat of the created universe as an outward sign and token of an inward and spiritual grace. Certainly Wilbur is more reticent of dogmatizing than Hopkins; confession of faith is not his prime motive in writing. But the Jesuit's homemade term for the patterned signatures of grace in nature, *inscape,* is one which happily defines the object of Wilbur's imagination. Through an intensity of focus he suggests the informing spiritual energy present in the appearances that capture his attention. A lively accuracy is habitual in his natural descriptions: his black November turkey, "The pale-blue bony head / Set on its shepherd's crook / Like a saint's death-mask," is not easily forgotten. Especially memorable are his readings of physical motion—something Wilbur can do more effectively than any other living poet. With an exquisite modulation he conveys a woman's solitary dance down the Spanish Steps "to the fountain-quieted square":

not then a girl,
But as it were a reverie of the place,
A called-for falling glide and whirl;

As when a leaf, petal, or thin chip
Is drawn to the falls of a pool and, circling a moment above it,
Rides on over the lip—
Perfectly beautiful, perfectly ignorant of it.

("Piazza di Spagna, Early Morning")

Just as evocatively, and in a very different mood, he recalls a childhood game
in "Running":

I ran with whacking keds
Down the cart-road past Rickard's place,
And where it dropped beside the tractor-sheds

Leapt out into the air above a blurred
Terrain, through jolted light,
Took two hard lopes, and at the third
Spanked off a hummock-side exactly right.

The early poem "Grace," which takes its cue from a passage in Hopkins's
Notebooks, celebrates not only "Nijinsky's out-the-window leap / And marvelous midair pause" but also

the dining-car waiter's absurd
Acrobacy—tipfingered tray like a wind-besting bird
Plumblines his swinging shoes, the sole things sure
In the shaken train.

To speak of grace in relation to such passages is really to invoke a triple pun,
referring at once to the observed bodily agility, to the spiritual force of which
the imagination finds it to be a figure, and to the poet's own seeming ease
in appropriating and reproducing the fleeting action. In another early poem,
"Juggler," the circus performer clad in sky blue may easily be taken as the
figure of a poet as he gracefully creates his miniature cosmos:

The balls roll round, wheel on his wheeling hands,
Learning the ways of lightness, alter to spheres
Grazing his finger ends,
Cling to their courses there,
Swinging a small heaven about his ears.

We need such artists, the poem says, "to shake our gravity up." Here "gravity" is used with as much a multiple sense as "grace" in other poems. "For him we batter our hands, / Who has won for once over the world's weight."

It is possibly because of such frank expressions of his view that one function of art is to divert the mind from suffering that certain readers have been quick to see and condemn in Wilbur an escapist or hedonistic tendency. Would they say the same of Samuel Johnson, to whom "the only end of writing" was that it helped men "better to enjoy life, or better to endure it"? It is true that some of Wilbur's earlier poems veer with disconcerting abruptness from the naturalistic to the esthetic, failing to effect the desired wedding of the two. Randall Jarrell had reason for his annoyance with the final stanza of "The Death of a Toad"—"So it was all only an excuse for some Poetry!" Wilbur himself, however, seems to have grown more alert to the danger of making his landscapes unrelievedly (and thus unconvincingly) pretty. He has never, in fact, avoided negative subject matter as completely as some critics have charged. Several of his earlier poems are squarely based on his armed service experience in World War II: "First Snow in Alsace," and "On the Eyes of an S.S. Officer" are examples. And his later books, from *Things of This World* on, provide instances of a humane concern with political issues in poems which rise above the documentary style that has elsewhere become all too familiar to us. "Speech for the Repeal of the MacCarran Act" manages to embrace a field of reference far wider than its title might suggest. "Advice to a Prophet" is the most memorable poem on nuclear war that I have met with, with the exception of "The Horses" by Edwin Muir. Wilbur's "Miltonic Sonnet" to Lyndon Johnson vigorously protests our involvement in Vietnam, and "On the Marginal Way," obliquely but powerfully, does the same.

I do not wish to imply that we ought to think of Wilbur as a political poet. But such political statements are an incidental sign of how his art has widened its inclusive range. It is as if he had come to discover ever greater degrees of freedom and potency in the sacramental imagination, which finds the material of poetry not merely in what is attractive and illustrious, but in the commonest things of the created order. Perhaps the key statement of such a discovery is the poem "Love Calls Us to the Things of This World," whose title is taken from St. Augustine. With a curious mixture of humorous charm and awe, the poem tells how a man, in the moment of waking, mistakes the laundry on a line outside his window for a flight of angels, "flying in place, conveying / The terrible speed of their omnipresence, moving / And staying like white water." In the face of this vision, "The soul shrinks / From all that it is about to remember, / From the perpetual rape of every blessed day." But finally,

> as the sun acknowledges
> With a warm look the world's hunks and colors,
> The soul descends once more in bitter love
> To accept the waking body.

The poem takes full measure of all that is meant by incarnation. It achieves a reconciliation of the ideal and the real, the soul and the body, of sudden, otherworldly intuition and steady, continuing observation of "the world's hunks and colors." This synthesis is represented in its final image, "the heaviest nuns [who] walk in a pure floating / Of dark habits, keeping their difficult balance."

The Mind-Reader, Wilbur's latest collection, is a solid addition to his achievement. The same tendencies of style and thought that I have been tracing throughout his work are present in it; his poems are still "keeping their difficult balance." They do so, moreover, with a tone more personal than Wilbur has previously used. In a poem like "In Limbo," about waking in the middle of the night and reviewing the scenes of the past, the poet seems, without greatly relaxing the formality of his style, to be admitting more of the circumstantial detail of his life into his verse. One gains a similar impression from "The Writer," about Wilbur's love and troubled concern for his daughter, and from "Cottage Street, 1953," about a meeting with Sylvia Plath. This last has stirred some controversy; some partisans of the dead confessional poet have found it condescending. But the aspect most prominent in the poem is, I should say, its self-questioning: Wilbur is moved to a confession of helplessness:

> It is my office to exemplify
> The published poet in his happiness,
> Thus cheering Sylvia, who has wished to die;
> But half-ashamed, and impotent to bless,
>
> I am a stupid life-guard who has found,
> Swept to his shallows by the tide, a girl
> Who, far from shore, has been immensely drowned,
> And stares through water now with eyes of pearl.

The poem's assessment of Plath's art is measured and exacting, but it is in no way condescending as it takes leave of

Sylvia, who condemned to live,
Shall study for a decade, as she must,
To state at last her brilliant negative
In poems free and helpless and unjust.

In his art and attitudes Wilbur has been called unduly cautious, and yet many of these poems show a readiness to respond to the new and the unexpected, and to question motives in the self that most men in middle age leave unexamined. In one of his new nature lyrics he celebrates the movement of earth during spring thaw, "As when a set mind, blessed by doubt, / Relaxes into mother wit." In "The Eye" he is "blessed by doubt" of his own artistry, of the exactitude of vision which, he now fears, may lead him to ignore his kinship with the things he observes. "Forbid my vision / To take itself for a curious angel," he prays to Lucy, patroness of eyesight:

Remind me that I am here in body,
A passenger, and rumpled.

Charge me to see
In all bodies the beat of spirit,
Not merely in the *tout en l'air*
Or double pike with layout

But in the strong,
Shouldering gait of the legless man,
The calm walk of the blind young woman
Whose cane touches the curbstone.

He shows himself aware here of the ever present danger of an art like his, which if it severs the sacramental bonds that unite it to nature can only become an estheticism that considers itself too good for this world.

The level of writing in this new book is so high that it is hard to choose which poems to single out for special mention. "A Sketch" does deftly for a goldfinch what Emily Dickinson did for the hummingbird in "A route of evanescence": taut-rhythmed, every word in place, it stands among Wilbur's finer evocations of natural vitality. "Peter" and "Teresa" perform the difficult feat (difficult for this century, at any rate) of making saints into humanly compelling subjects. "Children of Darkness," like many other poems of Wilbur's, is natural history with a strong undercurrent of natural theology: in this confluence it suggests the poet's affinities to Frost and Marianne Moore, who similarly consult the book of nature for prudential lessons. The poem is one of those which will be disliked by readers who find that Wilbur takes too sanguine a view of the universe. He is apparently beyond revision in this regard. In a later and more generous appraisal than the one quoted above, Randall Jarrell remarked that he "obsessively sees, and shows, the bright underside of every dark thing," and went on to suggest that it is the obsessiveness of this optimism which provides it with power and interest. Theodicy is a form that Wilbur sometimes falls into as if by reflex, but he brings all his intelligence to bear upon the argument when he finds himself once again taking it up. "Children of Darkness" presents a splendidly grotesque catalogue of fungi—its purported subject, although its broader concern is with the question why things which seem ugly and maleficent are suffered by the Creator to exist.

> If groves are choirs and sanctuaried fanes,
> What have we here?
> An elm-bole cocks a bloody ear;
> In the oak's shadow lies a strew of brains.
> Wherever, after the deep rains,
>
> The woodlands are morose and reek of punk,
> These gobbets grow—
> Tongue, lobe, hand, hoof or butchered toe
> Amassing on the fallen branch half-sunk
> In leaf-mold, or the riddled trunk.

The description proceeds with Gothic exuberance, glancing at the "parodically sexed" and "shameless phalloi . . . To whose slimed heads come carrion flies." This thoroughgoingness makes all the more dramatically effective the final reversal, in which these seemingly alien beings are perceived as occupying a fit place in the divine economy. Still Gothic, but at last benignly so, the last stanza circles back to the initial cathedral image, and accommodates the uncouth creatures as "gargoyles":

> Gargoyles is what they are at worst, and should
> They preen themselves
> On being demons, ghouls, or elves,
> The holy chiaroscuro of the wood
> Still would embrace them. They are good.

This is not an unreflective, but a meditated optimism. It subjects the things of darkness to a tasteful exorcism, placing them in a perspective worthy of the philosophic mind.

In concluding my praise, I must not neglect to mention the title poem.

Longer than the rest, in blank verse, it is a major effort, recalling "Walking to Sleep" in the inventive way it juxtaposes landscapes more eccentrically imagined and surreal than those which appear in the shorter poems. In description and in the smooth slide of their transitions both poems have a cinematic quality; "The Mind-Reader," being a dramatic monologue, has the additional interest of character. The speaker, part charlatan, part genuine seer, has come to regard his gift as more curse than blessing. It is an unusual affliction, and Wilbur has furnished him with a convincingly complex voice in which to lament—cynical, wry, at once self-pitying and vain. The piece exhibits a greater extention of negative capability than I would have expected from this poet.

I am not as pleased with the overall plan of the volume as I am with the majority of its contents. Slender as it is, it is unnecessarily padded with translations and humorous verses. Wilbur is a skillful translator, but he has in the past chosen more interesting pieces upon which to ply his skills. And his wit, I think, is more effective in incidental appearances than as the motive force of an entire poem. To judge from the examples here, his talent for pure comedy is limited—Lewis Carroll redivivus he is not. The presence of light or translated matter somewhat dissipates the impact of Wilbur's own serious pieces if the collection is taken as a whole. The physical slimness of the book reminds one of how much less frequently he has been publishing in recent years. Perhaps it is ungracious to notice this, since what he has published has so often been worth reading not once but innumerable times.

I can perhaps atone for my bit of carping by taking notice of the other book Wilbur published in 1976, the selection of his essays called *Responses*. Students of American literature, especially, will be grateful to have conveniently available so many of Wilbur's original and penetrating studies of Poe, as well as one of the best brief appreciations of Emily Dickinson ever written by a fellow poet. The more widely ranging discussions, such as "Poetry and Happiness" (courageous title!) and "Poetry's Debt to Poetry" (almost as courageous), manage to perform the double function we hope to find in a poet's critical prose. Besides being distillations of a lifetime's reading, furnishing discerning views of his predecessors and contemporaries, these pieces cast an oblique but steady light on Wilbur's own poetic themes and stylistic preferences. Having laid out my argument for this essay before reading *Responses*, I am bound to be pleased by passages which corroborate my interpretations, to find Wilbur for instance, articulating his urge for inclusiveness: "Every poet," he writes, "is impelled to utter the whole of the world that is real to him, to respond to that world in some spirit, and to draw all its parts toward some coherence." More pithily, he insists that the poet must "let no word or thing be blackballed by sensibility." An early essay defending formal techniques in poetry draws supporting analogies, more elaborately than I have done, from primitive religion:

> The rain-dancer casts down his fingers like rain shafts, or beats with his feet somewhat as the rain tramples the earth. But it isn't really like the rain; it can't begin to substitute for what it refers to. It is not a mere imitation, but a magic borrowing of the powers it wants to approach, and a translation of what is borrowed into a language of the dancing human body. . . . The difficulty and intricacy in the rain-dance arise not from emulation, and not from virtuosity in the dances, but from the difficulty—the impossibility—of achieving a direct expressive relationship with the rain, or with any other real thing. . . . The relation between an artist and reality is always an oblique one, and indeed there is no good art which is not consciously oblique. If you respect the reality of the world, you know that you can approach that reality only by indirect means.

Other critical theorists have offered similar analyses, but this one has the force of personal experience behind it: Wilbur has observed himself lying in ambush for nature, and he has observed his own satisfaction in taking her by surprise. His essays are meditative ventures, more inviting of the reader's participation than most criticism. Reading them does not merely augment our knowledge; it redirects our attention, and cleanses our minds of much that is trivial and stale. Wilbur's prose, like his poetry, engages with an able lucidity "the whole of the world that is real to him," and does so with such persuasive eloquence that we see his world as one we would like to share. Such mutuality happily maintained between poet and reader has a simple name: civilization. One wishes there were more of it around.

ASHLEY BROWN

The Poetry of Anthony Hecht

The Nightingale
What is it to be free? The unconfined
Lose purpose, strength, and at the last, the mind.
ANTHONY HECHT, a couplet to accompany Aesop

The American poets who were born up and down the 1920s have come into their full powers and fame well before now, though the contours of some careers have emerged rather slowly. Most of them were presented in Richard Howard's brilliant commentaries in *Alone with America* almost ten years ago. Mr. Howard didn't mean to write literary history, and indeed he avoided the issue and perhaps emphasized his forty-one subjects' aloneness by arranging them in alphabetical order. But there is something to be said for a sense of period; in recollection one thinks of the common urgencies and possibilities in the literary scene of a generation ago: the enveloping action, as it were, that the craft of poetry would make actual. As a contemporary, born in the same year as Anthony Hecht, Louis Simpson, Denise Levertov, Daniel Hoffman, and James Dickey (not a bad year), I can hardly pretend to be disinterested about poets whose work I have watched for three decades.

In the late 1940s those I read most immediately were Hecht, James Merrill, and Edgar Bowers, the latter in my opinion the most neglected member of his generation—neglected, that is, by almost everybody outside the circle created by Yvor Winters, his teacher and champion. They came together in one number of *The Hudson Review* in 1949, I remember. They were precocious in their different ways. They had been in the army during the war and had much to write about amidst the ruins of Europe, but I think

From *Ploughshares* 4, no. 3 (1978). © 1978 by Ploughshares, Inc.

that only Mr. Bowers had got hold of his subject at that time. His special
focus of experience comes out in the conclusion of "The Stoic," which is
addressed to a German friend:

> You must, with so much known, have been afraid
> And chosen such a mind of constant will,
>
> Which, though all time corrode with constant hurt,
> Remains, until it occupies no space,
> That which it is; and passionless, inert,
> Becomes at last no meaning and no place.

Earlier in the same poem he evokes

> Eternal Venice sinking by degrees
> Into the very water that she lights;
>
> Reflected in canals, the lucid dome
> Of Marie dell' Salute at your feet,
> Her triple spires disfigured by the foam.

Venice, after the war, became a kind of mise-en-scène for various states of
mind (Mr. Bowers returns to it in the second of his beautiful "Italian Guide-
Book" poems), just as it was the place for important premieres and exhi-
bitions. But who could have foreseen then that Mr. Merrill, with his dazzling
verbal gift, would eventually perfect the comedy of manners in our generation
and bring us, in the climactic sections of "The Book of Ephraim," the gran-
deurs and trivia of Venice as we know it? Or that Mr. Hecht would write
"The Venetian Vespers," a great meditation on the tragic displacements of
our century?

I have tended to put Mr. Hecht somewhere between Mr. Bowers and
Mr. Merrill all these years, just as a way of defining his special poetic qualities. He partakes of the moral penetration of the one and the wit of the
other, to my way of thinking. But this is too easily said, just as these qualities
are too easily named, and Anthony Hecht was his own man from the beginning. He is a New Yorker, born the day before St. Anthony's Day in January,
and he took his degrees at Bard College and Columbia. After Bard he went
to the war in Europe and Japan as an infantry rifleman for three years—an
experience that has deeply affected his poetry. Then he turned to John Crowe
Ransom at Kenyon College, like several others of his generation, and his first
poems that I read came out in *The Kenyon Review* for Spring 1947, where
he was Tony Hecht. These early pieces have not been reprinted, but they are
entirely competent and Mr. Hecht should certainly put them in a future

edition of his collected poems. They are called "Once Removed" and "To a Soldier Killed in Germany." Looking back at them from the vantage point of the later Hecht, one is inclined to say that they are very direct treatments of their subjects—quite understandably the work of a twenty-three-year-old recently under fire. The second poem begins with characteristic strength of feeling keyed up by a formal stanza:

> On a small town, twitching with life and death,
> The sun pours his consuming acid down
> On broken monuments, the shattered fist
> Of Hitler's figure, stoney carrion kissed
> By the devouring light, and near this town
> They stitched your lips and cut away your breath.

A recurring image in the poems, early and late, is "stone" or some variant of it: nature inert and shattered: "this broken landscape tied by the wind together." In retrospect this seems to point toward Mr. Hecht's first book, *A Summoning of Stones* (1954), which takes its title from a phrase by Santayana implying that the poet's duty is "to call the stones themselves to their ideal places, and enchant the very substance and skeleton of the world." (Mr. Hecht uses it as his epigraph.) Someone studying the poems might explore the imagery at length and observe its permutations, but just the titles of the three collections suggest a kind of progression: *A Summoning of Stones, The Hard Hours,* and *Millions of Strange Shadows.*

By autumn of 1947 Mr. Hecht was Anthony in *The Kenyon Review,* and he had moved on to the University of Iowa, another literary mecca of the period. I suppose it was his Kenyon year that left traces of Ransom in a few of the early poems and perhaps gentled them. "A Valentine," for instance:

> Surely the frost will gain
> Upon its essence, and execute
> Its little bravery of cardinal red.

Or "Songs for the Air":

> We may consider every cloud a lake
> Transmogrified, its character unselfed.

Few would dare to use "transmogrified" after Ransom's "Janet Waking," though I think Mr. Hecht gets away with it. These are only momentary details of style, however, an episode. Like Robert Lowell before him, he was affected more decisively by another Fugitive, Allen Tate. He never sounds like Tate nor assumes the high oratorical mode that is part of the southerner's inheritance. One might place his "Samuel Sewall" beside Tate's "Mr. Pope" to see the difference. What I have in mind is a certain "cut" in the poetic line:

> Now take him, Virgin Muse, up the deeper stream:
> As a lost bee returning to the hive,
> Cell after honeyed cell of sounding dream—
>
> Swimmer of noonday, lean for the perfect dive
> To the dead Mother's face, whose subtile down
> You had not seen take amber light alive.

These are the final tercets of Tate's "The Maimed Man," which opened *The Partisan Review* for May/June 1952, at a time when Mr. Hecht was perfecting his style. One line—"Swimmer of noonday, lean for the perfect dive"—represents the kind of poetry, taut and rhythmically alert, that he was already approaching. There is a further consideration here. In his prose tribute to Allen Tate (*The Sewanee Review*, Autumn 1959), Mr. Hecht says that what he finally realized from his teacher (which Mr. Tate was for a time) was "the way a poem's total design is modulated and given its energy, not by local ingredients tastefully combined, but by the richness, toughness and density of some sustaining vision of life." And this, I think, describes the way in which we should finally approach Mr. Hecht.

In 1952 there were other presences on the scene, notably Stevens and Auden. Stevens's rhetoric is occasionally overpowering for young poets, or it used to be. Mr. Hecht seems to have been playful about this older contemporary, who is often treated rather solemnly in the Age of Bloom; so I judge from the first group of poems in *A Summoning of Stones*. In "La Condition Botanique" he speaks of

> hopeful dreams,
> Peach-colored, practical, to decorate the bones, with schemes
> Of life insurance, Ice-Cream-After-Death.

Then "Divisions upon a Ground," which is a parody of "Le Monocle de Mon Oncle," was reprinted in *The Hard Hours* as "Le Masseur de Ma Soeur." "The Place of Pain in the Universe," an amusing meditation in a dentist's office, surely refers to the first section of *Esthétique du Mal*, where Stevens has his hero brooding at Naples in the shadow of Vesuvius:

> He tried to remember the phrases: pain
> Audible at noon, pain torturing itself,
> Pain killing pain on the very point of pain.

As for Auden, one might say that the big set pieces of *A Summoning of Stones*, "La Condition Botanique" and "The Gardens of the Villa d'Este," could not have existed as they do without the example of Auden's virtuosity from *The Sea and the Mirror* onward. Although the interest in elaborate, even "baroque" poetry during the 1950s was entirely characteristic of the period (James Merrill was an outstanding practitioner even then), Mr. Hecht had been reading Auden since 1937 at the age of fourteen and presumably was ahead of everyone else. But he never succumbed to the Auden manner of speech, which of course has always existed on several levels. It was a matter of formal perfection, the pleasure in the finished poem. (Mr. Hecht's interesting remarks on Auden can be found in *The Hudson Review* for Spring 1968.)

"The Gardens of the Villa d'Este" is a fifties poem in another obvious way. Around 1950, a Holy Year, the American literati moved over the Alps to Italy, which quickly became the great good place that France had been for the twenties. (Mr. Hecht was awarded a writing fellowship at the American Academy in Rome in 1951.) Poems about baroque fountains and gardens began to turn up in the literary quarterlies quite regularly. Mr. Hecht's garden is anything but *nature morte;* its delightful eroticism is immediately announced and carried through seventeen intricate stanzas. This is a serious poem, too, and toward the end of the movement slows down; the poet reflects:

> For thus it was designed:
> Controlled disorder at the heart
> Of everything, the paradox, the old
> Oxymoronic itch to set the formal strictures
> Within a natural context, where the tension lectures
> Us on our mortal state, and by controlled
> Disorder, labors to keep art
> From being too refined.

It is tempting to pursue the wit of this stanza in several directions, and no doubt some readers have taken it as a jeu d'esprit of the New Criticism (Brooks's paradox, Tate's tension, Warren's pure and impure poetry, etc.) long before now. But the stanza should direct our attention to Marvell's Garden (the important literary reference), hence back to Eden itself. Richard

Howard says that all the poems in A *Summoning of Stones* "are illuminated by a primal vision which asserts, beyond growth as beyond decay, beyond accident as beyond purpose, that there is a significant ordering in experience, fall from it as we must . . ." and this theme would naturally find its fulfillment in "The Gardens of the Villa d'Este." An analogous way of approaching the poem is by way of the water that pours over the stone and gushes from the fountains: "Clear liquid arcs of benefice and aid." This composes a counter-image to the "broken monuments" and "stoney carrion" of the earliest poems. I don't agree with some readers of A *Summoning of Stones* (for instance the late Louise Bogan in *The New Yorker*) who saw the Italian poems, especially the "Villa d'Este," as simply a celebration of elegance, however exuberant. The "controlled disorder" is really one phase of a larger and quite important subject, as Mr. Howard says.

In A *Summoning of Stones* and again in *The Hard Hours* (1967), Mr. Hecht places the "Villa d'Este" soon after "Christmas is Coming," a remarkable poem on several counts. It is one of the few things that he wrote in blank verse in those days (like Yeats and Tate he usually required rhymed stanzas), but certain words like *cold* and *pain* are carefully deployed half a dozen times in a poem of forty-nine lines, and the effect is almost formal. This procedure is continued by the old verse that is inserted and then repeated in fragments:

> *Christmas is coming. The goose is getting fat.*
> *Please put a penny in the Old Man's hat.*

The strange landscape of the poem isn't identified; it could be the setting for the Battle of the Bulge, where so many of one's contemporaries were frostbitten in December 1944:

> Where is the pain? The sense is frozen up,
> And fingers cannot recognize the grass,
> Cannot distinguish their own character,
> Being blind with cold, being stiffened by the cold;
> Must find out thistles to remember pain.
> Keep to the frozen ground or else be killed.
> Yet crawling one encounters in the dark
> The frosty carcasses of birds, their feet
> And wings all glazed. And still we crawl to learn
> Where pain was lost, how to recover pain.
> Reach for the brambles, crawl to them and reach,

Clutching for thorns, search carefully to feel
The point of thorns, life's crown, *the Old Man's hat*.

This almost refers back to "The Place of Pain in the Universe," with its
echo of *Esthetique du Mal*, and it could be considered a "tragic" version of
the same theme. By this time Mr. Hecht had begun to present his subject
through a kind of indirection: the old verse, a plea for charity out of the
more genial world of Dickens, say, cuts across the eerie landscape to maximum effect. And the serious wit of these last lines introduces a religious
perspective that is new in his poetry and that certainly anticipates a great
deal.

Leaving aside a number of fine individual achievements in *A Summoning
of Stones*, "La Condition Botanique" for one and "Alceste in the Wilderness"
for another, I turn to *The Hard Hours*. The title suggests a crisis or at any
rate a holding action in the poet's private life, but the general subject is much
larger than that, and eventually personal and public destinies merge. The
setting is usually urban now: Manhattan with its casual violence and its high
bourgeois culture on which the civilized mind can still draw: Central Park
and the Frick Collection:

> Daily the prowling sunlight whets its knife
> Along the sidewalk. We almost never meet.
> In the Rembrandt dark he lifts his amber life.
> My bar is somewhat further down the street.

The big set piece of the volume is "Rites and Ceremonies." Here the
poet reached beyond his own circumstances and the public atrocities of our
time toward the "richness, toughness and density of some sustaining vision
of life" that he mentions in his tribute to Allen Tate. The range of his subject
is large—say the whole sweep of western history. It is sometimes very un-
pleasant, and at one point he remarks: "The contemplation of horror is not
edifying, / Neither does it strengthen the soul." He has permitted himself a
new rhythmic and stanzaic freedom that carries him through ten pages, and
the intensity of feeling often pushes against the restraints of the stanzas, as
in the long passage on Buchenwald. But it is a "controlled disorder" at every
stage. The third section, which begins with the caustic lines I have already
quoted, is entitled "The Dream." After a preliminary passage, which touches
on the martyrdoms of three saints, we move to the Corso in Rome and the
homesick poet du Bellay at Carnival time; now we settle into a sequence of
five-line stanzas that concludes:

Du Bellay, poet, take no thought of them;
And yet they too are exiles, and have said
Through many generations, long since dead,
"If I forget thee, O Jerusalem, . . ."
Still, others have been scourged and buffeted

And worse. Think rather, if you must,
Of Piranesian, elegiac woes,
Rome's grand declensions, that all-but-speaking dust.
Or think of the young gallants and their lust.
Or wait for the next heat, the buffaloes.

Du Bellay, the homesick spectator, is I suppose a surrogate for Mr. Hecht
at this point, and in fact Mr. Hecht has already allowed him to speak in the
marvelous version of "Heureux qui, comme Ulysse, a fait un bon voyage . . ."
that he has placed just before "Rites and Ceremonies."

This is the most ambitious poem in *The Hard Hours*, its center, and
perhaps some tentative statement of Mr. Hecht's theme is in order at this
point. By far the best review of the book that I recall was Carol Johnson's
in *Art International* (Lugano, 1968). Miss Johnson said that "if it has seemed
nearly impossible for Americans to attain to tragedy without self-pitying
stridence or comedy without vulgarity, we now have Mr. Hecht's poem to
allay that pessimistic expectation and remind us in what proximity wit and
tragedy reside—providing civilization survives them." It is "the tragic vision," then, a term we are apt to be uncomfortable with, that we have to
take into account here. Many of the poems in this collection have public
subjects; I suspect the ones that have had the most impact are "Behold the
Lilies of the Field," which is placed near the beginning, and "More Light!
More Light!" which comes near the end. They remind us that human vi-
ciousness has been a recurring feature of history. (Occasionally, in reading
Mr. Hecht, I have thought of D. W. Griffith's panoramic movie *Intolerance*.)
In the first case the appalling execution of the Roman Emperor Valerian
(253–260 A.D.) erupts into a session on the modern psychiatrists' couch,
and the patient identifies himself with this ancient humiliation. The public
subject, that is, becomes the physical image of a private malaise. In "More
Light!" the poet juxtaposes the execution of a religious martyr in sixteenth-
century England ("Permitted at least his pitiful dignity") and a peculiarly
brutal incident at Buchenwald. He has insisted on confronting these horrors,
but in the second instance with a sardonic wit that governs, as Carol Johnson
says, the tragedy. "More light! more light!": these were Goethe's last words,
and light figures prominently throughout the poem.

But it would be mistaken to restrict Mr. Hecht to a bleak view of experience. The tragic vision itself, or rather the romantic melancholy which it could lead to, is beautifully parodied in "The Dover Bitch: A Criticism of Life." Although Mr. Hecht has the utmost respect for Arnold (I believe that when he reads to audiences he always takes up "Dover Beach" before his own poem), he seems to suggest that melancholy is a passive state of mind that could be otherwise dealt with by the modern intelligence. One might suppose that his main reference for the tragic vision would be *King Lear,* the play which has had a special fascination for the post-war world, but it seems to be the *Oedipus at Kolonos,* the great classic of reconciliation, which he is translating as a work-in-progress. His version of the chorus in praise of Kolonos has already appeared in *Millions of Strange Shadows,* and I quote the final stanzas, which I think bear out Richard Howard's thesis that in Anthony Hecht's poetry "there is a significant ordering in experience, fall from it as we must."

> O Lord Poseidon, you have doubly blessed us
> with healing skills, on these roads first bestowing
> the bit that gentles horses, the controlling
>   curb and the bridle,
>
> and the carved, feathering oar that skims and dances
> like the white nymphs of water, conferring mastery
> of ocean roads, among the spume and wind-blown
>   prancing of stallions.

An intensely personal poem, "The Vow," which stands just before du Bellay's "Heureux qui, comme Ulysse . . ." makes a connection with the *Oedipus at Kolonos* in another way. The subject is a dead unborn child. The poem is so carefully built up in forty lines that partial quotation would do it violence; I must refer the reader to *The Hard Hours.* About fifteen years ago Mr. Hecht picked this as his favorite for *Poet's Choice,* an anthology edited by Paul Engle and Joseph Langland. In the course of a short commentary he mentions a poem on the same subject in Lowell's first book, *Land of Unlikeness.* This would be "The Boston Nativity," a harshly satirical piece from Lowell's early Catholic period. Mr. Hecht's poem owes nothing to Lowell except, as he explains, the courage of the "difficult" subject. Where Lowell tends to contract his poem through his abrasive tone, Mr. Hecht expands backward, as it were, through the Judaic-Greek traditions, and the unborn child speaks with an "aged, bitter, Sophoclean wisdom." I quote a passage from Robert Fitzgerald's translation of the *Oedipus* to make the connection: a kind of background for Mr. Hecht's poem:

> Not to be born beats all philosophy.
> The second best is to have seen the light
> And then to go back quickly whence we came.
> The feathery follies of his youth once over,
> What trouble is beyond the range of man?
> What heavy burden will he not endure?

In "Three Prompters from the Wings," a triptych in which Atropos, Clotho, and Lachesis take us through the stages of Oedipus's career (they represent the future, the present, and the past), Clotho submits the "tragic vision" to this comment:

> Nothing is purely itself
> But is linked with its antidote
> In cold self-mockery—
> A fact with which only those
> Born with a Comic sense
> Can learn to content themselves.
> While heroes die to maintain
> Some part of existence clean
> And incontaminate.

Here Mr. Hecht approaches the later Yeats, as much in his assertive trimeters as in anything else. (Yeats of course also did a version of the *Oedipus at Kolonos* that is connected with *his* sense of the tragic.) Mr. Hecht's wit isn't always sardonic by any means. In the last lines of "The Vow," addressed to the unborn child, he remarks, audaciously yet tenderly:

> If that ghost was a girl's, I swear to it:
> Your mother shall be far more blessed than you.
> And if a boy's, I swear: The flames are lit
> That shall refine us; they shall not destroy
>   A living hair.
> Your younger brothers shall confirm in joy
>   This that I swear.

The poet's first two sons are named Jason and Adam, and in fact they have already appeared in a pair of charming poems where they reenact their mythical roles in random childish gestures. But the childhood world merges, through the television set, with the fearful possibilities of the public world,

and at the end of the last poem in *The Hard Hours* ("It Out-Herods Herod.
Pray You, Avoid It") the father offers this curt prayer:

> And that their sleep be sound
> I say this childermas
> Who could not, at one time,
> Have saved them from the gas.

The last decade has been a glorious period of creativity for Mr. Hecht.
A bit to one side of his poems, but closely related to them in ways that I
have already suggested, is the translation of *Seven Against Thebes* that he
did in collaboration with Helen Bacon (Oxford University Press, 1973). The
translation with its introduction is clearly an important event in classical
studies; that is, it makes accessible a dramatic masterpiece which hasn't been
treated as handsomely as Aeschylus's other works. As poetry, the Hecht-
Bacon version is superb: see, for instance, the long choral passage in trimeters
(lines 927–1109) with its pentameter interlude. I now think that Mr. Hecht,
after Yeats, is the master of the trimeter line in English poetry.

The translation was undertaken at the American Academy in Rome, and
modern unclassical Rome is the setting for "The Cost," the first poem in
Millions of Strange Shadows:

> Instinct with joy, a young Italian banks
>   Smoothly around the base
> Of Trajan's column, feeling between his flanks
>   That cool, efficient beast,
> His Vespa, at one with him in a centaur's race,
>   Fresh, from a Lapith feast,
>
> And his Lapith girl behind him. Both of them lean
>   With easy nonchalance
> Over samphire-tufted cliffs which, though unseen,
>   Are known, as the body knows
> New risks and tilts, terrors and loves and wants,
>   Deeply inside its clothes.

Although the barbarians are everywhere now, the poet seems to have relaxed
his severity, and indeed there is a kind of joy in physicality that runs through
many of the poems in this collection: "Somebody's Life" and "Swan Dive"
for instance. But youthful instinct could be "the secret gaudery of self-love,"
and in "The Feast of Stephen" physicality becomes sinister: Saul watches as
the young thugs move in on the first Christian martyr:

And in between their sleek, converging bodies,
Brilliantly oiled and burnished by the sun,
He catches a brief glimpse of bloodied hair
And hears an unintelligible prayer.

Youth and age figure prominently in these poems, and it is part of
Mr. Hecht's great talent to be able to move with ease among accumulated
memories. He does this as though he were riffling through a heap of photographs, deciding what to discard, what to preserve, and actual photographs
are the focal points of several poems. In "Dichtung und Wahrheit" he takes
up the subject with a certain hesitation:

The Discus Thrower's marble heave,
    Captured in mid-career,
That polished poise, that Parian arm
    Sleeved only in the air,
Vesalian musculature, white
    As the mid-winter moon—
This, and the clumsy snapshot of
    An infantry platoon,
Those grubby and indifferent men,
    Lounging in bivouac,
Their rifles aimless in their laps,
    Stop history in its tracks.

This poem is on a "high" subject: the "sacred discipline" that might "give
breath back to the past." In "Exile," dedicated to the Russian poet Joseph
Brodsky in America, his Egypt, the local scene is brought to the exile's
attention thus:

Look, though, at the blank, expressionless faces
Here is this photograph by Walker Evans.
These are the faces that everywhere surround you;
They have all the emptiness of gravel pits.

But this harsh first impression is gentled, and then one realizes that it would
be the poet's privilege, in this instance, to give breath back to the *present*:

This is Egypt, Joseph, the old school of the soul.
You will recognize the rank smell of a stable
And the soft patience in a donkey's eyes,
Telling you you are welcome and at home.

"A Birthday Poem," one of Anthony Hecht's finest achievements, is in
a sense about the act of perception itself. It is late June, and he peers through
the "golden dazzle" at a swarm of midges, his mind open to possibilities.
Perspective, the great invention (or was it discovery?) of the Renaissance,
sets off ranges of space, as in a crucifixion scene by Mantegna. The midges
give way to the "blurred, unfathomed background tint" in a Holbein group
portrait (a more secular age now). Then space shifts into time through "the
gears of tense," and the poet comes to rest with a photograph of his wife
as a child:

> You are four years old here in this photograph.
>   You are turned out in style,
> In a pair of bright red sneakers, a birthday gift.
>   You are looking down at them with a smile
> Of pride and admiration, half
> Wonder and half joy, at the right and the left.
>
> The picture is black and white, mere light and shade,
>   Even the sneakers' red
> Has washed away in acids. A voice is spent,
>   Echoing down the ages in my head:
> *What is your substance, whereof are you made,*
> *That millions of strange shadows on you tend?*

And the poet allows Shakespeare (Sonnet 53) to speak for him, as he has
previously brought du Bellay and the others into the conversation, as it were.
It is a moment of supreme poetic tact.

The longest poems in the new volume, "Green: An Epistle," and "Apprehensions," have already been much admired. "Apprehensions" especially
seems to mark the direction that Mr. Hecht's poetry is taking: the long
blank-verse monologue that admits a surprising amount of personal history.
The passage about the childhood experience on Lexington Avenue in "Apprehensions" bears out the idea of a "primal vision" or what Auden (who
is actually quoted) calls "The Vision of Dame Kind." It is beautifully sustained, a poem in itself, but Mr. Hecht has put it in a dramatic context that
makes it so much more than a moment remembered. It is true, as Richard
Howard remarks (in *Poetry*, November 1977), that prose is "no longer rejected" in these recent poems, but I think that the poet's impulse to write
lyric is as strong as ever. These are the final stanzas of "The Lull," the last
poem of all:

The seamed, impastoed bark,
The cool, imperial certainty of stone,
Antique leaf-lace, all these are bathed in a dark
Mushroom and mineral odor of their own,
Their inwardness made clear and sure
As voice and fingerprint and signature.

The rain, of course, will come
With grandstand flourishes and hullabaloo,
The silvered street, flashbulb and kettledrum,
To douse and rouse the citizens, to strew
Its rhinestones randomly, piecemeal.
But for the moment the whole world is real.

This lovely coda, a moment of repose before another onslaught of experience, makes the case for formal poetry as much as anything being written today. Its author has in many ways carried forward and modified a kind of tradition that I associate mainly with Tate and Auden, the leading members of the second generation of modernists (if we have Stevens, Pound, and Eliot in the first generation). He has dealt with the terrible divisiveness of the age with an extraordinary honesty and grace—what Auden called for in "The Shield of Achilles." My sense of the current scene is that his kind of poetry will matter a great deal from now on, after a period of rather shameless opportunism, and what is so reassuring is that he is writing better than ever.

HAROLD BLOOM

From "The Other" through
The Early Motion

I first read James Dickey's early poem, "The Other," some twenty years ago. Having admired his recently published book, *Drowning With Others,* I went back to his first book, *Into the Stone,* at the recommendation of a close friend, the poet Alvin Feinman. Though very moved by several of the earlier poems, I was affected most strongly by the one called "The Other." It has taken me twenty years to understand why the poem still will not let me go, and so I begin with it here. I don't think of Dickey as a poet primarily of otherness, but rather as a heroic celebrator of what Emerson called "the great and crescive self," indeed of the American self proper, which demands victory and disdains even great defeats. Dickey, as I read him, is like what Vico called the Magic Formalists or Blake named the Giant Forms. He is a throwback to those mythic hypotheses out of which strong poetry first broke forth, the bards of divination whose heroic vitalism demanded a literal immortality for themselves as poets. But even a Magic Formalist learns that he is at best a mortal god.

The pain of that learning is the central story of Dickey's poetry, and I choose to evade that pain here in order to emphasize Dickey's counter-song of otherness. Since I will take him scarcely into his middle years, I will be ignoring all of his most ambitious poetry, "the later motion," as he has called it. Though his work from 1965 to the present clearly is more problematic than the poems I will discuss, its achievement quite possibly is of a

From *The Southern Review* (Winter 1985). © 1984 by Louisiana State University. Originally entitled "James Dickey: From 'The Other' through *The Early Motion.*"

higher order. But it is too soon to prophesy Dickey's final stature, and criticism must discourse on what it loves before it broods upon the limits of the canonical. What I know and love best, so far, in Dickey's poetry is "the early motion," and the counter-song of otherness in that motion moves me most. I have circled back to that poem, "The Other," and turn to it now to locate an origin of Dickey's quest as a poet.

That origin is guilt, and guilt ostensibly of being a substitute or replacement for a brother dead before one was born. Freud, I think, would have judged such guilt to be a screen memory, and I am Freudian enough to look or surmise elsewhere for the source of guilt in the poems of *Into the Stone*. From the beginning of his poetic career, Dickey was a poet of Sublime longings, and those who court the Sublime are particularly subject to changeling fantasies. The poem he titled "The Other" is manifestly Yeatsian, whether directly or through the mediation of Roethke, but the argument already is Dickey's own, and in all respects it is the meter-making argument, and not the derived diction and metric, that gives this poem its great distinction. Indeed Dickey, an instinctive Emersonian from the start, despite his southern heritage, literalizes Emerson's trope of a meter-making argument by the extraordinary device of packing the seventy-seven lines of this lyrical reverie into what has always felt to me like a single sentence. How could there be a second sentence in a poem that identifies itself so completely with the changeling's will to be the other, when the other ultimately is the god Apollo?

Somewhere, Dickey identified his triad of literary heroes as the unlikely combination of Keats, Malcolm Lowry, and James Agee, presumably associated because of their early or relatively early deaths, and because of their shared intensity of belief in what could be called the salvation history of the literary art. But Dickey is very much a poet of Sensibility, in the mode that Frye once defined as *the* Age of Sensibility, the mode of Christopher Smart and of William Collins, among other doomed poets whose threshold stance destroyed them upon the verge of High Romanticism. The Keats who moves Dickey most, the Keats of the letters, is the culmination of the major theme of the poets of Sensibility, the theme that, following Collins, I have called the Incarnation of the Poetical Character. Lowry and Agee, though I don't recall Dickey mentioning this, were curiously allied as verse writers by the overwhelming influence that Hart Crane exerted upon both of them. Dickey seems to prefer Crane's letters to his poems, which oddly parallels his preference of Keats's letters. But Keats and Crane, like Lowry and Agee in their verse, represent fully in their poems the Incarnation of the Poetical Character, where the poet, in the guise of a young man, is reborn as the young god of the sun. That is clearly the genre of Dickey's "The Other," but the clarity is shadowed by Dickey's early guilt concerning what the poem accurately names as "my lust of self."

What self can that be except the magic and occult self, ontological rather than empirical, and in Yeatsian or Whitmanian terms, self rather than soul? The guilt that shadows Dickey's marvelous seventy-seven-line utterance is the guilt induced by what Freud came to call the above-I or the over-I (the superego), a rather more daunting though no less fictive entity than Emerson's Oversoul. Emerson had the shrewdest of eyes for anxiety, but Freud's eye, as Wallace Stevens once wrote, was the microscope of potency. The guilt of family betrayal must ensue from the changeling fantasy of the family romance, and for Freud (as for Kenneth Burke), all romance is family romance. But the family romance of the poet *as* poet tends to depart from the domain of the merely biographical family. Dickey's assertion of self as person was the desire to rise from the "strength-haunted body" of a "rack-ribbed child" to the Herculean figure he has been since, a titanic form among contemporary poets. But since poems can attempt the truth only through fictions or tropes, the poem of "The Other" is compelled to treat the child's aspiration as the drive toward becoming Apollo, poetry itself. The youthful Henry James, reviewing *Drum-Taps,* scorned Whitman as an essentially prosaic temperament trying to lift itself by muscular exertion into poetry. The elderly Henry James, weeping over the great *Lilacs* elegy, scorned his own youthful review; but, properly modified, it can give us a critical trope for reading Dickey: an essentially poetic temperament lifting itself by muscular exertion into poetry.

Dickey's most curious characteristic, from "The Other" through *Puella,* is his involuntary but striking dualism, curious because so heroic a vitalist ought not to exemplify (as he does) so Pauline and Cartesian a mind-body split, or even so prevalent a sense of what Stevens termed the dumb-foundering abyss between ourselves and the object. What the poem surprisingly shows for and to Dickey is that his own body becomes his brother, or Apollo, or "the other." If the body is the divine other, then pathos becomes both sublime and grotesque, because the body must change, and the final form of that change is death. "The Other" is almost the first of Dickey's poems, and in some ways he has never surpassed it, not because he has failed to develop, but because it is unsurpassable. The whole of Dickey is in it already, as the whole of Shelley is in *Alastor,* or the whole of Yeats is in *The Wanderings of Oisin.* I repeat that this does not mean that Dickey simply has unfolded; so restless and reckless an experimentalist is outrageously metamorphic. But all his changes quest hopelessly for a disjunctiveness his temperament refuses to allow him. The "holes" that space out the poems of his major phase never represent discursive gaps or even crossings from one kind of figuration to another. Instead, they impressively mark or punctuate the exquisite desperation of the will to live, the lust of self that is not to be railed at, because it does represent what Keats called "a sickness not ignoble": the sickness unto death of heroic poetry.

"The Other," like so much of Dickey's best work, is very clearly a Southern American poem, and yet its Incarnation of the Poetical Character is necessarily universal in its imagery and argument. This is the universal purchased at the high cost of what was to be a permanent guilt, the guilt of a poet who as poet greatly desired *not* to be egocentric, despite the demands of the mythology that found him from the start. Those demands are felt even in the opening movement of "The Other":

> Holding onto myself by the hand,
> I change places into the spirit
> I had as a rack-ribbed child,
> And walk slowly out through my mind
> To the wood, as into a falling fire
> Where I turned from that strength-haunted body
> Half-way to bronze, as I wished to.

Dickey's natural religion always has been Mithraism, the traditional faith of soldiers, and certainly the most masculine and fierce of all Western beliefs. Despite the Persian origins of Mithra, Rome assimilated him to Apollo, and Dickey's major alteration is to make the Incarnation of the Poetical Character into a Mithraic ritual. The "bronze" of this first stanza will be revealed, later in the poem, as both the statue of Apollo and the body of the sacrificial bull slain by Mithra. As the boy Dickey slings up the too-heavy ax-head, he prays

> To another, unlike me, beside me:
> To a brother or king-sized shadow
> who looked at me, burned, and believed me:
> Who believed I would rise like Apollo
>
> With armor-cast shoulders upon me:
> Whose voice, whistling back through my teeth,
> Counted strokes with the hiss of a serpent.
> Where the sun through the bright wood drove
> Him, mute, and floating strangely, to the ground,
> He led me into his house, and sat
> Upright, with a face I could never imagine,

> With a great harp leant on his shoulder,
> And began in deep handfuls to play it.

"Burned" is the crucial trope here, since the brother, as god of the sun, leads only into the heat and light that is the house of the sun. The oracular hiss is Pythian, though the voice truly becomes Dickey's own. What Dickey, *in the poem,* develops most brilliantly is the figure of downward movement, which is introduced in the second stanza as the combined fall of sweat and leaves, and further invoked in the fall of light. Later in the poem, music falls, followed in the final line by the casting down of foliage. All these fallings substitute for the hidden ritual in which the bull's blood falls upon the Mithraic adept, the warrior in the act of becoming Apollo:

> My brother rose beside me from the earth,
>
> With the wing-bone of music on his back
> Trembling strongly with heartfelt gold,
> And ascended like a bird into the tree,
> And music fell in a comb, as I stood
> In a bull's heavy, bronze-bodied shape
> As it mixed with a god's, on the ground,
> And leaned on the helve of the ax.

The "great, dead tree" of the poem's second stanza might be called Dickey's first major fiction of duration, the origin of his quarrel with time. Being Dickey's, it is the liveliest of dead trees, yet it cannot propitiate this poet's poignant longing for a literal immortality:

> Now, owing my arms to the dead
> Tree, and the leaf-loosing, mortal wood,
> Still hearing that music amaze me,
> I walk through the time-stricken forest,
> And wish another body for my life,
> Knowing that none is given
> By the giant, unusable tree
>
> And the leaf-shapen lightning of sun,
> And rail at my lust of self
> With an effort like chopping through root-stocks:
> Yet the light, looming brother but more
> Brightly above me is blazing,
> In that music come down from the branches
> In utter, unseasonable glory,

> Telling nothing but how I made
> By hand, a creature to keep me dying
> Years longer, and coming to sing in the wood
> Of what love still might give,
> Could I turn wholly mortal in my mind,
> My body-building angel give me rest,
> This tree cast down its foliage with the years.

"This tree" is at last Dickey himself as fiction of duration, the poet become his own poem, indeed "made / By hand," and so a house made by hands, a mortal body. When desire can turn monistic, for Dickey, it can become only a mortal turn, a trope knowing it is only trope. The other is divine, but only as Apollo or Mithra was divine, rather than as Jesus or Jehovah. A poem "about" a body-building child has transformed itself into the Sublime, into the body-building angel who has never since given Dickey any rest.

Retrospectively, I suppose that the poem "The Other" first moved me because so few American poems of twenty years ago had anything like Dickey's remarkable ability to be so humanly direct and yet so trustingly given to the potential of figurative language. The Dickey of the early motion seemed to have found his way back, almost effortlessly, to the secrets of poetry. I remember that the first poem by Dickey that I read was the title poem of *Drowning With Others*, a title that is itself an unforgettable trope, worthy of Emily Dickinson's apprehension that an acute consciousness, even when aware of neighbors and the sun, of other selves and outward nature, still died quite alone, except for its own identity, a totemic single hound. What is Sublime in the self finally is capable only of "drowning with others," but that is only part of what is central in what remains one of Dickey's most singular and enduring poems.

If I remember aright, Dickey himself doesn't much like this poem, and thinks it obscure rather than strong. Indeed, I recall his insistence that he wrote the poem only so as to give status to his book's title. His account of the poem's referential aspect was strangely literal, but I think this is one of his poems that sneaked by him, as it were:

> There are moments a man turns from us
> Whom we have all known until now.
> Upgathered, we watch him grow,
> Unshipping his shoulder bones
>
> Like human, everyday wings
> That he has not ever used,

Releasing his hair from his brain,
A kingfisher's crest, confused

By the God-tilted light of Heaven.
His deep, window-watching smile
Comes closely upon us in waves,
And spreads, and now we are

At last within it, dancing.
Slowly we turn and shine
Upon what is holding us,
As under our feet he soars,

Struck dumb as the angel of Eden,
In wide, eye-opening rings.
Yet the hand on my shoulder fears
To feel my own wingblades spring,

To feel me sink slowly away
In my hair turned loose like a thought
Of a fisherbird dying in flight.
If I opened my arms, I could hear

Every shell in the sea find the word
It has tried to put into my mouth.
Broad flight would become of my dancing,
And I would obsess the whole sea,

But I keep rising and singing
With my last breath. Upon my back,
With his hand on my unborn wing,
A man rests easy as sunlight

Who has kept himself free of the forms
Of the deaf, down-soaring dead,
And me laid out and alive
For nothing at all, in his arms.

I read this as another lyric of poetic incarnation, a rather less willing assumption of the divine other, perhaps even a defense against the Orphic predicament, but still a revision of the poem "The Other." Indeed, I wonder if one way of characterizing Dickey's obsessive strength as a poet is to say that he cannot stop rewriting that essential early poem. For the man who turns from us in the opening line of "Drowning With Others" is the Orphic

Dickey, poet and divine other. Like the rich-haired youth of Collins, or
Coleridge's youth with flashing eyes and floating hair, or Stevens's figure of
the youth as virile poet in "Mrs. Alfred Uruguay," this other Dickey has
hair released into "a kingfisher's crest, confused / By the God-tilted light of
Heaven." Apollo is reborn again, but as Orphic drowning man, fit version
of the poet of Sensibility in America, be he Hart Crane or Roethke or Agee
or Dickey. But if the man turning from us in this poem is Dickey in the act
of Sublime apotheosis, then whoever is that "I" rather desperately chanting
this hieratic spell? Perhaps that is why Dickey as commentator judged this
grand lyric too obscure, despite its palpable strength.

Our poet is weird in the true sense, one of the Fates (as Richard Howard,
lexicographer among bards, might remind us), and his natural mode is the
uncanny. What he has done here may be obscure to his spectral self, but his
magic or occult self gathers his spectral self, until even that "I" keeps "rising
and singing / With my last breath." And so truly neither self dies, or can
die, in this soaring lyric of divination. Perhaps there is a touch, not indeli-
berate, of Dylan Thomas in the metric here, and even allusive overtones of
Thomas at moments in the diction. That resemblance may even be a hidden
cause of Dickey's distaste for his poem, but I remark upon it to note the
difference between the poets, rather than their shared qualities. On mortality,
the warrior Dickey cannot deceive himself, but a poet whose totem seems
to be the albatross does not fear death by water. Few lines are as characteristic of Dickey as "And I would obsess the whole sea."

I take it that "drowning with others" is a trope for "winging with
others," and that the dominant image here is flight, and not going under.
Flight of course is Freud's true trope for repression, and an Orphic sensibility
never ceases to forget, involuntarily but on purpose, that its vocation is
mortal godhood, or not dying *as a poet*. Drowning with others, then, as a
trope, must mean something like dying only as the immortal precursor dies
or writing poems that men will not let die. Though its scale is small, this is
Dickey's *Lycidas*, even as *The Zodiac* will be his cosmological elegy for the
self. The child building up a Mithra-like body is still here in this poem, but
he is here more reluctantly, caught up in the moments of discovering that a
too-closely-shared immortality becomes mortality again, the stronger the
sharing is known.

Dickey, being one of our authentic avatars of the American Sublime,
exemplifies its two grand stigmata: not to feel free unless he is alone, and
finally to know that what is oldest in him is no part of the Creation. After
two poems wrestling with otherness, I need to restore his sense of solitude,
his Emersonian self-reliance, and the great poem for this in his early motion

is "In the Mountain Tent," which appropriately concludes the book *Drowning With Others*. I remember that Dickey contrasts this with the more famous "The Heaven of Animals," a lovely poem, but not one with the power of this meditation:

> I am hearing the shape of the rain
> Take the shape of the tent and believe it,
> Laying down all around where I lie
> A profound, unspeakable law.
> I obey, and am free-falling slowly
>
> Through the thought-out leaves of the wood
> Into the minds of animals.
> I am there in the shining of water
> Like dark, like light, out of Heaven.
>
> I am there like the dead, or the beast
> Itself, which thinks of a poem—
> Green, plausible, living and holy—
> And cannot speak, but hears,
> Called forth from the waiting of things,
>
> A vast, proper, reinforced crying
> With the sifted, harmonious pause,
> The sustained intake of all breath
> Before the first word of the Bible.
>
> At midnight water dawns
> Upon the held skulls of the foxes
> And weasels and touseled hares
> On the eastern side of the mountain.
> Their light is the image I make
>
> As I wait as if recently killed,
> Receptive, fragile, half-smiling,
> My brow watermarked with the mark
> On the wing of a moth
>
> And the tent taking shape on my body
> Like ill-fitting, Heavenly clothes.
> From holes in the ground comes my voice
> In the God-silenced tongue of the beasts.
> "I shall rise from the dead," I am saying.

Whether a Christian or not, this speaker appears to entertain a belief in the resurrection of the body. Even in this solitude of spirit, the uncanny in Dickey, his *daimon,* enters with the poem's implicit question: Whose body, mine or that of the other? Is it every man who shall rise in the body, or is it not a more Gnostic persuasion that is at work here? The Gnostic lives already in the resurrected body, which is the body of a Primal Man who preceded the Creation. What a Gnostic called the Pleroma, the Fullness, Dickey calls beautifully "the waiting of things." The dead, the animals, and Dickey as the poem's speaker, all hear together the Gnostic Call, a vast crying out of the waiting of things. Without knowing any esoteric Gnosticism, Dickey by poetic intuition arrives at the trope of the Kabbalistic holding-in of the divine breath that precedes the rupture of Creation. What Dickey celebrates therefore is "The sustained intake of all breath / Before the first word of the Bible." That word in Hebrew is *Beresit,* and so the vision of this poem is set before the Beginning. At midnight, not at dawn, and so only in the light of a rain image reflected from the beasts, Dickey speaks forth for the beasts, who have been silenced by the Demiurge called God by Genesis. In Dickey's own interpretation, the man experiences both a kinship with the beasts and a fundamental difference, since he alone will rise from the dead. But I think the poet is stronger than the poet-as-interpreter here. To rise from the dead, in this poem's context, is merely to be one's own magical or pneumatic self, a self that precedes the first word of the Bible.

It isn't very startling to see and say that Dickey, as poet, is not a Christian poet, but rather an Emersonian, an American Orphic and Gnostic. This is only to repeat Richard Howard's fine wordplay upon what could be called the Native Strain in our literature. What startles me, a little, is to see and say just how doctrinal, even programmatic, Dickey's early Orphism now seems. The Orphism has persisted, emerging with tumultuous force in the superbly mad female preacher of Dickey's "May Day Sermon," which I recommend we all read directly after each time we read Jonathan Edwards's rather contrary sermon, "Sinners in the Hands of an Angry God." Rhetorically, though, that is a very different Dickey than the poet of *The Early Motion,* whose Orphism perhaps is the more persuasive for being almost overheard, rather than so emphatically heard.

I turn my charting of the early motion to Dickey's next book, *Helmets,* which so far may be his most distinguished single volume, a judgment in which I would neither want nor expect him to concur. "Helmet," as a word, ultimately goes back to an Indo-European root that means both "to cover and conceal," but also "to save," which explains why "helm" and "helmet" are related to those two antithetical primal names, Hell and Valhalla. Dickey's book, of course, knows all this, Dickey being a preternaturally implicit knower, both as a poet and as a warrior—or, combining both modes, as an archer and hunter. Had I time and space, I would want to comment on every poem in *Helmets,* but I will confine myself to its two most ambitious meditations, "Approaching Prayer" and the final "Drinking from a Helmet." Certain thematic and agonistic strains that I have glanced at already can be said not to culminate but to achieve definitive expression in these major poems. I qualify my statement because what is most problematic about Dickey's poetry is that nothing ever is allowed to culminate, not even in *The Zodiac,* or "Falling," or "May Day Sermon." So obsessive a poet generally would not remain also so tentative, but Dickey's is a cunning imagination, metamorphic enough to evade its exegetes.

As a critic himself obsessed with the issue of belatedness, I am particularly impressed by the originality of "Approaching Prayer," which Dickey rightly called "the most complicated and far-fetched poem I've written." I should add that Dickey said that some fifteen years ago, but it is good enough for me that his observation was true up to then. The far-fetcher was the good, rough English term that the Elizabethan rhetorician Puttenham used to translate the ancient trope called metalepsis or transumption, and "Approaching Prayer" is certainly an instance of the kind of poem that I have learned to call transumptive. Such a poem swallows up an ever-early freshness as its own, and spits out all sense of belatedness, as belonging only to others. "Approaching Prayer" is at moments Yeatsian in its stance and diction, but what overwhelmingly matters most in it can only be called "originality." I know no poem remotely like it. If it shares a magic vitalism with Yeats and D. H. Lawrence, its curious kind of wordless, almost undirected prayer has nothing Yeatsian or Lawrentian in its vision. And it is less like Dickey's true precursor, Roethke, than it is like Robert Penn Warren's masterful "Red-Tailed Hawk and Pyre of Youth," which, however, was written long after it and perhaps may even owe something to it.

Originality in poetry, despite Northrop Frye's eloquent assertions, has little to do with the renewal of an archetype. Instead, it has to do with what I would call a struggle against facticity, where "facticity" means being so incarcerated by an author, a tradition, or a mode that neither author nor reader is aware of the incarceration. Dickey calls his poem "Approaching Prayer," but as his revisionist or critic, I will retitle it "Approaching Poetry" or even "Approaching Otherness." I grant that Dickey has said, "In this poem I tried to imagine how a rather prosaic person would prepare himself for the miraculous event which will be the prayer he's going to try to pray," but surely that "rather prosaic person" is a transparent enough defense for

the not exactly prosaic Dickey. No one has ever stood in Dickey's presence
and felt that he was encountering prose. The poem's speaker is "inside the
hair *helmet*" (my emphasis), and this helmet too both conceals and saves.
At the poem's visionary center, the boar's voice, speaking through the helmet,
gives us the essential trope as he describes his murder by the archer: "*The
sound from his fingers, / Like a plucked word, quickly pierces / Me again.*"
The bow, then, is poetic language, and each figuration is a wounding arrow.
Who then is slaying whom?

Like any strong poet, Dickey puts on the body of his dead father, for
him, let us say, the composite precursor Yeats/Roethke. Shall we say that the
strong poet, in Dickey's savage version, reverses the fate of Adonis, and slays
the boar of facticity? I hear the accent of another reversal, when Dickey
writes:

> My father's sweater
> Swarms over me in the dark.
> I see nothing, but for a second
>
> Something goes through me
> Like an accident, a negligent glance.

Emerson, in his famous epiphany of transmutation into a Transparent
Eyeball, chanted: "I am nothing; I see all; the currents of the Universal Being
circulate through me; I am part or particle of God." Dickey's surrogate sees
nothing, but for a second is all, since that something going through him,
glancingly negligent, accidental, also makes him part or particle of God.
Addressing beasts and angels, this not so very prosaic personage speaks both
as beast and as angel. But to whom? To part or particle of what is oldest,
earliest in him, to the beyond that comes straight down at the point of the
acceptable time. But acceptable to whom? The God of the hunt is hardly
Yahweh Elohim. Dickey's closing chant salutes the God through the trope
of "enough": a violent enough stillness, a brain having enough blood, love
enough from the dead father, lift enough from the acuity of slaughter—all
enough to slay reason in the name of something being, something that need
not be heard, if only "it may have been somehow said." The apocalyptic
Lawrence of the last poems and *The Man Who Died,* and the Yeats of the
final phase, celebrated and so would have understood that "enough." As an
American Orphic, as pilot and as archer, Dickey is less theoretic, more pragmatic, in having known just that "enough."

If I were writing of the later Dickey, the poet of "The Firebombing,"
"Slave Quarters," "Falling," and *The Zodiac,* then I would invoke Blake's

Proverbs of Hell on the dialectics of knowing enough by knowing more than enough. But I am going to conclude where Dickey himself ends *The Early Motion*, with the gracious approach to otherness that characterizes the nineteen fragments that constitute "Drinking from a Helmet." Dickey remarks that the fragments are set between the battlefield and the graveyard, which I suspect is no inaccurate motto for the entire cosmos of what will prove to be the Whole Motion, when we have it all. Though it is a suite of war poems, "Drinking from a Helmet," even in its title, moves toward meaning both of Dickey's major imaginative obsessions: divination through finding the right cover of otherness, and salvation from the body of this death through finding the magic body of the poet.

A survivor climbs out of his foxhole to wait on line at a green water-truck, picking up another's helmet to serve as a drinking vessel. Behind him, the graves registration people are laying out the graveyard for those still fighting. The literal force of this is almost too strong, and conceals the trope of divination, defined by Vico as the process of evasion by which the poet of Magic Formalism achieves godhood—a kind of mortal godhood, but immortality enough. Drinking from a helmet becomes the magic act of substitution, fully introduced in the luminous intensity of fragment VIII:

> At the middle of water
> Bright circles dawned inward and outward
> Like oak rings surviving the tree
> As its soul, or like
> The concentric gold spirit of time.
> I kept trembling forward through something
> Just born of me.

The "something" is prayer, but again in the peculiar sense adumbrated in the poem "Approaching Prayer." Dickey always has been strongest at *invention* (which Dr. Johnson thought the essence of poetry) and his invention is triumphant throughout the subsequent progression of fragments. We apprehend an almost Blakean audacity of pure vision, as the speaker struggles to raise the dead:

> I swayed, as if kissed in the brain.
> Above the shelled palm-stumps I saw
> How the tops of huge trees might be moved
> In a place in my own country
> I never had seen in my life.
> In the closed dazzle of my mouth

> I fought with a word in the water
> To call on the dead to strain
> Their muscles to get up and go there.
> I felt the difference between
> Sweat and tears when they rise,
> Both trying to melt the brow down.

I think one would have to go back to Whitman's *Drum-Taps* to find an American war poetry this nobly wrought. Vision moves from Okinawa to rural America, to the place of the slain other whose helmet has served as the vessel of the water of life:

> On even the first day of death
> The dead cannot rise up,
> But their last thought hovers somewhere
> For whoever finds it.
> My uninjured face floated strangely
> In the rings of a bodiless tree.
> Among them, also, a final
> Idea lived, waiting
> As in Ariel's limbed, growing jail.

Ariel, imprisoned by the witch before Prospero's advent, then becomes the spirit of freedom, but not in this poem, where only to "be no more killed" becomes freedom enough. "Not dying wherever you are" is the new mode of otherness, as vision yields to action:

> Enough
> Shining, I picked up my carbine and said.
> I threw my old helmet down
> And put the wet one on.
> Warmed water ran over my face.
> My last thought changed, and I knew
> I inherited one of the dead.

Dickey at last, though only through surrogate or trope, is at once self and other. What was vision becomes domesticated, touchingly American:

> I saw tremendous trees
> That would grow on the sun if they could,
> Towering. I saw a fence
> And two boys facing each other,
> Quietly talking,

> Looking in at the gigantic redwoods,
> The rings in the trunks turning slowly
> To raise up stupendous green.
> They went away, one turning
> The wheels of a blue bicycle,
> The smaller one curled catercornered
> In the handlebar basket.

The dead soldier's last thought is of his older brother, as Dickey's longing always has been for his own older brother, dead before the poet was born. Fragment XVIII, following, is the gentlest pathos in all of Dickey:

> I would survive and go there,
> Stepping off the train in a helmet
> That held a man's last thought,
> Which showed him his older brother
> Showing him trees.
> I would ride through all
> California upon two wheels
> Until I came to the white
> Dirt road where they had been,
> Hoping to meet his blond brother,
> And to walk with him into the wood
> Until we were lost,
> Then take off the helmet
> And tell him where I had stood,
> What poured, what spilled, what swallowed:

That "what" is the magic of substitution, and the final fragment is Whitmanian and unforgettable, being the word of the survivor who suffered and was there:

> And tell him I was the man.

The ritual magic of a soldier's survival has been made one with the Incarnation of the Poetical Character. Of all Dickey's poems, it is the one I am persuaded that Walt Whitman would have admired most. Whitman too would have said with Dickey: "I never have been able to disassociate the poem from the poet, and I hope I never will." What Whitman and Dickey alike show is that "the poet" is both an empirical self, and more problematically a real me or me myself, an ontological self, and yet a divine other. Both poets are hermetic and esoteric while making populist gestures. There the resemblance ends, and to pursue it further would be unfair to Dickey or any contemporary; it would have been unfair even for Stevens or for Hart Crane. The Dickey of the later motion is no Whitmanian; if one wants an American analogue, one would have to imagine Theodore Roethke as an astronaut, which defeats imagination. But I end by citing Whitman because his final gestures are the largest contrast I know to James Dickey's ongoing motions in his life's work. Whitman is up ahead of us somewhere; he is perpetually early, warning us: "Will you speak before I am gone? will you prove already too late?" The burden of belatedness is upon us, but if we hurry, we will catch up to him:

> Failing to fetch me at first keep encouraged,
> Missing me one place search another,
> I stop somewhere waiting for you.

Not Dickey; he cannot stop, yet he has taken up part of the burden for us. Whitman is larger, but then no one is larger, and that largeness is a final comfort, like Stevens's "Large Red Man Reading." Dickey speaks only to and for part of us, but that part is or wants to be the survivor; wants no more dying. Words alone, alas, are not certain good, though the young Yeats, like the young Dickey, wanted them to be. But they can help us to make "a creature to keep me dying / Years longer," as Dickey wrote in the poem of "The Other." I conclude by going full circle, by returning to the poem with the tribute that it could prove to contain the whole motion within it. Dickey cannot "turn wholly mortal in [his] mind," and that touch of "utter, unseasonable glory" will be his legacy.

DIANA COLLECOTT

Inside and Outside in the Poetry
of Denise Levertov

"We awake in the same moment to ourselves and to things." This sentence from Jacques Maritain was chosen by the Objectivist poet George
Oppen as an epigraph to his book *The Materials*. Its presence there accents
a paradox central to some of the most interesting American writing today.
"Objectivism" is a term very loosely used at present, and I can think of no
better way of giving it definition, than by recalling Louis Zukofsky's gloss
on the word "Objective" in the special number of *Poetry* (Chicago) he edited
in 1930. First he takes a definition from Optics; "An Objective—the lens
bringing the rays from an object to a focus." Then he offers its "Use extended
to poetry": "Desire for that which is objectively perfect." The Objectivist
movement initiated by Zukofsky in the thirties was a programmatic formulation of the poetic theory of Ezra Pound and the poetic practice of
William Carlos Williams over the previous twenty years. In particular, it
derived from Pound's effort, through the Imagist movement, to replace what
he called "the obscure reveries / Of the inward gaze" with a poetry concentrated on outward things. Hardness, edge, were the qualities that recom-
mended the work of H. D. and Marianne Moore to him; he praised in their
poems "[t]he arid clarity . . . of *le tempérament de l'Américaine.*"
   Yet neither Pound nor Zukofsky was so ignorant as to emphasize the
outward eye to the exclusion of what goes on inside the seeing mind. Indeed,
Zukofsky claims that, among the Objectivists: "Writing occurs which is the

From *Critical Quarterly* 22, no. 1 (Spring 1980). © 1980 by Manchester University
Press.

detail, not the mirage, of seeing, of thinking with the things as they exist.
. . . Shapes suggest themselves, and the mind senses and receives awareness."
It is implied here that the eye is the focal point in a two-way process. This
vivid commerce between inside and outside is a distinctive feature of the
poets of the Black Mountain school, who have assimilated the discoveries of
the Objectivists and their predecessors in the American avant-garde. Consider Robert Creeley's

> I keep to myself such
> measures as I care for,
> daily the rocks
> accumulate position.

Here, interpenetration between the inner world of the poet and the outer
world of objects establishes a mode of writing which Denise Levertov has
made hers also.

II

Denise Levertov is an American by adoption. She was born near London,
of Russian and Welsh parentage, in 1923. In 1948 she married the American
writer Mitchell Goodman, and went to live in the United States. By then,
she had already published a first book of verse in England; Kenneth Rexroth
has described her, at her debut in the Britain of Dylan Thomas, as "the baby
of the New Romanticism." These early poems were accomplished precisely
insofar as they were "obscure reveries / Of the inward gaze": weighted with
symbolism, they have a dream-like immobility. One is reminded of Charles
Olson's claim that Williams, following in the footsteps of Whitman, taught
American poets to *walk*. No "new measure" had reached British writers at
that time. Hence Levertov recalls: "Marrying an American and coming to
live here while still young was very stimulating to me as a writer, for it
necessitated the finding of new rhythms in which to write, in accordance
with new rhythms of life and speech." After first finding affinities with
academic writers such as Richard Wilbur, Levertov began the search for new
rhythms in the milieu of the Black Mountain poets. With Rexroth's encouragement, she submitted herself to a fresh apprenticeship with the work of
Williams; she wrote of this, around 1960: "I feel the stylistic influence of
William Carlos Williams, while perhaps too evident in my work of a few
years ago, was a very necessary and healthful one, without which I could
not have developed from a British Romantic with almost Victorian background, to an American poet of any vitality." "Vitality" strikes a keynote

here. It reminds us of Robert Duncan's contention that the essential difference between American and British poetry in our era is that the first is *active,*
it moves. "In American poetry," he writes, "the striding syllables show an
aesthetic based on energies." For Denise Levertov, the main transmitter of
this aesthetic was Charles Olson's essay "Projective Verse"—an essay, incidentally, which Williams thought so summative of his life's work, that he
included it intact as a chapter of his *Autobiography.* The most influential
formulation of this essay is not Olson's own, but a statement attributed to
Edward Dahlberg: "one perception must immediately and directly lead to a
further perception." Thus, a couple of decades after Zukofsky's "Objective,"
the new school of poets insisted afresh on the *act* of perception, or rather
on a series of acts which would shape the poem after their kind.

III

One poem of Levertov's which exemplifies these new influences, and her
own discovery of "new rhythms" is the title piece of *Overland to the Islands,*
the volume published by Jargon Books in 1958.

> Let's go—much as that dog goes,
> intently haphazard. The
> Mexican light on a day that
> —'smells like autumn in Connecticut'
> makes iris ripples on his
> black gleaming fur—and that too
> is as one would desire—a radiance
> consorting with the dance.
>   Under his feet
> rocks and mud, his imagination, sniffing,
> engaged in its perceptions—dancing
> edgeways, there's nothing
> the dog disdains on his way,
> nevertheless he
> keeps moving, changing
> pace and approach but
> not direction—'every step an arrival.'

This poem is "about" movement. It begins with the casual invitation "Let's
go" and then introduces the dog, as an example of movement; thereafter,
poet, poem and reader move with him, "intently haphazard"; one could
almost say that the dog *is* the projective movement of the poem: his interest

leads us from one perception to the next. Levertov has no inhibition about presenting the dog, "his imagination, sniffing, / engaged in its perceptions," as a model for the poet; but nor does she attempt to press this conclusion upon us. She does not stop to do this, as she too "keeps moving."

Anyone familiar with the poetry of Carlos Williams will feel at home here. In such poems as "Pastoral" or "The Poor" or "By the road to the contagious hospital," Williams is equally undemanding in relation to his environment, equally unwilling to press a comparison; he is content to record, and move on. The very dog of Levertov's poem is known to us from the opening lines of *Paterson, Book I,* where Williams declares his intent "To make a start, / out of particulars," and slyly presents himself as "Sniffing the trees, / just another dog / among a lot of dogs." Even the mannerisms in Levertov's poem—the quotation in the fourth line, the parenthesis by which she succeeds in all but keeping herself out of the poem ("and that too / is as one would desire")—are redolent of the master.

In a comment on "Overland to the Islands" Levertov says: "The last phrase, 'every step an arrival,' is quoted from Rilke, and here, unconsciously, I was evidently trying to unify for myself my sense of the pilgrim way with my new American, objectivist-influenced, pragmatic, and sensuous longing for the Here and Now." Later, Levertov identifies what she calls here "the pilgrim way" as "a personal fiction." It is certainly a *supreme* fiction, in Stevens's sense, since when she describes life as a pilgrimage, she is interested in the pursuit of a reality beyond that of the everyday, the "Here and Now." Yet Levertov's very sure-footedness in the *Here and Now* (the title, incidentally, of her first American collection) makes her refuse to leave behind the contingent world in pursuit of a transcendent reality. Thus the common dog, with its iridescently "gleaming fur" can act as an avatar to her, but thus also, the "rocks and mud" beneath its feet are essential to its imaginative progress.

IV

Denise Levertov's belief that one's inner discoveries should move hand in hand with one's outward perceptions has been the main impulse of her experiments in writing and her discussions of poetics. "Some Notes on Organic Form," dated 1965, is one of her earliest published statements on a re-thought Romanticism. In it, she emphasizes the concept that "there *is* a form in all things (and in our experience) which the poet can discover and reveal."

This essentially Platonic version of the artist's task is perhaps the last thing that one would expect from a confessedly "American, objectivist-influenced, pragmatic" writer. It leads Levertov to revive Hopkins's terms *inscape* and *instress,* and to add: "In thinking of the process of poetry as I know it, I extend the use of these words, which he seems to have used mainly in reference to sensory phenomena, to include intellectual and emotional experience as well." In another essay, she goes further than this, and argues that, just as "the *being* of things has inscape" so too does the poet's own being, and that the act of transmitting to others the inscape of things, is also the act of awakening one's own being.

It is by such steps that we arrive at that flow between inside and outside that Williams characterized as "an interpenetration, both ways." In the opening of *Paterson, Book II,* "Sunday in the Park," Williams presents such interpenetration in overtly sexual terms; "Dr. Paterson" is speaking:

> Outside
>> outside myself
>>> there is a world,
> he rumbled, subject to my incursions
> —a world
>> (to me) at rest,
>>> which I approach
> concretely—
>> The scene's the Park
>> upon the rock,
>> female to the city
> —upon whose body Paterson instructs his thoughts
> (concretely).

Here Paterson's role in relation to the rest of the world is obviously masculine: the objective world is "subject" to him; some lines further on, he "starts, possessive, through the trees"; yet within a page, he is describing himself as not merely possessive but "passive-possessive," and he seems to present this as a proper condition for the poet.

There are, in Levertov's writings, an almost equal number of descriptions of the poetic process as a passive and so-to-say "female" condition, as there are equations for a more aggressive and "male" activity. She appears to have taken to heart Williams's advice, in a letter he wrote her, that a poet must be "in essence a woman as well as a man." Indeed, she comments from her own experience, with unusual honesty: "Perhaps I don't know myself very well, for at times I see myself as having boundless energy and a savage will, and at other times as someone easily tired and so impressionable as to be, like Keats, weighed down almost unbearably, by the identities around me."

V

This combination of receptivity and creative energy appears to be essential not only to Denise Levertov's identity as a poet, but also to her sense of herself. In a comparatively recent poem, she records her delight at an interpretation of her name in its Hebrew meanings. D or Daleth means "door"; hence we get:

> entrance, exit,
> way through of
> giving and receiving
> which are one.

"Giving and receiving" are capable of becoming "one" in an American poetic which can incorporate somatic awareness—the body's sense of itself, as well as of the objects around it—in the disposition of words on the page.

Levertov has clearly cultivated such awareness at a subtle level. She speaks of *waiting* for the poem "in that intense passivity, that passive intensity, that passionate patience that Keats named Negative Capability." Reading her poetry and prose we realize that she writes best from that state of restful alertness in which, Wordsworth claimed, "we see into the heart of things." Hence "vision," "inscape," "revelation" are key words in her criticism, and she frequently cites such writers as Coleridge, Emerson, Rilke, in trying to identify the special value of such insights to poetic composition. One such passage, from Carlyle, is worth quoting, as it seems to express her own experience: "A musical thought is one spoken by a mind that has penetrated to the inmost heart of the thing; detected the inmost mystery of it, namely the melody that lies hidden in it; the inward harmony of coherence which is its soul, whereby it exists, and has a right to be, here in this world." "To write is to listen" says Levertov, on analogy with Picasso's "To draw is to shut your eyes and sing." Carlyle, Picasso, Levertov, all imply that the value they seek in art is *inside* as well as *outside,* that the song is "there" ready to be transcribed by him who hears it, that the composition exists already only to be seen by the artist.

VI

For Levertov, this knowledge does not undermine the outward senses, but substantiates them. Poetry requires, she says, the "utmost attentiveness," and the eye has a crucial part to play in bringing her poems into being. In "Pleasures," for instance, seeing is a means of discovering the hidden properties of ordinary objects:

> I like to find
> what's not found
> at once, but lies
>
> within something of another nature,
> in repose, distinct.

The rest of the poem gives specific instances of this kind of discovery of the unknown within the known:

> Gull feathers of glass, hidden
>
> in white pulp: the bones of squid
> which I pull out and lay
> blade by blade on the draining board—
>
> tapered as if for swiftness, to pierce
> the heart, but fragile, substance
> belying design.

Such lines are themselves acts of attention: their breaks indicate her careful scrutiny ("lay / blade by blade"); they record her reading of nature's book. We are reminded irresistibly of Thoreau, one of the American authors to whom Levertov constantly returns, and of Emerson, whose "Ask the fact for the form" was almost a slogan to the writers of the Black Mountain school.

Creeley, in fact, coined the expression: "Form is never more than extension of content." Levertov amends this to read: "Form is never more than a *revelation* of content." Thus the composition of the poem is itself regarded as a vehicle for revelation; indeed, Levertov argues that the very spaces on the page help the mind to fresh insights into the nature of things.

VII

If poetry is to become a simple act of transcription from nature, the poet must abandon his traditional role of supremacy over things. These writers believe that meaning is pre-existent in things: it does not depend on structures of thought and feeling imposed by the poet. Thus simple contingency offers a means to transcend itself, and Levertov can write: "A poetry that merely describes, and that features the trivial egotism of the writer (an egotism that obstructs any profound self-explorations) is not liberated from contingency." In castigating egotism here, Levertov echoes, perhaps, Olson's account of the modern poet's necessary relation to the world, for which he invents the term "Objectism." "Objectism [he writes in "Projective Verse"] is the getting rid of the lyrical interference of the individual as ego, of the "subject" and his soul, that peculiar presumption by which western man has interposed himself between what he is as a creature of nature . . . and those other creations of nature which we may, with no derogation, call objects." Olson's prime example of "Objectism" is W. C. Williams. Williams once described in a letter to Marianne Moore a youthful experience in which, he said, "everything became a unit and at the same time a part of myself." "As a reward for this anonymity," Williams concluded, "I feel as much a part of things as trees or stones."

Joseph Hillis Miller is surely right to see this "anonymity," this abandonment of the separate ego, as an abandonment also of that separation between the inner world of the subject and the outer world of objects which is a debased inheritance from Romanticism. "In Williams's poetry [Miller writes] there is no description of private inner experience. There is also no description of objects which are external to the poet's mind. Nothing is external to his mind. His mind overlaps with things; things overlap with his mind." Thus Williams may be placed at an extreme remove from the young T. S. Eliot who found in the philosophy of F. H. Bradley a congenial account of the prison of subjectivity: "My external sensations are no less private to myself than are my thoughts or my feelings. In either case my experience falls within my own circle, a circle closed on the outside; . . . In brief, regarded as an existence which appears in a soul, the whole world for each is peculiar and private to that soul." This ontological distinction between Williams and Eliot informs the modes of their writing and the attitudes they have to their readers. Where Eliot claims the artist's prerogative to pre-select experience for the reader, Williams complains that "There is a constant barrier between the reader and his consciousness of immediate contact with the world." He thus takes his stand with Whitman, who told his reader in "Song of Myself":

> You shall not look through my eyes either, nor take things from me,
> You shall listen to all sides and filter them for yourself.

For Levertov, as for Whitman and Williams, experience is a continuum. Geoffrey Thurley recognizes this, when he says of her work: "In place of the refined poetess sitting isolated among the teacups, socially aligned with her visitors but privately alienated from them, we encounter . . . the poet-housewife/mother . . . whose living-space coincides with [her] aesthetic space. The old separation of the avant-garde, in which the private world of poetic experience excluded the actual grubby world of social living, is replaced by a unified continuum."

VIII

In Levertov, as in Williams, there is no blurring of the edge between self and objects, but it is not a cutting edge: she is as free as he is of the angst that has dogged Romantic writers up to our own day. Hence the attitude with which she approaches the world is essentially one of wonder, of delight. Her poems bear out Williams's dictum that "There is a long history in each one of us that comes as not only a reawakening but a re-possession when confronted by this world."

For Levertov, writing is a way of recording such acts of "reawakening," of "repossession"; it is radiant with *recognition*:

> That's it, [she exclaims in "Matins"]
> that's joy, it's always
> a recognition, the known
> appearing fully itself, and
> more itself than one knew.

The perpetual problem of a poetry of recognitions is that it may only rarely get beyond exclamation. This poem, for instance, is punctuated by ejacula-tions of "the authentic!," and simply offers us fragments of experience that have struck the poet as in some way "authentic." Such writing remains obstinately Imagist, and lays itself open to the criticism of an early American review of Imagism, that: "Poem after poem of this sort is full of the simple wonder of a child picking up pebbles on the beach." However, if we can accept such naiveté as, in itself, "authentic," then we can begin to appreciate that it does not simply negate all our previous expectations of poetry, but offers a distinctively new mode.

IX

In order to describe this mode, I find myself falling back on Roman Jakobson's well-known distinction between the metaphoric and metonymic poles of discourse. You will recall that Jakobson associates metaphor, the assertion of similarity, with poetry, and with Romantic modes of experience. Metaphor and simile record the Romantic poet's efforts to identify *likeness* in the world about him, to impose his meanings on it, to span the felt distance between subject and object. Metonymy, on the other hand, rests on *contiguity*; it is enough for things to be associated in space for them to be placed together in discourse. Thus Jakobson identifies metonymy as the pole toward which prose, and in particular the literature of Realism, tends.

We can see then that Henry James, who argues that "Life is all inclusion and confusion; art is all discrimination and selection," would be inclined to metaphor and symbolism, by Jakobson's definition; whereas Balzac, who expressed his intent to "set forth in order the facts" is metonymic or Realist—if we may assume that, for him, the order in which the facts naturally occur is a sufficient order. Williams must undoubtedly be categorized with Balzac, since he overtly refuses the egotist's or artist's privilege of discrimination, in favor of transcription. "What is there to select?" he asks, "It *is*."

Williams explicitly rejected metaphor and simile early in his poetic career. Here is a significant passage from the Prologue to *Kora in Hell* (1917):

> Although it is a quality of the imagination that it seeks to *place together* those things which have a common relationship, yet the coining of similes is a pastime of a very low order. . . . Much more keen is that power which discovers in things those inimitable particles of dissimilarity to all other things which are the peculiar perfections of the thing in question. . . . This *loose linking* of one thing with another has the effects of a destructive power little to be guessed at. . . . All is confusion, yet it comes from a hidden desire for the dance.
>
> [my emphases]

This is a charter for the metonymic writer. It lies behind all Williams's efforts to establish a new mode of writing, in the face of Eliot's tremendous success as a symbolist poet. Confronted by that success, he wrote in *Spring and All*: "how easy to slip / into the old mode, how hard to cling / to the advance." The "old mode" is the mode of symbolism, of metaphor; the "advance," as Williams saw it, was the move beyond Romantic dualism into the metonymic mode.

The alternative to metaphor, in Williams's view, was a stress on particulars—hence the well-known slogan "No ideas but in things"; and hence, too, the injunction of *Paterson, Book III*:

> —of this, make it of *this,* this
> this, this, this, this.

Multiplicity, the listing of things without violating their particular existence, becomes a deliberate strategy, and is responsible for the shape of Williams's poems on the page. "By the brokenness of his composition," he wrote, "the poet makes himself master of a certain weapon which he could possess himself of in no other way."

The first poem of *Spring and All* demonstrates this strategy in its local detail:

> All along the road the reddish
> purplish, forked, upstanding, twiggy
> stuff of bushes and small trees.

It stops short of personification even then "sluggish / dazed spring approaches"; the poem continues:

> They enter the new world naked
> cold, uncertain of all
> save that they enter.

The reader may extrapolate from these lines a metaphor for the immigrant's bleak prospect of America, or for the baby's arrival in the world, but he is not *entitled* to do so by the mode of the poem.

This is a major difficulty for English students coming to Williams from a training in reading Eliot's poetry or indeed any poetry in the European metaphoric tradition—and in that we must include such writers as Wallace Stevens and Robert Frost. Because Williams is a metonymic poet, his work often seems, to the uninitiated, close to prose. His own development, indeed, involved a rejection of Keats's idiom in favor of the kind of Whitmanesque jottings that Allen Ginsberg has referred to as "prose-seeds." Metonymy was the natural medium in which he could set down the contiguous pattern of his perceptions. Hence the necessity of his work, and to that of the writers who followed him, of typographic freedom, of open form, which allows the "prose-seeds" to establish their own growth.

X

This is the context of Levertov's belief that "Form is never more than a *revelation* of content," and of her own poetic practice. In her writing, as in Williams's, there is no *depth,* no measurable distance between what is said and what is meant. In this, both differ from the most well intentioned of the Transcendentalists. Tony Tanner has pointed out the strain inherent in Thoreau's attempts to "move from the surface detail to the Universal benevolent One which underlay it," the evidence in his writing of "an effort of penetration, a will to seduce the larger meaning out of the small particular."

Levertov seems, like Williams, to have achieved a concatenation of the "surface detail" with the "larger meaning." Her poetry may be said to be *all surface*. I have attempted to show that this is not a matter of style alone, but of the poet's state of awareness. Thus she writes:

> life is in me, a love for
> what happens, for
> the surfaces that are their own
> interior life.

In passages such as this, it seems to me that Williams's phrase "passive-possessive" gets its full complement of meaning. Love is a precondition of Levertov's relaxed relationship with herself and with things. This persists in *The Sorrow Dance* at the very threshold of her poems against the Vietnam War. My last example, "Joy," is from this volume. It has an epigraph from Thoreau, which robustly insists:

> You must love the crust of the earth on
> which you dwell. You must be able to
> extract nutriment out of a sandheap.
> You must have so good an appetite as
> this, else you will live in vain.

> Joy, the 'well . . . *joyfulness* of
> joy'—'many years
> I had not known it,' the woman of eighty
> said, 'only remembered, till now.'

> Traherne
> in dark fields.
>   On Tremont Street,
> on the Common, a raw dusk, Emerson
> 'glad to the brink of fear.'
>   It is objective,

> stands founded, a roofed gateway;
> we cloud-wander

> away from it, stumble
> again towards it not seeing it,

> enter cast-down, discover ourselves
> 'in joy' as 'in love.'

In this poem, the very scraps of discourse are like the crusts from which Thoreau's nutriment must be extracted. Here the contiguity is not of things, but of "prose-seeds," disparate recognitions. The poet allows them to lie, like found-objects, on the page, and to offer a sense of revelation analogous to her own.

It is in this sense that the poem *moves*: that is, it moves *us,* just as the original experience moved the poet. It also moves, as "Overland to the Islands" moved, toward a final discovery. In Levertov's words "the metric movement, the measure, is the direct expression of the movement of perception." Here the measure enacts the meaning as "we / cloud-wander / away from it" and "stumble again towards it." The poem approaches its meaning in just such an oblique manner—via the words and experience of others, to a direct statement ("It is objective") which recalls the signal "It quickens" of Williams's "At the Ball Game." Like Williams, Levertov seems intent on using the brokenness of things as a vehicle for wholeness, and she does indeed offer an analogy for this wholeness, close to the center of the poem: "stands founded, a roofed gateway." Again, I restrain myself from the term "metaphor," since it seems to me that the gateway is *there,* just as the experience is there, to be entered—an entry which is not simply into the full value of the world outside, but also the full value of the world within oneself. This is what the poem ultimately "discovers" to us:

> and we discover ourselves
> 'in joy' as 'in love.'

JOHN HOLLANDER

Kenneth Koch

The appearance of Kenneth Koch's *Selected Poems, 1950–1982* is a long-overdue pleasure, and although those who admire his work as much as I do cannot help but regret certain favorites among his earlier poems that got lost in selection, this volume is of great value. It will allow unfamiliar readers to perceive, and knowing ones to reflect upon, the consistency of a joyful and energetic mode through over thirty years of, given that consistency, amazingly unrepetitive writing. Koch's continuing celebration of the playful sublime has always constituted a sort of gaudy tent, pitched among the ruins of high seriousness; a welcome sight in the intense heat, it has dispensed souvenirs and guidebooks (not to the ruins, but to itself) and orange juice, frequently blue in color, with such diligence and reliability that one has finally come to realize that the classical ruins were only random rubble, and that the tent was one of the unnamed goddess's authentic temples after all. The tent was striped with the bright, old colors of the New: Ariosto's proclaimed intention of writing of *cosa non detta in prosa mai, ne in rime*—what had not been said in prose before, nor verse—was inscribed on balloons in bunches. That the poet's true originality soared higher than those balloons of French modernist and *avant-gardiste* novelty may not have been discernible to most of the tourists over the years was, given the eternal nature of poetic reception, almost inevitable. But this lovely book should enable readers to participate more knowingly in the celebrations.

From *Yale Review* 74, no. 4 (Summer 1985), © 1985 by Yale University (originally entitled "Poetry in Review"); and from *Partisan Review* 27, no. 2 (Spring 1960), © 1960 by Partisan Review (originally entitled "Ko, or a Season on Earth by Kenneth Koch").

Koch's favorite kind of poem seems to be the set of variations, and the variation structure is itself varied and revised throughout his work. The first poem of his I ever read (in 1957?) was the wonderful "The Artist," a sort of visionary journal and scrapbook of a sculptor whose projects evolve from steel cigarettes and a cherrywood avalanche to a scheme of almost global proportions. Here, for example, is Koch's artist *in re* the question of *Bee*:

Pittsburgh, May 16th. I have abandoned the steel cigarettes. I
    am working on *Bee*.
Bee will be a sixty-yards-long covering for the elevator shaft
    opening in the foundry sub-basement
Near my home. So far it's white sailcloth with streams of
    golden paint evenly spaced out
With a small blue pond at one end, and around it orange and
    green flowers. My experience in Cleveland affected me
    so
That my throat aches whenever I am not working at full speed.
    I have never been so happy and inspired and
Play seems to me now like a juvenile experience!

                        *   *   *

June 8th. *Bee* is still not finished. I have introduced a huge
    number of red balloons into it. How will it work?
Yesterday X. said, "Are you still working on *Bee*? What's
    happened to your interest in steel cigarettes?"
Y. said, "He hasn't been doing any work at all on them since
    he went to Cleveland." A shrewd guess? But how much
    can they possibly know?

                        *   *   *

November 19th. Disaster! *Bee* was almost completed, and now
    the immense central piece of sailcloth has torn.
    Impossible to repair it!
December 4th. I've gone back to work on *Bee*! I suddenly
    thought (after weeks of despair!), "I can place the
    balloons over the tear in the canvas!" So that is what I
    am doing. All promises to be well!
December 6th. The foreman of the foundry wants to look at

my work. It seems that he too is an "artist"—does
sketches and watercolors and such. . . . What will he
think of *Bee*?

Plans, doubts, hopes, fears, the whole paraphernalia of confidences in
any artist's or writer's book of *son coeur mis à nu*, surround the records of
the creation and reception of what would look today like a series of examples
drawn from the fashionable art of the past two decades. But this poem was
not "influenced" by Pop Art; rather, so much of the framing of both objects
and hunks of environment which went on subsequent to its publication seem
to have been dully literal, even if unwitting, illustrations of it. (Here the
relation of true poetry to false art perhaps mirrors that of art to nature:
Whistler was once accosted by a lady who remarked that she had been
walking on the Embankment and that the Thames looked just like one of
his *Nocturnes*, to which the artist replied that Nature seemed to be creeping
up.) The elements of Koch's artist's oeuvre were mythological and paradigmatic, with the result that they became, in this Whistlerian-Wildean sense,
literally prophetic. "The Artist" is one mode of variation on the variation
theme, the "what next?"-ness that such patterns inevitably engender being
tied here to the narrative of an artistic career. From the early "Collected
Poems" to the more recent "In Bed," Koch is at work on what will be next.
The hilarious and beautiful "Lunch" from his first book is itself a Banquet
of Sense, what used to be called a "travelogue" of exotic lunches. I quote
from one of them as an instance of the author's superb ear and rhythmic
timing:

O launch, lunch, you dazzling hoary tunnel
To paradise!
Do you see that snowman tackled over there
By summer and the sea? A boardwalk went to Istanbul
And back under his left eye. We saw the Moslems praying
In Rhodes. One had a red fez, another had a black cap.
And in the extended heat of afternoon,
As an ice-cold gradual sweat covered my whole body,
I realized, and the carpet swam like a red world at my feet
In which nothing was green, and the Moslems went on praying,
That we had missed lunch, and a perpetual torrent roared into
    the sea
Of my understanding. An old woman gave us bread and rolls
    on the street.

The whole poem concludes with a consideration of, and a gleeful escape from, the problems raised by its own injunction. "Let us give lunch to the lunch." Both the problems and the injunction itself are more in the line of S. J. Perelman—one of the major unavowed influences on the fiction and poetry of a whole generation of American writers—than of French poetry. Koch's ongoing homage to Ariosto, in the ottava rima of his narrative poems *Ko* and *The Duplications* (alas, not included in this section: who could ever forget the opening of the former of these, the only epic or romance ever *literally* to begin in media res with the word "Meanwhile"?), is matched by his continual delight in the tones of poems like Whitman's "Respondez" or "Apostrophe," and in the parable that his free verse is always preaching about itself, in what is really a very neoclassical way of moralizing, as Pope did from the form and function of his couplets, about lines of life from lines of verse. Koch's characteristic scheme of apostrophe, particularly of long and awkwardly named things and beings, is perhaps ultimately Whitmanic as well, but only in style. More deeply, it may have been a poem like (but I suppose that there isn't any other poem "like") Stevens's "Someone Puts a Pineapple Together" that helped Koch see what there was to be seen; even more than the more obvious format of the "Thirteen Ways of Looking at a Blackbird," the series of exuberant misreadings of the pineapple on the table in the shaft of light from the planet of the imagination falling upon it remains a rhythmic model for his sequences of suprising verbal moves.

Koch's early (1960) *Ko, or a Season on Earth* is, as I mentioned before, not included in this volume. But it is worth considering in the light of his later work. It is a long, very funny, mock-heroic poem in five cantos of ottava rima, dealing with, but mostly digressing from, the rookie season with the Brooklyn Dodgers of a young Japanese pitcher of talents scarcely to be believed. The very first line is programmatically mock-epical, dutifully opening the poem strictly, by the book, in medias res, with a kind of ingenuous deadpan literalness: "Meanwhile at the University of Japan / Ko had already begun his studies" begins Koch, with nary an invocation of the muse. "Meanwhile," however, remains his favorite word throughout the poem, robustly shoving the divers episodes into their lines in a kind of narrative relay-race, guiding the reader about the face of the globe whereon the action rambles, substituting for structure and maintaining a semblance of order. These various episodes involve the adventures of, among others, a British proletarian named Huddel; a private detective named Andrews; a kind of Sax Rohmer international manipulator with a fixation on dogs; and a poet named Joseph Dah who is not content with metaphor but demands in life and art a real *becoming*—Koch calls him an "action poet," and, as his

daughter Doris explains to her lover Andrews as her father rushes into the
cabin of a yacht in the form of a dog,

> Dad's integrity
> Makes him, unlike most poets, actualize
> In everyday life the poem's unreality.
> That dog you saw on deck with steel-gray eyes
> Was but a creation of Dad's terrible musical potency.
> Then seeing the dog there made him realize
> That the dog was himself, since by himself created,
> So in this poem it's incorporated!

(Even this stanza, by the way, reveals some of the poem's most common
resources in the near Miltonic parody of the penultimate line as well as in
the strained gag-like humor in the "I-don't-care-if-it-doesn't-rhyme-or-scan-
very-well-the-last-three-words-are-a-*riot*" quality of the fifth one.) The plot
of the whole poem keeps cross-cutting from one of these stories to another,
returning to Ko and the Dodgers and a crucial game with Cincinnati from
time to time, and every once in a while bringing two or more of its strands
in a deliberately over-contrived fashion, while Koch crows with delight over
the coincidences he has engineered. The poem's narrative technique must be
traced back to Ariosto, I think, rather than merely to Byron (who is, of
course, obviously present here and there); the comic impulse is more toward
a rich, zany riot of improbability than toward the embodiment of a satiric
perspective in Don Juan's peculiar kind of innocence, for example. The confrontation of innocence and experience in various forms is present throughout *Ko*. But it is always used for local humor and never as a basic conceptual
framework for the narration. The characters in this poem have no inner lives
at all—perhaps Koch's reversal of Rimbaud for his subtitle constitutes a kind
of declaration of war on most contemporary writers' notions of what experience is. In general, though, it is never the poem's comic mechanism.

I think that it would be a mistake to compare *Ko* with, say, Auden's
Letter to Lord Byron, which is much more of a brilliantly skilled pastiche,
and, in its way, very much more serious. Koch's successes are of a different
sort, and occur whenever *Ko* erupts most naturally into imaginative excesses.
My favorite episode occurs in the first canto after Joseph Dah has locked his
daughter and her lover in a coffin and thrown them into the sea:

> Meanwhile in Kansas there was taking place
> A great upheaval. High school girls refused
> To wear their clothes to school, and every place

In Kansas male observers were amused
To see the naked girls, who, lacking grace,
Were young, with bodies time had not abused,
And therefore made the wheatfields fresher areas
And streets and barns as well. No matter where he is

A man is cheered to see a naked girl—
Milking a cow or standing in a streetcar,
Opening a filing cabinet, brushing a curl
Back from her eyes while driving in a neat car
Through Wichita in summer—like the pearl
Inside the oyster, she makes it a complete car.
And there were many sermons on the subject,
And autoists, come in to have the hub checked

On their old car, would stand and pass the day
With talking of the various breasts and waists
They'd seen throughout the week, and in what way
They thought the thing, according to their tastes,
Was right or wrong, that these young girls should stray
Through Kansas without even stocking pastes
Upon their legs . . .

As can be readily seen, Koch attains no "answerable style" here: he is often trapped into Ogden Nashisms or worse; half the time he triumphs over his demanding stanza form in expounding the story as he has obviously wanted to, the other part of the time using the form only to abuse it and to let it snarl back and take bites out of his story. He commits himself to a name for a character solely because of the exigencies of rhyme (a coach named De Bruins only enters the scene to rhyme with "ruins," but remains on throughout the poem, growing no more real at each mention of him). The stanzas are seldom end-stopped. One of the characters, we learn, had great skill "In juggling figures and in making millions. / At seventeen he joined the firm of Trillians, Trillians, Trillians, Trillians, Trillians, Trillians, / Trillians, Tull and Trillians, Limited:" But all this is calculated irresponsibility. The whole poem is quite like Terry Southern's indescribable novel, *Flash and Filigree,* in making a point out of keeping something up longer than could be believed possible. In going nowhere it stops at some outlandish and hilarious spots. But for a poem whose only conceivable subject is the accomplishment of its own completion, this is a real success. And its final success can be found in the remainder of Koch's poetry, wherein the parable of *Ko*'s quest for completion is played out in a variety of ways.

As I mentioned earlier, I miss some favorite poems here ("The Young Park," "The Scales," "The Interpretation of Dreams"—all from *The Pleasures of Peace*). But this volume includes almost all of the poems in *Thank You*, and all of them in the splendid recent volume, *The Art of Love*, whose title poem forms an Ovidian, didactic tetrad with three others ("Some General Instructions," "The Art of Poetry," "On Beauty"). Their late manner is more that of a teacher than of an eternal ephebe—one may compare the *Duck Soup*-like mise-en-scène of the poet's early "Fresh Air" with his more recent *ars poetica*, just as he himself invites you to look back at the early "The Circus" through (or is it past? over? under? around?) the later poem, which purports to try to remember the occasions on which the first was composed. In these poems, the wild turns of the earlier ones are there in smaller scale, and the parody of the didactic mode enables a literal one to work under the disguise of its own caricature. The shift in successive strophes toward the end of "The Art of Love" from the stand-up comic through the mellowed air of practical wisdom on the realm of the powers for which all poetry longs may be seen in

> Zombie-itis is love of the living dead. It is comparatively rare.
> If a woman likes it, you can probably find other things she likes
>   that you will like even more.
>
> Ten things an older man must never say to a younger woman:
> 1) I'm dying! 2) I can't hear what you're saying! 3) How many
>   fingers are you holding up?
> 4) Listen to my heart. 5) Take my pulse. 6) What's your name?
> 7) Is it cold in here? 8) Is it hot in here? 9) Are you in here?
> 10) What wings are those beating at the window?
> Not that a man should stress his youth in a dishonest way
> But that he should not unduly emphasize his age.
>
> The inability to love is almost incurable. A long sea voyage
> Is recommended, in the company of an irresistible girl.
>
> To turn a woman into a duck, etc., hypnotize her and dress her
>   in costume.
> To make love standing in water, see "Elephant Congress" in the
>   *Kama Sutra* (chap. iv).
> During a shortage of girls, visit numerous places; give public
>   lectures; carry this volume.

—where "a duck, etc.," is absolutely masterful. These poems, and "Days and Nights" and the very moving "With Janice" are marked by an imaginative maturity always wanting to brood on its own childhood, and never failing to startle us in old-new-old ways.

HAROLD BLOOM

"When You Consider the Radiance"

Nature centres into balls,
And her proud ephemerals,
Fast to surface and outside,
Scan the profile of the sphere;
Knew they what that signified,
A new genesis were here.
EMERSON, Circles

In 1955, A. R. Ammons, in his thirtieth year, published his first book of poems, *Ommateum, with Doxology*. *Ommateum* consists of thirty Whitmanian chants, strongly influenced by the metric of Ezra Pound (though by nothing else in Pound). *Doxology* is an intricate religious hymn, in three parts, more ironic in tone than in direction. In the lengthening perspective of American poetry, the year 1955 will be remembered as the end of Wallace Stevens's career, and the beginning of Ammons's, himself not Stevens's heir but like Stevens a descendant of the great originals of American Romantic tradition, Emerson and Whitman. Beyond its experimentation with Poundian cadences, *Ommateum* shows no trace of the verse fashions of the fifties; I cannot detect in it the voice of William Carlos Williams, which indeed I do not hear anywhere in Ammons's work, despite the judgments of several reviewers. The line of descent from Emerson and Whitman to the early poetry of Ammons is direct, and even the Poundian elements in *Ommateum* derive from that part of Pound that is itself Whitmanian.

Ommateum's subject is poetic incarnation, in the mode of Whitman's *Sea-Drift* pieces, Emerson's "Seashore," and Pound's "Canto II." The Whit-

From *The Ringers in the Tower*. © 1971 by the University of Chicago. The University of Chicago Press, 1971. Originally entitled "A. R. Ammons: 'When You Consider the Radiance.'"

man of "As I Ebb'd with the Ocean of Life" is closest, suggesting that poetic disincarnation is Ammons's true subject, his vitalizing fear. In the "Fore-word" to *Ommateum* he begins his list of themes with "the fear of the loss of identity." The first poem of the volume, the chosen beginning of this poet's outrageously and wonderfully prolific canon, is an assumption of another's identity. This other, "Ezra," is neither Pound nor the biblical scribe of the Return, but a suddenly remembered hunchback playmate from child-hood, brought back to the poet's consciousness by a report of his death in war. The whole of Ammons is in this first poem, but half a lifetime's imag-inings will be necessary to transfigure this shore-burst into the radiance already implicit here:

> So I said I am Ezra
> and the wind whipped my throat
> gaming for the sounds of my voice
>   I listened to the wind
> go over my head and up into the night
> Turning to the sea I said
>   I am Ezra
> but there were no echoes from the waves
> The words were swallowed up
>   in the voice of the surf
> or leaping over swells
> lost themselves oceanward
>   Over the bleached and broken fields
> I moved my feet and turning from the wind
>   that ripped sheets of sand
>   from the beach and threw them
>   like seamists across the dunes
> swayed as if the wind were taking me away
> and said
>   I am Ezra
> As a word too much repeated
> falls out of being
> so I Ezra went out into the night
> like a drift of sand
> and splashed among the windy oats
> that clutch the dunes
> of unremembered seas.

As in the "Ode to the West Wind" and "As I Ebb'd with the Ocean of

Life" so here the poet's consciousness is assaulted by the elements he seeks to address, reproved by what he hopes to meet in a relationship that will make him or keep him a poet. The motto of Ammons's first poem might be Whitman's:

> Nature here in sight of the sea taking advantage
> of me to dart upon me and sting me,
> Because I have dared to open my mouth to
> sing at all.

Later in *Ommateum*, Ammons echoes "As I Ebb'd" more directly, recalling its terrifying contraction of the self:

> Me and mine, loose windrows, little corpses,
> Froth, snowy white, and bubbles,
> (See, from my dead lips the ooze exuding at last,
> See, the prismatic colors glistening and rolling,)
> Tufts of straw, sands, fragments.

This becomes, in his ninth chant, Ammons's emblem of the last stage of "peeling off my being":

> but went on deeper
> till darkness snuffed the shafts of light
> against the well's side
> night kissing
> the last bubbles from my lips.

The Emersonian ambition to be possessed fully by the Transcendental Self is Ammons's early theme as it was Whitman's, and is still pervasive in Ammons's latest lyrics, but turned now in a direction avoided by his precursors:

> When you consider the radiance, that it does not withhold
> itself but pours its abundance without selection into every
> nook and cranny not overhung or hidden; when you consider
>
> that birds' bones make no awful noise against the light but
> lie low in the light as in a high testimony; when you consider
> the radiance, that it will look into the guiltiest
>
> swervings of the weaving heart and bear itself upon them,
> not flinching into disguise or darkening; when you consider
> the abundance of such resource as illuminates the glow-blue

bodies and gold-skeined wings of flies swarming the dumped
guts of a natural slaughter or the coil of shit and in no
way winces from its storms of generosity; when you consider

that air or vacuum, snow or shale, squid or wolf, rose or lichen,
each is accepted into as much light as it will take, then
the heart moves roomier, the man stands and looks about, the

leaf does not increase itself above the grass, and the dark
work of the deepest cells is of a tune with May bushes
and fear lit by the breadth of such calmly turns to praise.

This extraordinary poem, "The City Limits," marks one of the limits
of Ammons's art, and almost releases him from the burden of his main
tradition. "The guiltiest swervings of the weaving heart," for a poet as poet,
are those that swerve him away from his poetic fathers into an angle of fall
that is also his angle of vision. For an Emersonian poet, an American Romantic, the angle of vision becomes the whole of life, and measures him as
man. Sherman Paul, acutely measuring Emerson's own angle, provides the
necessary gloss for this Emersonian poem, "The City Limits":

> The eye brought him two perceptions of nature—nature en-
> sphered and nature atomized—which corresponded to the distant
> and proximate visual powers of the eye. These powers, in turn,
> he could have called the reasoning and understanding modes of
> the eye. And to each he could have assigned its appropriate field
> of performance: the country and the city.

We can surmise that the sorrow of all Emersonian poets, from Whitman
to Ammons and beyond, comes from the great central declaration: "I become
a transparent eyeball; I am nothing; I see all; the currents of the Universal
Being circulate through me; I am part or particle of God." But if "Thought
is nothing but the circulations made luminous," then what happens when
the circulations are darkening? The currents of the Universal Being do not
cease to circulate, ever, and the "mathematic ebb and flow" of Emerson's
"Seashore" is no consolation to temperaments less rocky than Emerson's
own (one thinks not only of Whitman, but of middle Stevens, and late
Roethke). To a grim consciousness like Frost's in "Directive," the wisdom
of the Emerson of The Conduct of Life is acceptable, admirable, even inevitable, and this late Emersonian strain may never be so worked out in our
poetry as to vanish. But Ammons has none of it, and the toughness of his

own consolations and celebrations comes out of another tradition, one that I do not understand, for everything that is Southern in American culture is necessarily a darkness to me. Ammons is a poet of the Carolina as well as the Jersey shore, and his relation to Whitman is severely modified by rival spirits of place. The Ezra-poet is as obsessed with sandstorms as any Near Easterner; for him the wind makes sheets of sand into sea mists. In "The City Limits" the radiance, despite its generosity, cannot reach what is over-hung or hidden, and what is wholly hidden cannot be accepted into the light it will not take. There is for Ammons a recalcitrance or unwilling dross in everything given, and this "loneliness" (to use one of his words for it) marks his verse from *Ommateum* on as more than a little distinct from its great precursors.

I am writing of Ammons as though he had rounded his first circle in the eye of his readers, and there is no other way to write about him, even if my essay actually introduces him to some of its readers. The fundamental postulates for reading Ammons have been set down well before me, by Richard Howard and Marius Bewley in particular, but every critic of a still emergent poet has his own obsessions to work through, and makes his own confession of the radiance. Ammons's poetry does for me what Stevens's did earlier, and the High Romantics before that: it helps me to live my life. If Ammons is, as I think, the central poet of my generation, because he alone has made a heterocosm, a second nature in his poetry, I deprecate no other poet by this naming. It is, surprisingly, a rich generation, with ten or a dozen poets who seem at least capable of making a major canon, granting fortune and persistence. Ammons, much more than the others, has made such a canon already. A solitary artist, nurtured by the strength available for him only in extreme isolation, carrying on the Emersonian tradition with a quiet-ness directly contrary to nearly all its other current avatars, he has emerged in his most recent poems as an extraordinary master, comparable to the Stevens of *Ideas of Order* and *The Man With the Blue Guitar*. To track him persistently, from his origins in *Ommateum* through his maturing in *Corsons Inlet* and its companion volumes on to his new phase in *Uplands* and *Brief-ings* is to be found by not only a complete possibility of imaginative expe-rience, but by a renewed sense of the whole line of Emerson, the vitalizing and much maligned tradition that has accounted for most that matters in American poetry.

Emerson, like Stevens and Ammons after him, had a fondness for talking mountains. One thinks of Wordsworth's old men, perhaps of the Virgilian Mount Atlas, of Blake's Los at the opening of Night V, *The Four Zoas*, of

Shelley's Mont Blanc, which obstinately refuses however to take on human form, and affronts the humane revolutionary with its hard, its menacing otherness. Emerson's Monadnoc is genial and gnomic:

> "Monadnoc is a mountain strong,
> Tall and good my kind among;
> But well I know, no mountain can,
> Zion or Meru, measure with man.
> For it is on zodiacs writ,
> Adamant is soft to wit:
> And when the greater comes again
> With my secret in his brain,
> I shall pass, as glides my shadow
> Daily over hill and meadow.
>
> . . . .
>
> Anchored fast for many an age,
> I await the bard and sage,
> Who, in large thoughts, like fair pearl-seed,
> Shall string Monadnoc like a bead."

Emerson is not providing the golden string to be wound into a ball, but one of a series of golden entities to be beaded on a string. Monadnoc awaits the Central Man, the redemptive poet of *Bacchus*. Thoreau, in his fine poem on the mountains, characteristically avoids Emerson's humanizing of an otherness, and more forcefully mountainizes himself:

> But special I remember thee,
> Wachusett, who like me
> Standest alone without society.
> Thy far blue eye,
> A remnant of the sky,
> Seen through the clearing or the gorge,
> Or from the windows of the forge,
> Doth leaven all it passes by.
>
> . . . .
>
> Upholding heaven, holding down earth,
> Thy pastime from thy birth;
> Not steadied by the one, nor leaning on the other,
> May I approve myself thy worthy brother!

Wachusett is not to be strung like a bead, however strong the bard and sage. Thoreau is a more Wordsworthian poet than Emerson, and so meets

a nature ruggedly recalcitrant to visionary transformations. Ammons, who
has a relation to both, meets Emerson's kind of mountains, meets a nature
that awaits its bard, even if sometimes in ambush. In *Ommateum*, there is
not much transformation, and some ambuscade, and so the neglect encountered by the volume can be understood. Yet these chants, setting aside ad-
vantages in retrospect, are remarkable poems, alive at every point in
movement and in vision. They live in their oddly negative exuberance, as the
new poet goes out into his bleak lands as though he marched only into
another man's phantasmagoria. One chant, beginning "In the wind my rescue is," to be found but mutilated in the *Selected Poems* (1968), states the
poet's task as a gathering of the stones of earth into one place. The wind,
by sowing a phantasmagoria in the poet's eyes, draws him "out beyond the
land's end," thus saving him "from all those ungathered stones." The shore,
Whitman's emblem for the state in which poets are made and unmade,
becomes the theater for the first phase of Ammons's poetic maturity, the
lyrics written in the decade after *Ommateum*. These are gathered in three
volumes: *Expressions of Sea Level* (1964), *Corsons Inlet* (1965), and *Northfield Poems* (1966), which need to be read as a unit, since the inclusion of
a poem in one or another volume seems to be a matter of whim. A reader
of Ammons is likeliest to be able to read this phase of him in the *Selected
Poems*, whose arrangement in chronological order of composition shows how
chronologically scrambled the three volumes are.

Ammons's second start as a poet, after the transcendental waste places
of *Ommateum*, is in this "Hymn":

I know if I find you I will have to leave the earth
and go on out
    over the sea marshes and the brant in bays
and over the hills of tall hickory
and over the crater lakes and canyons
and on up through the spheres of diminishing air
past the blackset noctilucent clouds
    where one wants to stop and look
way past all the light diffusions and bombardments
up farther than the loss of sight
    into the unseasonal undifferentiated empty stark

And I know if I find you I will have to stay with the earth
inspecting with thin tools and ground eyes
trusting the microvilli sporangia and simplest
    coelenterates

and praying for a nerve cell
with all the soul of my chemical reactions
and going right on down where the eye sees only traces

You are everywhere partial and entire
You are on the inside of everything and on the outside

I walk down the path down the hill where the sweetgum
has begun to ooze spring sap at the cut
and I see how the bark cracks and winds like no other bark
chasmal to my ant-soul running up and down
and if I find you I must go out deep into your
    far resolutions
and if I find you I must stay here with the separate leaves.

The chants of *Ommateum* were composed mostly in a single year, from
the spring of 1951 to the spring of 1952. In 1956, Ammons fully claims his
Transcendental heritage in his "Hymn," a work of poetic annunciation in
which the "you" is Emerson's "Nature," all that is separate from "the Soul."
The "Hymn's" difficult strength depends on a reader's recognition that the
found "you" is: "the NOT ME, that is, both nature and art, all other men
and my own body." Juxtapose a crucial passage of Emerson, and the *clinamen* that governs the course of Ammons's maturity is determined:

> The world proceeds from the same spirit as the body of man. It
> is a remoter and inferior incarnation of God, a projection of God
> in the unconscious. But it differs from the body in one important
> respect. It is not, like that, now subjected to the human will. Its
> serene order is inviolable by us. It is, therefore, to us, the present
> expositor of the divine mind. It is a fixed point whereby we may
> measure our departure.

Emerson's fixed point oscillates dialectically in Ammons's "Hymn."
Where Emerson's mode hovers always around metonymy, parts of a world
taken as the whole, Ammons's sense of the universe takes it for a symptom.
No American poet, not Whitman or Stevens, shows us so fully something
otherwise unknown in the structures of the national consciousness as Ammons does. It cannot be said so far that Ammons has developed as fluent
and individual a version of the language of the self as they did, but he has
time and persistence enough before he borrows his last authority from death.
His first authority is the height touched in this "Hymn," where everything
depends upon a precision of consequences "if I find you." "The unassimilable

fact leads us on," a later poem begins, the leading on being Ammons's notion of quest. If all that is separate from him, the "you," is found, the finding will be assimilated at the final cost of going on out "into the unseasonal undifferentiated empty stark," a resolution so far as to annihilate selfhood. One part of the self will be yielded to an apprehension beyond sight, while the other will stay here with the earth, to be yielded to sight's reductiveness, separated with each leaf.

This is the enterprise of a consciousness extreme enough to begin another central poem, "Gravelly Run," with a quietly terrifying sense of what will suffice:

> I don't know somehow it seems sufficient
> to see and hear whatever coming and going is,
> losing the self to the victory
>   of stones and trees,
> of bending sandpit lakes, crescent
> round groves of dwarf pine:
>
> for it is not so much to know the self
> as to know it as it is known
>   by galaxy and cedar cone.

But as it is known, it is only a "surrendered self among / unwelcoming forms." The true analogue to this surrender is in the curious implicit threat of Emerson's Orphic poet:

> We distrust and deny inwardly our sympathy with nature. We own and disown our relation to it, by turns. We are like Nebuchadnezzer, dethroned, bereft of reason, and eating grass like an ox. But who can set limits to the remedial force of spirit?

The remedial force of spirit, in this sense, is closest to being that terriblest force in the world, of which Stevens's Back-ache complains. Ammons, who knows he cannot set limits to such force, warns himself perpetually "to turn back," before he comes to a unity apparently equal to his whole desire. For his desire is only a metonymy, and unity (if found) compels another self-defeating question:

> You cannot come to unity and remain material:
> in that perception is no perceiver:
>   when you arrive
> you have gone too far:
>   at the Source you are in the mouth of Death:

you cannot
   turn around in
the Absolute: there are no entrances or exits
   no precipitations of forms
to use like tongs against the formless:
   no freedom to choose:

to be

   you have to stop not-being and break
off from *is* to *flowing* and
   this is the sin you weep and praise:
origin is your original sin:
   the return you long for will ease your guilt
and you will have your longing:

   the wind that is my guide said this: it
should know having
   given up everything to eternal being but
direction:

how I said can I be glad and sad: but a man goes
   from one foot to the other:
wisdom wisdom:
   to be glad and sad at once is also unity
and death:
   wisdom wisdom: a peachblossom blooms on a particular
tree on a particular day:
   unity cannot do anything in particular:

are these the thoughts you want me to think I said but
   the wind was gone and there was no more knowledge then.

The wind's origin is its original sin also; were it to give up even direction, it would cease to be "Guide," as this poem is entitled. If the wind is Ammons's Virgil, an Interior Paramour or Whitmanian Fancy remains his Beatrice, guiding him whenever wind ceases to lead. The poetic strength of "Guide" is in its dialectical renunciation of even this demonic paramour. For the wind speaks against what is deepest and most self-destructive in Ammons. "Break off from *is* to *flowing*" is a classic phrasing of the terrible dream that incessantly afflicts most of our poetic imaginations in America. "Unity cannot do anything in particular"; least of all can it write a poem.

   The wind, Ammons's way to knowledge, is certainly the most active wind in American poetry. In *Ommateum,* the wind is a desperate whip, doubting its own efficacy in a dry land. It moves "like wisdom," but its poet is not so sure of the likeness. In the mature volumes, it is more a blade than a whip, and its desperation has rendered it apologetic:

> Having split up the chaparral
> blasting my sight
> the wind said
>   You know I'm
>   the result of
> forces beyond my control
> I don't hold it against you
> I said
> It's all right I understand.

For the wind "dies and never dies," but the poet goes on:

> consigned to
> form that will not
> let me loose
> except to death
> till some
> syllable's rain
> anoints my tongue
> and makes it sing
> to strangers.

To be released from form into unity one dies or writes a poem; this appalling motive for metaphor is as desperate as any wind. Wind, which is "not air or motion / but the motion of air," speaks to a consciousness that is not spirit or making, but the spirit of making, the Ezra-incarnation in this poet:

> I coughed
>   and the wind said
> Ezra will live
> to see your last
>   sun come up again
>
> I turned (as I will) to weeds and
> the wind went off
>   carving
> monuments through a field of stone

> monuments whose shape
> wind cannot arrest but
> taking hold on
> changes
>
> While Ezra
>   listens from terraces of mind
> wind cannot reach or
> weedroots of my low-feeding shiver.

When the poet falls (as he must) from this Ezra-eminence, the terraces
of mind dissolve:

> The mind whirls, short of the unifying
> reach, short of the heat
>   to carry that forging:
>   after the visions of these losses, the spent
> seer, delivered to wastage, risen
>   into ribs, consigns knowledge to
>   approximation, order to the vehicle
> of change.

He is never so spent a seer as he says, even if the price of his ascensions
keeps rising. If from moment to moment the mode of motion is loss, there
is always the privileged "Moment" itself:

> He turned and
> stood
>
> In the moment's
> height,
>
> exhiliration
> sucking him up,
>
> shuddering and
> lifting
>
> him
> jaw and bone
>
> and he said
> what
>
> destruction am I
> blessed by?

The burden of Ammons's poetry is to answer, to name that enlargement of life that is also a destruction. When the naming came most complete, in the late summer of 1962, it gave Ammons his two most ambitious single poems, "Corsons Inlet" and "Saliences." Though both poems depend upon the context of Ammons's canon, they show the field of his enterprise more fully and freely than could have been expected of any single work. "Corsons Inlet" is likely to be Ammons's most famous poem, his "Sunday Morning," a successfully universalizing expression of a personal thematic conflict and its apparent (or provisional) resolution. But "Saliences," a harder, less open, more abstract fury of averted destructions, is the better poem. "Corsons Inlet" comforts itself (and us) with the perpetually renewed hope of a fresh walk over the dunes to the sea. "Saliences" rises past hope to what in the mind is "beyond loss or gain / beyond concern for the separate reach." Both the hope and the ascension beyond hope return us to origins, and can be apprehended with keener aptitude after an excursus taking us deeper into Ammons's tradition. Ammons compels that backward vision of our poetry that only major achievement exacts, and illuminates Emerson and all his progeny as much as he needs them for illumination. Reading Ammons, I brood on all American poetry in the Romantic tradition, which means I yield to Emerson, who is to our modern poetry what Wordsworth has been to all British poetry after him; the starting-point, the defining element, the vexatious father, the shadow and the despair, liberating angel and blocking-agent, perpetual irritant and solacing glory.

John Jay Chapman, in what is still the best introductory essay on Emerson, condensed his estimate of the seer into a great and famous sentence: "If a soul be taken and crushed by democracy till it utter a cry, that cry will be Emerson." In the year 1846, when he beheld "the famous States / Harrying Mexico / With rifle and with knife!," Emerson raised the cry of himself most intensely and permanently:

> Though loath to grieve
> The evil time's sole patriot,
> I cannot leave
> My honied thought
> For the priest's cant,
> or statesman's rant.
>
> If I refuse
> My study for their politique,
> which at the best is trick,

> The angry Muse
> Puts confusion in my brain.

The astonished Muse found Emerson at her side all through 1846, the year not only of the Channing Ode, but of "Bacchus" and "Merlin," his finest and most representative poems, that between them establish a dialectic central to subsequent American poetry. In "Bacchus," the poet is not his own master, but yields to demonic possession. In "Merlin," the demonic itself is mastered, as the poet becomes first the Bard, and then Nemesis:

> Who with even matches odd,
> Who athwart space redresses
> The partial wrong,
> Fills the just period,
> And finishes the song.

The poet of "Bacchus" is genuinely possessed, and yet falls (savingly) victim to Ananke—he is still *human*. The poet of "Merlin" is himself absorbed into Ananke and ceases to be human, leaving "Bacchus" much the better poem. To venture a desolate formula about American poetry: our greater poets attain the splendor of Bacchus, and then attempt to become Merlin, and so cease to be wholly human and begin to fail as poets. Emerson and his descendants dwindle, not when they build altars to the Beautiful Necessity, but when they richly confuse themselves with that Necessity. Poetry, Emerson splendidly observed, must be as new as foam and as old as the rock; he might also have observed that it had better not itself try to be foam or rock.

A strain in Ammons, ecological and almost geological, impels him toward identification with the American version of Ananke, and is his largest flaw as a poet. Robert Bly brilliantly parodied this strain by printing a passage from *The Mushroom Hunter's Field Guide* under the title, "A. R. Ammons Discusses The Lacaria Trullisata":

> The somewhat distant,
> broad, purplish
> to violaceous gills,
> white spore
>
> Deposit, and
> habitat
> on sand distingu-
> ish it. No
> part of the fruit-

Ing body is ever
glutinous.
Edibility. The question
is academic: It is

Impossible to get
rid of
all the sand.

And so on. The Ammonsian literalness, allied to a similar destructive impulse in Wordsworth and Thoreau, attempts to summon outward continuities to shield the poet from his mind's own force. "A Poem Is a Walk" is the title of a dark, short prose piece by Ammons that tries "to establish a reasonably secure identity between a poem and a walk and to ask how a walk occurs, what it is, and what it is for," but establishes only that a walk by Ammons is a sublime kind of Pythagorean enterprise or Behmenite picnic. Emerson, who spoke as much wisdom as any American, alas spoke darkly also, and Ammons is infuriatingly Emersonian when he tells us a poem "is a motion to no-motion, to the still point of contemplation and deep realization. Its knowledges are all negative and, therefore, more positive than any knowledge." "Corsons Inlet," "Saliences," and nearly a hundred other poems by Ammons are nothing of the kind, his imagination be thanked, rather than this spooky, pure-product-of-America mysticism. Unlike Emerson, who crossed triumphantly into prose, Ammons belongs to that company of poets that *thinks* most powerfully and naturally in verse, and sometimes descends to obscure quietudes when verse subsides.

"Corsons Inlet" first verges on, and then veers magnificently away from worshipping the Beautiful Necessity, from celebrating the way things are. "Life will be imaged, but cannot be divided nor doubled," might be the poem's motto; so might: "Ask the fact for the form," both maxims being Emerson's. Ammons's long poem, *Tape for the Turn of the Year,* contains the self-admonishment: "get out of boxes, hard / forms of mind: / go deep: / penetrate / to the true spring," which is the initial impulse of "Corsons Inlet." The poet, having walked in the morning over the dunes to the sea, recollects later in the day the release granted him by the walk, from thought to sight, from conceptual forms to the flowings and blendings of the Coleridgean Secondary Imagination. Released into the composition of "Corsons Inlet," he addresses his reader directly (consciously in Whitman's mode) to state both the nature of his whole body of poetry, and his sense of its largest limitation:

I allow myself eddies of meaning:
yield to a direction of significance
running
like a stream through the geography of my work:
   you can find
in my sayings

swerves of action
like the inlet's cutting edge:

there are dunes of motion,
organizations of grass, white sandy paths of remembrance
in the overall wandering of mirroring mind:

but Overall is beyond me: is the sum of these events
I cannot draw, the ledger I cannot keep, the accounting
beyond the account.

Within this spaced restraint, there is immense anguish, and the anguish
is not just metaphysical. Though this anguish be an acquired wisdom, such
wisdom proffers no consolation for the loss of quest. The anguish that goes
through "Corsons Inlet," subdued but ever salient, is more akin to a quality
of mind in Thoreau than to anything in Emerson or Whitman. What Transcendentalists wanted of natural history is generally a darkness to me, and I
resort to the late Perry Miller for some light on "the Transcendental meth-
odology for coping with the multifarious concreteness of nature. That
method is to see the particular as a particular, and yet at the same time so
to perceive it as to make it, of itself, yield up the general and the universal."
But that is too broad, being a Romantic procedure in general, with neither
the American impatience nor the American obsession of particularity clearly
distinguished from Wordsworthianism. Wordsworth was wonderfully patient with preparations for vision, and was more than content to see the
particulars flow together and fade out in the great moments of vision. Emerson scanted preparations, and held on to the particulars even in ecstasy. In
Thoreau, whatever his final differences with his master, the Emersonian pre-
cipitateness and clarity of the privileged moment are sharpened. When I read
in his *Journals,* I drown in particulars and cannot find the moments of
release, but "The Natural History of Massachusetts," his first true work,
seems all release, and very close to the terrible nostalgias "Corsons Inlet"
reluctantly abandons. William Ellery Channing, memorializing Thoreau
clumsily though with love, deluges us with evidences of those walks and talks
in which Overall was never beyond Thoreau, but came confidently with each

natural observation. But Ammons, who would want to emulate Thoreau, cannot keep the account; his natural observations bring him wholly other evidences:

> in nature there are few sharp lines: there are areas of
> primrose
>   more or less dispersed;
> disorderly orders of bayberry; between the rows
> of dunes,
> irregular swamps of reeds,
> though not reeds alone, but grass, bayberry, yarrow, all . . .
> predominantly reeds.

All through the poem beats its hidden refrain: "I was released from . . . straight lines," "few sharp lines," "I have drawn no lines," "but there are no lines," "a wider range / than mental lines can keep," "the waterline, waterline inexact," "but in the large view, no / lines or changeless shapes." A wild earlier poem, called "Lines," startlingly exposes Ammons's obsession, for there nature bombards him, all but destroys him with lines, nothing but lines:

> Lines flying in, out: logarithmic
>   curves coiling
> toward an infinitely inward center: lines
>   weaving in, threads lost in clustral scrawl,
>   weaving out into loose ends,
> wandering beyond the border of gray background,
>   going out of vision,
>   not returning;
> or, returning, breaking across the boundary
>   as new lines, discontinuous,
>   come into sight:
> fiddleheads of ferns, croziers of violins,
>   convoluted spherical masses, breaking through
>   ditchbanks where briar
> stem-dull will
>   leave and bloom:
>   haunch line, sickle-like, turning down, bulging, nuzzling
> under, closing into
>   the hidden, sweet, dark meeting of lips:
>   the spiraling out

or in
   of galaxies:
      the free-running wavy line, swirling
configuration, halting into a knot
   of curve and density: the broken,
      irreparable filament: tree-winding vines, branching
falling off or back, free,
   the adventitious preparation for possibility, from
      branch to branch, ash to gum:
the breaker
   hurling into reach for shape, crashing
      out of order, the inner hollow sizzling flat:
the longnecked, uteral gourd, bass line
   continuous in curve,
      melodic line filling and thinning:
concentrations,
   whirling masses,
      thin leaders, disordered ends and risks:
explosions of clusters, expansions from the
   full radial sphere, return's longest chance:
      lines exploring, intersecting, paralleling, twisting,
noding: deranging, clustering.

This is Ammons's Mad Song, his equivalent of Stevens's "A Rabbit as King of the Ghosts," another poem of the mind's mercilessness, its refusal to defend itself against itself. "Deranging, clustering" is the fear and the horror, from which "Corsons Inlet" battles for release, mostly through embracing "a congregation / rich with entropy," a constancy of change. The poet who insists he has drawn no lines draws instead his poem out of the "dunes of motion," loving them desperately as his only (but inadequate) salvation, all that is left when his true heaven of Overall is clearly beyond him. Yet this remains merely a being "willing to go along" in the recognition not of the Beautiful but the Terrible Necessity:

   the moon was full last night: today, low tide was low:
   black shoals of mussels exposed to the risk
   of air
   and, earlier, of sun,
   waved in and out with the waterline, waterline inexact,
   caught always in the event of change:
      a young mottled gull stood free on the shoals

and ate
to vomiting: another gull, squawking possession, cracked a crab,
picked out the entrails, swallowed the soft-shelled legs, a ruddy
turnstone running in to snatch leftover bits:

risk is full: every living thing in
siege: the demand is life, to keep life: the small
white blacklegged egret, how beautiful, quietly stalks and spears
        the shallows, darts to shore
        to stab—what? I couldn't
see against the black mudflats—a frightened
fiddler crab?

This great and very American passage, kin to a darker tradition than
Ammons's own, and to certain poems of Melville and Hart Crane, is "Corsons Inlet's" center, the consequence of the spent seer's consignment of order
to the vehicle of change. I remember, each time I read it, that Ammons is a
Southerner, heir to a darker Protestantism than was the immediate heritage
of the New England visionaries or of Whitman. But our best Southern poets
from Poe and Timrod through Ransom, Tate, Warren, have not affected his
art, and a comparison to a Southern contemporary like James Dickey indicates sharply how much Ammons is the conscious heir of nineteenth-century
Northern poetry, including a surprising affinity to Dickinson in his later
phase of *Uplands* and *Briefings*. But, to a North Carolinian one hundred
years after, Transcendentalism comes hard and emerges bitterly, with the
Oversoul reduced from Overall to "the overall wandering of mirroring
mind," confronting the dunes and swamps as a last resource, the final form
of Nature or the Not-me.

From the nadir of "every living thing in / siege," "Corsons Inlet" slowly
rises to a sense of the ongoing, "not chaos: preparations for / flight." In a
difficult transitional passage, the poet associates the phrasal fields of his
metric with the "field" of action on every side of him, open to his perception
"with moving incalculable center." Looking close, he can see "order tight
with shape"; standing back, he confronts a formlessness that suddenly, in
an extraordinary epiphany, is revealed as his consolation:

        orders as summaries, as outcomes of actions override
        or in some way result, not predictably (seeing me gain
        the top of a dune,
        the swallows
        could take flight—some other fields of bayberry

> could enter fall
> berryless) and there is serenity:
>
> no arranged terror: no forcing of image, plan,
> or thought:
> no propaganda, no humbling of reality to precept:
>
> terror pervades but is not arranged, all possibilities
> of escape open: no route shut, except in
> the sudden loss of all routes.

"No arranged terror" is the crucial insight, and if we wish to inquire who would arrange terror except a masochist, the wish will not sustain itself. The poem's final passage, this poet's defense, abandons the really necessary "pulsations of order," the reliable particulars, for what cannot suffice, the continued bafflement of perceiving nothing completely. For Ammons, the seer of *Ommateum* and the still-confident quester of the "Hymn," this bafflement is defeat, and enjoying the freedom that results from scope eluding his grasp is hardly an enjoying in any ordinary sense. The poem ends bravely, but not wholly persuasively:

> I see narrow orders, limited tightness, but will
> not run to the easy victory:
> still around the looser, wider forces work:
> I will try
> to fasten into order enlarging grasps of disorder, widening
> scope, but enjoying the freedom that
> Scope eludes my grasp, that there is no finality of vision,
> that I have perceived nothing completely,
> that tomorrow a new walk is a new walk.

Origin is still his original sin; what his deepest nature longs for, to come to unity and yet remain material, is no part of "Corsons Inlet," which grants him freedom to choose, but no access to that unity that alone satisfies choice. The major poem written immediately after "Corsons Inlet" emerges from stoic acceptance of bafflement into an imaginative reassurance that prompts Ammons's major phase, the lyrics of *Uplands, Briefings,* and the work-in-progress:

> Consistencies rise
> and ride
> the mind down
> hard routes

walled
with no outlet and so
to open a variable geography,
   proliferate
possibility, here
is this dune fest
   releasing,
mind feeding out,
gathering clusters,
fields of order in disorder,
where choice
can make beginnings,
   turns,
   reversals,
where straight line
and air-hard thought
can meet
unarranged disorder,
   dissolve
before the one event that
creates present time
in the multi-variable
   scope.

"Saliences" thus returns to "Corsons Inlet's" field of action, driven by that poet's need not to abide in a necessity, however beautiful. Saliences etymologically are out-leapings, "mind feeding out," not taking in perceptions but turning its violent energies out into the field of action. If "Corsons Inlet" is Ammons's version of "The Idea of Order at Key West" (not that he had Stevens's poem in mind, but that the attentive reader learns to compare the two), then "Saliences" is his *The Man With the Blue Guitar,* a discovery of how to begin again after a large and noble acknowledgment of dark limitations. "Saliences" is a difficult, abstract poem, but it punches itself along with an overwhelming vigor, showing its exuberance by ramming through every blocking particular, until it can insist that "where not a single single thing endures, / the overall reassures." Overall remains beyond Ammons, but is replaced by "a round / quiet turning / beyond loss or gain, / beyond concern for the separate reach." "Saliences" emphasizes the transformation of Ammons's obsessive theme, from the longing for unity to the assertion of the mind's power over the particulars of being, the universe of death. The Emersonianism of Ammons is constant; as did Whitman, so his final judgment of his relation to that great precursor will be: "loyal at last." But "Saliences" marks the *clinamen*; the swerve away from Emerson is now clarified, and Ammons will write no poem more crucial to his own unfolding. Before "Saliences," the common reader must struggle with the temptation of naming Ammons a nature poet; after this, the struggle would be otiose. The quest that was surrendered in "Guide," and whose loss was accepted in "Corsons Inlet," is internalized in "Saliences" and afterward.

"Saliences" approximates (indeliberately) the subtle procedure of a sub-tradition within Romantic poetry that goes from Shelley's "Mont Blanc" to Stevens's *The Auroras of Autumn*. The poet begins in an austere, even a terrifying scene of natural confrontation, but he does not describe the scene or name the terror until he has presented fully the mind's initial defense against scene and terror, its implicit assertion of its own force. So "Saliences" begins with a vision of the mind in action "in the multi-variable / scope." A second movement starts with the wind's entrance ("a variable of wind / among the dunes, / making variables / of position and direction and sound") and climaxes at the poem's halfway point, which returns to the image of the opening ("come out of the hard / routes and ruts, / pour over the walls / of previous assessments: turn to / the open, / the unexpected, to new saliences of feature." After this come seventy magical lines of Ammons upon his heights (starting with: "The reassurance is / that through change / continu-ities sinuously work"), lines that constitute one of a convincing handful of contemporary assurances that the imagination is capable always of a reno-vative fresh start.

The dune fest, which in the poem's opening movement is termed a provocation for the mind's release from "consistencies" (in the sense of Blake's Devourer), is seen in the second movement as "Corsons Inlet's" baffled field of action:

> wind, a variable, soft wind, hard
> steady wind, wind
> shaped and kept in the
> bent of trees,
> the prevailing dipping seaward
> of reeds,
> the kept and erased sandcrab trails:
> wind, the variable to the gull's flight,
> how and where he drops the clam
> and the way he heads in, running to loft:

wind, from the sea, high surf
and cool weather;
from the land, a lessened breakage
and from the land's heat:
wind alone as a variable,
as a factor in millions of events,
leaves no two moments
on the dunes the same:
  keep
free to these events,
bend to these
changing weathers.

This wind has gone beyond the wind of "Guide," for it has given up everything to eternal being, even direction, even velocity, and contents itself to be shaped and kept by each particular it encounters. Knowing he cannot be one with or even like this wind, knowing too he must be more than a transparency, an Eye among the blind particulars, the poet moves to a kind of upper level of Purgatory, where the wind ceases to be his guide, and he sees as he has not seen before:

when I went back to the dunes today,
  saliences,
congruent to memory,
spread firmingly across my sight:
the narrow white path
rose and dropped over
grassy rises toward the sea:
sheets of reeds,
tasseling now near fall,
filled the hollows
with shapes of ponds or lakes:
bayberry, darker, made wandering
chains of clumps, sometimes pouring
into heads, like stopped water:
  much seemed
constant, to be looked
forward to, expected.

It is the saliences, the outleapings, that "spread *firmingly* across my sight," and give him assurances, "summations of permanence." The whole passage, down through the poem's close, has a firm beauty unlike anything previous in Ammons. Holding himself as he must, firmly apart from still-longed-for unity, he finds himself now in an astonishing equilibrium with the particulars, containing them in his own mind by reimagining them there:

> in
> the hollow,
> where a runlet
> makes in
> at full tide and fills a bowl,
> extravagance of pink periwinkle
> along the grassy edge,
> and a blue, bunchy weed, deep blue,
> deep into the mind the dark blue
> constant.

The change here, as subtle as it is precarious, only just bears description, though the poet of *Uplands* and *Briefings* relies upon it as though it were palpable, something he could touch every way. The weed and the mind's imaginative constancy are in the relation given by the little poem, "Reflective," written just afterward:

> I found a
> weed
> that had a
>
> mirror in it
> and that
> mirror
>
> looked in at
> a mirror
> in
>
> me that
> had a
> weed in it.

In itself this is slight; in the context provided by "Saliences" it is exact and finely wrought. The whole meaning of it is in "I *found*," for "Saliences" records a finding, and a being found. Because of this mutual finding, the magnificent close of the poem is possible, is even necesary:

where not a single single thing endures,
the overall reassures,
deaths and flights,
shifts and sudden assaults claiming
limited orders,
the separate particles:
earth brings to grief
much in an hour that sang, leaped, swirled,
yet keeps a round
    quiet turning,
beyond loss or gain,
beyond concern for the separate reach.

I think, when I read this passage, of the final lines of Wordsworth's great Ode, of the end of Browning's "Love Among the Ruins," of the deep peace Whitman gives as he concludes "Crossing Brooklyn Ferry," and of Stevens closing "As You Leave the Room":

An appreciation of a reality

And thus an elevation, as if I left
With something I could touch, touch every way.

And yet nothing has been changed except what is
Unreal, as if nothing had been changed at all.

This is not to play at touchstones, in the manner of Arnold or of Black-mur, but only to record my experience as a reader, which is that "Saliences" suggests and is worthy of such company. Firm and radiant as the poem is, its importance for Ammons (if I surmise rightly) transcends its intrinsic worth, for it made possible his finest poems. I pass to them with some regret for the splendors in *Selected Poems* I have not discussed: "Silver," "Terrain," "Bridge," "Jungle Knot," "Nelly Myers," "Expressions of Sea Level," and for the long poem, *Tape for the Turn of the Year*, a heroic failure that is Ammons's most original and surprising invention.

Uplands, published in the autumn of 1970, begins with a difficult, almost ineluctable lyric, "Snow Log," which searches for intentions where they evidently cannot be found, in the particulars of fallen tree, snow, shrubs, the special light of winter landscape; "I take it on myself," the poet ends by saying, and repeats the opening triad:

    especially the fallen tree
    the snow picks
    out in the woods to show.

Stevens, in the final finding of the ear, returned to the snow he had
forgotten, to behold again "nothing that is not there and the nothing that
is." "Snow Log" seems to find something that is not there, but the reader is
left uncertain whether there is a consciousness in the scene that belongs
neither to him nor to the poet. With the next poem, "Upland," which gives
the volume both its tonality and title, the uncertainty vanishes:

    Certain presuppositions are altered
    by height: the inversion to
    sky-well a peak
    in a desert makes: the welling

    from clouds down the boulder fountains:
    it is always a
    surprise out west there—
    the blue ranges loose and aglide

    with heat and then come close
    on slopes leaning up into green:
    a number of other phenomena might
    be summoned—

    take the Alleghenies for example,
    some quality in the air
    of summit stones lying free and loose
    out among the shrub trees: every

    exigency seems prepared for that might
    roll, bound, or give flight
    to stone: that is, the stones are
    prepared: they are round and ready.

A poem like this is henceforth Ammons's characteristic work: shorter
and more totally self-enclosed than earlier ventures, and less reliant on larger
contexts. He has become an absolute master of his art, and a maker of
individual tones as only the greater poets can accomplish:

        the stones are
    prepared: they are round and ready.

"Upland" does not attempt to define "some quality in the air" that alters presuppositions and makes its stones prepared for anything at any time. The poem disturbs because it compels us to accept the conflicting notions (for us) of surprise and preparation as being no conflict for the intentionality held by those summit stones. It satisfies as much as disturbs because something in us is not wholly apart from the summit stone's state-of-being; a natural apocalypticism is in the air, and pervades our rare ascensions to the mind's heights. Ammons, who is increasingly wary of finalities, praises hesitation in the next lyric, "Periphery":

> One day I complained about the periphery
> that it was thickets hard to get around in
>   or get around for
> an older man: it's like keeping charts
>
> of symptoms, every reality a symptom
> where the ailment's not nailed down:
>   much knowledge, precise enough,
> but so multiple it says this man is alive
>
> or isn't: it's like all of a body answering
> all of pharmacopoeia, a too
>   adequate relationship:
> so I complained and said maybe I'd brush
>
> deeper and see what was pushing all this
> periphery, so difficult to make any sense
>   out of, out:
> with me, decision brings its own
>
> hesitation: a symptom, no doubt, but open
> and meaningless enough without paradigm:
>   but hesitation
> can be all right, too: I came on a spruce
>
> thicket full of elk, gushy snow-weed,
> nine species of lichen, four pure white
>   rocks and
> several swatches of verbena near bloom.

All the poems in *Uplands* have this new ease, but the conscious mastery of instrument may obscure for us the prevalence of the old concerns, lightened by the poet's revelation that a search for saliences is a more possible quest than the more primordial romancing after unity. The concerns locate

themselves still in Emerson's mental universe; Ammons's "Periphery," like
Dickinson's "Circumference," goes back to the astonishing *Circles* of 1840
with its insistence that "the only sin is limitation" and its repeated image of
concentricity. The appropriate gloss for Ammons's "Periphery" (and for
much else in *Uplands*) is: "The natural world may be conceived of as a
system of concentric circles, and we now and then detect in nature slight
dislocations which apprise us that this surface on which we now stand is
not fixed, but sliding." Ammons calls so being apprised "hesitation," and
his slight dislocation is the radiant burst of elk, snow-weed, lichen, white
rocks, and verbena that ends "Periphery" so beautifully.

In *Uplands* and the extraordinary conceptions of the recent volume,
Briefings, the motions of water have replaced the earlier guiding movements
of wind. "If Anything Will Level With You Water Will," the title of one fine
poem, is the credo of many. "I / mean the telling is unmediated," Ammons
says of a rocky stream, and his ambition here, enormous as always, is an
unmediated telling, a purely visionary poetry. It is not a poetry that dis-
courses of itself or of the outward particulars, or of the processes of the
poet's mind so much as it deals in a purer representation than even Wordsworth could have wanted. The bodily eye is not a despotic sense for Ammons
(as it became for Thoreau) who has not passed through a crisis in perception,
but rather has trained himself to sense those out-leapings later available to
the seer (like Emerson) who had wisdom enough to turn back from Unity.
For pure representation in the later Ammons, I give "Laser" (from *Uplands*)
as a supreme example:

> An image comes
> and the mind's light, confused
> as that on surf
> or ocean shelves,
> gathers up,
> parallelizes, focuses
> and in a rigid beam illuminates the image:
>
> the head seeks in itself
> fragments of left-over light
> to cast a new
> direction,
> any direction,
> to strike and fix
> a random, contradicting image:

but any found image falls
back to darkness or
the lesser beams splinter and
go out:
the mind tries to
dream of diversity, of mountain
rapids shattered with sound and light,

of wind fracturing brush or
bursting out of order against a mountain
range: but the focused beam
folds all energy in:
the image glares filling all space:
the head falls and
hangs and cannot wake itself.

I risk sounding mystical by insisting that "an image" here is neither the poetic trope nor a natural particular, but what Ammons inveterately calls a "salience"; "the image glares filling all space." Not that in this perception there is no perceiver; rather the perceiving is detached, disinterested, attentive without anxiety or nostalgia. Perhaps this is only Ammons's equivalent of the difficult "half create" of "Tintern Abbey" or Emerson's "I am nothing; I see all," but it seems to ensue from the darker strain in him, that goes back to the twenty-sixth poem in *Ommateum*, "In the wind my rescue is," which stated a hopeless poetic quest: "I set it my task / to gather the stones of earth / into one place." In *Uplands*, a profound poem, "Apologia pro Vita Sua," makes a definitive revision of the earlier ambition:

I started picking up the stones
throwing them into one place
and by sunrise I was going far away
for the large ones
always turning to see never lost
the cairn's height
lengthening my radial reach:

the sun watched with deep concentration
and the heap through the hours grew
and became by nightfall
distinguishable from all the miles around
of slate and sand:

during the night the wind falling
turned earthward its lofty freedom and speed
and the sharp blistering sound muffled
toward dawn and the blanket was
drawn up over a breathless face:

even so you can see in full dawn
the ground there lifts
a foreign thing desertless in origin.

"Distinguishable" is the desperate and revelatory word. To ask, after death, the one thing, to have left behind "a foreign thing desertless in origin," the cairn of a lifetime's poems, is to have reduced rescue into a primordial pathos. Yet the poem, by its virtue, renders more than pathos, as the lyric following, on the same theme, renders more also:

Losing information he
rose gaining
view
till at total
loss gain was
extreme:
extreme & invisible:
the eye
seeing nothing
lost its
separation:
self-song
(that is a mere motion)
fanned out
into failing swirls
slowed &
became continuum.

"Offset" is the appropriate title; this is power purchased by the loss of knowledge, and unity at the expense of being material. *Uplands,* as a volume, culminates in its last lyric, "Cascadilla Falls," placed just before the playful and brilliant long poem, *Summer Session 1968,* in which Ammons finds at last some rest from these intensities. Despite its extraordinary formal control and its continuous sense of a vision attained, *Uplands* is a majestically sad book, for Ammons does not let himself forget that his vision, while uncompromised, is a compromise necessarily, a constant knowing why and how "unity cannot do anything in particular." The poet, going down by Cascadilla Falls in the evening, picks up a stone and "thought all its motions into it," and then drops the stone from galactic wanderings to dead rest:

> the stream from other motions
> broke
> rushing over it:
> shelterless,
> I turned
>
> to the sky and stood still:
>
> I do
> not know where I am going
> that I can live my life
> by this single creek.

From this self-imposed pathos Ammons wins as yet no release. Release comes in the ninety delightful lyrics gathered together in *Briefings* (first entitled, gracefully but misleadingly, *Poems Small and Easy*), this poet's finest book. Though the themes of *Briefings* are familiarly Ammonsian, the mode is not. Laconic though transfigured speech has been transformed into "wasteful song." The first poem, "Center," places us in a freer world than Ammons would give us before:

> A bird fills up the
> streamside bush
> with wasteful song,
> capsizes waterfall,
> mill run, and
> superhighway
> to
> song's improvident
> center
> lost in the green
> bush green
> answering bush:
> wind varies:
> the noon sun casts
> mesh refractions
> on the stream's amber

> bottom
> and nothing at all gets,
> nothing gets
> caught at all.

The given is mesh that cannot catch because the particulars have been capsized, and so are unavailable for capture. The center is improvident because it stands at the midmost point of mind, not of nature. *Briefings* marks an end to the oldest conflict in Ammons; the imagination has learned to avoid apocalyptic pitch, but it has learned also its own painful autonomy in regard to the universe it cannot join in unity. With the confidence of this autonomy attained, the mind yet remains wary of what lurks without, as in "Attention":

> Down by the bay I
> kept in mind
> at once
> the tips of all the rushleaves
> and so
> came to know
> balance's cost and true:
> somewhere though in the whole field
> is the one
> tip
> I will someday lose out of mind
> and fall through.

The one particular of dying remains; every unmastered particular is a little death, giving tension to the most triumphant even among these short poems. "Hymn IV," returning to the great "Hymn" and two related poems of the same title, seals up the quest forever:

> You have enriched us with
> fear and contrariety
> providing the searcher
> confusion for his search
>
> teaching by your snickering
> wisdom an autonomy
> for man
> Bear it all
> and keep me from my enemies'

wafered concision and zeal
I give you back to yourself
whole and undivided.

I do not hear bitterness in this, or even defiance, but any late Emersonian worship of the Beautiful Necessity is gone. With the going there comes a deep uncertainty in regard to poetic subject, as "Looking Over the Acreage" and several other poems show so poignantly. The ironically moving penultimate poem of *Briefings* still locates the poet's field of contemplation "where the ideas of permanence / and transience fuse in a single body, ice for example, / or a leaf," but does not suggest that the fusion yields any information. The whole of *Briefings* manifests a surrender of the will-to-knowledge, not only relational knowledge between poetic consciousness and natural objects, but of all knowledge that is too easy, that is not also loss. Amid astonishing abundance in this richest of his volumes, I must pick out one lyric as representative of all the others, for in it Ammons gives full measure of a unique gift:

He held radical light
as music in his skull: music
turned, as
over ridges immanences of evening light
rise, turned
back over the furrows of his brain
into the dark, shuddered,
shot out again
in long swaying swirls of sound:

reality had little weight in his transcendence
so he
had trouble keeping
his feet on the ground, was
terrified by that
and liked himself, and others, mostly
under roofs:
nevertheless, when the
light churned and changed

his head to music, nothing could keep him
off the mountains, his
head back, mouth working,
wrestling to say, to cut loose

from the high, unimaginable hook:
released, hidden from stars, he ate,
burped, said he was like any one
of us: demanded he
was like any one of us.

It is the seer's horror of radical light, his obduracy to transcendence, that moves the seer himself, moves him so that he cannot know what he should know, which is that he cannot be like ourselves. The poem's power is that we are moved also, not by the horror, which cannot be our own, but by the transcendence, the sublime sense we long to share. Transcendent experience, but with Emerson's kind of Higher Utilitarianism ascetically cut off by a mind made too scrupulous for a new hope, remains the *materia poetica* of Ammons's enterprise. A majestic recent poem like "The City Limits" suggests how much celebration is still possible even when the transcendent moment is cruelly isolated, too harshly purified, totally compelled to be its own value. Somewhere upon the higher ridges of his Purgatory, Ammons remains stalled, unable for now to break through to the Condition of Fire promised by *Ommateum,* where instead of invoking Emerson's Uriel or Poe's Israfel he found near identity with "a crippled angel bent in a scythe of grief," yet witnessed a fiery ascent of the angel, fought against it, and only later gained the knowledge that "The eternal will not lie / down on any temporal hill."

J. D. McCLATCHY

Lost Paradises

At this point in our poetry's time, it is probable that Robert Lowell most decisively displays the ambitions of its traditionalist voice, and John Ashbery most incisively deploys the ambiguities of its characteristic speech. But if we grant that such strategies—the structures of voice and the situations of speech—are often compromises with the origins of either, then priority belongs to that artist who can discover the convergence of both, who can reveal expression as experience itself. And more than any other poet of his generation and few in our history, James Merrill has both rendered and renewed the primary language of poetry: the world inherent in the word. It is not merely that he is, since the loss of Auden, the master of verse technique, and in the face of contrary fashions has persisted in an affirming formalism capable of the elegant humanity of a Pope or the witty exuberance of a Byron. Nor is it only the subtle virtuosity of his diction, which works with self-conscious brilliance to release the subconscious depths in a poem's means and meanings—a language he once called "'English' in its billiard-table sense—words that have been set spinning against their own gravity." Beyond these exquisite disciplines there exists an exacting freedom of range, where an often light touch disguises the intense intellectual and emotional pressures used to refine his own experience into lines that allow us to find ours.

And, at the same time, each of his most important collections has marked a decisive change in his career, not so much of theme or perception, but of presence and performance. Beginning with *Water Street* (1962), he moved away from the anonymous opalescence of his early verse, which was

From *Parnassus* 5, no. 2 (Spring 1977). © 1977 by the Poetry in Review Foundation.

intricately imaged and shimmered with metaphysical foreplay. He moved to
make his poetry available to his own experience. The result was a more
immediately personal and relaxed voice which spoke in longer, usually narrative, forms whose variety sustained their patterns of exposition and epiphany. *Nights and Days* (1966) is a still more daring exploration of the
possibilities implicit in the long poem, though here his narratives are re-
fracted through myths, both traditional and imagined, that lend them a
heightened resonance. And in this book too, he perfected an idiosyncratic
verse form, at once dramatic in its extensions and arresting in its course,
that modulated from blank verse to couplets to quatrains and could accommodate incidental sonnets or prose excerpts. The best poems in his last book,
Braving the Elements (1972), a summary of these advances, gather into a
demanding, occasionally oblique and spare series of evocations of "meaning
relieved of sense," and achieve their force as telling meditations on Merrill's
most consistent concern, the flow and flaws of time as it constitutes, inter-
sects, undoes, and fulfills a life and its relationships. Such distinguishing
tactics and themes have accustomed us to expect, or rather to appreciate,
the enduring individuality of a Merrill poem which, under its art's own spell,
effects its disenchantments, the antiromantic transformation of experience
into self-revelation by means of recognition and acceptance.

But it is doubtful that anyone could have anticipated the high romance
of *Divine Comedies,* a book astonishing in its ambition and achievement.
Insofar as it counterpoints the burden of Merrill's career, this new book
confirms certain tendencies that revalue his previous attempts to articulate
important aspects of his experience, even as it reveals the poet in command
of a verse that combines the conversational fluency of *The Fire Screen* (1969)
with the almost oracular density of *Braving the Elements* into a language as
translucent, rich, and moving as any that has yet been fathered on our mother
tongue. Of equal significance is the substantiality of the book, which is
divided into two sections: the first with nine poems, six of them of some
length; the second, a narrative of nearly 100 pages, called "The Book of
Ephraim," which by any standard is one of the most remarkable poems in
memory. Together, the two sections, by cross-reference and accumulation,
constitute a single long work which I did not hesitate to rank as a signal
event in American literature. How often, after all, has a poet of such assured
gifts risked them to reach, with a contradictory grace, the depths of true
feeling and the necessary verges of felt truth that this book brings to us,
brings us to? It is Merrill's most complex and insistent work, and the elegant
maze of its narratives, the torsion of its topics and anomalous material, its
metrical array and daunting range of allusions, make unparalleled demands

on its readers. Perhaps it is these difficulties alone that account for the hesitant tone of the several initial reviews of the book—even including one by
Merrill's most perceptive advocate, Helen Vendler—that have failed to sense
the emphatic seriousness and consequence of this book's intentions and effects. In the limited space available to me here, I would like briefly to suggest
their outlines, and to do so by starting at the end, with the major poem that
anchors the collection, "The Book of Ephraim."

The poem's titular protagonist is a Greek Jew, born in Asia Minor in
8 A.D., later a favorite of Tiberius on Capri, and killed by the imperial guard
at age 28 for having loved the monstrous Caligula. The stuff of lurid costume
drama. But then, Ephraim is not the hero but a medium, the contact established through a ouija board by Merrill and his companion David Jackson,
and the poem recounts two decades of their adventures in revelation and
literal enthusiasm, arranged into 26 abecedarian installments. There are pre-
cedents among poets for this sort of spiritualism—one recalls Victor Hugo's
sessions at the *table parlante* or Yeats's correspondence with his familiar
spirit Leo Africanus—but still it is a risky subject. (As Auden once wrote of
Yeats's occult studies: "but mediums, spells, the Mysterious Orient—*how*
embarrassing." Someone else, I suppose, could say the equivalent of Auden's
own orthodox Christianity, but both these problematic beliefs are psychic
facts, and as such beyond the pale of proof or contention. At the very least—
and it would be less than necessary or appropriate—Merrill's apparatus can
be regarded as literary convention rather than sectarian conviction.) Merrill
himself has hinted at his interest in the phenomenon before, in such poems
as "Voices from the Other World," "Words for the Familiar Spirit," perhaps
parts of "From the Cupola," in his short story "Driver," and most notably
in an episode in his 1957 novel, *The Seraglio,* where Ephraim is renamed
Meno and as much of his story as Merrill had then been dictated is rehearsed.
In this new poem, we have the whole of it. Its telling transpires over the
course of a year (1974) which includes the four score seasons of the events
it portrays as they converge toward the occasion of composition. The story
began—and I use the word "story" as a convenient abbreviation for "history," since what happens in the poem was real, or "real"—in 1955, not
long after Merrill and Jackson had retreated into the isolation of a relationship: "We had each other for communication / And all the rest. The stage
was set for Ephraim." Slowly, the formula of The Other World is divulged—
a scheme not dissimilar from Orphic, Platonic, or Vedic analogues, though
Plato, Dante, and Yeats are echoed in Merrill's version not as metaphysical
systems but as its emotional logic. While alive, each of us is the representative
of a patron Beyond, who attends to us only when, after death, we are recycled

into other lives—"the quick seamless change of body-stocking"—which re-
curs until we are sufficiently purged (of life? by life?) to begin the divine
nine-stage ascent, where we assume the age "AT WHICH IT FIRST SEEMS
CREDIBLE TO DIE" and, patrons now ourselves, rise in station through
degrees of "PEACE FROM REPRESENTATION." But none of this becomes
dogmatic; as Ephraim, a blithe spirit himself, tells them: "U ARE SO QUICK
MES CHERS I FEEL WE HAVE / SKIPPING THE DULL CLASSROOM
DONE IT ALL / AT THE SALON LEVEL." In fact, the economy of this
Marriage of Heaven and Here is reassuringly sociable: we are, or are in touch
with, the dead: nothing is ever lost—such friends of Merrill's as Maya Deren
or Maria Mitsotáki or Auden himself are always "there."

   Though his gossip about the greats, from Mozart to Montezuma, is
never less than engaging, it is less to talk about himself or his home-away-
from-home that Ephraim spells out his answers, than to guide his devotees
toward an understanding of themselves, to prompt them in their parts on
the world's stage. For Merrill and Jackson, their life with Ephraim parallels
their life with each other—gradually domesticated in two villages (Stoning-
ton, Connecticut, and Athens, Greece), on Grand Tours (for which long
passages of the poem provide a magic lantern), undergoing the difficult dy-
namics of intimacy, disillusion, and endurance. Ephraim begins as a gentle
educator:

> TAKE our teacher told us
> FROM SENSUAL PLEASURE ONLY WHAT WILL NOT
> DURING IT BE EVEN PARTLY SPOILED
> BY FEAR OF LOSING TOO MUCH   This was the tone
> We trusted most, a smiling Hellenistic
> Lightness from beyond the grave.

and eventually becomes friend and co-conspirator in ways too fascinating
and complicated for a paraphrase to capture. There is minimal resistance on
their part. They admit the possibility that "his lights and darks were a
projection / Of what already burned, at some obscure / Level or another, in
our skulls." And when the poet consults a psychiatrist who terms it a *folie
à deux,* Merrill himself offers him guilt's own jargon:

> "Somewhere a Father Figure shakes his rod
>
> At sons who have not sired a child?
> Through our own spirit we can both proclaim
> And shuffle off the blame
> For how we live—that good enough?" Tom smiled

And rose. "I've heard worse. Those thyroid
Pills—you still use them? Don't. And keep in touch."

But the poet knows too, knows better, that even if we half-create what we
perceive, compensation is also the origin of vision, whose signifying "systems" are as varied and as valid as the ways the imagination can body forth
the form of things unknown:

> We were not tough-
> Or literal-minded, or unduly patient
> With those who were. Hadn't—from books, from living—
> The profusion dawned on us, of "languages"
> Any one of which, to who could read it,
> Lit up the system it conceived?—bird-flight,
> Hallucinogen, chorale and horoscope:
> Each its own world, hypnotic, many-sided
> Facet of the universal gem.
> Ephraim's revelations—we had them
> For comfort, thrills and chills, "material."
> He didn't cavil. *He* was the revelation
> (Or if we had created him, then we were).
> The point—one twinkling point by now of thousands—
> Was never to forego, in favor of
> Plain dull proof, the marvelous nightly pudding.

A structuralist reading of that passage would suggest that Merrill's own
canny sense of the experience is that his transcriptions from the ouija board
are yet another *code*—synchronic and paradigmatic—another structure by
which we attempt to see life whole, another "language" analogous to poetry
itself. A small detail extends this point. For Ephraim to "see" Merrill and
Jackson, "We prop a mirror in the facing chair, / Erect and gleaming, silver-
hearted guest, / We saw each other in it." By making spectacles of themselves,
they focus the life beneath the life, for which reality itself is the medium, to
something beyond mere reflection. And to push the point further—perhaps
too far—the book's dust jacket is dominated by a cartouched mirror—
indicating, I suppose, that the poem is meant to function for us as the
board has for the poet.

Two references within the poem are crucial glosses on the significance
of these matters, and on the whole question of "belief"—the poet's and a
reader's—in the poem. At one point, Merrill reminds us that "Stevens imagined the imagination / And God as one; the imagination, also / As that which

presses back, in parlous times, / Against 'the pressure of reality.'" But he is
quoting only half of the apposite adage; Stevens writes: "Propositia: 1. God
and the imagination are one. 2. The thing imagined is the imaginer. The
second equals the thing imagined and the imaginer are one. Hence, I suppose,
the imaginer is God." At face value, this might encourage us to read the
poem as an intricately displaced hymn of praise to the creative power—at
an abstract level, of the imagination itself, and at an autobiographical level,
of Merrill's own. This sense of the poem is supported not only by its highly
self-reflexive nature, its continuous references to the process by which the
poet's past products were invented from his life, but also by the original
pretext for "The Book of Ephraim"—the poem is a novel in ruins. Another
poem in *Divine Comedies*, "The Will," explains Ephraim's angry role in the
designed disappearance of a novel Merrill was writing about his medium.
The pale fire of that abandoned project flickers through the poem as an
alternative and doubly displaced version of the story. Set in the Southwest,
it tells of . . . well, the fragments we are given are less important than their
reminder of Merrill's interest in The Other Life Within Us and Abroad: how
fictions, even supreme fictions, are the natural impulse of an artist's necessary
mythologizing of himself. There may be reasons other than Ephraim's dis-
pleasure that the novel was destroyed; for instance, as a play within the
poem's play, it is a logical successor to Merrill's 1965 experimental novel
The (Diblos) Notebook. But I would like to think that it was because, as
Stevens observed, "in the presence of extraordinary actuality, consciousness
takes the place of imagination." The "lost novel" does, however, offer a clue
to be transferred to the poem proper. It was, says Merrill, to have had a
theme

> Whose steady light shone back, it seemed, from every
> Least detail exposed to it. I came
> To see it as an old, exalted one:
> The incarnation and withdrawal of
> A god.

And the god's name is not Ephraim but Eros, who, we should remember,
Plato tells us was born of Need and Resource as spiritual mediator between
the real and ideal worlds to bring forth the beautiful. That seems one appropriate identity for Ephraim himself, as he mediates between Merrill and
his world and his art.

One further reference within the poem draws us, I think, still closer to
its deeper purposes, and allows us to shift our attention from ritual to ro-

mance. Late in the poem, Merrill echoes the earlier citation: "Jung says—
or if he doesn't, all but does— / That God and the Unconscious are one.
Hm. / The lapse that tides us over, hither, yon; / Tide that laps us home away
from home." Among the many prospective patrons for this poem—Plato,
Dante, Proust, Stevens, or Auden—it is Jung who presides, especially the
later sage of *Answer to Job* and *Memories, Dreams, Reflections*. Again, Merrill has obscured his source's qualification, for Jung himself says that "strictly
speaking, the God-image does not coincide with the unconscious as such,
but with a special content of it, namely the archetype of the self." It is worth
pausing here to recall that that mythographer of the psyche thought of us
all as "representatives" of the collective unconscious—what the ancients
called the "sympathy of all things"—personified in the anima-figure who
communicates with consciousness in primordial images that reveal as much
of life as has ever been lived or imagined. To that extent, each of us contains
and transmits "another world"—that of the dead living in us. And the dead
themselves, Jung says, figure as potential images. Even as their state partakes
of the "maximum awareness which has been attained anywhere," so, too,
our contingent human destiny is to create more and more consciousness to
reveal life. A crucial part of that revelation is the prior process of self-
realization, Jung's concept of individuation by which a person comes to
know and embody the definitive uniqueness of his personality within the more
impersonal character of the collective past which exists in him. If we were
to translate these patterns and motifs into a traditional and generic literary
perspective, then "The Book of Ephraim" is decidedly a high internal romance. To be sure, it is a contemplative adventure—as Ephraim insists:
"WILL / U NEVER LEARN LOOK LOOK LOOK LOOK YR FILL / BUT
DO DO DO DO NOTHING." But the order of the poem's existence is of
a Prelude or The Growth of a Poet's Mind, a manifestation of Merrill's own
adult quest for a fulfillment that both yields to and transcends the real
world—a quest for self-realization pursued through the unconscious reaches
of memory to create identity. As Harold Bloom has noted about the major
Romantic prototypes of Merrill's poem: "The hero of internalized quest is
the poet himself, the antagonists of quest are everything in the self that blocks
imaginative work, and the fulfillment is never the poem itself, but the poem
beyond that is made possible by the apocalypse of imagination." With
Ephraim as psychopomp, the poet struggles against the dragons of self-
consciousness (whether neurotic distress or aestheticizing distance) toward
the hidden hoard of wisdom and power, treasures which instead of coming
at the expense of self-knowledge are dependent upon it. Merrill is rather
reticent to confront his struggle directly—itself evidence of its moment:

What I think I feel now, by its own nature
Remains beyond my power to say outright,
Short of grasping the naked current where it
Flows through field and book, dog howling, the firelit
Glances, the caresses, whatever draws us
To, and insulates us from, the absolute—
The absolute which wonderfully, this slow
December noon of clear blue time zones flown through
Toward relatives and friends, more and more sounds like
The kind of pear-bellied early instrument
Skills all but lost are wanted, or the phoenix
Quill of passion, to pluck a minor scale from
And to let the silence after each note sing.

That singing silence of art's instruments is, throughout the poem, contrasted
with the perversions of power, whether the insane destruction at Hiroshima
or the inflated rhetoric of Watergate, the paralyses of narcissism or regression
or the heart's dark secrets. As in Wagner's dialectic of power and love, the
fate of the Heavenly City (and hence, of the archetype of self) is in the end
indistinguishable from that of our earthly paradise of temptations to the
extremes of self-destruction. And the "minor scale" to which Merrill has
tuned the absolute, his "something evermore about to be," is his deliberate
and characteristic trope on the apocalyptic, whose space becomes time,
whose self becomes others, whose lonely love becomes itself. The "baldest
prose reportage" is its final representation, a transcription that doubles the
force of the adjective in Plato's definition of time as "a moving image of
eternity":

AM I IN YR ROOM   SO ARE ALL YR DEAD WHO HAVE
NOT GONE INTO OTHER BODIES   IT IS EASY TO CALL
THEM BRING THEM AS FIRES WITHIN SIGHT OF EACH
OTHER ON HILLS   U & YR GUESTS THESE TIMES WE
SPEAK ARE WITHIN SIGHT OF & ALL CONNECTED TO
EACH OTHER DEAD OR ALIVE   NOW DO U UNDER-
STAND WHAT HEAVEN IS   IT IS THE SURROUND OF
THE LIVING ... & NOW ABOUT DEVOTION   IT IS
I AM FORCED TO BELIEVE THE MAIN IMPETUS
DEVOTION TO EACH OTHER TO WORK TO REPRODUC-
TION TO AN IDEAL   IT IS BOTH THE MOULD & THE
CLAY   SO WE ARRIVE AT GOD OR A DEVOTION TO
ALL OR MANYS IDEAL OF THE CONTINUUM   SO WE

CREATE THE MOULDS OF HEAVENLY PERFECTION &
THE ONES ABOVE OF RARER & MORE EXPERT USEFUL-
NESS & AT LAST DEVOTION WITH THE COMBINED
FORCES OF FALLING & WEARING WATER PREPARES A
HIGHER MORE FINISHED WORLD OR HEAVEN

What my description of the poem has scanted, of course—and still can only suggest—is any detailed discussion of its parquetry and prosody. Not far along in the poem, Merrill compares the give-and-take between realms, ours and Theirs, to the texture of verse itself: the enlightened power of art's own second nature like "rod upon mild silver rod." And his poem disposes its verbal dominion in dazzling fashion. Auden's *The Sea and the Mirror* comes to mind as a similar, though less ambitious, example of a long poem whose cumulative impact derives, in part, from its dramatic variety of styles and verse forms. Merrill here deploys an array of conventional forms—blank verse, couplets, quatrains, sonnets, terza rima, even a brief anthology of epigraphs—to articulate and define his story. But these conventions have, as well, an emblematic significance, by amplifying the narrative content with the traditional associations of the form in which it is framed. Late in the poem, for instance, there is a section describing an encounter in Venice, and its triplets are obviously poised as a homage to Dante—a tribute which, in turn, lends added weight and poignance to Merrill's final lines by echoing Dante's:

> But that our struck acquaintance lit no drowned
>
> Niche in the blue, blood-warm Palladian
> Sculpture maze we'd surfaced from, which goes
> Evolving Likeness back to the first man,
>
> Forth to betided lineaments one knows
> Or once did. I lose touch with the sublime.
> Yet in these sunset years hardly propose
>
> Mending my ways, breaking myself of rhyme
> To speak to multitudes and make it matter.
> Late here could mean, moreover, In Good Time
>
> Elsewhere; for near turns far, and former latter
> —Syntax reversing her binoculars—
> Now early light sweeps under a pink scatter
>
> Rug of cloud the solemn, diehard stars.

Or take the following passage—a guess at the way of the other world—as typical of Merrill's ability to control his lines:

> Ephraim had resumed his volunteer
> Work in that dimension we could neither
> Visualize nor keep from trying to:
> For instance (this March noon) as a fogswept
> Milk-misty, opal-fiery induction
> Center where, even while *our* ball is kept
> Suavely rolling, he and his staff judge
> At a glance the human jetsam each new wave
> Washes their way—war, famine, revolution;
> Each morning's multitude the tough
> Tendril of unquestioning love alone
> Ties to dust, a strewn ancestral flesh
> —Yet we whose last ties loosened, snapped like thread,
> Weren't we less noble than these untamed dead?—
> Old falcon-featured men, young skin-and-bone
> Grandmothers, claw raised against the flash,
> Night-creatures frightened headlong, by a bare
> Bright Stage, into the next vein-tangled snare.

These lines, like the whole poem, demonstrate this poet's genius for using his metrics and darting rhymes to explicate the elaborate syntax, for using puns or enjambment to create an enriching lexical ambivalence for individual words and phrases, and for pursuing images until they yield to subject. Let me offer one more example: part of Merrill's meditation on the Venetian crowds:

> The wooden bridge, feeling their tread no longer,
> Grumbles: per me va la gente nova.
> Gente nova? A population explosion
> Of the greatest magnitude and brilliance?
> Who are these thousands entering the dark
> Ark of the moment, two by two?
> Hurriedly, as by hazard paired, some pausing
> On the bridge for a last picture. Touching, strange,
> If either is the word, this need of theirs
> To be forever smiling, holding still
> For the other, the companion focusing
> Through tiny frames of anxiousness. There. Come.

> Some have come from admiring, others are hurrying
> To sit out the storm in the presence of Giorgione's
> *Tempesta*—on the surface nothing less
> Than earthly life in all its mystery:
> Man, woman, child; a place; shatterproof glass
> Inflicting on them a fleet blur of couples
> Many of whom, by now, have reproduced.

The timing and tone, the focus and resolve, there are perfect. And the sheer brio of word-play is indicative of Merrill's method of allowing experience to discover itself in language. Merely on the prosodic level, "The Book of Ephraim" is a virtual handbook of technique. To watch the poet exchange clarifying image for revealing paradox gives us a privileged sense of his craft. But Merrill's art consists in working that craft in service to luminous details of landscape and heartscape. Together, they avow the poem's most profound sense of its own myth, as that term is defined in a book invoked by Merrill's text, Maya Deren's *Divine Horsemen*: "the facts of the mind made manifest in a fiction of matter." And if, as I have been suggesting, we mind the matter of this poem as romance, then the essentially nostalgic cast of that genre is equally apparent in the volume's other poems, whose autobiographical facts are subsumed by the fictional longings of memory for the pastoral and primitive, for an idealized childhood and a sentimentalized heroism, the paradises lost to maturity and contingency. The four preeminent poems in the book's opening section—"Lost in Translation," "Chimes for Yahya," "Yánnina," and "Verse for Urania"—are all reminiscences or reveries, their narratives shuttling between past event and present meditation, their recollections poised between past emotion and present tranquillity. Likewise, their tone is one of autumnal resignation, rather like that of those last harmonic romances of Shakespeare—and can it be merely accidental that the publication of *Divine Comedies* should coincide with Merrill's fiftieth birthday, with the intimations of mortality such a date presumes?

Each of the poems involves some sort of trip, literal or figurative, so that their recurring plot is the voyage of self-discovery, during which the poet tours his own past, in settings local or exotic. "Chimes for Yahya," for instance, opens and closes in Merrill's Athens home, but it opens out to and closes in on a recuperative stay in Isfahan, decades ago, with a Wise Young Prince who initiated the poet into mysteries of "Unlikeness to myself I knelt embracing." It is a *dramma giocoso*, though, an elaborate parody of Yeats's "The Second Coming," a mock nativity ode whose playful epiphany becomes an emblem of "the pain so long forgiven / It might as well be pleasure I rise in." Yahya is the mild, beneficent counterpart to another father-figure in Merrill's continuing calculation of the family romance—the compelling last-century tyrant Ali Pasha, whose outsized figure dominates the poem about Merrill's visit to his now sleepy capital "Yánnina." Screened by images of dream, shadow play, and magician's tent, the poem reconstructs the large shifting imagos of Feminine and Masculine, each split between the destructive and the seductive. Like the boxed woman the provincial magician has sliced in two and who "to a general exhalation heals / Like anybody's life, bubble and smoke / In afterthought," those versions of sexuality are reconciled in the child of them both, who is father to the poet who now can balance their opposing demands by relinquishing their allure:

> Ali, my father—both are dead.
> In so many words, so many rhymes,
> The brave old world sleeps. Are we what it dreams
> And is a rude awakening overdue?
> Not in Yánnina. To bed, to bed.
> The Lion sets. The lights wink out along the lake.
> Weeks later, in this study gone opaque,
> They are relit. See through me. See me through.
>
> For partings hurt although we dip the pain
> Into a glowing well—the pen I mean.
> Living alone won't make some inmost face to shine
> Maned with light, ember and anodyne,
> Deep in a desktop burnished to its grain.
> That the last hour be learned again
> By riper selves, couldn't you doff this green
> Incorruptible, the might-have-been,
>
> And arm in arm with me dare the magician's tent?

Those lines recall, as well, the "broken home" that is one of Merrill's favorite themes, the title of one of his best previous poems, and the setting of "Lost in Translation," the most immediately appealing poem in the volume. The jigsaw puzzle which the young Merrill and his "French Mademoiselle" piece together—during a time when "A summer without parents is the puzzle / Or should be"—is a tableau of yet another "Sheik with beard / And flashing sword hilt," attended by "a dark-eyed woman veiled in mauve." The child wonders

> whom to serve
> And what his duties are, and where his feet,

And if we'll find, as some before us did,
That piece of Distance deep in which lies hid
Your tiny apex sugary with sun,
Eternal Triangle, Great Pyramid!

The way we translate life to art, art to life, as if they were languages indif-
ferently learned but unhesitatingly spoken, is the animating energy behind
this brilliant, deceptively affecting work, which resolves itself in language—
a scene of instruction in which Rilke puzzles out a translation of Valéry's
"*Palme,*" sacrificing felicity for sense.

But nothing's lost. Or else: all is translation
And every bit of us is lost in it
(Or found—I wander through the ruin of S
Now and then, wondering at the peacefulness)
And in that loss a self-effacing tree.
Color of context, imperceptibly
Rustling with its angel, turns the waste
To shade and fiber, milk and memory.

The subject of "Lost in Translation"—the poet's recovering relationship
to his own past—is slightly deflected in "Verse for Urania" but only in order
to provide a still more penetrating and embracing meditation on time. The
poem is addressed not to Merrill's own childhood but to the infant daughter
of his Greek-born, too-Americanized tenants on the occasion of her baptism.
She is the poet's godchild—perhaps even a type of the Divine Child which
Jung considered a most constant and potent symbol of the self in fullest
potentiality, and thus a poignant reminder of one's unfulfilled desires. That
this child's name is also that of the Muse of astronomy and cosmological
poetry allows the poet's reflecting consciousness to relate its second cos-
mogony. Since "the first myth was Measure," the rhythms of life, like those
of verse, "Prevail, it might be felt, at the expense / Of meaning, but as well
create, survive it." All things pass—"Such is the test of time that all things
pass"—but only to return upon themselves, and Merrill would hold with
Nietzsche that he "who consents to his own return participates in the divinity
of the world." That is what this poem—indeed, this book—finally celebrates.
We are the time we pass through, in a measured design greater than either—
as Merrill tells his godchild:

It was late

And early. I had seen you through shut eyes.
Our bond was sacred, being secular:
In time embedded, it in us, near, far,
Flooding both levels with the same sunrise.

To have a share in that bond, by reading *Divine Comedies,* is to be convinced
that our literature has secured for itself a book with the temperament for
patient, exalted vision, and a poet in the tradition of greatness.

DIANE MIDDLEBROOK

Bound Each to Each

"All that I have done is a program, consciously or not," Allen Ginsberg
wrote William Carlos Williams in 1949. The program appears in retrospect
to have been growing up. Shakespeare says there are seven ages of man; the
modern child psychologist Erik Erikson says there are eight. Whatever the
number, the process itself has plateaus and escalations we are prone to count.
Here I shall count two of them in the work of Allen Ginsberg: the first (in
The Gates of Wrath) and the most recent (*The Fall of America*).

I

Erikson agrees with Shakespeare that the first age of man is ingestive:
a stage of taking in and biting down. This appears to be the case with
intelligence as well. Ginsberg's first stage, as revealed in *The Gates of Wrath*,
was a mouthful of Blake, Shelley, Crane, and Yeats. The poems in this book
almost did not survive to be printed. Ginsberg says that the book was carried
off in typescript to London "by a lady friend" in the early fifties, and returned, mysteriously, by Bob Dylan in 1968. The return to its author of *The
Gates of Wrath* by a musician represents one of the profound coincidences
that followers of the Divine Light call "*lila*"—the games life plays with us—
for Ginsberg was at the time Dylan gave him this lost book just learning to
annotate music in order to set some of Blake's poetry. The splendid result
of this effort was a record: "Blake's Songs of Innocence and of Experience

From *Parnassus* 2, no. 2 (Spring 1974). © 1974 by the Poetry in Review Foundation.

Tuned by Allen Ginsberg" (MGM / Verve FTS 3083). But this is to look ahead. In *The Gates of Wrath* we see Allen Ginsberg in 1948, trying not to set but to *be* the William Blake of *Songs of Innocence and of Experience.* Ginsberg's strategy as a poet was imitation; he reproduces Blake's short, rhymed lines and uses a diction which sounds anachronistic because it is Blake's diction. He has a fuzzily visionary subject matter which he acknowledges is derivative:

> What everlasting force confounded
> In its being, like some human
> Spirit shrunken in a bounded
> Immortality, what Blossom
> Inward gathers us, astounded?
> Is this the sickness that is Doom?
> ("On Reading William Blake's
> 'The Sick Rose'")

As frequently, the spirit bringing metaphors for poetry is Yeats out of Shelley:

> Dread spirit in me that I ever try
> With written words to move,
> Hear thou my plea, at last reply
> To my impotent pen:
> Should I endure, and never prove
> Yourself and me in love,
> Tell me, spirit, tell me, O what then?

But always this spirit tells Ginsberg to write in rhymed stanzas. Some of the poems in *The Gates of Wrath* are lovely, and all of them are interesting in retrospect, especially those in which Ginsberg is boldly repetitious: often he writes a good line but knows it's in the wrong poem, so he sets up another poem to give the line a home. We now know that the grownup Allen Ginsberg is a writer of the long free prophetic line associated, in American poetry, with Walt Whitman. So to hear Ginsberg speak initially the language of the English Romantic and metaphysical poets binding themselves to stanzas gives unanticipated delight when he achieves what they were after—as in "The Voice of Rock" or "Stanzas Written at Night in Radio City":

> Art is short, nor style is sure:
> Though words our virgin thoughts betray,
> Time ravishes that thought most pure,
> Which those who know, know anyway;
> For if our daughter should endure,

When once we can no more complain,
Men take our beauty for a whore,
And like a whore, to entertain.

Still, *The Gates of Wrath* represents in Ginsberg's work the stage of poetic slavery, a period described by Wordsworth in "Immortality": the poet acts "As if his whole vocation / Were endless imitation." Wordsworth was lamenting his own alienation from The Child we have all been; but "Immortality" goes on to affirm that this Child survives in our very souls as the "fountain-light" of vision, even though he has a period of disguise as a mere imitator of dreary adult competence. This imitative stage is useful, too, as Erikson observes. To write like somebody else is Play, in the psychologist's definition: it prepares for the point at which, no longer protected, the self moves forward to enact its own unrepeatable dance in the context of time, where every action is fraught with consequence.

Dependence, in Ginsberg's early poetry, is not merely dependence on older poets, but dependence on a few talismanic words which he often gives the emphasis of rhyme position in a stanza. "Bone," "wrath," and "rose" recur as the mental geometry of this book, the formulae, or sometimes the points of departure, for the visionary art the young Ginsberg treasured. The quality of firmness in these monosyllabic nouns anchors the poems in a consistent metaphysic and a consistently prophetic stance toward the urban locale which thrusts its misery into even the most abstract poems:

Sometime I'll lay down my wrath,
As I lay my body down
Between the ache of breath and breath,
Golden slumber in the bone.

A tendency to aphorism strengthens the poems of *The Gates of Wrath* rhetorically. Like the poet of *Poetical Sketches* (Blake's first book), Ginsberg might have gone on to write short lyrics all his life, if an early lyric like this one is indicative of his talent for concision and handling of the line:

I speak of love that comes to mind:
The moon is faithful, although blind;
She moves in thought she cannot speak.
Perfect care has made her bleak.

And, like Blake, Ginsberg appears to have written these strict poems in order to acquire his poet's license—the authorization of the untidy consciousness which lies below this stanza-speaker's view of what can be let into the line, and where it should go.

II

It may be that only poets concerned with the "unconscious program" of the mind's growth into utterance share the Wordsworthian obsessive dread of imitation ("Full soon thy soul shall have her earthly freight, / And custom lie upon thee with a weight, / Heavy as frost, and deep almost as life!"). But all the modern poets we call Romantic—with the exception of Yeats—share the belief that the growth *up* is growth away from traditional English stanza forms into a verse as free as they can think to make it. Yet free verse too has its impressive fathers. In Allen Ginsberg's case the generative parents are the biblical psalm as rendered in English by the King James translators; Blake; Christopher Smart in "Jubilate Agno"; the majestically enjambed blank verse of Milton, Shelley, and Wordsworth; finally, the poetry of Walt Whitman. Whitman is especially important, because he adds to the ecstatic mode of the long poem in Romantic English verse a tone of righteous democratic American anger as an alternative to meditative affirmation. *The Fall of America* is dedicated to the angry Whitman of *Democratic Vistas* (1871).

Ginsberg profited from all these influences, but by the time of writing the "poems of these states" which make up *The Fall of America,* he has abandoned his early models. Finding one's own way to *be* in words is a hard job. "What's to be done with my life, which has lost its idea?" Ginsberg asks in the *Indian Journals.* "I don't even have a good theory of vegetarianism." What to take in, then? Ginsberg's solution is "attention to the actual movie of the mind." "Then you see what a man is, you know what he has in him," Whitman said in "Song of Myself," Ginsberg describes his technique of writing now as a complete abandonment of the sense of structure which dominates *The Gates of Wrath.*

> Such craft or art as there is, is in illuminating mental formations, and trying to observe the naked activity of my own mind. Then transcribing that activity down on paper. So the craft is being shrewd at flash lightning mental activity. Trapping the archangel of the soul by accident, so to speak.

Hence, Allen Ginsberg's mature poems are complicated only by the amount of his personality they contain. In the best of them, as in Whitman, egotism is, movingly, a form of demoting the merely personal:

> I will haunt these States
> with beard bald head
> eyes staring out plane window,

           hair hanging in Greyhound bus midnight
           leaning over taxicab seat to admonish
               an angry cursing driver
               hand lifted to calm
                 his outraged vehicle
           that I pass with the Green Light of common law.
                                           ("A Vow")

But Ginsberg is frequently obscure, as Whitman never is. This attribute of his poetry is a direct product of his aesthetic, as he describes it: "If you can actually keep track of your own head movie, then the writing down is just like a secretarial job, and who gets craft about that? Use dashes instead of semicolons." A reader with enough good will can then simply not puzzle over puzzling references (usually from esoteric sources) but simply pass on, since another feature of Ginsberg's sort of writing is amplitude. The obscurity of any one line is merely the obscurity of the mind's momentary distraction into self-delight; in another instant another more accessible metaphor might have occurred as the expressible form of the same perception.

Attending "the movie of the mind" means noticing things rather than mulling them over. Its poetic form becomes the catalogue in long lines, as Ginsberg describes it, "a giant sentence which will include the whole associational mobile." It's not surprising that Ginsberg should have sought out the wisdom of Eastern religions to cultivate this emotional condition, "trapping the archangel of the soul." Writers of English poetry since the nineteenth century have approached the tantalizing but nearly incomprehensible texts of Eastern wisdom with profitable hopefulness. Matthew Arnold, for example, despairing of Wordsworth's radical model of natural mysticism, found in the Bhagvadgita a more useful form of enlightenment. Thoreau and T. S. Eliot had comparable relations with the East, converting the texts, so to speak, by naturalizing them on unfamiliar intellectual ground. It was bold of these writers to seek philosophic and spiritual enrichment from sources so distant from Christianity, and therefore, from cultural respectability: further, comprehending these teachings at all requires enormous effort of the sort we see Ginsberg performing day by day in the *Indian Journals*. All these writers have enriched the genres they've written in by subsuming Eastern mysticism into their own personal forms of mysticism, demonstrating that the particular is the only source of revelation available to the Eternal.

This is the point of view we find in *The Fall of America,* poems of Ginsberg's return from India to his homeland which reflect a matured view of the application of vision to contemporary reality. In *The Gates of Wrath* Ginsberg was preoccupied with having a visionary perception of reality: in *The Fall* he is interested in using it.

Ginsberg is hopeful about the future of poetry as America falls. "Wouldn't it be best," he asks, "if one were interested in what would survive, wouldn't it just be best if one were to deal only in the forms which are memorizable and singable and could survive beyond the printing press? . . . art which is perennial, useful, that is, useful in caves." But Ginsberg in this book gives us little of that useful sort of art. For one thing, his lines are too diffuse and undeliberated to be memorizable. But more important, Ginsberg as a poet does not—with one exception—seek to memorialize things in poetry *because* they are worth keeping. When we look at the imagery of reindeer and wolves surviving in the caves at Lascaux and Altamira we know we are beholding objects sacred to their creators. But Ginsberg's picture-making is, by his own acknowledgment, as unselective as possible. Like the TV cameras monitoring the aisles of supermarkets and discount stores, the poems of *The Fall of America* register abundant temporary intersections between objects and the eye as Ginsberg crisscrosses North America by car, bus, and plane. The camera's eye and Ginsberg's are both on the watch for outrageousness, too, though Ginsberg is capable of irony and passionate delight. Nonetheless, after reading only a little of *The Fall*, the reader felt she could put down the book and make her own poem merely by taking a walk. Ginsberg's poetry at its most effective has this influence, the power of awakening a reader to the unfailing sufficiency of his own imagination; and since Ginsberg's idea of poetry is so much like Whitman's, the reader's feeling of not needing the book may very well have been Ginsberg's point in writing it. Still, such an aesthetic does not make for the kind of art Ginsberg ascribes with admiration to bards and prophets, the kind "useful in caves."

I said there was an exception to Ginsberg's genial tendency to include whatever comes along as subject matter in *The Fall of America*. The exception is Ginsberg's obsession with the figure of a young male who appears some-times in his true identity as Neal Cassady, sometimess generalized into

> The hero surviving his own murder,
>   his own suicide, his own
>   addiction, surviving his own
>   poetry, surviving his own
>   disappearance from the scene—
> returned in new faces, shining
>   through the tears of new eyes.

New small adolescent hands
    on tiny breasts,
pale silken skin at the thighs,
    and the cherry-prick rises hard
        innocent heat pointed up
        from the muscular belly
of basketball highschool English class spiritual Victory,
    made clean at midnight in the bathtub of old City,
        hair combed for love.
                            ("Kansas City to St. Louis")

Neal Cassady's death in February 1968 intrudes violently into Ginsberg's chronological record of "these states 1965–1971." The poems lamenting Cassady are of two types: one elegiac, the other political. The
intensity of Ginsberg's grief over the loss of this idealized former lover produces the elegiac poems, which are moving and personal. But because Ginsberg is inescapably a Romantic, thoughts that lie too deep for tears are a
mental necessity; he therefore seeks transcendence of the personal by linking
Cassady's death thematically to the Vietnam War and the Siege of Chicago,
with an effect of surrealism occasionally declining into silliness:

Denver without Neal, eh?
        . . . when the Earth Angel's dead
    the dead material planet'll revolve robotlike
    & insects hop back and forth between metallic cities.
                                ("Over Denver Again")

Largely because of his deep feeling for Cassady, Ginsberg's tender lyrical
voice is well represented in The Fall of America. But his ambition in this
book to speak, like Whitman, from the self-transcendent perspective of a
prophet doesn't come off very well. The data remain data, conceptually
unmanaged; the mood of outrage seems childishly insufficient as a mode of
emotional mastery over the horrors he describes. As in The Gates of Wrath,
Ginsberg's strength in this latest book is the strength of his belief in the art
of poetry itself. Ginsberg remains an imitator, a disciple whose work is
always reminding the reader of the nineteenth-century Romantic masters. As
their disciple, however, Ginsberg has no peer: perhaps it is his own form of
maturity as a poet. In any case, Ginsberg's whole working life has been an
illustration of the capacity of that poetry to revitalize itself in the consciousness of people seeking through every mode of communal effort to find grace,
a way to survive with others.

CHARLES MOLESWORTH

"The Rank Flavor of Blood"

When Ezra Pound called for the "direct, objective treatment of the thing itself," he was in some sense echoing the historicism of late nineteenth-century thought. Historicism implicitly rejects systems, whether of an ideological or a theological sort; and, in attempting to understand historical events without the benefit of any transcendent framework, it tacitly accepts the end of absolute value and absolutist authority as signaled by the French Revolution. Though Pound's polemic addressed itself to eradicating the "emotional slither" he identified with late Victorian poetry, it inadvertently limited the poet almost exclusively to the ironic mode. Since mythical statements, and expressions of direct sentiment, would be curtailed by any rigorous adoption of "direct, objective treatment," the lyric poem might well lose the chief sources of its resonance. One way for the poet to render some justice to the complexity of experience is by turning to his own divided consciousness as his chief subject and presenting the consciousness directly while ironically qualifying the mind that observes it. Or the poet might take different, fragmentary, but conflicting values inherent in an experiential situation, relate them one to another, dampening his own intentions and judgments, and energize the poem through an ironic interplay of multiple but partial "truths." Poets, especially ironic poets, became in some sense historicists of imagination.

From such impulses we can trace the development of the typical Amer-

From *The Fierce Embrace*. © 1979 by the Curators of the University of Missouri. The University of Missouri Press, 1979. Originally entitled "'The Rank Flavor of Blood': The Poetry of Galway Kinnell."

ican poem of the two decades that span the Second World War: Eberhart's "The Groundhog," Nemerov's "The Goose Fish," and Shapiro's "Auto Wreck." Few poets produced much work outside this dominant mode, marked as it was by logical structure, "tension," and ironic verbal surfaces. The two major exceptions are Randall Jarrell and Theodore Roethke, though both of these, with poems like "Death of the Ball-Turret Gunner" and "Elegy for My Student Jane," respectively, showed they had mastered the ironic idiom. But changes began to occur: Olson's "Projective Verse" and Allen Ginsberg's "Howl" were clear signs, at least with the comfort of retrospection, that a new poetics was developing. It might be instructive to trace some of the lineaments of this new idiom by focusing on one poet's career for a certain period, namely that of Galway Kinnell in the 1960s.

Kinnell's poetry of this period involves itself with a virtual rediscovery of how to view objects intensely, while continuing to avoid any prescribed system. Even as early as his long poem "The Avenue Bearing the Initial of Christ into the World," which falls outside the scope of the present study, though it deserves an essay of its own, Kinnell's poetry has been celebratory and inclusive in its characteristic attitude toward the world of objects. "There are more to things than things," says one modern French philosopher, and the contemporary poet instinctively agrees; but how to discover that "more" without falling into mere attitudinizing remains problematic. Pound taught his successors, who include most American poets, that no authority could replace personal testament, especially when such testament involved accurate perception and attentive apperception. But poets could still remain estranged from things; they might fall into a glorified listing of the mundane, or make the operations of the mind so dominant that the poems would lose their subjects in a welter of "impressions." Pound's influence dominated developments in American poetry so completely that poets as diverse as, say, Robert Creeley and William Meredith could easily refuse to yield to each other in their admiration for Pound's accomplishments. Kinnell took from Pound, however, only so much as could fruitfully be grafted onto the traditions of Blake and Whitman; and, though for some Pound's concern with "technique" might seem inimical to inspiration, such need not be the case. Pound's concern with objective "vision" on the physiological level corrects rather than replaces the concern with the "visionary." But Kinnell was still faced with the problem of how to bring his poetry out of the modernist cul-de-sac of irony into a postmodernist aesthetic. He did this in large measure by two actions, which may appear contradictory but are in fact complementary: self-discovery and self-destruction, the heuristic and the incendiary actions of poetry. Kinnell became a shamanist, rather than a historicist, of the imagination.

The first volume to contain poems Kinnell wrote in the sixties was *Flower Herding on Mount Monadnock* (1964), a book divided into two parts, the first heavily concerned with cityscapes and urban consciousness, and the second almost totally rural in its subjects and locales. The last poem of the first section, "For Robert Frost," offers a convenient transition into the second section, a transition important for the next volume, *Body Rags* (1969), filled as it is with a poetry of nature rather than of history. Such a reductive distinction can be misleading, of course, and it may help to look briefly at the poem for Frost to see in part how Kinnell views America's most famous "nature poet." The pastoralism of Frost both echoes and disjoins Kinnell's sensibility:

> When we think of a man who was cursed
> Neither with the mystical all-lovingness of Walt Whitman
> Nor with Melville's anguish to know and to suffer,
> And yet cursed . . . A man, what shall I say,
> Vain, not fully convinced he was dying, whose calling
> Was to set up in the wilderness of his country,
> At whatever cost, a man, who would be his own man,
> We think of you.

The qualified praise here may well bring to mind Auden's elegy for Yeats, a typically modern poem in the way it refuses to follow the ordinary "rules" for elegiac praise and insists on an honesty that threatens to dislocate the very discourse of the poem and move down to the level of verse epistle or even satire. Still, Kinnell sees Frost as "cursed," not perhaps as the same sort of *poète maudit* as Melville, but as someone tied to, perhaps bound down by, his bourgeois virtues of self-reliance and rugged individualism. The obverse of those virtues reflects the loneliness, the alienation, in Frost's life, the "desert places," against which confusion the poems offer only a "momentary stay." This surely is the side of Frost that most attracts Kinnell (as the third section of the poem makes clear), and he almost appears to be exorcising those other, civilized virtues of Frost that made him such a master ironist. When we look back on this poem from the perspective of Kinnell's two latest books, the most stringent criticism of Frost he proposes may be when he says that the older poet was "not fully convinced he was dying." Such an affirmation of life *against* death will become for Kinnell a weakness, a mark of the weak self-love, an unwillingness to accept the "last moment

of increased life." As he says in "The Poetics of the Physical World," "The
poetics of heaven agrees to the denigration of pain and death; the poetics of
the physical world builds on these stones."

Along with death, Kinnell places pain at the base of his poetics, and
pain plays a large part in the poems of Flower Herding. The first section of
the book is concerned with pain as a subject, or at least as a surrounding
condition of other subjects. Chief among these subjects, Kinnell places an
awareness of time's ongoingness, an intense awareness that this particular
moment, this now is isolate, thrown up by itself to baffle and defeat human
expectations. Here is a passage from "The River That is East," the first
poem of the book:

> We stand on the shore, which is mist beneath us,
> And regard the onflowing river. Sometimes
> It seems the river stops and the shore
> Flows into the past. Nevertheless, its leaked promises
> Hopping in the bloodstream, we strain for the future,
> Sometimes even glimpse it, a vague, scummed thing
> We dare not recognize, and peer again
> At the cabled shroud out of which it came,
> We who have no roots but the shifts of our pain,
> No flowering but our own strange lives.

All New York poems with bridges in them, such as this one, must recall
Hart Crane, though part of the success of this poem lies in how effectively
it uses its poetic forebears without being strangled by them. This is true of
much of Kinnell's poetry and is one of the several ways in which he resembles
Theodore Roethke. The images here of mists, scum, and shrouds should
remind us of how early Kinnell was involved in a poetry obsessed with death
and pain, a product of a consciousness in which sharp juxtapositions and
sudden changes of perspective appear endemic. The root and the flower of
his experience exist without any system except what they may discover for
themselves in an existential framework.

It is in section II of Flower Herding that we find the first seeds of
Kinnell's "poetics of the physical world," as that poet concentrates on natural as opposed to urban objects, moments, and landscapes. Here, too, pain
and death are present, almost omnipresent. But the isolate moments, the
"leaked promises" of continuity, or of wholeness, become, in the rural setting, moments of ecstasy. The perspective of the future as "a vague, scummed
thing / we dare not recognize" fades into a more empty perspective, perhaps;
but it is that very emptiness that constitutes such promise for Kinnell. As

Kinnell suggests in "The Poetics of the Physical World," death represents the last, absolute perspective; its very finality makes it a magnificent possibility, or rather, the source of magnificent possibilities.

> We may note that the desire to *be* some other thing is itself suicidal; it involves a willingness to cease to be a man. But this is not a simple wish for extinction so much as it is a desire for union with what is loved. And so it is a desire for more, not less, life.

Reading *Flower Herding* as part of a putative spiritual autobiography, the reader will decide that it is only when Kinnell escapes the city for the country that the possibilities of mortality become positive rather than negative. When we regard *Flower Herding* as the barometer of other, larger currents at work in American poetry in the sixties, it clearly stands with Bly's *Silence in the Snowy Fields* (1962) and Wright's *The Branch Will Not Break* (1963). These three books can be seen as developments away from the ironic mode practiced and perfected by, among others, Ransom, Tate, Nemerov, and Wilbur, and toward a poetic mode first announced by Theodore Roethke as early as 1950, but largely unheeded until ten years later. Here is Roethke characterizing the lyric poet in "Open Letter," from *On the Poet and His Craft*:

> He must scorn being "mysterious" or loosely oracular, but be willing to face up to a genuine mystery. His language must be compelling and immediate: he must create an actuality. He must be able to telescope image and symbol, if necessary, without relying on the obvious connectives: to speak in a kind of psychic shorthand. . . . He works intuitively, and the final form of his poem must be imaginatively right.

Such phrases as "psychic shorthand" and "telecop[ing] image and symbol" illuminate the shifts in perspective and the imagistic density that make the typical Kinnell poem. Here are the final lines of the title poem of *Flower Herding*:

> It burns up. Its drift is to be nothing.
>
> In its covertness it has a way
> Of uttering itself in place of itself,
> Its blossoms claim to float in the Empyrean,

A wrathful presence on the blur of the ground.
The appeal to heaven breaks off.
The petals begin to fall, in self-forgiveness.
It is a flower. On this mountainside it is dying.

Heaven and the void vie with each other to be the flower's proper domain; the flower makes claims it cannot demonstrate, and yet it forgives itself; it needs its covertness in order to survive, and yet it must utter itself, make known and articulate its "invisible life." All of these contradictory impulses suggest that we can "interpret" the flower as an image from the processes of nature and as a symbol for the act of writing the poem, or even for the psychic paradoxes of the poet himself.

Nowhere are such leaps from the imagistic to the symbolic made clear; in fact, the tone of the poem occasionally works against such leaps, especially in the last line. But the pain and the ecstasy of the consciousness that employs such telescopings tell us that aspiration and acceptance are two aspects of the same intentionality. We might even say that the dialectic between aspiration and acceptance provides the central energy of the poem and that that dialectic reveals its terms most clearly in the tone of a line such as "A wrathful presence on the blur of the ground," where overtones of an almost biblical phrasing terminate in the flatness of the final five words. But the flatness of such a termination, along with phrases like "breaks off," can't be called ironic, at least not if we use irony to mean a kind of qualifying defensiveness. If anything, the variations in texture in these lines reflect quite openly the actuality of the circumscribed transcendence in the poem, circumscribed because it sustains itself only through an acceptance of death. And the persistence of fire and death imagery throughout Kinnell's poetry forces us to disregard, or at least to minimize, the habitual expectation of ironic distance that we bring to much modern poetry. His obviously attempts to be a poetry of immersion into experience rather than of suspension above it.

Kinnell's next book after *Flower Herding* presents several difficulties; these result in part simply because several of the single poems in *Body Rags* are difficult ("The Last River" and "Testament of the Thief"), but also because the mode of expression throughout can seem half-formed, occasionally alternating between the densely remote and the flatly commonplace. At least seventeen (out of twenty-three) of the poems are constructed in "sections," and the section becomes the organizing principle of *The Book of Nightmares* as well as of the best poems in *Body Rags*: "The Poem," "The Porcupine," and "The Bear." But eight of the poems in *Body Rags* contain only two sections each, and these represent, I think, some of Kinnell's least successful poems. At the same time, the concentration of imagery and attention that they contain, along with the multiple and shifting perspectives, eventually culminates in what remains Kinnell's typical strength. Here is one poem that has some strength but finally fails to be as powerful as several others in the same format:

> Night in the Forest
>
> 1
> A woman
> sleeps next to me on the earth. A strand
> of hair flows
> from her cocoon sleeping bag, touching
> the ground hesitantly, as if thinking
> to take root.
>
> 2
> I can hear
> a mountain brook
> and somewhere blood winding
> down its ancient labyrinths. And
> a few feet away
> charred stick-ends surround
> a bit of ashes, where burnt-out, vanished flames
> absently
> waver, absently leap.

Postmodernist poetry insofar as it rejects or moves beyond irony, runs the risk of sentimentality on the one hand and of being "loosely oracular" on the other. Here, the "blood winding / down its ancient labyrinths" is susceptible to either charge, though perhaps especially the latter. Such resonance as the poem does have originates in the subtly controlled tone and syntax of the last few lines. But, considering the total statement of the poem as a dialectic between its two "sections" doesn't particularly increase our appreciation of it. The poem goes beyond descriptive prettiness only by hinting at emotions that would probably be mawkish if further explored.

But it is ungracious to consider at too great a length any failings in *Body Rags* when that volume contains at least three poems that have already come to enjoy a wide and deep esteem: "The Poem," "The Porcupine," and "The Bear." These are the three poems in which Kinnell moves most clearly beyond the suspension of irony toward the immersion of empathy, and they are, I believe, sure indicators of a new postmodern aesthetic in contemporary American poetry. By empathy I mean something other than Keats's "negative capability," though that concept forms part of Kinnell's poetics. Empathy in Kinnell's poetry, however, results in an important way at the edges of experience, that boundary along which the organism and the environment become interdefinitional. Irony occurs at the center of opposing vectors, at the point of greatest cumulative tension. On the other hand, empathy results from a systemic consciousness, an awareness of the field on which and through which the forces of experience act and make themselves visible. In some ways this accounts for Kinnell's feelings that the self, the ego, hinders true poetry, since the ego so often defends itself rather than adapts to new experience, thus effectively delimiting the consciousness instead of surrendering it to new forms. Such a poetics of empathy, however, stops short of aesthetic anarchy by insisting that reality itself has forms inherent in it, or at least that the mind will instinctively develop such forms for itself, out of its own powers, its own thirst for order. Robert Creeley quotes Allen Ginsberg as saying "Mind is shapely." And Denise Levertov gives the following definition of organic poetry:

> It is a method of apperception, i.e., of recognizing what we perceive, and based on an intuition of an order, a form beyond forms, in which forms partake, and of which man's creative works are analogies, resemblances, natural allegories. Such poetry is exploratory.

In order to complete its explorations, such a poetry must avoid an entrapping irony and make maximum use of empathy.

Each poet's method of exploring will be different, and the various forms of control he exercises will be based on his own method of apperception. For Kinnell, this reflexive act of sensory consciousness often takes shape, as I have suggested, along the edges, the margins of perception. Such consciousness need not be purely spatial in form, either; and Kinnell often uses a temporal marginality, a sense of the "just occurred" or imminent event as crucial in the discovery of the "form beyond forms, in which forms partake." As he says in "The Poem":

> On this hill crossed
> by the last birds, a sprinkling
> of soil covers up the rocks
> with green, as

the face
drifts on a skull scratched with glaciers.

The poem too
is a palimpsest, streaked
with erasures, smelling
of departure and burnt stone.

Along with the images of burning, "build-soil," and painful scars that occur
frequently in Kinnell's work, this poem has two other images: the human
face and a written text. Both of these latter figures recur with increasing
frequency in *Body Rags* and *The Book of Nightmares,* and their resonances
are indicative of Kinnell's attempts to "register" experience with the most
sensible recorders available. In his essay "Poetry, Personality, and Death,"
Kinnell offers the following observations on the American face, a face he
thinks has literally been marked and transfigured by the technological age:

> Contrast the ancestral faces one still sees in Europe, contrast the
> faces in old paintings and photographs. Is it just my imagination
> that the American chin has thickened, its very bones swollen, as
> if to repel what lies ahead? And those broad, smooth, curving,
> translucent eyelids, that gave such mystery to the eyes—is it my
> private delusion that they have disappeared, permanently rolled
> themselves up, turning the eyes into windows without curtains,
> not to be taken by surprise again? And that the nose, the feature
> unique to man, the part of him which moves first into the un-
> known, has become on our faces a small neat bump?

Concern with the face in large part springs from a concern with sensuous
experience, with receiving the primary data of our environment, with ex-
ploratively moving "into the unknown." The face offers a force field of
sensitively registered changes and dispositions; it also provides a collection
of "edges" that take shape according to our willingness to immerse ourselves
in our experience. Speaking in "The Porcupine" of the "clothespins that
have / grabbed our body-rags by underarm and crotch," Kinnell describes
the animal in these terms:

> Unimpressed—bored—
> by the whirl of stars, by *these*
> he's astonished, ultra—
> Rilkean angel!

for whom the true
portion of the sweetness of earth
is one of those bottom heavy, glittering, saccadic
bits
of salt water that splash down
the haunted ravines of a human face.

Physiognomy takes on the scope of geography, and again, in proper Rilkean fashion, the transcendence of the poem's desires springs from contact with the earth, as the human face becomes the source of the porcupine's intensely craved salt and becomes of more interest than "the whirl of the stars." The larger systems of signification are replaced by pain.

Kinnell had begun *Body Rags* with a poem called "Another Night in the Ruins," which has the following terminal section:

How many nights must it take
one such as me to learn
that we aren't, after all, made
from that bird which flies out of its ashes,
that for a man
as he goes up in flames, his one work
is
to open himself, to *be*
the flames?

The volume ends with "The Bear," a shamanistic immersion in the unknown, a "dance of solitude" that describes in great detail the hunting of the animal with "the chilly, enduring odor of bear." I think one phrase that might adequately hint at how the poem achieves its power over us is Denise Levertov's *natural allegory*. Pursued so intensely, the bear must end up "meaning something else," but only the briefest of analogical touchstones appears at the end of the poem, after the speaker has killed the bear and is watching a dam bear give birth to her cubs, "lumps of smeared fur":

the rest of my days I spend
wandering: wondering
what, anyway,
was that sticky infusion, that rank flavor of blood, that
                    poetry, by which I lived?

Exploration and attentiveness provide the grounds of existence for the hunter of bear, for the poet; and those grounds are both the occasion and the subject of his most insistent questionings.

The hunter kills the bear by coiling a bone and freezing it in blubber; when the bear ingests it, the bone uncoils and pierces his inner organs. The resultant internal bleeding dominates the images of the poem, and the speaker eventually tracks down the bear, hacks "a ravine in his thigh," tears him "down his whole length," and climbs inside. Once the hunter is inside, his empathetic identification with the bear becomes literal, and the poet recapitulates by dreaming the bear's death. The final death agony of the poet-shaman-dreamer can easily be read as the moment of greatest artistic risk, when the flux of experience yields to the stasis of form.

> and now the breeze
> blows over me, blows off
> the hideous belches of ill-digested bear blood
> and rotted stomach
> and the ordinary, wretched odor of bear,
>
> blows across
> my sore, lolled tongue a song
> or screech, until I think I must rise up
> and dance. And I lie still.

Only by digesting the blood that leaked into his stomach, that is, only by destroying himself, could the bear have lived; and such self-transcendence, Kinnell seems to be saying, can only be achieved by someone tracking down and recording the experience. Such evidence as becomes available for this act may only be a carcass, a remnant of what has "just occurred"; but, through emphatic dream-work, through poetry, such exploration and attentiveness can be the source of new life. Again, from "Poetry, Personality, and Death":

> The death of the self I seek, in poetry and out of poetry, is not a drying up or withering. It is a death, yes, but a death out of which one might hope to be reborn more giving, more alive, more open, more related to natural life. . . . For myself, I would like a death that would give me more loves, not fewer. And greater desire, not less.

The song may be no more than a screech, but it still expresses the organism's need to come to terms with its environment, and for Kinnell such a coming to terms involves growth. Throughout his poetry there flows the awareness that growth involves a kind of dying, and *The Book of Nightmares* becomes the fullest statement of this theme. Though the theme itself might be expressed as a paradox, the mode of its expression in the poems remains that of empathetic immersion, rather than that of ironic suspension.

Empathy as Kinnell employs it in *The Book of Nightmares* makes most statements about his "themes" appear reductive. In a poem that uses ironic tension suspended throughout a logical structure, the thematic argument still constitutes a weakened paraphrase of what the poem "really says," but this difficulty of determining what the poem "says" is geometrically increased when the poem uses an affective structure, articulated more by associative links than by a deductive sequence. When Susan Sontag called for an "erotics rather than a hermeneutics" of art, she was asking for a method much more suited for a postmodernist, nonironic literature. Such an approach might best lead us into this book of Kinnell's, a book densely palpable in its concern with the suffering flesh and peaked with frequently climactic longings. As Robert Bly says, "in poems ideas lie curled under tree roots, only a strong odor of fur indicating anything is there," though we should add that this is certainly truer for the poems of which Bly approves than for other, more "thematically consistent" poetry. It might be possible to indicate the change from a thematic, "argued" poetry to an associative poetry, of which *The Book of Nightmares* represents such a brilliant example, by considering as symptomatic the change from a predominant use of visual imagery to a more and more frequent use of olfactory and gustatory images. "The rank flavor of blood" in "The Bear" controls the affective energies in that poem much more strongly than do any of the visual images it contains. But perhaps the best way to appreciate *The Book of Nightmares,* or rather our experience of it, is to plunge into it, gathering and sorting ideas only as they become dominant.

There are ten poems in *The Book of Nightmares,* each with seven sections. Like the Commandments with alchemical glosses, the poems are about holiness grossly apprehended in a world charred by ignorance and intensity. The titles of the individual poems—"The Dead Shall Be Raised Incorruptible," "The Call Across the Valley of Not-Knowing," "Lastness"—are like titles of religious tracts or gnostic testaments; yet enough narrative fragments and images recur and develop from poem to poem to make the book a considerable whole. Inside each of the ten poems, the sections vary in texture, pace, intensity, and mode. Some are exacting transcriptions of climactic moments; others are quiet, loving exempla, or mysterious, mystically symbolic constructs. The subtle syntax, often articulating the curve of a perception or the morphology of an emotion, echoes the sort of thing that we saw at the end of "Night in the Forest."

Complex and rich as all this is, the voice that sustains itself and discovers itself throughout the poems remains somehow straightforward. It's almost as if Kinnell constantly and innocently surprises himself, finding, "as he obeys the necessity and falls," that "the dead lie, / empty, filled, at the beginning, / and the first / voice comes craving again out of their mouths." The young daughter who "puts / her hand / into her father's mouth, to take hold of / his song" is the initial addressee of the book (if such a spirit can be described by that rhetorical term), and her innocent grasping after the human voice stands for the central mystery that is both the cause and the occasion of Kinnell's book. Again, the human face and the work of art are the key traces of emotion.

In Kinnell's poetry, deeply human utterances are like animals. They are best witnessed as expressive gestures. The bear that concluded *Body Rags* makes several reappearances in this book, in several guises. Nowhere does he speak, but he is witness to human speech whether he "sits alone / on his hillside, nodding from side / to side" or is "floundering through chaos / in his starry blubber" as Ursa Major. Notice too the shifting perspective, the sudden awareness of infinite extension for the bear, something that happens frequently in these poems. Other images besides the bear recur, each equally part of the failed flesh of the world as well as of its fulfillment. A decapitated hen becomes a henflower, filled with a "mass of tiny, / unborn eggs, each getting / tinier and yellower as it reaches back toward / the icy pulp / of what is." An unborn child can "rouse himself / with a huge, fishy thrash, and resettle in his darkness."

The Book of Nightmares, filled with obsessive images, carries back from the darkness a "languished alphabet." But this set of characters can spell more than objects; it speaks as well of people and events. The daughter who appears in the first and the son who hears the final reflections of the poem are just two, though the two most important, of the people with whom Kinnell converses. Indeed, if one were to formulate a thematic statement equivalent to the poem's energies, that statement would have to recognize the daughter's birth and the poet's own imagined death as the terminal points of the work. There is also a "stranger extant in the memory" though extinct from the palpable world, perhaps a suicide, but certainly a possessed individual who defines for the poet not only the limits of pain but also the body that suffers, "all bodies, one body, one light / made of everyone's darkness together."

Again, it should be pointed out that the book succeeds beautifully as a whole; but what makes the total more than the sum of the parts is the tough, but complexly responsive, sense of form that Kinnell has discovered for his own voice. Each of the ten poems is variously incendiary and heuristic. The poet's attention burns through level after level, each vision catching up sparks and flashes from other sightings. The fires of the world must be met with fire if the poet is to truly discover all the edges of his possibilities. "Somewhere / in the legends of blood sacrifice / the fatted calf / takes the bonfire into his arms, and *he* / burns *it*."

Destructive though the element of fire may be, Kinnell's forms are always instructive. There is an almost didactic tone in some parts of this book, a didacticism close to the evangelical. (That alone should make the book distinct from the dominant modern mode of irony.) But the poet draws back from priesthood because he continually rediscovers himself, and discovers in himself "the hunger to be new." Proposing new visions, like Adam he awakes to find them true: "The witness trees heal / their scars at the flesh fire." Nightmares are incendiary, but the book is heuristic. Or, to put it another way, what we see in our nightmares will surely char us unless we can transcribe it. The shaman-speaker of the last poem in *Body Rags* ends his days wondering; but in this later book, the shaman-speaker is closer to the answer to that question, "what . . . was the rank flavor of blood . . . by which I lived?" Again, it is through dream that the answer is formulated:

> a face materializes into your hands,
> on the absolute whiteness of pages
> a poem writes itself out: its title—the dream
> of all poems and the text
> of all loves—"Tenderness toward Existence."

Once more the human face and the poetic text coincide to register the vision. Learn, he tells his child, "to reach deeper / into the sorrows / to come," anticipate the "still undanced cadence of vanishing." Then, with the child soothed and put back to sleep, he adds a promise. The promise is to learn, even if the lesson is preceded by destruction, and the promise constitutes Kinnell's testament.

> Little sleep's-head sprouting hair in the moonlight,
> when I come back
> we will go out together,
> we will walk out together among
> the ten thousand things,
> each scratched too late with such knowledge, *the*
> *wages of dying is love.*

Kinnell has discovered his own way of looking at things here, and though irony may be weakened, certainly American poetry is the stronger for it.

ALFRED CORN

A Magma of Interiors

"To create a work of art that the critic cannot even talk about ought to be the artist's chief concern," John Ashbery has said (*Art News,* May 1972). This statement was made about painters, but there's every chance Ashbery would appropriate that concern for poetry as well. He said, in another review, "Poets when they write about artists always tend to write about themselves." The ambition to outdistance criticism can arise simply as a human dislike of being pinned down—"Is that all there is?"—but mainly indicates a commitment to innovation and evolution in art. A recurrent problem in the evolution of twentieth-century art is that so many writers, not content with being *absolument moderne,* have then supposed they ought to be futuristic; and what is more poignant than yesterday's imagination of the future? In practice, the will to innovation often produces works nobody can talk about, yes, but more to the point, works that nobody *cares* to talk about.

This does not apply to John Ashbery. His originality is, unmistakably, the kind that comes as a by-product of sincerity. One feels that Ashbery would consider it somehow "false" to write with any greater reliance on conventions of communication as they already exist—even if those conventions included some established by the early work of John Ashbery. In short, his achievement is a *surpassing* achievement.

All of Ashbery's books have been difficult to talk about, and *Self-Portrait in a Convex Mirror* resists analysis and evaluation as valiantly as the

From *Parnassus* 4, no. 1 (Fall 1975). © 1976 by the Poetry in Review Foundation.

others. Still, the merit of his work now seems to be evident to just about everybody, at least the work beginning with *The Double Dream of Spring,* including *Three Poems,* and culminating with the poems now collected in this volume. In this climate of admiration and critical hesitation it's possible to conclude that some kind of corner has been turned in the movement—I don't say progress—of literature. Although Richard Howard, Harold Bloom, and David Kalstone have broken or are breaking important critical ground in Ashbery criticism, at present, and of necessity, it remains largely a project. What's most obvious to me now is simply the great pleasure, interest, and even the amazement *Self-Portrait* affords; and of course my assignment here is not an overall assessment, but rather the review of a book.

It's tempting to fall back on the methods of apophantic or "negative" theology and list everything the poems in this volume are *not,* but I think I'll plunge right in and say what they are, at least how the majority of them function for one reader. The poems seem to be imitations of consciousness, "meditations" about the present, including the moment of writing. Their ambition is to render as much of psychic life as will go onto the page— perceptions, emotions, and concepts, memory and daydream, thought in all of its random and contradictory character, patterned according to the "wave interference" produced by all the constituting elements of mind—a "magma of interiors," one of the poems puts it.

Ashbery's method is allusive, associative, and disjunctive, rather than logical, dramatic, or narrative. A typical extended poem will launch itself, or maybe wake up to find itself already in transit, throw out a fertile sugges- tion, make connections, go into reverse, change key, short-circuit, suffer en- lightenment, laugh, nearly go over the edge, regard itself with disbelief, irony, and pathos, then sign off with an inconclusive gesture. The texture of many of the poems reminds me of Gaudí's mosaics in the Barcelona Parque Guell, where broken-up fragments of colored tile with all kinds of figurations— Arabic-geometrical, floral, pictorial—are carefully reassembled in a new and satisfying whole:

> Nathan the Wise is a good title it's a reintroduction
> Of heavy seeds attached by toggle switch to long loops leading
> Out of literature and life into worldly chaos in which
> We struggle two souls out of work for it's a long way back to
> The summation meanwhile we live in it "gradually getting used to"
> Everything and this overrides living and is superimposed on it
> As when a wounded jackal is tied to a waterhole the lion does come
>
> ("Lithuanian Dance Band")

It's possible of course to consider this kind of poetry not simply an "imitation of consciousness" but rather a new synthetic kind of experience too underdetermined or maybe overdetermined to render consciousness accurately, and so existing on a purely contemplative, aesthetic plane. Obviously, these two efforts overlap and blend: "imitation" in art is never duplication, and it always involves some synthesis; but nothing lifelike can be synthesized in art unless it can seem to belong to consciousness. In the measure, then, that an imitation becomes more stylized and synthetic, its resemblance to anyone's consciousness proportionately decreases—it becomes more purely artful. I don't see the poems in *Self-Portrait* as all occupying a fixed point on the spectrum that moves from direct representation of a stream of consciousness to a purely composed and synthetic experience. It's like the new mixed suiting materials—some are more synthetic than others. Nor would I assume that any of the poems were pure products of "automatic writing." If there's an automatic writer that can rap out phrases like the following, one wants the thing installed immediately:

> This was one of those night rainbows
> In negative color. As we advance, it retreats; we see
> We are now far into a cave, must be. Yet there seem to be
> Trees all around, and a wind lifts their leaves, slightly.
>
> ("Märchenbilder")

In a sense, all good writing is an "imitation of consciousness" insofar as that is compatible with the selectivity required for effective, beautiful communication. A special quality of consciousness as imitated by Ashbery, however, is its inclusiveness, or, more precisely, its magnification: into these poems come minute or translucent mental events that would escape a less acute gaze, an attention less rapt. It's the same degree of magnification, I think, used to apprehend the *tropismes* in Nathalie Sarraute's early fiction, though Ashbery lacks the fury and venom characteristic of her work. In this poetry, the unconscious—that misnomer—is in agreeable tension with the conceptual, composing mind; the free interweaving of the known and the about-to-be-known makes for a rich experiential texture in which guesswork, risk, and discovery contribute almost a tactile quality to the overall patterning.

Imitating consciousness, or the stream of consciousness, as a writing method is sown with thistles for any writer without genius or at least without a mental complexion as special and original as John Ashbery's. Zany, elegiac, informed—and sometimes interestingly deformed—by an acquaintance with arcane or demotic or technological subject matter, it's a sensibility one thread of which has been described by the narrator of *A Season in Hell*:

> I liked idiotic paintings, carvings over doorframes, vaudeville drop-scenes, sign-boards, dimestore prints, antiquated literature, church Latin, pornographic books with bad spelling, novels by our grandmothers, fairy tales, children's books, old operas, silly lyrics, uncouth meters.

Cultural allusion in Ashbery goes high as well as low—classic and sometimes obscure works of music, painting, and literature come into mention, without, however, being presented as "letters of credit," as they sometimes are with insecure writers; so that it would be wrong to call Ashbery's poetry "literary." The charge more often than not is made disingenuously, by the way. No subject matter, I think, is safely out of poetry's reach, even literary subject matter. It strikes me as unnatural, even artificial, to proscribe literary or cultural allusion from poetry in the age of the paperback, the LP, and color reproduction. If recondite allusion is a fault, then it ought to be acknowledged that, at present, readers of poetry are more likely to have accurate perceptions and definite feelings about, say, the *Pastoral Symphony,* or *The Cherry Orchard,* or *The Twittering Machine,* than about the Snake River, the hornbeam tree, or the engine of a Diamond Reo. It's true that art can come to conceal the world around us and act as a filter to unmediated experience (not necessarily a bad thing—who would *always* take his experience unmediated?) so that too many people get described as looking like "Bronzinos," and too often office routines are summed up as "Kafkaesque"; but Ashbery avoids that kind of triteness—or any kind of creative abdication. I'd say the cultural allusions were brought in simply as part of an environment, the nuts and bolts of daily life in a cultural capital.

I haven't made a survey, but I believe most of the allusions in this volume have to do with music; in fact, many of the poems take their titles from music: "Grand Galop" (Liszt), "Tenth Symphony" (Mahler's unfinished one?), "Märchenbilder" (the Schumann Opus 113), and "Scheherazade," which could be Rimsky-Korsakov or possibly Ravel, if we allow for English spelling. The texts of the poems include many other musical allusions; and, in a published interview, Ashbery has stated that he often writes with music playing, as a stimulant. All of this ought to be a tip-off. The Symbolist (and Paterian) doctrine that all the arts aspire to the condition of music has been, implicitly, a point of departure for development of modernist art in this century and stands behind the two distinctive tendencies in that art—the drive toward abstraction and the absolute fusion of form and content.

Ashbery is something of an American Symbolist, and his poem "The Tomb of Stuart Merrill" is by way of an *hommage* to a not too well-known American poet of the fin-de-siècle who expatriated, wrote in French, and enlisted in the Symbolist movement. (Incidentally, if mention of the French tradition always comes up in any discussion of Ashbery, nonetheless his Americanness remains obvious and inescapable, as Wallace Stevens's does. Ashbery only occasionally reproduces the formal restraint, sensuousness, and lucidity of characteristically French art; more often his work exhibits the sincerity, distrust of artifice, and studied awkwardness we associate with achievement in the American grain.)

Valéry, a good Symbolist and word-musician, said that content in art was only impure form, and Ashbery's poem "Soonest Mended," two books ago, suggested that meaning might be "cast aside some day / When it had been outgrown." Of course meaning is never outgrown—*magari*—until life is; nor can meaning ever be cast aside, really, because the act of doing so then becomes the "meaning" of a text. No, John Ashbery's poetry does retain content, a content, however, radically fused with form—the result is that paraphrases of the poems are more than usually lame, if not downright impossible. Anyway, I'd rather listen to the *Bagatelles* than read an account of them.

The poems in *Self-Portrait* don't attempt to resemble music by taking the false lead of "verbal music" and onomatopoeia in the manner of, say, Poe, or even of Stuart Merrill. Instead, they find a poetic equivalent of music—a kind of abstraction of argument and theme in which the reader follows a constantly evolving progression of mood, imagery, and tone, with sudden shifts and modulations, and a whole rainbow of emotive and conceptual sonorities; none of this logical or foreseeable and yet, at its best, embodying, in its engagement with chaos—as with Beethoven—an elusive, convincing necessity. Sounds improbable, but, in support, I offer this anecdote: to someone not an expert in poetry I read several pages from *Self-Portrait*; his comment was, "It's like music."

Strangely enough, but rightly, the poems make their music mainly out of visual materials: they are crowded with images, colors, silhouettes. Ashbery has the intense gaze of the child, the divine, or simply the poet, whose vision so absorbs him that the line between the visible world and the self begins to dematerialize, subject to fuse with object. In Mae West's words, "I've been things and seen places."

> The shadow of the Venetian blind on the painted wall,
> Shadows of the snake-plant and cacti, the plaster animals,

Focus the tragic melancholy of the bright stare
Into nowhere, a hole like the black holes in space.
                                                    ("Forties Flick")

I hope I haven't given the impression that these poems lack conceptual
themes altogether. Argument, though not presented directly or logically, fuels
and supervises the poetic proceedings, especially in the title poem. Because
of the great ambiguity (surely more than seven kinds come into play) an
Ashbery poem is likely to become a sort of *auberge espagnole*, to be furnished
out in different schemes by every reader who stops with it; but that's usual
even with less ambiguous poetry. My notion is that everyone ought, according to his lights and darknesses, forge ahead with interpretations—responsible and as little "forged" as possible, of course. Also, I'd suggest that it's
better to talk about the general *area* of meaning being explored, rather than
about hard and fast aphoristic conclusions. But back to our sheep.

The phrase "tragic melancholy" from the above lines sums up for me
the prevailing tone of the book. The tragedy arises from dilemmas of
epistemology and solipsism; and Ashbery's characteristic response to those
dilemmas is neither rage nor despair, but melancholy—a melancholy well
acquainted with terrible necessity but one whose most frequent gesture is a
cosmic, valedictory shrug: things are like that, we have to move on. In good
Pierrot fashion, Ashbery often transmutes melancholy into laughter; *Self-
Portrait* is grandly comic. Anyone who has seen one of the old cartoons in
which cat, coyote, or *luftmensch* walks over the edge of a cliff and navigates
successfully until he perceives it was by blind faith alone knows that laughter
may be metaphysical—and this scenario is one that occurs, varied and
abstracted, in many of Ashbery's poems. Humor in *Self-Portrait,* if often
crackerbarrel or camp, is also cosmic. To describe it, one wants to adapt
Rilke's definition of beauty and say that, for Ashbery, laughter is the beginning of terror we're still just able to bear.

His last book, *Three Poems,* made a kind of secular religion out of
necessity: random and hopeless as our experience is, this book says, we are
nonetheless "saved," and, in some sense, whatever is is OK. This benign
vision has mostly been abandoned in the new book or temporarily supplanted
by an agonized awareness of solipsism and radical uncertainty: Who or
what is "I"? How is it that experience is nothing but ourselves and still,
supremely, *not* ourselves? How can "I" be known to anyone else when "I"
is already a conundrum to itself? To answer these questions is an unrealizable
and therefore noble project. In a number of the new poems Ashbery performs
the poetic equivalent of dead reckoning, whereby the subject moves from

steppingstone to unsteady steppingstone, from bright, fading image to disembodied idea, from recollection to speculation, as if it all might lead to a
conclusion, and not simply an ending. So much inconclusive striving, such
a strenuous inertia, is very painful—all the more because the poems present
the narrator as a kind of Tantalus who both believes and disbelieves in some
final release, a privileged moment just about to occur in which all opposites
will be united:

> The pageant, growing ever more curious, reaches
> An ultimate turning point. Now everything is going to be
> Not dark, but on the contrary, charged with so much light
> It looks dark, because things are now packed so closely together.
> We see it with our teeth. And once this
>
> Distant corner is rounded, everything
> Is not to be made new again. We shall be inhabited
> In the old way, as ideal things came to us,
> Yet in the having we shall be growing, rising above it
> Into an admixture of deep blue enameled sky and bristly gold stars.
>
> ("Voyage in the Blue")

Privileged moments such as this one are presented as evanescent; they solve
nothing permanently and function largely to make us realize the abjection of
ordinary, "underprivileged" consciousness.

When we come to the end of one of these poems we would feel dis-
satisfied, I think, at not having been provided with some kind of resolution
or wisdom if it weren't for the poems themselves, which are, when good,
enough. Two endings:

> The night sheen takes over. A moon of cistercian pallor
> Has climbed to the center of heaven, installed,
> Finally involved with the business of darkness.
> And a sigh heaves from all the small things on earth,
> The books, the papers, the old garters and union-suit buttons
> Kept in a white cardboard box somewhere, and all the lower
> Versions of cities flattened under the equalizing night,
> The summer demands and takes away too much,
> But night, the reserved, the reticent, gives more than it takes.
>
> ("As One Put Drunk into the Packet Boat")

> Yet we are alone too and that's sad isn't it
> Yet you are meant to be alone at least part of the time

You must be in order to work and yet it always seems so unnatural
As though seeing people were intrinsic to life which it just might be
And then somehow the loneliness is more real and more human
You know not just the scarecrow but the whole landscape
And the crows peacefully pecking where the harrow has passed.
                                                ("Lithuanian Dance Band")

So far I've avoided quoting from the title poem (which I take to be the greatest in the volume) because, well, partly because, like any great monument, it has to be approached with caution, you may stumble as you climb up to it. Extraordinary achievement is likely to be greeted with silence—you simply want to point, even though there's an element of rudeness in doing so. Let me try then to do a little more. "Self-Portrait in a Convex Mirror" is an extended poem (reminding one again that in recent years, for whatever reason, the best poems written in America are long poems), and takes its title and subject from an early work of the Mannerist Francesco Parmigianino. The self-portrait is an "anamorphic" painting, that is, one that distorts normal perspective rendering by reproducing either a slant view of the subject or mediating it through non-plane reflecting surfaces such as cylindrical, conic, or convex mirrors. Examples of "slant" rendering (imagine looking at a movie screen from the first row) are found in the notebooks of Leonardo, and they almost always come into play in the trompe-l'oeil effects in late-Renaissance and baroque ceiling frescoes. The first major treatise on anamorphic art was Jean Niceron's *La Perspective curieuse* (1638), which gives techniques for making paintings to be reconstituted in non-plane reflecting surfaces. Jan van Eyck's *Arnolfini marriage group* (1434) and other Renaissance paintings include a convex mirror as a detail in a larger decor, but Parmigianino's self-portrait is the first—as far as I know, the only—portrait in a convex mirror.

Why did he paint himself this way? Why has Ashbery chosen this painting as a subject for poetic meditation? Call it happy accident, and then simply applaud the results—a painting of extraordinary psychological richness and a poem with passages like the following:

But there is in that gaze a combination
Of tenderness, amusement and regret, so powerful
In its restraint that one cannot look for long.
The secret is too plain. The pity of it smarts,
Makes hot tears spurt: that the soul is not a soul,
Has no secret, is small, and it fits
Its hollow perfectly: its room, our moment of attention.

When I read this poem I'm reminded of a slide projector with a button-operated focus. A picture appears, sharp in outline; then another replaces it, out of focus—the vague forms, as they ooze toward clarity, suggest numerous possibilities, but, no, the picture is something different from anything we'd imagined, though the final image now seems inevitable. The next picture is blurred, too, and so engaging in its abstract form, we're tempted to leave it; but, reluctantly, we bring it into focus. When the show is over we realize that all the pictures shared something—they recorded a summer in Italy, or a trip to the National Gallery, or the building of a bridge.

I don't understand every line in "Self-Portrait," nor do I mind much; the coming and going of understanding as managed here is an interesting, involving experience. And poetry is much more a matter of pleasure than it is of argument: we are more readily seduced than convinced, I think. In any case, the freehand development of this poem's principal theme—that art is like a distorting mirror wherein we discover a more engaging, mysterious, and enduring image of ourselves than unmediated experience affords—is carried out with great assurance and variety; gradually, as one reads, the poem attains a supernatural, slow-motion grandeur seldom encountered in poetry in any language, or in art in any medium:

> A peculiar slant
> Of memory that intrudes on the dreaming model
> In the silence of the studio as he considers
> Lifting the pencil to the self-portrait.
> How many people came and stayed a certain time,
> Uttered light or dark speech that became part of you
> Like light behind windblown fog and sand,
> Filtered and influenced by it, until no part
> Remains that is surely you. Those voices in the dusk
> Have told you all and still the tale goes on
> In the form of memories deposited in irregular
> Clumps of crystals. Whose curved hand controls,
> Francesco, the turning seasons and the thoughts
> That peel off and fly away at breathless speeds
> Like the last stubborn leaves ripped
> From wet branches? I see in this only the chaos
> Of your round mirror which organizes everything
> Around the polestar of your eyes which are empty,
> Know nothing, dream but reveal nothing.

Or, finally:

                                    Is there anything
To be serious about beyond this otherness
That gets included in the most ordinary
Forms of daily activity, changing everything
Slightly and profoundly, and tearing the matter
Of creation, any creation, not just artistic creation
Out of our hands, to install it on some monstrous, near
Peak, too close to ignore, too far
For one to intervene? This otherness, this
"Not-being-us" is all there is to look at
In the mirror, though no one can say
How it came to be this way. A ship
Flying unknown colors has entered the harbor.

HAROLD BLOOM

The New Transcendentalism:
The Visionary Strain in Merwin

I mean we have yet no man who has leaned entirely on his character,
and eaten angels' food; who, trusting to his sentiments, found life
made of miracles; who, working for universal aims, found himself fed,
he knew not how; clothed, sheltered, and weaponed, he knew not how,
and yet it was done by his own hands.

EMERSON, *The Transcendentalist* (1842)

M y subject is a still little-noted phenomenon, the revival of the Native Strain or Emersonian vision, in the poetry of my own generation of American poets, born in the decade 1925–1935. I know it could be argued that the true continuators of the Emersonian strain are to be located elsewhere, not so much in the School of Stevens and Frost as in that of Williams and Pound. But I am troubled by the equivocal nature (as it seems to me) of the achievement of Olson, Duncan and their fellows, down to Ginsberg, Snyder and younger figures. Emersonian poetry is a diffuse though recognizable tradition: it includes Jeffers as well as Hart Crane, the Pound of *The Pisan Cantos* together with the Stevens of "The Auroras of Autumn," middle Roethke just as much as the later Aiken. The problem of American poetry after Emerson might be defined as: "Is it possible to be un-Emersonian, rather than, at best, anti-Emersonian?" Poe is not an Emersonian poet, but then he is also not a good poet. Perhaps only our Southern poets, down to Tate and Warren, could be as un-Emersonian as they were anti-Emersonian; the best of them

From *Figures of Capable Imagination.* © 1976 by Harold Bloom. Seabury Press, 1976. Originally entitled "The New Transcendentalism: The Visionary Strain in Merwin, Ashbery, and Ammons."

now (Dickey and Ammons) are wholly Emersonian. Even in Emerson's own time, irreconcilable poets emerged from his maelstrom: Dickinson, Thoreau, Whitman, Very, even Tuckerman, whom Winters judged to be as firm a reaction against Emerson as Hawthorne and Melville were. American Romanticism is larger than Emersonianism, but in our time it may no longer be possible to distinguish between the two phenomena. The prophet of a national poetic sensibility in America was the Concord rhapsode, who contains in the dialectical mysteries of his doctrines and temperament very nearly everything that has come after.

[I will treat here] a representative text by the indubitably representative poet of my generation, the Protean Merwin. The poem is the wonderful "The Way to the River" from the volume, *The Moving Target,* of 1963. As the poem is about fifty lines, I will summarize rather than quote it entire. Addressed to the poet's wife, the poem is a kind of middle-of-the-journey declaration, a creedal hymn reaffirming a covenant of love and a sense of poetic vocation. Historically (and prophetically) the poem sums up the dilemma of "the Silent Generation" of young Americans, on the eve of the astonishing change (or collapse) of sensibility that was to begin at Berkeley in 1964. After nearly a decade, one sees how brief an episode (or epicycle) this Time of Troubles was. Merwin, with his curious proleptic urgency, memorably caught the prelude to that time:

> The way to the river leads past the names of
> Ash the sleeves the wreaths of hinges
> Through the song of the bandage vendor
>
> I lay your name by my voice
> As I go
>
> The way to the river leads past the late
> Doors and the games of the children born looking backwards
> They play that they are broken glass
> The numbers wait in the halls and the clouds
> Call
> From windows
> They play that they are old they are putting the horizon
>
> Into baskets they are escaping they are
> Hiding
>
> I step over the sleepers the fires the calendars
> My voice turns to you.

This is the "poverty" of Emerson and Stevens: imaginative need. Merwin joins a tradition that includes the E. A. Robinson of "The Man Against the Sky," the Frost of "Directive," the Stevens of "The Auroras of Autumn" as he too follows Emerson in building an altar to the Beautiful Necessity:

> To the city of wires I have brought home a handful
> Of water I walk slowly
> In front of me they are building the empty
> Ages I see them reflected not for long
> Be here I am no longer ashamed of time it is too brief its hands
> Have no names
> I have passed it I know
>
> Oh Necessity you with the face you with
> All the faces
>
> This is written on the back of everything
>
> But we
> Will read it together.

The Merwin of this—still his present phase—began with the central poem, "Lemuel's Blessing," which follows the Smart of "Jubilate Agno" for its form (as do so many recent American poets, including Ginsberg, Strand, Donald Finkel) but which is also an Emersonian manifesto. Addressing a Spirit ("You that know the way") Merwin prayed: "Let the memory of tongues not unnerve me so that I stumble or quake." This hymn to Self-Reliance expanded into the most ambitious poem of *The Moving Target*, a majestic celebration of what Emerson called the Newness, "For Now": "Goodbye what you learned for me I have to learn anyway / You that forgot your rivers they are gone / Myself I would not know you." In *The Lice*, his next volume (and his best), Merwin defined the gods as "what has failed to become of us," a dark postscript to the Emersonian insistence that the poets are as liberating gods. The poems of *The Lice* are afflicted by light, as in this wholly characteristic brief lyric, the poignant "How We Are Spared":

> At midsummer before dawn an orange light returns
>   to the mountains
> Like a great weight and the small birds cry out
> And bear it up.

With his largest volume, *The Carrier of Ladders*, Merwin appears to have completed his metamorphosis into an American visionary poet. The book's most astonishing yet most problematic poems are four ode-like

"Psalms," subtitled: "Our Fathers," "The Signals," "The September Vision" and "The Cerements." No recent American poet, not even the Roethke of *The Far Field* or Dickey in his latest work, has attempted so exalted a style:

> I am the son of hazard but does my prayer reach you O star of
>   the uncertain
> I am the son of blindness but nothing that we have made
>   watches us
> I am the son of untruth but I have seen the children in Paradise
>   walking in pairs each hand in hand with himself
> I am the son of the warder but he was buried with his keys
> I am the son of the light but does it call me Samuel or Jonah
> I am the son of a wish older than water but I needed till now
> I am the son of ghosts clutching the world like roads but
>   tomorrow I will go a new way.

The form is again that of the "Jubilate Agno," but the most important line in this first "Psalm," and in all of Merwin, is very far from Smart's pious spirit:

> I am the son of the future but my own father.

As a poet, this latest Merwin hardly approaches that impossible self-begetting; the accent of the Pound-Eliot tradition hovers everywhere in even the most self-consciously bare of these verses. Merwin is more impressive for his terrible need, his lust for discontinuity, than for any actual inventiveness. The poignance of his current phase is the constant attempt at self-reliance, in the conviction that only thus will the poet *see*. Merwin's true precursors are three honorable, civilized representative poets: Longfellow and MacLeish and Wilbur, none of whom attempted to speak a Word that was his own Word only. In another time, Merwin would have gone on with the cultivation of a more continuous idiom, as he did in his early volumes, and as Longfellow did even in the Age of Emerson. The pressures of the quasi-apocalyptic 1960s have made of Merwin an American Orphic bard despite the sorrow that his poetic temperament is not at home in suffering the Native Strain. No poet legitimately speaks a Word whose burden is that his generation will be the very last. Merwin's litanies of denudation will read very oddly when a fresh generation proclaims nearly the same dilemma, and then yet another generation trumpets finality.

Merwin's predicament (and I hope I read it fairly, as I am not unsympathetic to his work) is that he has no Transcendental vision, and yet feels impelled to prophesy. What is fascinating is that after one hundred and thirty years, the situation of American poetry is precisely as it was when Emerson wrote his loving but ironic essay on his younger contemporaries and followers, *The Transcendentalist*, where they are seen as exposing our poverty but also their own. With that genial desperation (or desperate geniality) that is so endearing (and enraging) a quality in his work, Emerson nevertheless urged his followers out into the wilderness:

> But all these of whom I speak are not proficients; they are novices; they only show the road in which man should travel, when the soul has greater health and prowess. Yet let them feel the dignity of their charge, and deserve a larger power. Their heart is the ark in which the fire is concealed which shall burn in a broader and universal flame. Let them obey the Genius then most when his impulse is wildest; then most when he seems to lead to uninhabitable deserts of thought and life; for the path which the hero travels alone is the highway of health and benefit to mankind. What is the privilege and nobility of our nature but its persistency, through its power to attach itself to what is permanent?

Merwin prays to be sustained during his time in the desert, but his poems hardly persuade us that his Genius or Spirit has led him into "uninhabitable deserts of thought and life." Readers distrustful of *The Carrier of Ladders* either emphasize what they feel is a dominance of style over substance or they complain of spiritual pretentiousness. What I find more problematic is something that Emerson foresaw when he said of his Transcendentalist that "He believes in miracle, in the perpetual openness of the human mind to new influx of light and power; he believes in inspiration, and in ecstasy," and yet went on to observe that such a youth was part of an American literature and spiritual history still "in the optative mood." Merwin's optative mood seems only to concern his impersonal identity as poet-prophet; instead of a belief in an influx of light and power, he offers us what we might contrive to know anyway, even if we had not been chilled with him by his artful mutations:

> To which I make my way eating the silence of animals
> Offering snow to the darkness
>
> Today belongs to few and tomorrow to no one.

Emerson's favorite oracular guise was as an Orphic poet. Of the Orphic deities—Eros, Dionysus, and Ananke—Merwin gives us some backward glances at the first, and a constant view of the last, but the Dionysiac has gone out of his poetry. Without the Bacchic turbulence, and haunted by a light that he presents as wholly meaningless, Merwin seems condemned to write a poetry that is as bare of true content as it is so elegantly bare in diction and design. Only the *situation* of the Emersonian Transcendentalist or Orphic Poet survives in Merwin; it is as though for him the native strain were pure strain, to be endured because endurance is value enough, or even because the eloquence of endurance is enough.

RICHARD HOWARD

"The Body Wakes to Burial"

Not margins but centers, not edges but spaces, not contiguities but distances: the thematic insistence of this poet—who by forty had written four volumes of poetry, two in verse and two (it is tempting to say) inversely—is plain, indeed is plane: from Martins Ferry, Ohio, to Stateline, Nevada, with significant stopovers in Minneapolis and in Fargo, North Dakota, it is a landlocked, borderless life whose terms are *spread out,* articulated by James Wright in a dialect of dispossession and deprival, "a vowel of longing" unique among his contemporaries for its final bleakness, singular in its ultimate solitude:

> To speak in a flat voice
> Is all that I can do . . .
> I have gone forward with
> Some, a few lonely some.
> They have fallen to death.
> I die with them.

The wonder, though, and in this case the reward, is that when a poet's diction, his controlled utterance, has come—or has over immense portages been brought—to a true accommodation of his desire (*his* desire, not the desire of the poem, which is for completion, for repetition, for return; and not the desire of the culture, which is for comfort, for confirmation, for

---

From *Alone with America.* © 1980 by Richard Howard. Atheneum, 1980. Originally entitled "James Wright: 'The Body Wakes to Burial.'"

repose), it should thereupon be adequate as well to fulfillment, to realization, to the ecstasy which is beyond desire because it is unknown to desire; at these moments—they are only moments, of course, and they are few enough in any man's poetry, readily singled out in James Wright's—poverty and riches change place, altitude and expanse are transformed into each other, and the very immensity of space is concentrated into incandescence:

> Miles off, a whole grove silently
> Flies up into the darkness.
> One lamp comes on in the sky,
> One lamp on the prairie.

The point is to reach a point, literally, of no return, a true event which would be one that cannot recur—as Wallace Stevens calls it, "an escape from repetition, a happening in space and the self that touched them both at once and alike." For this escape, for this event the instruments of a *convention* are felt to be thereby not instruments but obstacles. Traditional versification, rhyme, the discourse which submits itself to an asymptotic norm sensed to govern *the line* however great the departures from it—these are, for James Wright's ultimate art, no means at all. Yet it is an *art*, not merely a compliance, not merely a rapture, which we are entitled to see as Wright's achievement. An art constituting itself out of what it gives away, and out of the very process of giving itself away. It is René Char's dictum that Wright quotes (Char, of whom he writes: "one passes inevitably from a perception of the form to a sense of the man," a passage we must make in Wright's own case) in his effort to constitute an *ars poetica: "to escape the shameful constraint of choosing between obedience and madness."* And the wisdom which sees a shameful constraint not only in obedience—in a subservience to the instruments—and not only in madness—in eschewing the instruments—but in the obligation to choose between them, the wisdom which would avoid that alternative and fashion out of its very abjuring what James Wright calls his "just devotions," conscious that "the spirit thrives / out of its own defeat"—that chastened wisdom is what we may most admire, I think, and what we must in any case admit in this poet's ecstatic apprehension, his final solution.

But I am getting ahead of myself, or ahead of him, for that exact calling of the turn, or of the unreturning, was not to be within James Wright's reach, not even within his range, for a long time; the true vocation of this poet, "a meagre Art /acquired by Reverse," in Dickinson's phrase, follows after not a false calling but an impertinent one, as Wright himself has insisted ("whatever I write from now on will be entirely different . . . I am finished with what I was doing"). Though it is the "art acquired by reverse" that we must enter upon and, in the wrestler's sense, close with, we must not ignore what the poet reversed *from*. We must not succumb to the temptation of despising a poet's created world just because he has desisted from it; indeed it is rather our obligation, when a conversion has been effected and another covenant vouchsafed, to trace connections, to show the Old Adam lurking about the confines of the New Jerusalem:

> A man ought to hide sometimes on the banks
> Of the sky,
> And some human beings
> Have need of lingering back in the fastidious half light
> Even at dawn.

What counts, then, and what is to be accounted for, when a man divides himself into a Before and an After, is the evidence throughout the change, at every stage of the transformation scene, of a great constancy, of a loyalty to the altering self which informs equally these six lines of longing for a lost *pietas* ("we have coddled the gods away"), addressed to a singer of the old religion in the first book, *The Green Wall* (1957), lines indulging, a little, the alternative of "obedience" in their rhythmic docility:

> The sounds go on, and on,
> In spite of what the morning
> Or evening dark has done.
> We have no holy voices
> Like yours to lift above us,
> Yet we cannot be still

and these six lines, or rather loops, of the dénouement, the unknotting of links from the latest book, *Shall We Gather at the River* (1968), lines running, in their slack caprice, the other risk, the risk (by a like aspiration to ascent and to release from earth) that only the grave can afford:

> I want to be lifted up
> By some great white bird unknown to the police
> And soar for a thousand miles and be carefully hidden
> Modest and golden as one last corn grain,
> Stored with the secrets of the wheat and the mysterious lives
> Of the unnamed poor.

What makes common ground, though, between Wright's early and outward *vision of landscape* and his ultimate and endogenous *landscape of vision*; what is partaken of equally by the luxuriant account of

> things that lured me to decay:
> The ground's deliberate riches, fallen pears,
> Bewildered apples blown to mounds of shade

and by the harsher, internalized accents, a decade and three books beyond, or rather inside of

> shattered hillsides of yellow trees
> In the autumn of my blood where the apples
> Purse their wild lips and smirk knowingly
> That my love is dead;

what binds the outer version of natural process ("things that lured me") to the inner one ("trees in the autumn of my blood") is, precisely, *common ground,* the earth which "knows how to handle the great dead," the earth which is "this only place / we ever dared believe, for all its scars." That is why so many of these poems, early and late, require the hard ground ("the living need not seek / for love but underfoot"), require what Wright calls "the perpetual savagery of graves" to ballast and sustain his enormous spiritual yearning:

> Walking here lonely and strange now, I must find
> A grave to prod my wrath
> Back to its just devotions.

It is not until the poet is able to see the entire earth and all its processes of fruition and decay *inside* himself, contained by the arena of his own body just as "earth contains . . . a remembrancer of wild arenas we avoid," that he can stop separating, can stop alienating himself from "our gathering of the cheated and the weak," the ghosts and criminals and lunatics and perverts, the dispossessed who haunt him from the start ("My Grandmother's Ghost," "She Hid in the Trees from the Nurses," "A Poem About George Doty in the Death House," "To a Fugitive," "Sappho," "At the Executed Murderer's Grave," "The Poor Washed Up by Chicago Winter"—this is only a partial list). It is not until Wright has made himself over, from *The Branch Will Not Break* (1963) onward, converted himself from an elegiast into an apocalypst, discovering the whole of nature not as a rhythmical series of sad events but as the singular content of a ceaseless human soma:

How many scrawny children
Lie dead and half hidden among frozen ruts
In my body, along my dark roads?

—that he can mount to that ecstasy so marvelously his own, momentarily
given and not repeated but possibly followed by yet another, which is the
achievement of his later poems.

Few poets, one may say, enable us to take the expression *ground form*
so literally as James Wright enforces, implants the acceptation: the easy
sorrows, the more difficult splendors of earth engender his utterance; the
wrecked landscapes of the Ohio strip-mines and the ruined lives scattered
upon them compel a recognition, once the enemy is discovered within rather
than projected upon the surrounding sordor, that mortality is its own re-
compense, that "bodiless yearnings make no music fall" and that

Only the living body calls up love,
That shadow risen casually from stone
To clothe the nakedness of bare desire.

The moment of discovery, of acknowledgment that the arena is the self and
not the sociology of Midwestern erosion, is recorded pointedly in *Saint Judas*
(1959), in the final couplet of a poem called "A Prayer in My Sickness":

I have lain alien in myself so long,
How can I understand love's angry tongue?

The recognition that one must be a naturalized inhabitant of the self in order
to converse with love is crucial to Wright's persistence as a poet—"the main
thing is not to get on in the world but to get home," Wright says of Theodor
Storm, and of himself in that somatic landscape of his own discovery:

Close by a big river, I am alive in my own country
I am home again.

When what you have always thought was outside yourself and therefore
against you is found to be within and therefore with you, you can deal with
its mortal as with its ecstatic consequences. For the creating mind, Wright
has remarked of Char, there is no such thing as irrelevancy—the corporeal
and the chthonic are collected into "a single human word for love of air."
"The hero," as Wright says of Gabriel Oak in Hardy's *Far from the Madding
Crowd*, "is always surrounded by things that fill him with inexorable affection and with which, at last, he becomes miraculously identified." We are
reminded, too, that Hardy is one of those few poets of the "voiceless earth"

who has helped Wright on to his "secret he learned from the ground," as he says in his early poem "At Thomas Hardy's Birthplace, 1953." Few poets, then, except the Hardy whom Wright so beautifully apostrophizes in a characteristically self-accusing poetics have had the revelatory sense ("earth is a door") of significant soil:

> We may turn for nourishment to authors who humbly take walks in the evening over fields and under trees, hold out their words and stand patiently until the night fills them. But our usual impatience is our blindness, our abstraction is our coarseness, and our sloth is our starvation. We fail in the grace to stand still. We want devoutness: the grace to see.

Impatience, abstraction and sloth are the adversaries here, and as well as the Hardy buried at Stinsford who knew, Wright says, "the hidden joy, the secret hurt," we might deduce from this remarkable little passage other masters, native practitioners of the opposing virtues which afford "the grace to see": endurance, exactitude and labor. "Authors who humbly take walks in the evening over fields and under trees"—it is easy enough to divine that the author of

> A sense of ocean and old trees
> Envelops and allures him;
> Tradition touching all he sees,
> Beguiles and reassures him

would beguilingly and reassuringly rehearse for James Wright the stoicism he required to sustain his suffering; and that the author of "Acquainted with the Night" is precisely the man—

> When far away an interrupted cry
> Came over houses from another street,
> But not to call me back or say good-by

—to hold out his words and stand patiently until the night fills them. We have divined the more easily, of course, because Wright names his nourishing authors: "I have tried very hard to write in the mode of Edward Arlington Robinson and Robert Frost," he says about his first two books—it is after *Saint Judas* that whatever he writes is intended to be "entirely different." And when we read a poem like "The Alarm" in the latter book, a poem as scrupulously patient with suffering, a suffering without hope of anything better, as anything in Robinson, as carefully decasyllabic, concrete and deliberate as anything in Frost, then we must recognize the success of the effort ("I have tried very hard . . ."), the adequacy of the means to the meaning, and the voice entangled, as Frost puts it, in the words and fastened to the page for the imagination's ear:

> When I came back from my last dream, when I
> Whirled in the morning snowfall up the lawn,
> I looked behind me where my wings were gone,
> Rusting above the snow, for lack of care,
> A pile of rakes and shovels rotted away.
> Tools of the world were crumbling into air,
> And I, neither the living nor the dead,
> Paused in the dusk of dawn to wonder why
> Any man clambers upward out of shade
> To rake and shovel all his dust away.

Yet what if a poet discovered, in the very comforts of a recurrent natural order,

> Where the sea moves the word moves, where the sea
> Subsides, the slow word fades with lunar tides

—what if a poet discovered that he was after not adequacy ("and things were as they were") but ecstasy ("you wake in a book that is shining"), not the lament of encirclement (what else is such verse as the stanza from "The Alarm" I have quoted here?) but the luminosity of a breakthrough ("the moon suddenly stands up in the darkness / and I see that it is impossible to die")?

Shakespeare, of course, accounts best for what we might call the consolation-theory of a poetry by natural analogy. "Praising what is lost / makes the remembrance dear . . . We are reconciled," says the King in *All's Well that Ends Well*—yet what if it is precisely the impulse to end well, to praise what is lost and to cherish memory, the impulse to be *reconciled* that a poet wants to be rid of? The poetry of recurrence (which most of us think of as poetry itself, for we all prefer, most of the time, expedience to ecstasy), the traditional pattern which alone can accommodate an experience of the negative, can transform what is a known loss into at least the comfort of elegy— Wright rejects these things as a betrayal of the life he knows to be within him; he does not want *his* poetry to be a consolation any more, an anesthesia, as it is shown to be at the end, say, of "The Alarm":

And I was home now, bowing into my dust,
To quicken into stupor one more time,
One of the living buried like the dead.

He wants his poetry to be a *finding*, an *invention* in the literal sense of
the word, not a loss comforted by rite but a discovery, however brutal, made
bearable by art. It is of course other men's art which helps him to his own
performance. I have already mentioned Storm as one of Wright's mediating
figures, but it is important to see that Storm—like Hardy, and like Frost and
Robinson, though more intensely, more nakedly—points backward to the
negative experience, the endured suffering, the alienation of self in a *tragicall*
nature ("the autumn landscape where we lay and suffered"). Still, in Storm
there is an ellipsis, a rejection of comfort that suggests, in Wright's translation, for example, of the *Frauen-Ritornelle*, the preliminary to release, the
prelude by comfortless acedia to the real illumination:

Nutmeg herb,
You blossomed once in my great-grandmother's garden;
That was a place a long way from the world, over there.

Dark cypresses—
The world is too interested in gaiety;
It will all be forgotten.

The fragmentary poems in *The Branch Will Not Break* afford many analogies
to this kind of poem, in which the energy of constatation is not allowed to
run out into verse, into some kind of normative, reboant movement, but is
instead checked, baffled, splintered:

The unwashed shadows
Of blast furnaces from Moundsville, West Virginia
Are sneaking across the pits of strip mines
To steal grapes
In heaven.
Nobody else knows I am here.
All right.
Come out, come out, I am dying.
I am growing old.
An owl rises
From the cutter bar
Of a hayrake.

That is not ecstasy, but it is without resignation, and in its silences (the spaces the voice must leave, particularly in the last five lines) affords the likelihood, I think, for a new apprehension, generates a kind of comfortless grief, even an unknown eros. Compare, for example, the first lines of this same poem ("A Message Hidden in an Empty Wine Bottle that I Threw into a Gully of Maple Trees One Night at an Indecent Hour"—the title is certainly a jolt from the frosty pieties, "the cold divinities of death and change" to be met with in the first two books), lines of an insistent cruelty:

> Women are dancing around a fire
> By a pond of creosote and waste water from the river
> In the dank fog of Ohio.
> They are dead.
> I am alone here,
> And I reach for the moon that dangles
> Cold on a dark vine

with these lines from "On the Skeleton of a Hound" from the first book, lines of the same visionary dedication, but self-pitying, plangent, over-determined in their adjustment of lilt to longing:

> Then, suddenly, the hare leaped beyond pain
> Out of the open meadow, and the hound
> Followed the voiceless dancer to the moon,
> To dark, to death, to other meadows where
> Singing young women dance around a fire,
> Where love reveres the living.
>   I alone
> Scatter this hulk about the dampened ground;
> And while the moon rises beyond me, throw
> The ribs and spine out of their perfect shape.

In the phrasing, the fractured but still bleeding bones of *statement* in the later version ("They are dead. I am alone here") we are not permitted to dissolve, as the earlier iambics insist we dissolve, into a cloud, a nimbus of gorgeous condolences, "handy resurrections." Nothing so attractive (and so unreal) as "meadows where singing young women dance around a fire where love reveres the living" is now vouchsafed, but instead "a pond of creosote and waste water from the river in the dank fog of Ohio": the gain in precision, in purpose, is a gainsaying, too, of consolation. The ground is cleared.

In the third and fourth books, *The Branch Will Not Break* and *Shall We Gather at the River,* James Wright reaches occasionally—but it is the occasions which justify the effort, which ransom the expense—beyond even

such rectitude of desolation which is the self's first calisthenic in the achievement of recognition, or identity made ecstatic. And the guide to this final or
at least fulfilling mode of his poetry is an elusive Virgil indeed, the "silence-
haunted" Georg Trakl, whose poems Wright calls—and the relevance to his
own enterprise is patent—"attempts to enter and to recognize one's very
self." With Robert Bly, James Wright has translated twenty of Trakl's poems
"from which all shrillness and clutter have been banished," and the still
raptures of these interior landscapes, with their abrupt drops and ascents
into the "merely personal" and beyond it, certainly qualify and prepare all
that Wright creates in his own broken but incandescent later poems, gen-
erated from moments of beatitude like the one recorded in "Today I Was
So Happy I Made This Poem" and concluding—it is the *summum bonum*
of Wright's whole undertaking—with these lines:

> Each moment of time is a mountain.
> An eagle rejoices in the oak trees of heaven,
> Crying
> *That is what I wanted.*

The aphoristic resonance of this ("aphorisms, representing a knowledge broken," Bacon says), the elliptical *sentences* of some seraphic wanderer, suggest
what Wright found in Trakl's mysterious verses, his statements of stillness:

> I am a shadow far from darkening villages.
> I drank the silence of God
> Out of the stream in the trees.
>
> Cold metal walks on my forehead.
> Spiders search for my heart.
> It is a light that goes on in my mouth.
>
> At night I found myself on a pasture,
> Covered with rubbish and the dust of stars.
> In a hazel thicket
> Angels of crystal rang out once more.

In "Milkweed," for example, the apocalypse is not only invoked, it is *experienced,* reminding us of Éluard's great discovery: "there is another world,
but it is in this one." Wright's ecstasy is earned by a tremendous renunciation, the abjuring of ritual—and in consequence his poems are not lovely,
are not conveyed in a language of polished facets; rather they are splinters,
jagged cleavages on which the sun, momentarily, explodes:

While I stood here, in the open, lost in myself,
I must have looked a long time
Down the corn rows, beyond grass,
The small house,
White walls, animals lumbering toward the barn.
I look down now, It is all changed.
Whatever it was I lost, whatever I wept for,
Was a wild, gentle thing, the small dark eyes
Loving me in secret.
It is here. At a touch of my hand,
The air fills with delicate creatures
From the other world.

In the same book, Wright stands just off the highway to Rochester, Minnesota (a guarantee these epiphanies are real, Wright always locates them in the home counties) watching two Indian ponies; he joins them, plays with them in the pasture at twilight, and suddenly—

Suddenly I realize
That if I stepped out of my body I would break
Into blossom.

By a sensitive enjambment, Wright indicates both the breaking *and* the blossoming here, the surrender of perfection necessary to achieve . . . identity. And in the fourth book, following upon many utterances of despair and deadly terror—

I ride the great stones,
I hide under stars and maples
And yet I cannot find my own face.
In the mountains of blast furnaces,
The trees turn their backs on me

—and upon a discouragement with these United States which is all the more powerful for its regional particulars:

For the river at Wheeling, W. Va.,
Has only two shores:
The one in hell, the other
In Bridgeport, Ohio.

And nobody would commit suicide, only
To find beyond death
Bridgeport, Ohio

—comes one of Wright's finest poems, "Northern Pike," a wonderful con-
jugation of the spoiled and the splendid which *underwrites,* in every sense,
the crippling illumination of the everyday:

> We paused among the dark cat-tails and prayed
> For the muskrats,
> For the ripples below their tails,
> For the little movements that we knew the crawdads were making
>   under water,
> For the right-hand wrist of my cousin who is a policeman.
> We prayed for the game warden's blindness.
> We prayed for the road home.
> We ate the fish.
> There must be something very beautiful in my body,
> I am so happy.

Less rapturous only because it is more inclusive, in its final vision not only
of the possibilities of gratification but of depletion too, is Wright's ultimate
anthem to his body, apostrophized as metonymy and synechdoche at once,
product and arena of his ground form, container and thing contained: "A
Late Autumn Daybreak," in which the poet sets himself free not only from
the fear of death but from the craving for life, not only from the ritual but
from the random, reinventing the very conventions—even rhyme!—he had
had to expunge, and assuming once again the toys as well as the toils of his
art:

> I sat upright and saw the moon
> Blurred in the agony of cold.
> I knew it would be daylight soon.
> Agony, agony, I grew old
> When I dared force my gaze outside
> To the great bough bleeding on dead grass
> To death. My God, I thought, and died.
> That was my branch that broke, alas.
>
> Suddenly I left my body
> And flew straight up into the dawn,
> Crying out holy, holy, holy
> Be the next death I light upon.
> If there be trees, oh waft me down
> Into a body lovingkind;

Leave me aloft, if there be none
To bear me but a leafless wind.

TWO CITIZENS

At the end of his *Collected Poems* (1971), whose motto might well be
a retrospective phrase from *Two Citizens*: "I love myself the ground," James
Wright added some thirty uncollected poems, raucous and even rakish, for
they included a blank page dedicated to his horse which had eaten that
particular poem, and they described with an apposite leer what they were
doing:

> not a poem
> not an apology to the Muse
> but the cold-blooded plea of a homesick Vampire.

The satisfaction of having in one volume most of the best poems of one of
our best poets made me overlook the nature—fragmentary, inchoate, the
vibrato out of control—of those "new poems" at the time, though now I
see they were an alluvial deposit on which *Two Citizens* draws heavily,
manifesting "a deep identity / with something under / the bare stones."
    All these poems are of course written in "the one tongue I can write in
. . . my Ohioan," and they are concerned, as Wright has always been, with
that mythology of the insulted and injured to be located alike in southern
Ohio and the poet's body ("helpless and miserable / dreaming itself / into an
apparition of loneliness"). And they exploit that mythology with the inso-
lence of utter conviction:

> The cracked song
> Of my own body limps into the body
> Of this living place. I have nobody
> To go in with
> But my love who is a woman,
> And my crude dead, my sea,
> My sea, my sepulcher, the crude
> Rhythms of my time.

But so deeply is the poet identified with something which has happened to
him outside the poem that he cannot be bothered to make it into a coherence
within the poem; the divine event is a déjà vu; it is as he says, "a secret of
blossoms we had no business / to understand, only to remember." As no

more than a reader of poems, we remember, certainly—we remember that
particular *stimmung* of James Wright's past,

> That lonely thing
> That fears him, yet comes out
> To look through him and sing;

and we note certain clues toward what is dimly apprehended as a sort of
Ohio Osiris Complex here, the sense of disintegration in dark waters, the
embrace of a tree, and a resurrection ("I rose out of my body so high into /
that sycamore tree that it became / the only tree that ever loved me"). But
my suspicion of Wright's legend of himself as the Torn God is confirmed by
no more than scattered limbs, perhaps appropriately—"wound after wound,
I look for / the tree by the waters"—and in the arrogance of these disjunct,
choking poems, there are but glimpses, for me, of what I divine to be gathering on the far shore, the other side of "that water I rose from." In *Two
Citizens* (Tammuz and Astarte, they are) and the thirty poems which precede
them, I can discern only the night journey, the *sparagmos,* except for sacred
moments like this one:

> There used to be a sycamore just
> Outside Martins Ferry,
> Where I used to go.
> I had no friends there.
> Maybe the tree was no woman,
> But when I sat there, I gathered
> That branch into my arms.
> It was the first time I ever rose.

Years ago, writing about Wright's early work, I spoke of his approach to
"the ecstasy which is beyond desire because it is unknown to desire"; that
is the ecstasy made up to here, but it is not *made* in the poems, it stands
outside them, as of course ecstasy does.

TO A BLOSSOMING PEAR TREE

It has been four years since James Wright's last book, and I had better
loiter a little, I think, over the situation of this most rapt, even stupent of
our lyrists, halting first to say what I mean by calling Wright—whose poems
are so unconcerned with repetition, refrain, or regularity that they are often,
now, in prose—a lyrist at all. Lyric cancels out time, confirms and sustains
a "now" which is invested with significance as long as the lyric structure

(the voice itself, raised, looming and looped about the broken sentences, a narrow rivulet of print between ample meadows of margin) endures, releasing us from the pressure of ulterior things. It is a significance of the divine event, a secret, as Wright says, "of blossoms we had no business / to understand, only to remember." (One figure, here, is the source of Wright's new apostrophe, the object of his attentions, and the subject of his *askesis*: blossoming.) Out of time, the poems are so many clues toward what I have called a sort of Ohio Osiris Complex: the sense of disintegration in dark waters, the embrace of a tree, and a resurrection. But the ecstatic apprehensions of *Two Citizens* (Tammuz and Astarte, they are, though Wright always disguises his theophany as himself and his wife, even giving her a voice, a poem of her own, in this new book) are dimmed now; chastened and cautious ("Saguaro, you are not one of the gods"), a little darkened from—perhaps *by*—his old exaltations, his peerless apocalypse (in which of course the entire earth found its death and rebirth inside the poet's own body, conceived as infinite and eternal), Wright addresses himself, loyal still to his plain chant, his ground bass, to those energies and impulses in nature which are effervescent, fecund and even prodigal. Fifteen years ago, this was his identification:

> Suddenly I realize
> That if I stepped out of my body I would break
> Into blossom.

By a characteristically sensitive emjambment, Wright thus indicated both the breaking *and* the blossoming. But now, in the tormented title poem which confronts, which invokes these same energies and impulses, a discrepancy, an alienation is powerfully mourned; there is no release into ecstasy, merely its notation as otherness, and the human humiliation:

> Young tree, unburdened
> By anything but your beautiful natural blossoms
> And dew, the dark
> Blood in my body drags me
> Down with my brother.

The pear tree is still there, splendid but separate, and the man, in his brotherhood with the wrecked and ruined of his kind, is here:

> How I envy you.
> For if you could only listen

> I would tell you something,
> Something human.

The poems in Wright's lovely new book are all such attestations—diffident yet explicit, careful yet fervent, defeated yet proud—of disjunction, of negation, of (we must say it) failure in his vast project. If he were to succeed, after all, we should not have the poems—we should have silence. But he has failed, and the confession of his failure ("a half-witted angel drawling Ohioan / in the warm Italian rain") constitutes his new book, its resonance greatly enlarged by the poems about Italy, the region around Verona in particular: "It is all right with me to know that my life is only one life. I feel like the light of the river Adige. By this time, we are both an open secret." The poet must still locate the landscape in his own soma, and the fact that Dante has been there before him somehow makes his task if not easier, surely then more alluring:

> In the middle of my own life
> I woke up and found myself
> dying, fair enough, still
> alive in the friendly city
> of my body, my secret Verona,
> milky and green,
> my moving jewel, the last
> pure vein left to me.

By discovering (and perhaps that is why so many of the pieces must be prose here: they are *on the way,* they are not realizations, they are aspirations: lyrical prose) the impossibility of his project (I am not Osiris, after all), Wright has discovered as well the possibility of his poetry ("I know what we call it / most of the time / but I have my own song for it / and sometimes, even today, I call it beauty"). No American poet is so consistent as Wright, so consigned to his peculiar, beautiful doom. The further nuance here is of course the exchange of the ruined American midlands (and the repugnant American public mentality):

> A black crust, America is
> A shallow hell where evil
> Is an easy joke, forgotten
> In a week

for the Italian locus, the places and objects of Verona which afford the poet, which furnish him, his apocalyptic transformations not more easily or more readily, but more ripely; it is here in Italy that the asseveration is most richly to be made:

> it was hard to name
> Which vine, which insect, which wing,
> Which of you, which of me.

Something in his own country has the more painfully cast James Wright out of his own body, and the moments when he finds himself, when he *comes to,* as we say, are more likely to be elsewhere, abroad:

> I am sitting contented and alone in a little park near the Palazzo Scaligeri in Verona, glimpsing the mists of early autumn as they shift and fade among the pines and city battlements on the hills above the river Adige. The river has recovered from this morning's rainfall. It is now restoring to its shapely body its own secret light, a color of faintly cloudy green and pearl.

Now surely such perceptions can be made back home, but there is some function of the self which is available to Wright *over there* and only so: the function is one of transformation, which he has gainsaid among the strip-mines, and the scrap-iron, or which has gainsaid him. "What can I do to join him?" Wright asks about the garter snake basking on a rail, and it is his very question, the interrogation proposed to a condition where being can be shared or participated in more broadly, more fully. The blossoming pear tree is no longer to be found in Wright's own veins and vesicles. The wonder of the book named for this tree is that he has put away any bitterness, any *ressentiment* about the collapse of the eager transaction as it was reported in so many other poems, so many earlier books. There is nothing to do but sit still and look very closely, very carefully at what is in front of your eyes, his eyes; the acknowledgment of the separate life, the contours which are not shared but merely shards, fragments of a unity, a totality inaccessible even to wishing—this acknowledgment makes for a poetry which, by immense repudiations, has come to accept itself, has resigned itself (what else is prose but the resignation of poetry, the submission to an element which makes no stay against that ebbing tide?) to a constatation of being which he cannot become, or rather a becoming which he cannot be; call it an acceptance of mortality rather than a god's estate, of death rather than eternal life. As James Wright asks (in prose): "What color is a hungry shadow?"

RICHARD HOWARD

"Who Will Call
These Things His Own?"

The principal advantage of belonging to, and even—belatedly—of being owned by, a rather traditionless country like America is that the poet has to fall back on the Universe, or at least on the university. Thus a curriculum vitae which appears, as Irving Feldman's does, to be altogether a matter of studying and teaching, of listening in one classroom and lecturing in another, can in fact disguise a heroic conquest of identity, a private anabasis through Western Culture, whose deities and dooms crowd the self with choices, or at least with refusals, until at last one comes in sight of the sea (some vision of a life governed by meaningful limits, measures, repetitions), exultantly shouting "Tenure! Tenure!" but meaning, really, rebirth.

Of course falling back on the Universe, *and* on the university, is not always or even often regarded as an advantage at all for a man's poetry; poetry is so much a matter of local attachments, even when, as in Irving Feldman's case, the poet feels attached to no localities—language itself is a local attachment, and there are no poems written in the universal languages. Yet the universal, and the abstract, and the impersonal as they are accommodated in learning—in the university, in other words—are precisely what the American Jewish poet, by this half of the century, must come to terms with, must master in a life and a country acknowledged to be dispossessed of the past.

Appropriately dedicated to his parents, Feldman's first book, an inves-

From *Alone with America*. © 1980 by Richard Howard. Atheneum, 1980. Originally entitled "Irving Feldman: 'Who Will Call These Things His Own?'"

tigation of the sources of power, a search for the attitude, the posture of survival—

> For me, the line I cannot cross.
> In exile, mourning I endure
> Every dying, every loss.
>
> My eye runs on! my heart clings.
> I wait upon the blackened shore,
> Remembering the time of kings.

—was published in 1961 and called *Works and Days and Other Poems*. The title group is named, I suppose, after Hesiod's caustic maxims intended to inculcate righteousness and efficiency, but in this instance memorializing, rather, the world of Henry Roth and Saul Bellow:

> A liver lounging in a pot;
> Mama boiling the kitchen runes.
> Always I see her face a blot
> In the sacred oval of the spoons.
>
> Grey and sweet and shining eyes,
> Freckled arms that took with ardor
> The scalds and bundles of sacrifice
> —To fill again love's larder.
>
> She kneeled to dust the furniture,
> But rose with an abstracted eye.
> What was it she had seen there?
> In spite of all, people die . . .
>
> The radiator knocked like a ghost,
> Outside, the wind and bawling cats.
> My father nodded at his post,
> Messiah thundered fireside chats.
>
> That all proclaimed the quotidian,
> And should the day ache with glory,
> Prescribed a little medicine.

The novelistic mishmash of housework endured and mortality anticipated, the infirmity which "saw Israel's shining tents / fold up like a doctor's bag" is the *medium,* the substantive level on which Irving Feldman seeks to repossess or repopulate his heritage by a series of dramatic and philosophical personations, emblems of the history he must invent, since nothing, evidently, is given to him outright:

> Here I am stupidly living in sackcloth and ash.
> Why was I born just a year before the Crash?
> Why'd my father lose his lots and his cash
> And go jobless till a gentle lack of courage
> Was inbred? Then why'd I grow in this image?
> How can I be a hero if I'm not half a fake
> Like my cousins Joe and Jake?
> To be Chosen—that means having only one part.
> But if I'm Elect, why all this fat around my heart?
> Why was I born in Brooklyn with the lower middle-classes?
> Is that a hero's place? Was Moses freckled! Samson wear glasses!
> Why me? Haven't You had F.D.R. and Cecil de Mille?
> (Pardon me, O Lord, if I question Your will,
> But wouldn't Seymour or Sherman have done just as well?)
> Why do you tell me to build when I want to destroy?

This instance of the poet as stand-up Jewish tragic (even Lennie Bruce would have had no difficulty finding the appropriate ethnic rhyme for "destroy") suggests how much Feldman has to overcome, how much chattering and whining, before he can confront himself. He is in the vexing situation of the artist who must move from the suburbs to the center of civilization, the center being always the most isolated place—and who must move by his own devices, under his own steam. Yet his devices are remarkable, and the steam he gets up is often powerful enough to whelm the poet's poverty of doctrine by his wealth of dramatic detail. Not only Moses and Samson (without glasses, though isolated: "where's the drunk idolatrous crowd?"), but Prometheus and Narcissus, Adam and Abraham, Theseus and of course the Wandering Jew clutch at his stupent imagination, force him to refashion the myths of heroism from an anti-heroic metal, contaminated by modern plumbing and even a college education: his Prometheus, "alone, and nailed through the heart into nature" suffers "of all things the worst: / to be a victim and have no torturer"; his Samson finds it "better to fall among the evil / than turn to stone standing alone"; his Wandering Jew demands of God:

> Why for the pure task these tools of dirt?
> This abstracted heart, this fever, this world?

Inevitably, gratefully, annihilation appears the proper path to heroic stature—or as one of Feldman's saints puts it, "Self-denial is the self's strongest wine."

Happiest in its dramatic voice, this copious first book—endorsed like a blank check by John Crowe Ransom, who "would not care to limit the extent of [Feldman's] triumph when I think about his promise as a poet," and by Lionel Trilling, who finds "the considerable size of the production in itself a virtue"; in other words, not positively detested by these cautious men— *Works and Days* affords the young poet many occasions to transcend his situation; he is possessed, evidently, by figures of religious authority—saint, prophet, god, and martyr. With the authority of desperation, he speaks in their voices, offers his mewing handful of sacred and mythic negatives ("Although like Theseus I fought, / I have become what I have slain"), perverse, compulsive, haunted by a failure to have acted or even suffered heroically which is the endemic complaint of the American Jew of Feldman's generation; when a god (and it is, characteristically, "a god," not God, that the stage directions specify) speaks to his city "After the Judgment," we hear the poet condemning himself to his identity:

> The destiny you bear! to be as you are.

> To live was always to be judged, and what
> Was hardest: to be judged as right. For all things
> Are so, even you. And now you cannot
> Hide from the sunlight of your beings.

Selfhood has its satyr-plays, of course. After so much sucking-up to the Sublime, there comes, gratifyingly for the poet's sanity, we must feel, a terrible Bronx cheer. Not always speaking about "Dying" in the noble character of Oedipus:

> How will you know your chest from the night?
> —When the sphinx has come there asking
> Its inexorable question. How will you raise it up?
> How will you call? The night is here, asking
> 'Where are you? You, where are you?'
> How will you inform the night? . . .
> How will you say, 'I am here. Here I am?'
> Breath is a question, breath the answer.
> But when your heart's hammerstrokes
> Stutter, I, I, I am,
> And your voice calls out, 'Where are you?'

> You!
> How will you know yourself from the night?

nor about "Birth" in that of Theseus:

> if only
> We can praise the moment and what is given
> In it, even ourselves dying, then must
> We move by our heart's desire and all
> Its blest fatalities, and, living that
> Perfected hope, the sense of oneself moving,
> Cannot misstep, if only we hallow
> And will not violate.

Irving Feldman has a grotesque impersonation in his repertoire as well: in his treatment of the Flood, one of his finest poems, it is only to be expected that his speaker would be not Noah but one of his doomed fellow-townsmen, outraged by the patriarch's greed for heroics:

> One comes telling us Noah has built a boat
> That through the flood he may ride about,
> And filled it all with animals.
> Just like the drunken fool, that slut-
> Chaser, to think of no one else.

> I feed my friends and kin; twenty nine thrived
> In my home. But mad Noah harangues the air
> Or goes muttering in his cuff
> As though a god were up his sleeve.
> Who is Noah to get saved? . . .

> Out of its harness the mind wild as a horse
> Roams the rooms and streets. There are some that say
> Noah sits amid the rude beasts in his ark
> And they feed one upon the other in the dark
> And in the dark they mate. And some say worse . . .

> Some here say a dove has come,
> Sure, they think, the sign of a god.
> And others say that Noah walks the street
> Puffed with news. But bid him wait!
> We are busy with our flood.

The wit and energy of the verse here, the vitality of the *contraption,* is a product of a successful ventriloquism: when he speaks for himself, Feldman is often slack, often slow to come to the point. Only at the end of this first book, looking back at these funny stories and tragic fables, the long series of poems in which solemnity is incurred like a disease, and the grotesque furthered in a saving series of literally gnomic verses where "The Gnome" speaks:

> My Favorite Flower Is: the Red Rose.
> My Favorite Occupation Is: Repose.
> My Favorite Game: Articulation.
> My Favorite Fear: Suffocation.
> When I Grow Up I Want To Be: the Same,
> Only endlessly and more fascinatingly more so!
> My Favorite Element Is: Earth.
> My Ultimate Aim
> Is (without further ado):
> Rebirth.

—is Feldman able, wryly, reluctantly, deprecatingly ("I have eaten all my words, / and still I am not satisfied!") to speak out not as some Giant Form, not as some archetypal trope in that art of mistaken identities which is myth, but as his own man:

> *Après le déluge, moi.*
> There it is, all the sad tale—
> A perfect post-diluvian male,
> And other humanist ta ran ta ra.
> For after all, it's only disgrace,
> At the very best, to outlive
> (Half-monadnock, half sieve)
> The saddest thing in the life of the race.

Irving Feldman's second book, *The Pripet Marshes and Other Poems,* published in 1965, leaves us in no doubt, from the first lines of the "Prologue," that the cue of that final poem in the first book had been taken, the self forced out of its camouflaging, buck-passing mythologies, the speaker identified:

> I in the foreground, in the background I,
> And the stone in the center of all,
> I by the stone declaiming, I
> Writing here, I trundling in

> The moody mountain scene, the cardboard
> Couples, the dusty star, I turning
> From the page, my hand staying moonlit,
> My pen athwart the light, I dimming
> The moon with cloud . . . Thinking,
> Thinking . . . And, still by the stone, I
> Attent to my declamation, taking it down.

The poem claims his responsibility, "pen athwart the light," to account for the world in his own person. Where in the first book the poet's vocation was explicitly mocked—"his Master File of Forms, Norms, and Storms"— and accommodated only faute de mieux:

> It is to be doubted we live as well or die better.

—Feldman can now summon his forces, enriched probably by the orders of the very figures he once mimicked and now assimilates to his own substance, "because I love dialectic and song," can bear to face "The Six Million":

> Survivor, who are you?
> Ask the voices that disappeared,
> The faces broken and expunged.
> I am the one who was not there.
> Of such accidents I have made my death.

We must not allow the heroism of this admission to pass unremarked— Feldman's survival as a poet is in it. There is, further, a wonderful courage in the long poem of this name, when Feldman accepts the burden laid upon him by his unparticipating history, an acceptance unmediated by myth or personation, a self-acceptance:

> I heard the air (that was
> To be ashen) and the flesh
> (That was to be broken), I heard
> Cry out, Possess me!

> Dear ones, what can I say?
> I must possess you no matter how,
> Father you, befriend you,
> And bring you to the lighthearted dance
> Beside the treasures and the springs,
> And be your brother and your son . . .
> Come in your widow's raiment of dust and ashes,

Bereaved, newborn, gasping for
The breath that was torn from you,
That is returned to you . . .
My heart is full, only the speech
Of the ritual can express it.
And after a little while,
I will rouse you from your dawn sleep
And accompany you in the streets.

Much of the rest of this book——not all of it; no one element of a body of poetry can be as preemptive as it appears in discussion: if I detach certain notions which I call basic, it may turn out only that they are detachable—is devoted to an investigation of the ritual that alone can express a full heart, most brilliantly, I think, in a witty series of poems "after Picasso's Suite de 180 dessins" and in another such series "after Picasso's Portrait de Femme" (the solemnities of Goya and Michelangelo in the earlier book are exchanged for the contemporary's "spoor of anecdotes, vestigia, mask-droppings"; the myth of greatness and the myth of madness are dropped in favor of the artisan's "motley of loss"). In "vocations of hammer, stylus, string," Feldman now sees the possibility of "the small change of relation," as in the case of Picasso:

Quickly, this ease he translates
to opportunities, discovers answers,
Landfalls, clues to something hidden.

And in a further poem, "Clown and Destiny," the problem of role-playing, of part-taking is worked out explicitly: Feldman addresses himself as a kind of comedian, trying masks, haunted by a tragic identity ("the dead one among the shifting figures") which cannot be beguiled by mere impersonations ("the renewals of your painted face"); in them he thereby discovers what he must oppose and so *becomes* the dead one:

Armored to battle what killing thing appears:
Starlight or dog or turning ocean.

Willing to speak as "the dead one," to assume the identities of the dead— "I am my dead brother (and I am you), / I survive"—this poet turns and confronts his life with an astonishing nakedness of statement; his language is often, in the nature of his undertaking, abstract, his lines often have no metrical norm, despite the typographical appearance of initial capitals and rhymes, yet in them there is always what Hopkins called the rhythms of prose, that is, the native and natural rhythm of speech, the least forced, the most marked of all possible rhythms:

> Many smile, but few are happy; my friends,
> Their lives hardening about them, are stern
> With misery, knowing too well their ends . . .

> Despair brutalizes. That is the law. (But
> Is there music in that?) My friends, feeling
> Their lives hardening, grow harder, less appealing;
> Almost the past condoning, almost a pleasure
> Finding there they cannot in their harder future,
> Though they know, as we say, the two go together.
> So wise men have said all things return.

> (Many smile, but few are happy; my friends,
> With misery, knowing too well their ends,
> Their lives hardening about them, are stern.)

This is another kind of poetry than the personating voice, the dramatic monologues of *Works and Days*. There is a poetry that says one thing is another thing, which is the poetry of metaphor, of recognition; but there is also an ultimate poetry that says a thing is itself, which is the poetry of statement, of cognition. This poetry of cognition is what Irving Feldman has arrived at, has earned. In the title poem of his second book, a dream of persecution and death in which the oneiric elements, by the rhythm of the poet's voice, have penetrated so far into experience as to seem supremely *natural*, and in the final "Song" of that book, in which the nature addressed has become supremely *formal*:

> So you are

> Stone, stone or star,
> Flower, seed,
> Standing reed,
> River going far

> So you are

—in these acknowledgments there is a beautiful visionary exactitude; in such "speech of the ritual" we may hear the expression of a full heart, the longed-for rebirth. For it is only, Irving Feldman shows us—and how perfectly in those three syllables: "so you are"—it is only when we have identities that we can have transformations.

MAGIC PAPERS

A decade ago, Irving Feldman's first book, *Works and Days,* articulated an identity in two ways: wry, brilliant, as a stand-up tragic; plangent, even solemn, as the puppet of enormous mythological personations (Oedipus, Moses, the Wandering Jew). In *The Pripet Marshes,* his second book, Feldman directed these voices upon the holocaust of contemporary history, sought relations between what survives and what is consumed. Under such pressure, the resonances fused, and Feldman forged an utterance which in his new book is unmistakable, though happily not invulnerable: that twist of the natural idiom we call a style.

The first thing to notice about these demanding, rewarding poems— generally long, generally low-pitched—is their sentences, that word itself a clue, for it meant, once, a discernment by the senses and the mind. Difficult as these poems are, if you listen simply to the modulated voice in which they are stated—even chanted, even sung—you are led through the toils of subject matter and out into understanding:

> I detest the wryness of my voice,
> Its ulteriority, its suffering—
> What is not lived only
> Can suffer so. I wish to give birth to the deep,
> Deliver myself on this darkness, this devil.

The accent is of wisdom. We are so used to cleverness, to knowingness, even to learning—and Feldman has helped us to be used to them—that the accent of wisdom, reticent, observant, matte, comes as a shock, a disquietude. Whether he is watching the fanatic girl who lives across the airshaft, or lovers on the Brighton Beach Local, whether he is moralizing his own childhood or his wife's nightmares, observing a girl dressing hornpout or partridges for a meal or merely—merely!—celebrating his unbelief, there is a gravity in Feldman's new poems that pinions the mind. It is not a gravity alien to wit, or even to fun, and it is wonderfully nimble in tracing a figure. Still, it is the gravity which is heavy with grief, for that is what gravity ultimately means: "Oh why is the soul sent on its errands / in the dark? with its list / of names, its fist of pennies, / its beating heart?" Feldman cannot answer, that is the entire burden of his book, but he goes on asking, interrogating the world, and his reward is to speak it: "eternity emerges at its growing point."

LOST ORIGINALS

Together, as the children say, is where it's at: the very word, which at its root means not only the *gate* through which we gather but the *good* which we gather for, exactly describes Feldman's achievement, his risk and his reward. Always till now in his work there has been a yoking together of what is felt—or known, or not even suspected—to be disjunct. Our shrewd Minos of poetry, R. W. Flint, has referred to Feldman driving pairs in tandem—Heine and Maimonides up front, Kafka and Blake behind. In speaking of the poet's earlier (three) books, I myself have referred to his "articulating an identity in two ways," and indeed if Flint and I have been right, the poet now drives right past us in that handsome equipage. If there has always been the tug between wit and wisdom, the war of survival against consumption or even against consummation in Feldman's two-chambered heart, what is fascinating here and now is the fused, annealed singularity of the voice, the energy of a diction which—out of so many refusals and losses—gets it all together: "the missing world, / the hidden heart-attack were one."

The poet is released by his singular lack of duplicity into two kinds of energy inaccessible to him when he suffered the divisions of comment and criticism: he is enabled to wield, with stunning effect, a kind of polymorphous perversity of language, of words, of syllables: he can *play* more profitably than any other poet among us:

> to hear
> love's lithe youngtongue's shaping son

> mouthoozemuse
> titwitwoostalk
> mamadrama
> stablebabelburble
> sleeperslupper
> bloomballoomboom
> sayseedsomescatterthing

and he can *mythologize* on his own, lost originals indeed, which have found the poet and forced him, as the original does, to the source. It is no accident that so many of the myths are of children—"The Jumping Children," "The Air Children," "The Marvel was Disaster"; indeed it is an intention that even the poems which are about the end—are "about" death, dissolution and destruction—return (where else could they go?) to the beginning, to

what childhood may loom up as or illumine: "Dying, Morton saw a child
who was / the child he'd been, who would become / the man he is."

Finest, because fiercest, of these new myth-makings which so melt birth
and becoming into bereavement is "My Olson Elegy." The insistent posses-
siveness of the very title suggests at once the kind of organized violence (and
what else is poetry?) being done to a great tradition, acknowledged here as
great and gradually operative in the enterprise of mourning: at the end, a
means of releasing the elegist into his own powers, his own primacy. Astonishing in its decorum, a recuperation of baroque diction, it is, among other
things, the source of his book's ominous title:

> you plunge to the primitive deep
> where satire's puny dreadful monsters,
> its Follies and its Vices, cannot reach,
> and swim among their lost originals
> —free, forgotten, powerful, moving
> wholly in a universe of rhythm—
> and re-enter your own first Fool,
> inventing happiness out of nothing.
> You are the legend death and the sea have seized
> in order to become explicable.

Feldman's elegy asserts its incomparable modernity not by any surrender of
magniloquence, not by a modish shrinking (or sinking) from "superlative
song," but by its reversal of conduct: whereas the movement of "Lycidas,"
say, is from despair through a series of insights to triumphant joy, that of
"My Olson Elegy" is from *ressentiment* through a series of submissions to
a dispersed, dispensing illumination: death becomes an acceptance of earth
(and water) so enormous that what had appeared to be an immortal triumph
of poetry turns out to be merely another action of mortality, and that is the
true triumph—Adonis recycled. "The swimmer like the sea reaches every
shore."

Though I have admired, and indeed addressed myself to, each of Feldman's books with the conscientiousness which fine work must elicit from
any fair reader, I admit that I should never have suspected anything so incandescent to come from the author of those first three collections. *Lost
Originals* is not a collection, it is a triumph of identity; it is, in pleasure and
myth, one thing, "one with the world's danger / that now is nothingness and
now a tooth." He has made himself a master, and what is most astonishing
of all, Irving Feldman is a master of joy.

HELEN VENDLER

Ghostlier Demarcations, Keener Sounds

Adrienne Rich's memorable poetry has been given us now, a book at a time, for twenty-two years. Four years after she published her first book, I read it in almost disbelieving wonder; someone my age was writing down my life. I felt then, as I feel now, that for each reader there are only a few poets of whom that is true, and by the law of averages, those poets are usually dead or at least far removed in time and space. But here was a poet who seemed, by a miracle, a twin: I had not known till then how much I had wanted a contemporary and a woman as a speaking voice of life:

> Strength came where weakness was not known to be,
> At least not felt; and restoration came
> Like an intruder knocking at the door
> Of unacknowledged weariness.

When I look back now through *A Change of World* (1951), I try to remember which of the pages so held me and why; and I find four sets of poems I greet with the sense of déja vu. One set had simply lovely lines, seeming today almost too decorative, too designed, but presenting to me then the poetry of the delicately apprehended and the exquisitely remembered, poetry of "the flecked leaf-gilded boughs," and "paths fern-fringed and delicate," orna- mented with "whisking emerald lizards." I did not mind, in some of these solacing poems, echoes of Auden or Yeats, feeling that what was beautiful

From *Parnassus* 2, no. 1 (Fall 1973). © 1973 by the Poetry in Review Foundation.

was beautiful no matter who invented it; but there was, it was true, an ominous note which kept being interlaced with the poised rhythms.

A second group of poems set the status quo against some threatened future time; yet the danger was contained, and in fact the action of containing danger was gravely obligatory, a sacred trust. The poems articulated their own balance between danger and decorum in imagery of rebellion (which usually lost) against tradition (which usually won, at least tonally). The speaker for tradition in one poem is "the uncle in the drawing room"; gesturing toward "crystal vase and chandelier," knowing the "frailties of glass," he points seriously to the duties of the custodians of culture:

> Let us only bear in mind
> How these treasures handed down
> From a calmer age passed on
> Are in the keeping of our kind.
> We stand between the dead glass-blowers
> And murmurings of missile-throwers.
> ("The Uncle Speaks in the Drawing Room")

The poet-observer creating the uncle may see him ironically in part, but there is no denying the ethical imperative of his last claim. Equally subversive of tradition but yearningly attached to its honor, "For the Felling of a Tree in Harvard Yard" ends ambiguously on a double set of responses:

> The second oldest elm is down.

> The shade where James and Whitehead strolled
> Becomes a litter on the green.
> The young men pause along the paths
> To see the axes glinting bold.

> Watching the hewn trunk dragged away,
> Some turn the symbol to their own,
> And some admire the clean dispatch
> With which the aged elm came down.

Though revolution may end this poem, nostalgia rules it, nostalgia for the "roots enormous in their age," for "the great spire . . . overthrown." In 1955 I read this poem purely as elegy (no doubt confusing it in my undiscriminating admiration with "Binsey Poplars" and the spreading chestnut tree) and I was unable as yet, myself, to conceive of revolutionary impatience. But even now its tone seems to contain far more of the pang of elegy than of the briskness of destruction. So the poems played with fire, yet did not burn: I must have liked that.

The third set of poems that moved me then were poems on the identity and lot of women. I had no conscious thoughts on the topic, the natural order of the universe seeming then to be the inequality of man and woman; and yet some strains of discord in the book must have seemed an external documentary to those inarticulate strains in myself. On the one hand, woman was to be Patience on a monument, a Hermione-statue always there when her husband chose to come back:

> She who has power to call her man
> From that estranged intensity
> Where his mind forages alone,
> Yet keeps her peace and leaves him free,
> And when his thoughts to her return
> Stands where he left her, still his own,
> Knows this the hardest thing to learn.
> ("An Unsaid Word")

Hard it may be, but learn it she must, says this poem; and it assumes that there is no such "estranged intensity" where *she* could be mentally foraging alone, and whence he might forbear to call *her* back. And yet, in other poems, the imperative of exploration, separation, private discovery, is equally felt:

> Each his own Magellan
> In tropics of sensation. . . .
> These are latitudes revealed
> Separate to each.
> ("Unsounded")

In still other poems, needlework, that laborious confection of female artistry, becomes the repeated symbol of the ambiguously triumphant womanly lot. While their lords left for "harsher hunting on the opposite coast," Norman ladies

> sat at home
> To the pleasing minor airs of lute and hautbois,
> While the bright sun on the expensive threads
> Glowed in the long windless afternoons.

But what is left of the Anglo-Norman battles but the Bayeux tapestry, which "prove[d] / More than the personal episode, more than all / The little lives" ("Mathilde in Normandy"). And, in spite of the seductive evenings in "The

Kursaal at Interlaken," the female speaker, while playing her social role, nonetheless casts longing eyes toward a solitary virginity:

> Jungfrau, the legendary virgin spire,
> Consumes the mind with mingled snow and fire.

This sentimental image, though there is no reason to doubt its sincerity, cannot equal, in poetic success, the trivialities so adeptly and ironically sketched earlier in the poem:

> What is the world, the violins seem to say,
> But windows full of bears and music boxes,
> Chocolate gnomes and water-color mountains,
> And calendars of French and German days—
> *Sonntag* and *vendredi*, unreal dimensions,
> Days where we speak all languages but our own?

The Jungfrau, no matter how symbolically laden, loses out, and that loss means that this poem wished to be what we would nowadays call a feminist poem and had not the emotional force to carry it off. The impulse toward a feminist stance arises in "The Kursaal" because the speaker is not in love with her lover:

> You will perhaps make love to me this evening. . . .
> Reality would call us less than friends
> And therefore more adept at making love.

But most of *A Change of World* is written by a girl in love, a girl "receiving marvels, signs":

> There is a streetcar runs from here to Mars.
> I shall be seeing you, my darling, there,
> Or at the burning bush in Harvard Square.
>
> ("Vertigo")

This seems too easy an apotheosis now, but it seemed bold at first reading, and drew me by the same authority as the lines in "For the Conjunction of Two Planets" which imperiously declared for myth against astrophysics:

> Whatever register or law
> Is drawn in digits for these two,
> Venus and Jupiter keep their awe,
> Warders of brilliance, as they do

Their dual circuit of the west—
The brightest planet and her guest.

Not only was our feminism only an occasional shadow over our expectation
of the ecstatic, our sense of permanent location in our lot was only incipient,
too. The fourth set of poems that kept me standing in the library stacks
reading this new and revelatory book was the set about Europe. In *A Change
of World* Rich struck all the notes of her generation's inchoate responses to
Europe: an attachment, a disloyalty; beauty, decadence; the perfect, the tired;
art, the artificial. Alienated by a lengthily educated childhood from the American scene, and yet invisibly, visibly, and irrevocably American, the students
who went abroad like Rich wandered tranced in the deceptive paradises of
the transatlantic escape.

Now, six books later, almost two decades older, Rich's readers encounter
her newest book, *Diving into the Wreck*. If we suspend knowledge of what
came between, we may ask what has happened to the girl of 1951, that girl
who wanted everything suffused by the delicate and the decorative, who
questioned her passivity even while exhorting herself to that virtue, who
mourned change and yet sensed its coming, who feared her own alienation
in her native country, who, above these cares and anxieties, took pains that
all her poems should turn out right, that there should be no ragged edges,
that chimes should chasten discords—what has become of her? She has forgotten, or repudiated, her dream of Europe: Beethoven makes a fugitive
appearance in the new book, but even he is not permitted to represent nineteenth-century European high culture; Rich calls her Beethoven poem "The
Ninth Symphony of Beethoven Understood at Last as a Sexual Message."
Passivity, too, is repudiated in principle, but returns in surreptitious forms,
as life is consumed by that which nourished it:

Time takes hold of us like a draft
upward, drawing at the heats
in the belly, in the brain

. . . the mirror of the fire
of my mind, burning as if it could go on
burning itself, burning down

feeding on everything
till there is nothing in life
that has not fed that fire
("Burning Oneself Out")

The overtones here come from Williams's "Burning the Christmas Greens," but Williams's poem is about the desire for change which consigns the greens to the fire, while Rich is helplessly suspended in the fires of time and thought. The old decorativeness reappears in the intricate ending, but this time not in the service of a scrim-curtain prettiness. As for the questions of female identity and the rival claims of change and tradition, they have merged into one inextricable and apparently insoluble problem. In the first book, change could be chosen or not; by now, Rich utters ruin (and resurrection) as inevitable law:

> I don't know who we thought we were
> that our personalities
> could resist the failures of the race.
>
> Lucky or unlucky, we didn't know
> the race had failures of that order
> and that we were going to share them
>
> Like everybody else, we thought of ourselves as special . . .
>
> Next year it would have been 20 years
> and you are wastefully dead
> who might have made the leap
> we talked, too late, of making
>
> which I live now
> not as a leap
> but a succession of brief, amazing movements
> each one making possible the next
>
> ("From a Survivor")

It is easier to believe in the failures of the race than in the amazing movements, and in fact the fine title poem of this volume proposes, with resolute courage, the exploration of those failures:

> I came to explore the wreck.
> The words are purposes.
> The words are maps.
> I came to see the damage that was done
> and the treasures that prevail.

These declarative pallors give way to a rich sense of the state of the wreck, in which we recognize an old vitality:

I am she: I am he

whose drowned face sleeps with open eyes
whose breasts still bear the stress
whose silver, copper, vermeil cargo lies
obscurely inside barrels
half-wedged and left to rot
we are the half-destroyed instruments
that once held to a course
the water-eaten log
the fouled compass

There is a visible continuity between the phosphorescent wreck and the orderly gardens and villas of early Rich, but the complacency of tone, so earnestly assuring the intellectual resolution of the early poems, is conspicuously stricken from this new exploration.

Oddly, it is not stricken from other poems, where complacency has become an unthinking assault on plain reasonableness. Because this new volume has provoked such hostile and intemperate criticism, it is probably just as well to mention its most extreme poem: a poem called "Rape," which begins by announcing that "There is a cop who is both prowler and father," and ends by claiming that as you describe your rape to him "your details sound like a portrait of your confessor" (who has been carefully described in SS terms, as, with boots on, gun in hand, "he and his stallion clop like warlords"). This cliché (the cop whose eyes "grow narrow and glisten" as "his hand types out all the details") is really unworthy of a poet, as is the incrimination of all men in the encapsulation of brothers and fathers in the portrait of this rapist super-cop. Rich would be the first to object to an equally stereotyped description of women—as shrew, as castrating mother, or whatever. The poem, like some others, is a deliberate refusal of the modulations of intelligence in favor of an annulling and untenable propaganda, a grisly indictment, a fictitious and mechanical drama denying the simple fact of possible decency (there are decent cops and decent fathers, and decent brothers, too, but they have no place in the consciousness producing this poem).

It is not hard to imagine someone writing a poem like "Rape," but it is hard to see how such poems pass muster months later when a volume is being gathered for publication. The truth of feeling ("I felt this way, I wrote it down") has never been coterminous with the truth of art. And since the truth of art has always been Rich's securest claim on our attention even in her tidiest poems, it gives a reader a wrench of pain to see her play false to her own standard. But criticism has so fastened on these lapses that the tense fineness determining the tactics of many of these poems has been ignored. Unwelcome though some of Rich's sentiments may be to those who do not share her recent activist feminism and other political activities, it would be unfair to let ideological differences obscure the presence, felt and conveyed in these poems, of finely-discriminated emotions—of the numbed, the stricken, the defrauded, the miserable. Rich feels all of these, and finds metaphors for them, this "living in the cave," as one poem has it. The poem seems to me to be about being a mother with children, but it will do for any one with dependents:

> These things around me, with their
> daily requirements:
> > fill me, empty me
> talk to me, warm me, let me
> suck on you
>
> Every one of them has a plan that depends on me
>
> stalactites want to become
> stalagmites
> veins of ore
> imagine their preciousness
>
> candles see themselves disembodied
> into gas
> and taking flight
>
> the bat hangs dreaming
> of an airy world
>
> None of them, not one
> sees me
> as I see them.

This ending may seem reductive of others, but I do not believe the poet need grant consciousness equivalent to her own to those surrounding her; especially if those people are children with their indisputable "daily requirements" and their innocent but monstrous egotism. And yet the virtue of the poem is the respect accorded those "other minds"—they are real, they have dreams, wishes, plans, hopes. Are we not all urged to contemplate our own preciousness, to aspire to the condition of luminousness, to dream of life outside the cave, to hope to grow up to stand on our own two feet (like stalagmites) instead of hanging dependently (like stalactites)? Who would

want anything else for her children but those dreams, those plans? And yet—
that the means to all these ends should be the one consciousness "arranging
all in one clear view" gives that consciousness at least the right to wish that
someone else could see the whole geography, flora and fauna, of the cave, to
bear her company. There are many poems of this sort, in which the poet's
grief does not encroach upon the rights of others, and the feminist consciousness is mitigated by the real demands of life: the final perplexity of the
poem is simply the misery of contending rights and needs in human existence.

The complicity of women in their own plight is, in the better poems,
admitted: though a man depends on a woman for "protection" as she on
him, and though "it all seems innocent enough, this sin / of wedlock," there
is something in her perpetual self-abnegating servitude that atrophies one
portion of the woman—yet she participates in the infliction of that atrophy:

> your wife's twin sister, speechless
> is dying in the house
> You and your wife take turns
> carrying up the trays,
> understanding her case, trying to make her understand.
> ("A Primary Ground")

Fair enough. For someone who finds the present world "a world masculinity
made / unfit for women or men" poetry will often express "the phenome-
nology of anger." And yet the desolate poems seem to me better than the
ones preoccupied with fantasies of murder (becoming a human acetylene
torch, etc.). I do not know why this should be, but the poetry of pure anger
is a relatively rare phenomenon. The dialogue with men, which provokes
Rich's anger (a dialogue dating from adolescence, perpetuated through courtship, desiccated in marriage, renewing itself in affairs, exploding in betrayal
or abandonment) is artificial when uninflected by grief, loss, and incredulity.
When Rich is genuinely "trying to talk with a man" (the title of one poem)
she allows for mixed emotions; out in the desert with the man, she recapitulates with exhausted irony the whole long trip that has brought them to
this ghost town:

> What we've had to give up to get here—
> whole LP collections, films we starred in
> playing in the neighborhoods, bakery windows
> full of dry, chocolate-filled Jewish cookies,
> the language of love-letters, of suicide notes,

afternoons on the riverbank
pretending to be children.

Which of us, at forty, will not wince at the fluoroscopic truth of that list:
we can name our own LPs, our fantasy PTA neighborhood self-projections,
our parents' cookie jars, our dramas of love and self-pity, our slides into
regressive and delusory role-playing. Critics who represent Rich's recent poetry as the utterance of exaggerated feminism alone seem not to have read
these plainspoken passages, returning throughout this book, passages showing (in the jargon of today) where we are all at.

There is more to look at in *Diving into the Wreck,* notably its last poem;
but first, in order to see the place of this book in Adrienne Rich's continuing
writing, writing unflaggingly done through youth, marriage, motherhood,
solitude, employment, political engagement, and fame, we must look back
to earlier works. Except for youth, any one of these phases, not to speak of
all of them, can be destructive of writing: we all recall Jane Austen's years
of silence when her father had to give up his house and take the family into
lodgings; we remember Sylvia Plath's hectic early-morning sleepless composition before her babies awoke; and there are doubtless other examples.
A writer who persists, phase after phase, usually has some intrinsic and
compelling self and style demanding expression. If we try to isolate the self
and style which appeared in *A Change of World* and which have continued,
through age and variation, all the way up to *Diving into the Wreck,* we are
asking, really, which are Rich's best poems, how her voice makes itself both
remarkable and beautiful.

Rich hit her stride, and wrote her first "perfect" poem (of her voice at
that time) in her second volume, *The Diamond Cutters* (1955). The poem
in question, "The Middle-Aged," is one of a distinguished group, including
"The Tourist and the Town," "Lucifer in the Train," "The Wild Sky," "Villa
Adriana," and "Landscape of the Star," which all, in some way, deal with
homelessness; and that homelessness, with its accompanying ache of filial
nostalgia, is the new theme, coming into the ascendant, which distinctly
marks *The Diamond Cutters* as an advance over the first volume. Sometimes
the pain of departure and separation is overt and unmediated:

> Imperceptibly
> That landscape altered; now in paler air
> Tree, hill and rock stood out resigned, severe,
> Beside the strangled field, the stream run dry.
>   ("Lucifer in the Train")

In a passage that recalls the (independently conceived) Plath poem "The Colossus," we see another child reconstructing the parental domain:

> We come like dreamers searching for an answer,
> Passionately in need to reconstruct
> The columned roofs under the blazing sky,
> The courts so open, so forever locked.
>
> And some of us, as dreamers, excavate
> Under the blanching light of sleep's high noon,
> The artifacts of thought, the site of love,
> Whose Hadrian has given the slip, and gone.
>
> ("Villa Adriana")

Moon explorers, in a desolate new landscape, long for their terrestrial home:

> We speak the names we learned as we were bred,
> We tell of places seen each day from birth—
> Obscure and local, patois of the Earth!
>
> ("The Explorers")

And finally, identifying herself with the Magi for whom "the palaces behind have ceased to be / Home," Rich walks, on Christmas morning, in "an unaccustomed city" and says bravely that though this is the "night that calls all travellers home, / The prodigal forgiven and the breach / Mended for this one feast," for her, denied this solace, there is another; the passage is prophetic:

> Yet all are strange
> To their own ends, and their beginnings now
> Cannot contain them . . . Once-familiar speech
> Babbles in wayward dialect of a dream.
>
> Our gifts shall bring us home: not to beginnings
> Nor always to the destination named
> Upon our setting-forth. Our gifts compel,
> Master our ways and lead us in the end
> Where we are most ourselves.
>
> ("Landscape of the Star")

All of these poems of exile, separation, breach, and, most explicitly, the deprivation of native speech, are both made and marred by their sense of shivering phantomhood; like Lucifer, the poet is banished—to the moon, to "ashen prairies of the absolute," to a ruined villa, to an endless desert jour-

ney. But recovery, though hoped for, and vowed, and even prophesied, is still
spectral, unseen—recovery as anodyne, not fact. But the poem called "The
Middle-Aged" has mastered its exile, and has taken the larger view: no longer
outcry alone, it includes analysis as well. If it has a fault, it is that it bends
backward, away from its companions; it tries so bravely not to be bitter that
it is not bitter enough. Nonetheless, it points to the attempt at the conquering
of experience which is the ground of the aesthetic, writing "till all's arranged
in one clear view." Here is Rich on the suffering of being young:

> To be young
> Was always to live in other people's houses
> Whose peace, if we sought it, had been made by others,
> Was ours at second-hand and not for long.
>
> They were so kind;
> Would have given us anything; the bowl of fruit
> Was filled for us, there was a room upstairs
> We must call ours: but twenty years of living
> They could not give. Nor did they ever speak
> Of the coarse stain on that polished balustrade,
> The crack in the study window, or the letters
> Locked in a drawer and the key destroyed.
> All to be understood by us, returning
> Late, in our own time—how that peace was made,
> Upon what terms, with how much left unsaid.

When I copied that poem down in 1955—I still have the copy, and have
retyped it time and again for others—I did not know why, since I liked all
the other poems too, I liked this one the best. Now I would say that it holds
its position of preeminence among the companion poems that share its theme
not only because of its analytic mastery of the situation, but also because of
its simplicity. All of the paraphernalia—Lucifer, Hadrian, the Mare Crisium,
the Magi, Constable, San Miniato al Monte—have been swept away, and we
meet the bowl of fruit, the upstairs room, the secondhand peace, the affliction of the young who have "to live in other people's houses." There is a lot
to be said, I suppose, for objective correlatives, but Magi treks and moon
journeys go rather far afield and threaten to render the experience more
fancifully than accurately, as the correlative becomes more interesting to the
poet than its origins.

The shape of *The Diamond Cutters* suggests that Rich may need to
write explicit *cris du coeur* as sketches, so to speak, for a more contained

and disciplined later poem. It is odd that some readers will so placidly receive and even praise such unmediated cries of filial longing, but will become irrationally damning about a single cry of unmediated anger. These hysterias only prove that Rich is touching intense and widely diffused feelings; a poet could hardly ask for more. In her poems, Rich sees more deeply than in her recent prose propaganda; poetry makes her more reflective and more self-corrective, less inflexible, more pained.

In *Snapshots of a Daughter-in-Law* (1963), we find that marriage has turned the earlier filial exile-in-space into something considerably more bitter—separation under the same roof, a sense of separate-and-not-equal lives bequeathed to men and women, with women's only claim that of a more arcane insight into Nature:

> has Nature shown
> her household books to you, daughter-in-law,
> that her sons never saw?

The silent isolation of minds in marriage is followed by a choking, deprived speech. The central poem in this volume is without doubt "A Marriage in the Sixties," a poem still hoping for the best and yet unwilling to dissemble the worst:

> Today we stalk
> in the raging desert of our thought
> whose single drop of mercy is
> each knows the other there.
> Two strangers, thrust for life upon a rock,
> may have at last the perfect hour of talk
> that language aches for; still
> two minds, two messages.

"My words," says Rich, watching those words drop unheard and neglected, "reach you as through a telephone / where some submarine echo of my voice / blurts knowledge you can't use" ("The Lag"). In this volume, Rich's lines loosen up into free verse; we may assume various influences, from Eliot to Lowell to Plath, but since the modern movement as a whole was on its way toward dispensing with rhyme, it was inevitable that Rich should forsake her sweetness, cadence, and stanzas once her life began to refuse its earlier arrangements. Nervous, hardened, noting harshly that only cutting onions can provoke her unwept tears into her eyes, she moves under a "load of unexpired purpose, which drains / slowly." Rich's effects now depend only on metaphor, juxtaposition, and adroit lineation; she vomits up "dead gobbets" of herself, "abortive, murdered, or never willed" for new recognition; she crawls out of her cocoon like a fish attempting the grand evolutionary trick of becoming a bird:

> like a fish
> half-dead from flopping
> and almost crawling
> across the shingle,
> almost breathing
> the raw, agonizing
> air
> till a wave
> pulls it back blind into the triumphant
> sea.
>
> ("Ghost of a Chance")

At about this time, Rich's dilemmas make for unresolved poems, ending in the defeat of the fish or a flight of a naked man across roofs of houses:

> Was it worth while to lay—
> with infinite exertion—
> a roof I can't live under?
> —All those blueprints,
> closing of gaps,
> measurings, calculations?
> A life I didn't choose
> chose me:—even
> my tools are the wrong ones
> for what I have to do.
> I'm naked, ignorant,
> a naked man fleeing
> across the roofs.
>
> ("The Roofwalker")

The weakness of the book is its explicitness and its irresolution. The nerves it touches are raw and recognizable ones; but it leans on words like "ache" and "agonizing" which preempt our responses. "If Rich were a great poet," said a friend reading these poems, "which of us could bear to read her?" Rich's transcriptions of pain, wholly accurate, are to be prized even if only as documentaries: and these unhappy limbo poems ending in stalemate are an honorable and possible form, but a whole book of them inevitably sets the reader on a slide downhill at the bottom of which he anticipates a crash.

And yet the crash is staved off for one more book, Rich's most beautiful and accomplished single volume, *Necessities of Life* (1966).

If, as Rich's early pattern suggests, blunter poems are followed by subtler ones, *Necessities of Life* derives its power from its absorption of all past phases into its present one. In "Autumn Sequence," Rich forces herself to that generosity toward past selves:

> Generosity is drying out,
>
> it's an act of will to remember
> May's sticky-mouthed buds
> on the provoked magnolias.

But that act of will makes this volume almost an obituary; at least it is the obituary of a whole section of life. The title poem—a second talisman, at least for me, to join with "The Middle-Aged," shows a new self emerging and seeking a new place in the world:

> Piece by piece I seem
> to re-enter the world: I first began
>
> a small, fixed dot, still see
> that old myself, a dark-blue thumbtack
>
> pushed into the scene,
> a hard little head protruding
>
> from the pointillist's buzz and bloom.

We cannot help noticing how free from compulsion Rich's images have become. The early poems were so neat in their useful skeins of imagery; if a color appeared in the upper left of the tapestry, it was sure to reappear, economically but predictably, in the lower right. Now precision of feeling and exactness of recollection govern the correlative, and though the visual reference apparent in the thumbtack and the pointillist is maintained, it is allowed considerable freedom. In adolescence come passion and ambition, melting the pigments:

> After a time the dot
>
> begins to ooze. Certain heats
> melt it.
>   Now I was hurriedly
>
> blurring into ranges
> of burnt red, burning green,

> whole biographies swam up and
> swallowed me like Jonah.
>
> Jonah! I was Wittgenstein,
> Mary Wollstonecraft, the soul
>
> of Louis Jouvet, dead
> in a blown-up photograph.

There is a hiatus in the poem at this point, as though the self-devouring of adolescence were nameable, but the other-devouring of marriage and child-rearing were not. The "hard little head" become photograph loses its painterly dimension and becomes a dry bulb waiting out its time of deprivation, "gone underground" like Herbert's flower, through "all the hard weather":

> Till, wolfed almost to shreds,
> I learned to make myself
>
> unappetizing. Scaly as a dry bulb
> thrown into a cellar
>
> I used myself, let nothing use me.
> Like being on a private dole
>
> Sometimes more like kneading bricks in Egypt.

In this poverty of slavery—and the comparisons tell us that even the "privileged" life of a Cambridge wife and mother can feel like that—the poem reaches its central minimal state in an exhausted miserliness keeping others at bay:

> What life was there, was mine,
>
> now and again to lay
> one hand on a warm brick
>
> and touch the sun's ghost
> with economical joy,
>
> now and again to name
> over the bare necessities.

This beautiful passage, though it could perhaps not have been written before Stevens's poetry of poverty, has the touch of the physical in it that Stevens's poetry lacked: that warm brick and its ghostly heat did not inhabit Stevens's universe. Those "certain heats" of adolescence have dwindled to this spectral form: passion and ambition alike almost expire in this daily kneading of the bricks, this being "wolfed almost to shreds" by others. But the devouring demand has, with time, eased; a tentative green shoot rises from the root cellar; "Who would have thought my shrivel'd heart / Could have recover'd greennesse?" asks Herbert under similar conditions. But Rich's resurrection is not Herbert's cyclical one; she will never again be a flower. However, she can be a cabbage, an eel, something sturdy and slippery at once (and female and male at once, the androgynous imagery suggests):

> So much for those days. Soon
> practice may make me middling perfect, I'll
>
> dare inhabit the world
> trenchant in motion as an eel, solid
>
> as a cabbage-head. I have invitations:
> a curl of mist steams upward
>
> from a field, visible as my breath.

Encouraging, brisk lines: they tell what every depleted mother must feel when the haze and stumbling of physical and psychic tiredness finally lift after a decade of babies. But where is the new society to join, when child-bearing is over? Where but among the old wives?

> houses along a road stand waiting
>
> like old women knitting, breathless
> to tell their tales.

In these lines, acquiescence and rebellion compete: that the little dark-blue thumbtack should come to this; that the girl who dreamed of being Wittgenstein should join the garrulous crones. And yet, what else can the normal lot be; given the submission of the soul in all those years of Egyptian bondage, given the confines of the root-cellar, is it not enough to sit on the doorstep and knit?

That was as far ahead as Rich could see in 1962, and, as always, she told us life as she saw it. It is with an almost desperate vertigo that we come from this poem and others like it to the poems of violent change in the later books, when Rich feels picked up and thrown by life into jangling new positions, unforeseen, unasked-for, but welcomed as they come. The more reproachful of her critics have assumed that her revolutionary stances are chosen and therefore blameworthy; I see them rather as part of the inexplicable ongoingness of life, to be reported like the rest. Better a change than

the falsely "mature" acceptance of the unacceptable, a stance that Rich falls
into off and on in *Necessities of Life,* notably in the increasingly expedient
"literariness" of the poem "After Dark" on her father's death, and in the
forced ending of the fine poem "Like This Together," where Rich declares
that love can be kept alive by our working at it, that the dry scaly bulb can
be pried into life:

> Only our fierce attention
> gets hyacinths out of those
> hard cerebral lumps,
> unwraps the wet buds down
> the whole length of a stem.

This "solution" won't work for a destroyed city, and a destroyed city is the
problem of this poem:

> They're tearing down, tearing up
> this city, block by block
> Rooms cut in half
> hang like flayed carcasses,
> their old roses in rags,
> famous streets have forgotten
> where they were going. Only
> a fact could be so dreamlike.
> They're tearing down the houses
> we met and lived in,
> soon our two bodies will be all
> left standing from that era.

These lines have that power of the best sort of metaphor, that they pierce
equally in two directions, until we scarcely know whether we are flinching
from the tearing up of Cambridge or from the decay of a marriage. The
death of Rich's husband since the poem was written gives the last line an
edge it did not have in the writing; but even without that added wreckage,
all the king's horses and all the king's men cannot put this Cambridge together again, and the final forced hyacinths are an evasion of reality.

The two books preceding *Diving into the Wreck* are waiting out some
murky transition: the most explicit poem in *Leaflets* (1969) jettisons every
past except the residual animal instinct of self-preservation, and every future
except death; comparing herself to "the red fox, the vixen" and denying any
connection to the ascetic New England settlers (like the Israelites, a "chosen
people") with their "instinct mortified in a virgin forest," Rich says:

what does she want
with the dreams of dead vixens,
the apotheosis of Reynard,
the literature of fox-hunting?
Only in her nerves the past
sings, a thrill of self-preservation. . . .
and she springs toward her den
every hair on her pelt alive
with tidings of the immaculate present. . . .
She has no archives,
no heirlooms, no future
except death
and I could be more
her sister than theirs
who chopped their way across these hills
—a chosen people.

("Abnegation")

This vixen ("wise-looking in a sexy way" in Rich's unfortunate description) has none of the vitality of torn-down Cambridge, and so is allegorical rather than convincingly metaphorical, but this rather weak poem makes the clear point of the book; jettison the past, live in sex and the present, forget the mind, tradition, and sublimation. "All our high-toned questions / breed in a lively animal" Rich had said in "Two Songs," and now the animal is trying to get rid of the questions; but of course they are bound to recur. That they recur in angry declarations (quoted at length by hostile critics) rather than as questions does not, to my mind, make them any the less the old questions. And so I do not terribly mind if Rich writes, "I have learned to smell a *conservateur* a mile away: / they carry illustrated catalogues of all that there is to lose" (a couplet that enraged one reader), because all that these lines mean is that Rich is still bothered by tradition and its claims. How much more can we ask of a living poet than that he should be engaged with the old questions and new ones? Must we always approve his answers if we are to admire his work?

The Will to Change (1971) take too much credit to itself in its title. Change is our lot whether we will it or not, and though we like to think we have willed what has happened, a sterner eye might see us as motes blown by the zeitgeist. In fact, Rich does see the roots of mystery in human states. In an anti-Wordsworthian version of a Wordsworthian thought ("O mystery of man, from what a depth / Proceed thy honors!") she sees the "depth" as the Freudian upstream of a river. Addressing someone else, she writes unsparingly of his present state, reserving condemnation by the imputation of mysterious damage done long ago. The slow, accretive metaphors describing the river in the poem "Study of History" mirror ecological despair, and are a harrowing picture of a mind so silted over and trampled upon that it can barely make its clouded way through the narrows of present experience:

> Out there.   The mind of the river
> as it might be you.
>
> Lights   blotted by unseen hulls
> repetitive shapes passing
> dull foam crusting the margin
> barges sunk below the water-line with silence.
> The scow, drudging on.
>
> Lying in the dark, to think of you
> and your harsh traffic
> gulls pecking your rubbish   natural historians
> mourning your lost purity
> pleasure cruisers
> witlessly careening you.

(I pause only to say that Rich's "music," so praised by her earlier reviewers and so ignored by most of her later ones, seems to me to reach its height of accomplishment in lines like these, as "hulls," "dull," "crust," "sunk," and "drudge" play one note while "margin" and "barges" play another, both soon to be reinforced by "gulls" and "rubbish" for the first, and "dark" and "harsh" for the second. The unobtrusiveness of these choices, choices perceived as such only when we ask why the lines adhere so to each other, is worth all the prettiness sacrificed in favor of their reticence.)

After the description of the river comes the Freudian exculpation:

> but this
> after all
> is the narrows and after
> all we have never entirely
> known what was done to you upstream
> what powers trepanned
> which of your channels diverted
> what rockface leaned to stare
> in your upturned

                    defenseless
                    face.

The ending may be sentimental, but the river and the mind to which it corresponds are heavy with truth. But *The Will to Change* as a volume is tortured by its own frequent disbelief in language. In "Snow" Rich asks herself:

> was it a whole day or just a lifetime
> spent studying crystals
>
> on the fire escape while the 'Sixties
> were running out.

As the snow crystals melt, as every unique "star [becomes] a tear," Rich asks about the adequacy of a common language:

> if no two are alike
> then what are we doing
> with these diagrams of loss.

The impotence of language forces recurring descriptions of itself:

> this name traced on a window
>
> this word I paste together
> like a child fumbling
>
> with paste and scissors
> this writing in the sky with smoke
>
> this silence
>
> this lettering chalked on the ruins
> this alphabet of the dumb
>
> this feather held to lips
> that still breathe and are warm.
> ("The Photograph of the Unmade Bed")

In search of a new style, Rich refuses the old structural model of problem-and-resolution, and lets all the crystals turn to tears:

> the mind of the poet is changing
>
> the moment of change is the only poem
> ("Images for Godard")

The refusal of articulation arises at its most complete at the beginning of "Shooting Script," the remarkable 15-page poem closing *The Will to Change*. I am not certain that "Shooting Script" is one poem, beginning as it does with fragmented single images, continuing with a translation of the Persian poet Ghalib, and going on to complete poems recognizably Rich-like. Composed from November of 1969 through July of 1970, "Shooting Script," for all its awkwardness, still seems to me to mark a conclusive new beginning, as the first poem in which Rich is willing—in fact is compelled as by a vow—to let her descriptions float entirely free, uncoerced by any will to make things neat and orderly, whether for herself or for her readers. It is ironic that a volume labeled *The Will to Change* should abandon the will to shape, but Rich's new poetic—the faithful transcription of what the new generation calls "vibes," without faking them together into premature sense—is announced in the third poem of the volume, "Planetarium":

> I am bombarded yet   I stand
>
> I have been standing all my life in the
> direct path of a battery of signals
> the most accurately transmitted most
> untranslateable language in the universe . . .
>   I am an instrument in the shape
> Of a woman trying to translate pulsations
> into images   for the relief of the body
> and the reconstruction of the mind.

Now, in "Shooting Script," composed in "midwinter and the loss of love," those pulsations are allowed to occur, or rather to resurface from the past, like potsherds from a dig. The painful task of "reconstruction of the mind" forbids any convenient alterations which might force the shards to fit together; the heap of broken fragments must instead be patiently accumulated, patiently sorted and recorded; only at night can one dream of a primitive wholeness, the wholeness of a more direct and primitive sort of people, those who originally made the pots. The poem using this metaphor (number 5 of "Shooting Script") tells us once more of the post-Wordsworthian experience of the civilized man meeting the solitary reaper: "Will no one tell me what she sings?" But the immediacy of the song, of the potter's wheel, is hidden from the poet, who can only "dream of the unformed, the veil of water passing over the wet clay, the rhythms of choice, the lost methods." Rich has abandoned the sentimental fantasy of being a purely animal vixen, but she still wishes for a hypothesized primitive physical human self, like the villagers whose ancestors made the pots:

> Of simple choice they are the villagers; their clothes come
> with them like red clay roads they have been walking.

> The sole of the foot is a map, the palm of the hand a letter,
> learned by heart and worn close to the body.

In the new primitivism, the poet must abandon his magic lantern and give up "the temptations of the projector": but in fact the projector itself had come to grief, refusing to move on to the next slide, projecting one image "over & over on empty walls." One must "see instead the web of cracks filtering across the plaster":

> To read there the map of the future, the roads radiating
> from the initial split, the filaments thrown out from
> that impasse.

> To reread the instructions on your palm; to find there how
> the lifeline, broken, keeps its direction.

> To read the etched rays of the bullet-hole left years ago
> in the glass, to know in every distortion of the light
> what fracture is.
>
> ("Shooting Script," number 14)

Giving up the prism, the lens, the map, and pulling herself up by her own roots, Rich, as *The Will to Change* closes, eats the last meal in her own neighborhood and prepares, deprived of all instruments, to move on, guided only by the fortuitous cracks in the plaster, the innate lifeline, the traumatic rays of the bullet-hole. She could hardly have been more frank; from formalism to—not freedom, but, as always—a new version of truth. If this is a revolution, it is one bound like Ixion on the wheel of the past—environmental past in the plaster, genetic past in the lifeline, traumatic past in the bullet-hole. And if it is revolution, it is one which does not wish to deny the reality of past choices and past modes of life. Putting off in her boat, Rich watches "the lights on the shore I had left for a long time; each one, it seemed to me, was a light I might have lit, in the old days" ("Shooting Script," II, number 13). Houselights and hearthfires, abandoned, remembered, light the departure.

And so, in *Diving into the Wreck,* the old questions are still mining like moles underneath: tradition, civilization, the mind and the body, woman,

man, love, writing—and the war added as a metaphor, so far as I can see, for illustration of the war between the sexes rather than for especially political commentary. In the most meditative and searching poem (besides the title poem) in *Diving into the Wreck*, Rich forsakes distinctions between men and women, for the most part, and sees us all as crippled creatures, scarred by that process of socialization and nurture which had been, when she began writing, her possession, her treasure; tapestries, Europe, recorders, Bach— the whole edifice of civilization, of which she now sees the dark side—war, exploitation, and deadening of instinct. The fable of civilization and its discontents is drawn from the account of the taming of a savage child told in *The Wild Boy of Aveyron* by J-M Itard. The poem begins in a reminiscence of "The Middle-Aged"—"They were so kind; / Would have given us anything":

> In their own way, by their own lights
> they tried to care for you
> tried to teach you to care
> for objects of their caring.

The seductive interchange by which parents barter "care for you" in exchange for your "caring" for "objects of their caring" is glossed by Rich's pun. Other details from "The Middle-Aged" (and other poems) seem to haunt this beginning, as we see the list of things the parent-figures, who captured the wild child, want to make him care for: the "polished balustrade" of the earlier poem becomes "glossed oak planks"; the "letters locked in a drawer and the key destroyed" become "locks, keys / boxes with coins inside"; the "dead glass-blowers" whose precious works the uncle in the drawing room still protected reappear in "glass / whirled in a fire / to impossible thinness": but the deepest slight to civilization comes in the vision of a book seen through savage eyes:

> they tried to make you feel
> the importance of
>
> > a piece of cowhide
> > sewn around a bundle
> > of leaves impressed with signs
>
> to teach you language:
> the thread their lives
> were strung on.

The repudiation of the pattern of parental lives leads to the repudiation of books, their life-thread. And yet, this poem uses the medium it distrusts, attempting to

> Go back so far there is another language
> go back far enough the language
> is no longer personal.

The possibility is enough to justify the attempt, and it is an attempt not half so strange as it has been made, by some critics, to appear: what else have artists attempted to find in returning to motifs drawn from tribal painting and sculpture but some level at which language is no longer personal? Rich's myth is now the primitive—therefore her notions of trips in solitary kayak-like skiffs, of caverns, of the primeval forest, of indigenous villagers. The long exposure of most women to the more primitive experiences still remaining in civilized life—menstruation, intercourse, pregnancy, miscarriage, childbirth, nursing, toilet training, and child-rearing—make any woman feel as if she has spent ten or fifteen years in a Cro-Magnon cave. It is natural to ask what the irremediable substructure of life is, and what is overlaid upon it: not a new question, but a perennial one in any attempt to get at the truth of human relations.

The wild child was discovered with many scars, bearing witness, as Itard writes, "against the feebleness and insufficiency of man when left entirely to himself, and in favor of the resources of nature which . . . work openly to repair and conserve that which she tends secretly to impair and destroy." Rich writes another of her cavern poems on Itard's hint, entering "that part of the brain / which is pure survival":

> The most primitive part
> I go back into at night
> pushing the leathern curtain
> with naked fingers
> then
> with naked body
>
> There where every wound is registered
> as scar tissue
>
> A cave of scars!
> ancient, archaic wallpaper
> built up, layer on layer
> from the earliest, dream-white

to yesterday's, a red-black scrawl
a red mouth slowly closing . . .

these scars bear witness
but whether to repair
or to destruction
I no longer know.

It is not surprising that the poem, although some later tidying up is done,
can get no further in insight than this. Since the efficient moral is, or ought
to be, in Itard's view, better care of the child, "the attention of scientists,
the solicitude of administrators, and the protection of the government," Rich
is surely within her rights to flash on her screen of language a picture from
Vietnam (a war waged by scientists, administrators, and the government):

is the child with arms
burnt to the flesh of its sides
weeping eyelessly for man.

Diving into the Wreck ends asking:

why do the administrators

lack solicitude, the government
refuse protection,

why should the wild child
weep for the scientists

why.

Though the official reproof from the poet is directed against those face-
less bureaucracies, the primary offenders are still the parents—those first
administrators and original governors, who inflict, by their scientific "teaching the child to care for what they care for," a conditioning regardless of
individual needs, and inflict thereby those first scars which determine in large
part the rest. The forcefulness of *Diving into the Wreck* comes from the wish
not to huddle wounded, but to explore the caverns, the scars, the depths of
the wreckage. At first these explorations must reactivate all the old wounds,
inflame all the scar tissue, awaken all the suppressed anger, and inactivate
the old language invented for dealing with the older self. But I find no betrayal
of continuity in these later books, only courage in the refusal to write in
forms felt to be outgrown. I hope that the curve into more complex expression visible in her earlier books will recur as Rich continues to publish, and

that these dispatches from the battlefield will be assimilated into a more complete poetry. Given Rich's precocious and sustained gifts, I see no reason to doubt her future. The title poem that closed *The Diamond Cutters* says that the poetic supply is endless: after one diamond has been cut, "Africa / Will yield you more to do." When new books follow, these most recent poems will I think be seen as the transition to a new generosity and a new self-forgetfulness.

Robert Pack

Leonard Baskin might do his portrait, using the Clifford photograph on the paperback cover of Pack's *Waking to My Name*. The shadows darkened, the weathered lines of the poet's face at fifty etched in, the rock set of the jaw, the slight downturn of the lips, the eyes peering out from behind the bone fortress with that quizzical mixture of irony and vulnerability. You come away from reading this volume of 250 pages that cover Pack's life as a poet—twenty-five years of it—with the sense that a man has dressed over some deep wound with an extraordinary array of bandages. At times he can make even his early masters—Keats and Stevens and Hardy and especially Robinson and Frost—seem light and gay, for he refuses to look away from the fact of death in the same way that Baskin's drawings refuse any consolations before the same fact. Pack's own death (waiting for him somewhere down the line), his father's death, his children's eventual deaths, the death of everything he treasures now even as he understands that someday he will have to let it all go. "On what premise might an art be based that would free it from a dependence on violence as its primary source of energy and thus lead the artist from the maker's happiness back again into life?" Pack asks. In returning to something believable, some supreme fiction, he suggests in his 1975 essay, "Art and Unhappiness," "the artist might become a model for us all, adding a tranquil perspective out of his ordering power" so that he might free his "voice from dependence on irony or cynicism."

From *A Usable Past: Essays on Modern and Contemporary Poetry.* © 1984 by the University of Massachusetts Press.

Pack means what he says, and he has tried to establish a poetics based
on creating a Wordsworthian tranquility for our time which he demands
and needs. When Pack reads modern fiction and nonfiction and poetry (and
as director of the Bread Loaf School of Writing he is inundated with it), I
can imagine his ironic smile as he reads of violence and more violence, of
murder, suicide, rape, incest, fellatio, sodomy, and the thousand strange faces
violence can be made to wear. His answer to these faces is the counter-
proposition of limitation and its promise: the Vermont countryside (though
he is an ex-New Yorker in the way Frost was an ex-Californian), a wife of
twenty years, three children, a mother, a sister, and a father who in a sense
"deserted" him by dying when Pack was sixteen. Out of this recognizable
world Pack has chosen to build his classical, anti-Romantic world, snatching
what domestic pleasures he can against the lengthening shadows of death
and oblivion. Like Candide, like Stevens's Crispin, Pack wants to cultivate
his small garden in relative stability and peace. Ironically, critics and some
of his fellow poets have taken him at his word. But what they have not
gauged sufficiently—and what Pack himself has underplayed—is a potential
for anger and violence in himself which he has had to learn to control.
Wordsworth is indisputably somewhere in the background as Pack's progen-
itor, but Pack's world is a lot darker than that Romantic's ever was, as
relentlessly dark, perhaps, as Frost's was.

Pack's real father is Keats rather than Wordsworth, in spite of what
Pack has said to the contrary. I mean the Keats of the late odes, fronting the
fact of death, the Keats we hear in the odes to melancholy and the nightingale
and the urn, the poet hopelessly trying to make time stand still, trying to
warm himself by the fire of the imagination (and even succeeding for a few
brief moments), a man trying to wrestle with his own death (in spite of
whatever he can find to say to the contrary) and trying to console himself—
and others—as he inevitably goes on losing that battle. And therein lies
Pack's terrible strength, which makes him harder to read sometimes than
Hardy. (I once heard Pack recite Frost's "Out, Out. . . ," about the death of
a boy whose hand is ripped off by a mill saw. I was gasping by the time
Pack had finished, stunned for days after by Pack's evocation of that small
death. I had heard Frost's poem before, had even taught it, but for the first
time I deeply felt that boy's irretrievable loss at the marrow.)

Anger. Consider for example the poem that begins Pack's new selected,
a recent poem called "After Returning from Camden Harbor." The speaker
is recalling a sullen trip back home to Middlebury with his wife after a few
days at the shore. He is angry with her for whatever reason (since in a
marriage of any duration anything can be enough to start an argument). He

has turned defensive and sullen and inward, wanting to speak, needing to speak, but afraid that speech would be speech seeking the wrong thing. Worse, it has rained at the seashore, turning this vacation ground into a landscape exactly duplicating Pack's own troubled mind, so that inner and outer weather have once again conspired. Sadly, the speaker realizes the futility of his own anger, does not want to stay angry since anger is itself wasteful, poisoning more of the limited time he knows he has left with his wife. He tries therefore substituting one image—the roiling sea "with sailing boats / rearing like horses against the flat slap / of foaming waves"—with another domesticated image: "a plain, translucent pitcher, quiet with milk, on a yellow tablecloth / brightened by morning sun." This in turn becomes a "green pitcher of milk" and the image is meant to replace the impinging reality of a green chaotic sea. The realization of love, like the realization of the poem, Pack insists, is a matter of choice and thus a matter of words, of giving order to the chaotic turmoil of chance swirling within and without. The garden *must* replace the wild, insane sea both around and—even worse—within us. For this measure of order, limited as it is, is really all we have.

The poem's happy surprise of form is concealed until the close when we realize that, in all this furious disorder, Pack has managed to provide us with an intricate sestina. Pack's poems are filled with such difficult forms used deftly, masterfully, and I find myself admiring his use of them almost in spite of myself. Perhaps it is the heritage of Whitman and Pound and Williams, but I distrust such forms in American verse, and from their actual practice I would guess most American poets writing today (with a few notable exceptions) feel the same way. But Pack uses the sonnet, the rondo, the villanelle, the ballad, the sestina, the blank verse dramatic monologue—with urgent rightness. As here, where he has his wife break the sullen silence of the trip back to Vermont by communicating the neutral information that a computer, "given six random words / and the idea each sentence must include them, / all repeating in the final line— / composed a poem that furiously made sense." Those six words—three nouns and three descriptive modifiers—Pack, true to the furious logic of his sestina, repeats together as the last line of his poem: "*idea water asleep furiously green words.*" We go back to the opening of the poem and find that, sure enough, all six words have already been introduced in the first four lines of the poem and then repeated over and over in the poem's succeeding lines. This is not mere cleverness but the demonstration of a civilized and passionate wit, choosing to order those six random words, uttered by his wife/muse, into a poem celebrating his love, in spite of his very real anger, for the very real woman sitting there beside him. Like Robert Hass's "Meditation at Langunitas" with its final repetition of the single word, "blackberry," a word that has come by poem's end to carry so much meaning, Pack's poem dares even more in terms not of nostalgia for an early love but rather of celebration of something so much more difficult to do convincingly: to choose to praise married love in the midst of anger itself. Not idealized love, then, but a love, frayed, tired, committed to the long haul, a love that means trying to compose a sense of domestic order—of *choosing* to do just that—when every fiber and nerve end in us feels like throwing the whole relationship with its crushing human limitations over the side and beginning again with the chimera men sometimes call, to their own chagrin—and the woman's—the Perfect Woman.

Marriage and poetry go hand in hand in Pack's poetics. Out of the chaos of anger and confusion and the illusion of infinite choices before us, we choose this word and that woman, composing day by day an order so that we may realize the good we can possess rather than plunging after what Pack sees as the short-term pleasure and long-term vacuity of essentially anonymous sexual liaisons. Pack may well be a proponent of the Paterian aesthetic; he may be in some senses a latter-day Marius the Epicurean attuned to the various registers of the pleasure scale (as a poem like "The Last Will and Testament of Art Evergreen," with its rich sensual catalogues, will attest to), but out of that aesthetic he has created a fierce moral construct which informs—*in-forms*—the very core of the man's poetics. For Pack, the decision to create a circumscribed happiness out of the dark void of Genesis, in other words the choice to create the poem, is at heart a moral choice reflecting on our very humanness. *I choose, therefore I am what I am.* Call it the Cartesian fable of Popeye.

One reason Pack has not received more critical attention is that, though he cannot have escaped being a Romantic, he has tried very hard to write a classical poetry in a Romantic age. It is as though he knew that this age is the age of Lucifer the over-reacher, spawning another generation of sons and daughters swerving from their poetic fathers. We live with another generation of poets whose strongest voices appear to deny the limits of language, intent on the distinctive sounds each can make. We still want distinctive, individuating voices; we want to sound ourselves as John Cage, breaking all the traditional values of music, is able to sound himself. We still want, as Hopkins knew in his own heart, to taste ourselves no matter what the cost. And this denial of our place in the chain of humanity, the necessary realization that we are children of very human progenitors and not of the gods, leads us, in Pack's view, to the dangerous illusion that we are immortal, that we are gods as the serpent in the garden promised us we would be if only we rejected the father.

But Pack places himself boldly against such illusions. He is painfully aware that we are limited by ourselves. Having lost his own father early, Pack knows—chillingly—that this makes him next in generation to go into the silence. Like his masters, Keats and Hardy, Frost and Stevens and Yeats, he has been made aware of his own limitations. Bloom has already brilliantly observed that the knowledge of limitation is itself a temptation to be overcome; too great a preoccupation with limitation, with the shadow of death, renders us powerless. Pack has wrestled with the shadow of this covering angel in that his formal patterns of image and syntax have rendered some of his earlier poems static and unrealized, their energy straining for release but caught by the cold serpent's medusa gaze. Hopkins—another of Pack's favorites—ran the same risks and for some of the same reasons: that he was placing himself squarely against over-reachers whom he admired while he struggled to set up an antithetical poetic. For Hopkins it was Shelley and Byron and Keats and especially young Swinburne just as for Pack it would seem to be Berryman and Lowell, Plath and Sexton, and—more recently— Ashbery and Merrill, as much as he might seem to admire these poets for their own demonic energy.

I don't think any less anger or fear informs Pack's poetry than theirs; he can see as well as anyone the verbal pyrotechnics of an Ashbery, a Merrill, even a Tate. But he has opted—this repressed Romantic—for another kind of poetry somewhat out of favor now in the United States: a poetry of statement, of formal complexity aligned to an older tradition, a poetry of moral purpose which insists on returning the reader to the world as we live it, better able to live in that world ambiguous because we have come to better terms with it. Readers naturally feel uncomfortable when someone has designs on them. But every poet has designs on the reader. What helps Pack particularly is the distance of formal design, the distance of wit, the distance of irony. And yet, ironically, it is against this same mask of irony that Pack has tried to distance himself so that we may believe what he says. Repeatedly he has divested his protective masks to reveal himself in all his human limitations. It is a paradox that the anger Pack would transform reveals itself in his poetry as a demonic energy, an energy, thankfully, which even prose statements and poetic maxims or witty and convoluted word games cannot quiet or tame.

This is why a poem like "The Kiss," dedicated to the youngest of his three children, Kevin, evokes such strong emotions in us. It is early April in

Vermont in this poem. It is still cold and the ground frozen, but there is the promise of another planting season in the air. Pack is at home with this Vermont countryside; he has made it as much a part of his poetry as Frost and Robinson once made New Hampshire and Maine a part of theirs. It is a rugged pastoral we are offered, Pack presiding here as Pan, his "boot-grooves packed with mud" until they have become "cold cleft toes." Like a latter day Franciscan, he helps apple trees through yet another harsh New England winter. There are fresh turds on the ground near the trees where starving deer have come to strip the bark for food and Pack takes in "the faint waft of skunk" carried by the wind: visual and olfactory images he cherishes because they sharpen the edge of his pleasure while reminding him of the human limits of our pleasure. As in other poems, he sees the "female curves" of distant hills and gives his mind to sexual fantasies until he realizes the cost to spirit of such illusions and remembers "what thoughts I must / hold back to let my careful body thrive / as bone by bone it was designed to do."

He is the presiding genius of this scene, tending the apple trees "as if to dress / a child for school" and he must husband his energies wisely. Suddenly he is visited by his youngest son, trying to launch a huge bat kite in the April wind until it takes a nose dive and crashes into one of Pack's apple trees. Then, like Vito Corleone in *The Godfather,* Pack takes, not a serrated orange peel, but some of the protective aluminum foil from the apple tree he has been tending, makes two enormous fangs, and goes running after his son across the field until, his heart banging in his chest from the unaccustomed activity, he catches his boy and wrestles him to the ground. The boy is both delighted and terrified by that passionate force and the father, no longer Pan now but a very demon, is overcome with longing for his youngest. Here is his own flesh, his own blood, he sees, and he sinks his mock vampire fangs into his son's warm neck to suck "deeper / than I have known." Raw violence, transformed by a father's need to possess what he knows must quickly move away from him if the son is to flourish in his own time. The boy cannot understand his father's longing, will not understand until he himself has earned his own fatherhood, but many of us who are parents will know at once what Pack intends. "In our struggle to survive with purpose," Pack tells us, "what we need is an art in which the indigenous happiness of art, its order-giving power, is wedded to an idea of goodness—a goodness that is attainable in daily life. When this idea of goodness is passionately held, the theme and spectacle of evil may be treated without exploitation, for the deprivation or loss of good feelings (as in friendship or love) will be powerfully felt, and the power of the longing for their restoration will replace the increasing need for shocking stimulation that the imagery of violence generates." This desire to evoke and restore good feelings is what Wordsworth calls the "tranquilizing power," and it possesses the "wondrous influence of power gently used."

Pack's ostensible strategy in "The Kiss" would seem to follow his prose formula here completely. Yet the poem does not finally behave in a Wordsworthian fashion for me. One reason, I think, is that Wordsworth's pantheism with its benign nature has been replaced in Pack with a psychological ambivalence we associate with Freud and Otto Rank. Rather than end with an image of tranquility and of power gently used, Pack closes this fine poem with the powerful and poignant image of a father trying to sustain his own too mortal life by usurping his son's. He is in fact fed by the boy's warmth, an image the more poignant because Pack has once again become aware that his own world is so quickly gone. But in the poem he has not yet given over, not yet made the sacrifice he understands he must someday make of letting go so that his son may flourish. Instead, he desperately clings to what he loves, knowing, even as he composes his poem at his typewriter, that the scene he is reenacting is already in the past. And it is that saving ambivalence, that dissonance in Pack's formal constructs, that saves him. In short, his poems are greater than his own prose criticism tells us the poem can and cannot be and go beyond the limits Pack has told us the poem should not be able to go.

To read through *Waking to My Name* from beginning to end is to come to an understanding of the ways in which, over the past quarter century, Pack has matured as a poet and as a man. This volume gives a representative selection—containing about two-thirds of the poems that have appeared in seven previous volumes beginning in 1955. In Pack's case this presentation has been crucial because it shows how the darker side of this poet is defined in gradual stages, thus revealing by stark contrast the special light Pack has also earned for himself. I have read Pack's poetry regularly since the publication of *Home from the Cemetery* in 1969 and long ago came to admire his toughness, his paradoxical tenderness, his irony, his composed, sardonic, witty surfaces, his unusual civility (in the sense in which, say, Richard Wilbur and Charles Tomlinson would understand that term). Reading Pack I see one possible successor to Frost and Stevens in terms of tone, colloquial strategy, formal imperative. It is time now for a reassessment of the man, something Pack has not yet adequately been given, though his poems certainly deserve it. For the man is hardly written out, and his latest work, which I have read in manuscript—a volume consisting of a series of complex, interwoven dramatic monologues spoken by what I can only call a representative human family placed in Vermont—shows that Pack at fifty is still working, and still waking into his own name.

What we hear in him is a voice that has been struggling over the years, despite the polished surfaces, to come into its own, beginning in 1955—the year Wallace Stevens died—with a competent collection written when Pack was still only in his early twenties: *The Irony of Joy*. It is a derivative voice we hear in this book (for how except in a handful has it ever been otherwise?). But already Pack's signature is upon these poems. His is a strong voice, the poems tough, poignant, declamatory, hard-edged in their structure. Like so much poetry written in the academic mode in America at that moment of our literary history, Pack's is a poetry aligned to figures like Nemerov, Wilbur, Jarrell, and Bishop. Here is poetry with a moral grain which depends on the fathers, on the traditional structures and recognizable voices passed down by them. The close of "To the Family of a Friend on His Death" catches the tone of this first book, a first effort so much better in spite of its limitations than the first efforts of many young poets:

> A man
> Is not the sum of fortune of his gifts;
> You want his life. Somewhere some still break
> Familiar bread in happiness,
> Draw in the sweetness of abundant breath.
> What good is it to know your early joy
> Depended on his death?

But Pack was not satisfied with a poetry of detachment and irony masking a real sensitivity and so—in spite of the academic vogue for irony in the 1950s—Pack's next volumes show a development in a formal mastery wedded to a colloquial line, together with a new calculus of emotional responses. The Pack who wrote *A Stranger's Privilege* (1959) and *Guarded by Women* (1963) shows the impact of Freud and of Yeats, the Yeats we recall in Roethke's Yeatsian poems. This is Pack in his late twenties and early thirties, a poet very much involved in his craft and already capable of writing some very good poems. There are poems of social protest here, poems of an apocalyptic baroque verging on Bosch, Freudian and grim fairy tales, poems that rewrite the biblical myths of Genesis (in fact the whole Pentateuch), to give voice to Pack's own need for beginnings. Among my own favorites here are "Neanderthal," "Adam on His Way Home," "The Shooting," and especially "South Beach," this last for its combination of strong rhetoric and the colloquial in a poem that realizes a setting in the way early Wilbur or Snodgrass or the Lowell of *Life Studies* did:

Two children splash along this beach
As if this summer's day will have no end.
I lie back on my towel, cover my face
With the *New York Times,* and think things through
As the ocean rasps upon the shore
By the breaker where our dog was killed.
In the blown sand and the water's spray,
I tell myself that all is vanity,
Even accepting vanity is vain;
I do five extra push-ups, take a dip,
Relieved at last by the absence of hope,
And feel then, tightening on my lips,
The white, determined smile of the drowned.

Whether we accept our fate or refuse it is of little consequence to fate itself. No poem can alter our fate by even a hair; it can only release us, release our muscular tensions by giving us a moment of pleasure and a glimpse into the truth of our human condition. And for Pack that is quite enough. One of the things therefore I take pleasure in is the way Pack has co-opted and subdued Yeats's late tragic gaiety in his own lines: "I tell myself that all is vanity, / Even accepting vanity is vain."

With *Home from the Cemetery* (1969)—his fourth book of poems— Pack arrives at his maturity. This is still for me his strongest single volume, as important for his development as *Spring and All* was for Williams's development, both books published too in their makers' fortieth year. There is not a throwaway poem in the entire book and some of Pack's best lyrics— sardonic, mordant, bitter, wry—are here. This volume contains the beautifully touching poem to the poet's infant son, the baby's arrival in the midst of the father's own angers and frustrations. "Welcoming Poem for the Birth of My Son" closes with the baby's coming at Christmastime, just the worst time of all for the poet. And yet, finally, perhaps the best time of all:

He comes, crowned in his ears and fuzz,
In a dazzle of fingers and toes, making
Miracles with his glad eyes;
He walks in the sun-struck kingdom of penguins
Enraptured on their eggs, crying GOOD WILL
To that angered city where my love hides.

There are also several very good social fables here, registering Pack's anger and dismay at what was happening to America in the late sixties, poems like "The Unificationizer" and "Burning the Laboratory" and—one of my favorites—"Love," which I understand more only as I grow older. Another is "The Stone," which may owe something to Ted Hughes's gothic animism or to Roethke's infantile animism but which makes particular sense when one considers the Vermont landscapes and the old stone walls which line the country roads with their dark shadows. And—too—when one understands the nature of Pack's own hunger for life and motion. The volume contains two major poems. The first is "Home from the Cemetery," a haunting Rothkean pastoral meditation which recounts the poet as a young man moving among the final landscapes surrounding his father's death in 1945, an attempt made twenty-five years after the event to come to terms with that wounding loss. The other poem is Pack's most ambitious—though not his most successful: "The Last Will and Testament of Art Evergreen."

"Last Will," seventeen-pages long, is a testament in thirty parts; it has been justly praised by figures as different as Anne Sexton and Lawrence Raab. A complex effort, it deserves a careful and extensive reading impossible here. Essentially, however, the poem is a dialogue between an old man who is near death named Art Evergreen (the name of course suggesting the poet's own sense of how we survive our own extinction) and a younger man named Jack who records Art's wishes and in so doing, it turns out, may well be Art's real son. One of Pack's preoccupations here as elsewhere is with the sense of continuity, the older poet handing on to the son (or daughter) what has already been handed on to him. It is a broadly, weirdly comic poem in which Art, over the course of a day (any day, since our lives are a succession of days anyway ending in the final and shortest day), gives away his body— his eyes, ears, nose, mouth, the rest of it at the same time teaching his amanuensis, Jack, how to use the very senses life gives us to enjoy. "I leave my eyes to you, Jill, both nearsighted," he quips, trying to teach his wife— one of four who all happen to be named Jill—to

> Wonder back through them to sunlight whipping
>   white on tacking sailboats;
> Or sledding over the dip of a hill,
> See the unfurling smoke of children's voices.
>   Past rainbow conch shells,
> See salt-shiny toes of sandpiper girls
>   swinging hands;
> Yellow trefoil fields; masquerading skunks;
>   the clown-glee of raccoons
> Parading through their moony paradise
>   of garbage pails.

In turn young Jack Jackson (Jack son of Jack) tries to comfort the old man, who is soon to lose a world of things finely seen, by telling him that really he shall not miss such things since the "advantage of being dead / is that one sees nothing," that his eyes then will float like stars in the vast interstellar darkness, "boneless body / Spiralling away" and that moon craters will form where once his ears were so that self "will never enter them again / To hear sand slushing" as it did when once he walked the shores. Cold comfort that; yet, if we are to enjoy the light, Pack warns us as others have earlier, we must first become aware of our own deaths. And so Art Evergreen comes finally to lash out at what he considers the idea of God himself, that false father in Pack's world. Or, better, the ideas of God we have inherited over centuries: Egyptian, Greek, and Roman deities, various beast gods, even Jahweh with his "fire-fanning wings with feathers overlaid / hue upon brightening hue / Into a rainbow spanning the covenant, seascape, / breath-filled void." Thus does Art dismiss the second-rate imagination of Genesis to replace it with his own world. And though Pack admires Hopkins, he parts with him on the comfort of the resurrection, for in his world there is no resurrection beyond a comic re-creation (out of Stevens) where Art might leap up "naked hi ho / out of bed, prancing erect / On your pet hog, your cape streaming, singing / *The Star-Spangled Banner*," where he may finally embrace the Perfect Woman, who—it turns out—would still be another woman named Jill. For Pack it will never happen, though we may hope for a kind of immortality in the millions of sons and daughters Art can affect by his evergreen words, including these words of his major comic pronouncement, a *last* will and a last testament meant to replace the Old and New Testaments themselves. "How long can I go on writing this," the poem ends, "keeping you alive?" And for once the voices of Art and his son and heir Jack and the Maker of this poem and of this world—a god-figure named Pack—collapse into one. By looking at the worst life has to offer we can hope for renewal, for some happiness in our own time. This comic / moral mode recalls at times the exacerbated voice of Stevens at forty-two, composing his own early last will and testament: "The Comedian as the Letter C."

    Nothing But Light (1972) is a consolidation of what Pack had achieved in *Home from the Cemetery*. It is a satisfying volume with poems like "The Pack Rat" (the artist as comic collector of things, the artist as lover, as father, as husbandman), the moving and evocative "My Daughter," the terrible poem, "The Children," about casualties among children all over the world, as in that still green memory of Vietnamese children running down a road, their clothes, skin and hair on fire from an American napalm shell exploded on top of them. And there is the inexorable pressure of "The Plea of the Wound." Two poems in this book stand out powerfully above all the others: "Prayer to My Father While Putting My Son to Bed" and "Now Full of Silences." Harold Bloom has described them as "unique consolations in the abysses of family romance, firm achievements of a deliberately 'reasonable romancer' who has individualized his own distinguished middle way." Both are exquisitely moving, quiet and tender, almost Virgilian in their resonances. Listen to the opening of the first:

> Father of my voice, old humbled ghost,
>   ragged with earned earth,
> Teach me to praise those joys your last sleep
>   still wakes in me.
> What can I hold to? What can I tell this boy
>   who at moonrise
> Picked a vase of asters, purple and white,
>   now holding back from sleep
> Another trusting moment, listening
>   to my voice,
> To what it says?

Pack will not be hurried in his meditations, in the earned fruits of what he has disciplined himself, cell by cell and word by word, to say. And for one who would question the metaphysical efficacy of prayer, he does a good job of understanding the silent places of the heart and the heart's affections. Here we are, he says in "Now Full of Silences," "keeping watch over the stony fields / we are learning to forego" as the poor, dumb innocent animals in Noah's menagerie climb up the planks of the ark to "leave for the last spaces / full of silences / Which our words fill emptying themselves, / watering the final pity / We once taught the gods when we walked / among them." We no longer walk as gods now but rather with the animals, sharing their common fate as we all go into that same silence uttering even as we do the talismanic words the gods themselves once spoke to us. Perhaps, Pack hopes, we too go up the ramp in pairs like the animals, confirmed in our deaths as,

> hand in hand, as we have always done,
>   we walk into the past.

Pack's poetry lacks the insistent egobeak of so many American poets, crying out with their thin wares: *hear me, hear me.* His civility has cost him, probably, much critical attention. Nevertheless these poems rest secure in their achieved craft and human wisdom. In that sense Pack is truly one of the sons of Wallace Stevens.

Keeping Watch (1976) consolidates Pack's achievement. There is, for example, "Pruning Fruit Trees," with its two voices intersecting in a harrowing dithyrambic counterpoint, the voice of the stoic fronting death and the voice of elegy. There is the cosmic joy of "A Spin around the House," as the father, in a spontaneous and happy mood, begins to dance and whirl around the kitchen after dinner until his children, caught up in his dervish mood, lift "their blue glasses / over the spinning table / as their laughter splurges through the galaxy." There is the Stevensian sequence, "Maxims in Limbo," recalling "Like Decorations in a Nigger Cemetery," though Pack's 101 maxims and axioms are both more blooded and more accessible than Stevens's, if less challenging. There is, too, the poem, "Feeding the Birds," which captures the essential Franciscan spirit of the late Williams of "For Daphne and Virginia" and "The Mental Hospital Garden."

Finally, there are two poems that need special mention. The first is "Jeremiah," a love poem responding subtly to Williams's "Asphodel" and employing Williams's step-down triads, first moving to the right and then reversing themselves and moving to the left. The second is "The Ring," that touching prothalamion, a lyric of continuities employing the circular strategies of the greater English ode. Pack is a master of layering and manipulating time to reveal what is so essential to his poetic vision: the circular patterns through which we all move, repeating in our lives the gestures of our parents, which will in time be repeated by our own children. For whatever individuality we may achieve must be seen in conjunction with the way we repeat and repeat and repeat. Pack suggests this in his rhetorical patterns, his syntactic echoings, dependency on refrain, repetition of sound patterns, end rhymes, assonance, the repetition of entire lines, the repetition of key images. As here in the figure of the ring, which is first of all the wedding ring passed down from parent to poet, and which will someday be passed on to the poet's daughter. But the ring is also the arc of the apple branch reflected (and completed) in the pond, the circle of the moon and time, the halo of the necessary angel who guards the household, the arc of epithalamion completed in the death of the parent who gives himself or herself so that the child in turn may live out his or her days fully and the pattern we call life may continue. Perhaps, Pack suggests, his own father saw his daughter's eyes reflected in his own wife before he died, as now he sees in his mind's eye his own daughter's eyes, the arc of anticipation thus completed (in time) in the arc of memory:

> I hand the groom the ring
> and step back in the house
> an angel guards, beside the moonlit window
> where my mother paused,
> when her husband died, and turned the ring half-circle
> where the lord and lady
> cannot see. And there, reversed, again
> she waits in apple light,
> as slow wind shifts the laden petals
> in her hair, the pond,
> under the tree, for him to wed her now,
> as I do thee.

I have already spoken about some of the new poems in *Waking to My Name,* but a number of others besides "Camden Harbor" and the title poem need mentioning. I single out "The Twin," "Learning to Forget," "The Stained Glass Window," and particularly the finely modulated "Looking at a Mountain-Range While Listening to a Mozart Piano Concerto." This last reveals something of Pack's long attention to classical music, to Bach and Mozart especially and their genius for repetition and variation which Pack has sought for in his own poems, which, he has said, have at their core a "musical soul." Musical repetition, he tells us, means returning "to the crucial scenes of one's past, or the compulsion to face apprehensions and fears that have not been (and may never be) resolved." So in his poems where repeating phrases and images recall those scenes that bring us happiness, though they can also "be the dramatic necessity of returning to memories or ideas that still cause distress or even dread." The act of returning brings with it the concomitant hope of mastering emotions that threaten us, showing us at least how we may learn to endure them. Poetry, then, as Stevens would have agreed, "by affirming design, can celebrate the mind's power to confront its own despair" since that despair is grounded in what we are and in what we as a species have done to ourselves. "Brightly the piano asserts its melody," Pack's Mozart poem has it, and it is a melody we can hear in the poem's finely achieved blank verse lines:

> the orchestra gathers its colors to reply,
> true to the law that everything responds,
> nothing is left unanswered, that variation
> extends the self—as if one's life were made
> essential in a piano's theme, departing
> then returning one to what one is.

And now again it is the piano's turn,
and now the separate instruments, again
as one, move onward to their chosen end
beyond which nothing else will be desired.

Thus, in a meditation on the nature of Mozart's art, Pack reveals his
own penchant for a Paterian aestheticism Stevens himself understood: the
amassing harmony of one's life under the shadow of the urn, life understood
in its essential and repeating patterns so that even our own deaths can come
to be accepted as part of that unalterable pattern. In accepting such limitations Pack has found sufficient light by which to make his way and make his
ars poetica. His poems proclaim that he has come to accept the human and
necessarily limited aspects of the love he can give—and receive—from wife
and friends and children. It is not the frenetic anonymity and shadow fruit
which he believes Romantic love holds out for us to eat. In a sense Pack has
become his own maker, his own final father, an aging Adam in a postlap-
sarian world, waiting for the flood to engulf him as he knows it must at last,
but choosing in the meantime to walk with a very real Eve (or Jill) who
shares his mortality and his warmth with him. It is a vision that must suffice,
and will. We could do worse than listen to what Pack's poems have to teach
us.

Intimacy has become Pack's consuming theme in middle age, a consoling
intimacy which I rarely find in American poems, either because the wisdom
and the difficult ability to record that wisdom is lacking, or because most
contemporary poets seem capable of dealing adequately only with what Hopkins once called the dull dough of selfyeast. There is danger in Pack's working
with these quiet themes, of course; the danger that the poem will become
trite, unconvincing, bourgeois in the Marxist sense. Characteristically, Pack
avoids the frenzied, the Dionysiac, the ecstatic, for something quieter and
more solidly in the middle ranges. Because he has, many have read his stoic
control as a comfortable prosiness. Yet Pack is anything but a comfortable
poet. He knows darkness intimately, and has opted, like Williams before
him, for the light. And he can sing, exquisitely, as in his new poems appearing in the little magazines and quarterlies. They are dramatic monologues which belong to the tradition (too long left in disuse) Frost made
available to us more than half a century ago. With the dramatic monologue
Pack extends his own voice to include father and mother, sister and brother,
son and daughter: in short the whole human family tree. *Faces in a Single
Tree*, containing Pack's most recent work, is (at present) composed of some
thirty long poems which together provide us with a world in the sense in

which Hardy and Faulkner and Anderson earlier composed worlds out of Wessex and Yoknapatawpha and Winesburg. Pack has naturally chosen Vermont and its people, and though that world is sketched in rather than painted in great detail, he has managed to make these poems resonate with a complex of feelings that, while they sometimes evoke Frost's presences and sometimes Browning's grotesques, are very much a part of Pack's circumscribed but distinctive experience. Together these monologues comprise an extended poem on the theme of intimacy. Some of the new pieces are sardonic, some scarifying, others poignant; many of them reverberate long and hard in the imagination. One comes away from these poems feeling one has heard these voices before, seen these words revealed somewhere else. For they are the same preoccupations we have found in Pack's earlier lyrics. But, as Pack's variations on intimacy are played out now in these dramatic monologues, we become aware of new currents of feeling, new patterns, new realizations.

I am impressed by the control and convincing quality of many of Pack's new poems, but a few I find stunning. These newest poems do not lend themselves to excerpting. They are too interwoven, depend too much on subtle repetition and variation. The language is familiar, colloquial, quiet, prosaic, unhurried. "Inheritance," for example, is a Wordsworthian poem in the tradition of "Michael." A father is talking to his son about the young man's future, trying to explain why he must disappoint him by not letting the son get into heavy debt at the beginning of his business career. It would not, he tells his son, be fair to be indebted to the father. No, the young man should not be mortgaging his future to pay off his past but should rather think about what he owes to the son he himself will someday have. We pay the father back by passing on ourselves to our own children and someday, the father tells his son, come

> cool October afternoon, when he
> is splitting wood with you, and you
> are resting on a stump beside the sumac
> blazing in the last warmth of the sun,
> he'll take his T-shirt off, and as the axe
> descends, you'll watch his shoulder muscles flex
> and then release beneath his flawless skin.
> A waterfall, you'll flow out of yourself.

Even as he speaks, this father has been splitting wood with his own son. The talk goes on, things are said and left unsaid. At the poem's close the speaker remarks that another long, cold winter is coming on. Which reminds him then of something *his* father once told *him,* that earth is first our home and finally our grave. He remembers it was a day like this and he was raking leaves when his father told him that:

> I stood
> before him, naked to the waist, sweating,
> thinking of your mother, trying to decide
> what I would say when I proposed to her.

What has been so poignantly left unsaid is the realization—long after the fact—that the speaker's father had in his time seen the inevitable separation of his son from the nest and—in that sudden realization—had willed to empty himself of himself. Call it a celebration of the fact of familial pattern repeating itself, as here, tactfully, tacitly, the father tells his son how much he loves him and that he too is ready to empty himself for him, giving him now his real inheritance: the covenant of a future at one with the past from which it stems.

Pack began publishing in the same year Allen Ginsberg, three years his senior, read "Howl" to a crowd in San Francisco. He has survived to see the Confessionals rise and tragically set in their own short red sun. He has bided his time, trying to find a way through the same world that Plath and Sexton and Jarrell and Lowell and Berryman each tried to find a way. The results of that search, having shaped themselves over a quarter of a century, have now been gathered in *Waking to My Name*. One feels the fact of mortality everywhere in these poems, the sense of loss, the calculus of costs, the seriousness of all that life in the pause between birth and death has to offer us. Nature giveth and taketh away. And even as phoebe and chickadee clash in the radiant summer fields around him, even as he knows that his own name—poet—is pulsing now at fifty, Pack also knows that his own heartbeat is there to remind him "that most of the full of my life is behind me." Pack is more than a veteran craftsman. He is a poet of the Penates, the old, despised but still-vital household gods whom we ignore at our own peril. He is a health-giving presence, this leech-gatherer. Read him.

DAVID LEHMAN

The Sound and Sense
of the Sleight-of-Hand Man

with rumors of
The ocean's legerdemain, which by mere sleight of land
Keeps taking back what ground it appeared to have given.
HOLLANDER, *Powers of Thirteen*

Two voices are there, of wit and despair, from the start. Both are inde-
fatigable; neither will rest until it finds a hearing. In the dialectic between
the two is the Jewish literary imagination, and at his best John Hollander
fuses the impulses so that his excess of joy weeps, his excess of sorrow laughs.
[For references to individual texts, I shall use the following abbreviations:
SE = Spectral Emanations: New and Selected Poems; IP = In Place;
BW = Blue Wine and Other Poems; RR = Rhyme's Reason: A Guide to
English Verse; FE = Figure of Echo: A Mode of Allusion in Milton and
After; PT = Powers of Thirteen.] Reversing Pope's terms, Hollander asserts
that "the sense must seem an echo to the sound" (*RR*), and since an echo
is a secondary event there is usually an air of sadness about it; sadness, at
any rate, can function as a catalyst in the conversion of cleverness into wit,
and wit in turn sharpens language into "a direct sensuous apprehension of
thought." The phrase, from Eliot's essay on the metaphysical poets, exactly
describes Hollander's aspirations for his verse. If he can claim a unique place
in contemporary letters, that is due in large part to his success at integrating
erudition with sensibility, as Eliot commended.

Hollander can, it often seems, transmute ideas into sensations, obser-

---

From *Parnassus* 12, no. 1 (Fall/Winter 1984). © 1985 by the Poetry in Review
Foundation.

vations into mental landscapes. What enters his work from outside, as echo
or shadow, ends as something made over, made his own, a part of a new
whole. His first volume, *A Crackling of Thorns* (1957), sounds the characteristic note of melancholy—an echo made aware of its lateness, "transumed"
into levity, as in this playful allusion to Shakespeare's melancholy Jacques:

> Europe, Europe is over, but they lie here still,
> While the wind, increasing,
> Sands teeth, sands eyes, sands taste, sands everything.
>   ("Late August on the Lido," *SE*)

In a later poem, an inversion of Keats produces the desired effect: the poet
and college cronies have assembled at the West End bar in Columbia territory, "half in / Death with easeful love" (*SE*). More lately still, in one of the
poems in *Blue Wine,* a painted moon

> Sets and leaves dark night with a
> Valediction forbidding
> Morning or the like, and which
> The faithful darkness may try
> To observe, for all we know,
> Its failure being our light.
>   ("Pictures in a Gallery," *BW*)

Such a gesture, down to the object lesson in enjambment, is nothing if not
literary, at least at its base, even when as here the lines modulate into a
version of paradox that leaves behind their immediate source in John Donne.

Literary has become a dirty word in some circles these days, but it
oughtn't to be: is our generation so hooked on "deep" imagery that it cannot
savor the sophisticated wordplay of "Mount Blank" or "A Season in Hellas"
or "Crocus Solus," to cite just three ingenious Hollander titles? One would
like to think otherwise. For a bias against the literary, as against the sleight-
of-hand man's way with words, would amount in this case to a bias against
ambition. Hollander's repertoire of stratagems and tropes goes hand in hand
with an intellectual curiosity that obeys few bounds. With his assured dex-
terity, he has managed to sqeeze more and more of the universe into a ball;
and his mythmaking is itself informed with the weight of a people's heritage.
It may even be argued that Hollander's poems affirm their Jewish identity
not at the expense of his literary imagination but by dint of his having placed
it at the vital center of his cosmos. Jews, after all, are people of the Word—
the earsplitting Word that cannot be uttered by human voices; in the after-
math of its echo, exegesis becomes both a sacred and a necessary act. That

is one reason why so many of Hollander's poems resemble midrashim, or rabbinical commentaries. His habit of smuggling into his poems the tactics of his critical prose is evidence not so much of an academic hangover but of the profound, and profoundly Jewish, conviction that an unmediated vision is an impossibility. In an essay on Gershom Scholem, Robert Alter succinctly states the case. Scholem, Alter notes, "emphasizes the mediated nature for rabbinic Judaism of every experience after the initial revelation. As a result, exegesis becomes the characteristically Jewish means to knowledge and perhaps even the characteristically Jewish mode of religious experience."

In Hollander's most frankly autobiographical collection, *Visions from the Ramble* (1965), the secular and the religious realms are kept separate if in fearless symmetry. "The Ninth of July" chooses its moment "in the darkness between two great explosions of light, / Midway between the fourth of July and the fourteenth, / Suspended somewhere in summer between the ceremonies / Remembered from childhood and the historical conflagrations / Imagined in sad, learned youth" (*SE*). Trying to find an order in memories associated with these "two great explosions of light," the poet defines a consciousness divided between the European past ("Europe, Europe is over") and "The American moment." The sexual fireworks of advanced adolescence are identified with those of Independence Day celebrations; boyhood's declarations of independence echo those of history. The world and the poet come of age together:

> Burning, restless, between the deed
> And the dream is the life remembered: the sparks of Concord
>   were mine
> As I lit a cherry-bomb once in a glow of myth
> And hurled it over the hedge. The complexities of the Terror
> Were mine as my poring eyes got burned in the fury of Europe
> Discovered in nineteen forty-two. On the ninth of July
> I have been most alive; world and I, in making each other
> As always, make fewer mistakes.
>
> (*SE*)

Characteristically, a rhetorical trick uncovers a truth: "Europe / Discovered in nineteen forty-two" stands opposed to America discovered in fourteen ninety-two.

From the ceremonies of innocence described in "The Ninth of July" we move to "The Ninth of Ab" with its rites of anguish. We move as well from the secular to the Hebrew calendar, to *Tisha b'Ab*—the Jewish fast day second in solemnity only to Yom Kippur. The fast commemorates the destruction of the holy temple. *Lamentations* supplies the synagogue text:

"what was wailed at a wall / In the most ruined of cities" enters the poet's pores as, still a child, he sits "perspiring / Among the intonations of old tropes of despair." This music shall be his own, these rituals his poetry shall observe. The geography of Hollander's imagination, which takes absence and loss, exile and diaspora, as basic preconditions, will revert frequently to such biblical models. Already the specter of Jerusalem casts its shadow on the "sweltering" sidewalks of Manhattan. "The City, a girl with the curse, / Unclean," defiled as the temple was:

> Only the baking concrete, the softening asphalt, the wail
> Of wall and rampart made to languish together in wild
> Heat can know of the suffering of summer.
>
> (SE)

Two more voices are there, then: the voice of Judaic sorrow and that of the lifelong student of English poetic history. These work well together even when nothing on the surface suggests a linkage. Hollander has, virtually as a moral obligation, honored poetry as a craft and discipline (in *Rhyme's Reason*), done some original work on poetic allusion (in *The Figure of Echo*), and given us our best shaped verse since Apollinaire (in *Types of Shape*, 1968, examples from which appear in *Spectral Emanations*). In all this he has acted as the heir presumptive to an English laureate. But the Jewish character of his verse remains a constant. In some of his poems Hollander is, like Stevens's "rose rabbi," a scholar of love. Many others give explicit treatment to a Jewish theme or motif. Hollander has, in fact, a range of Jewish accents to choose from. The talmudic commentator in "Blue Wine" had previously been the joyous cabalist of "The Ziz" and, before that, Allen Ginsberg's city-boy sidekick in "Helicon"; the Hebraic lamentation of "The Ninth of Ab" gives way to gallows humor with a Jewish nose for the noose in "On the Calendar." The latter, a prose poem, is divided into 31 mock-journal entries corresponding to the month of Hollander's birth: October 1929, which coincided precisely with Tishrei 5690. (Hollander was born on the 28th, the day the stock market crashed.) With the logic peculiar to Jewish wit, each entry tells of a different form of execution. On the tenth of the month, Yom Kippur,, "I will beat my breast in remorse so hard that it caves in." On the twelfth, Columbus Day, "I will discover a new continent," before a quick dissolve turns the hero into an Odysseus whose script has been changed on him: "washed up on its beach, lying there naked and exhausted, the Princess of the Shore surrounding me with her laughing companions, I shall look up at her eyes into the smile of her father, the Lord of Hell" (SE). On the fifteenth, as the festival of Succoth begins, "I will enter a tabernacle in the wilderness of the city; the tabernacle, poorly built and tended, will collapse." Hollander borrows from "The Garden" of Andrew Marvell to tell of his protagonist's fate during the Jewish holiday of the harvest: "ripe apples will drop upon my head" (*SE*).

"On the Calendar" presented Hollander with a seemingly perfect occasion to let scriptural and literary references intermingle. Similarly, in "New York," secular and religious signs and symbols are allowed to merge. Here Hollander contrives to canter in Augustan hoofsteps while delivering a monologue such as one associates with Bickford's cafeteria in days gone by. The poet's "dear old friend is leaving town," marking his exodus with an acerbic farewell of some satirical bite:

> I've had it all; let those remain who need
> The grinding crowds and the great mills of greed:
> The thieving steel of the Triborough Bridge
> Authority spans Pelham and Bay Ridge,
> Whose Moses may have slain an overseer
> Once long ago—but see his late career,
> Cornering the straw market, and his boast,
> Outliving Pharaohs, a rich palace ghost.
>
> (*SE*)

And just as the rhetorician and Jewish tale-teller meet in Hollander's night mirror, so the Miltonic and Mosaic modes feed off one another in the difficult title poem of *Spectral Emanations,* which aims to kindle a feast of dedication, sustaining the consecrated oil on the brigh menorah of poetic invention.

Spectral Emanations is really two books in one: it contains a gathering of new poems (superseded in turn by *Blue Wine*), to which it adds selections from all of the poet's previous collections, excepting the unexcerptable *Reflections on Espionage* (1976). *Spectral Emanations* thus facilitates a retrospective look at the growth of this poet's mind, a tailor-made opportunity for revaluation. And perhaps the first fact to be noted, annotated, pondered, is Hollander's virtuosity, evident from the start—and his periodic attempts to pursue visionary projects that require him to subordinate his powers of craft to the possibilities of trope. Again one has the sense of a fork in the road that this peripatetic poet visits more than once. Hollander describes the crossroads in his essay on Ben Jonson in *Vision and Resonance* (1975):

> Modern poets can take one of two directions, it seems, in moving
> toward a characteristic use of form, in seeking to "learn a style

from a despair" of belated arrival in a world where forms are not
given, where style is not canonical. One of these is that of American Modernism, following the Emersonian injunction to "mount
to Paradise / By the stairway of surprise"—in short, to seize early
enough upon a poetic tessitura of one's own, to frame a mode
of singing, as it were, that would make any other formal style
impossible. . . . The other tradition is best exemplified by Auden,
and in this he was Ben Jonson's heir in our age. His grasp of the
competing necessities of the public and private realms was mirrored not only in his poetic morals but in his stylistic practice;
using a vast array of forms, styles, systems, differentiating between private messages, songs, sermons, inscriptions, pronouncements, and so forth, he made of his technical brilliance more than
merely a matter of his own delight. In craft began, for him as
well as for his predecessor Jonson, responsibilities.

Hollander has most avidly obeyed the "Emersonian injunction" in such
works as "Spectral Emanations" and "The Head of the Bed," which proceed
from his wish to write poems that would take their creator by surprise and
defeat conventional attempts at explication. Both poems concern elements of
Judaic legend—"The Recovery of the Sacred Candlestick" in the one case,
"A filthy myth of Lilith" in the other—though less for their own sake than
as pretexts, tropes around which to organize a discourse.

It is the Emersonian side of the poet that most interests his friend and
colleague Harold Bloom, whose analysis of the angst caused by "belated
arrival" applies with a vengeance to Hollander's poetry. To Bloom, Hollander
remains "the very witty neoclassical lyricist and verse essayist . . . but . . .
only occasionally, and with the work of his left hand." If anyone could make
"what's left sound right," Hollander can:

> Here's a *caesura:* see what it can do.
> (And here's a gentler one, whose pause, more slight,
> Waves its two hands, and makes what's left sound right.)
>   (*RR*)

Bloom might argue that with *Rhyme's Reason,* as with such earlier perfor-
mances as "Upon Apthorp House" or "New York," Hollander satisfies an
irrepressible urge toward the shimmering surfaces of "stylistic practice"; by
absorbing the urge, these works make it possible for the poet to devote other
occasions, undistracted, to acts of "organized imagining." In the past, critics
have taken Hollander to task for his allegedly "disembodied virtuosity"

(Robert Alter), for indulging his "terrifying knowledgability" (Donald Davie), and for employing "complication for complication's sake" (Helen Vendler), but the evident complication and erudition and technical skill of such a poem as "Spectral Emanations," while terrifying in some ways, do in fact body forth a subject. "Spectral Emanations," as Bloom argues, is "a self-proclaimed replacement for an irrecoverable Jewish lamp"; Hollander's epigraph, from Hawthorne's *The Marble Faun,* explains the elaborate artifice that follows:

> There was a meaning and purpose in each of its seven branches, and such a candlestick cannot be lost forever. When it is found again, and seven lights are kindled and burning in it, the whole world will gain the illumination which it needs. Would not this be an admirable idea for a mystic story or parable, or seven-branched allegory, full of poetry, art, philosophy, and religion?

With its system of correspondences, "Spectral Emanations" aspires to achieve what Yeats called "unity of culture"; it is Hollander's project to substitute man-made artifice for the sacred objects that have been lost forever. Tropes are trumps: a polymathic range of references furnishes the figures through which the poet can commune with his imagination, casting his nerves in polychromatic patterns on a screen, with the anomalous twist that the dream-texts come equipped with their own interpretative apparatus.

Much of Hollander's work, ever since *Visions from the Ramble,* becomes newly available when considered within a high romantic context; Hollander himself has endorsed the line of reasoning Bloom proposes. Still, Bloom's right-handed compliment may lead to misunderstandings, based as it is on the tenable but not necessarily valid assumption that the romantically sublime is superior in kind to the classically restrained. In his scrupulous examination of successive Hollander collections, Richard Howard takes a not-unrelated stand but puts a significantly different emphasis on it. Howard praises *Visions from the Ramble* for its departures from the impregnable fortress of intellect—or, more exactly, for the intellectual leverage that can bear an autobiographical burden, the poet's "entire confrontation with himself"; *The Night Mirror* (1971) is in its turn celebrated as a "glyph of self-disclosure." One senses in Howard's commentary, as in Bloom's, an admonition and a piece of advice. It is as though, according to either view, Hollander's prodigious gifts and broad range of references carry with them the danger that he may misdirect his efforts.

It might almost be averred that any critic of Hollander must choose between Howard's way and Bloom's; does Hollander go wrong when he fails to toe one or the other line? Ought he to turn his energies to autobiographical enterprises or, contrarily, to what Bloom calls "a kind of bardic ordeal . . . in search of a late sublimity linking form and subject"? Yet, because a peace treaty between the rival positions should not be ruled out, one is inclined to suspend judgment. And perhaps one ought to complicate matters further by putting the case for Hollander's "other tradition," whose Dioscuri are Jonson and Auden. Though Hollander himself might value the less what comes as second nature to him, surely there is something to be said in favor of a poetry that can invest rhetorical flourishes with moral responsibility—that can make "stylistic practice" a matter of "poetic morals," as *Rhyme's Reason* does by exemplifying and thereby renewing the forms and conventions of English verse. To what else does this marvelous manual testify if not to happy stewardship of the "talent which is death to hide"? This is pedagogy at its best:

> Even as when some object familiar to us all—
> A street, a spoon, a river, a show, a star, a toothache—
> Is brought to our attention, called up from our memory
> To light up the darkened surface of something we've barely known of
> —So did the epic simile sing of a silent past.
>
> (RR)

Auden would have loved it.

It would be impossible, and scarcely desirable, to consider Hollander without reference to his "other tradition"—and indeed to the idea of tradition itself, the sense of the past as a heavy weight which, when set down, haunts with its absence. One way to read *The Figure of Echo* and, to a less pronounced degree, *Rhyme's Reason* involves thinking of them as parts of a serial study of poetic influence, the "anxiety" more or less displaced by scholarly zeal in the former and by the playfully didactic impulse in the latter. And one way to read Hollander's recent poems, from "Spectral Emanations" and "Blue Wine" to the recently completed *Powers of Thirteen,* is to discern in them the poet's deliberate effort to reinvent his influences, to trade Auden for Stevens and to subordinate both to a style of wit learned from despair, a mode of speech filtered through a funnel of silence. "When styles one had to find could be / The ultimate morality, / I worked progressions on the late," Hollander writes in "Upon Apthorp House" (*SE*), acknowledging an early commitment to Ben Jonson's "poetic morals" but putting it in the past tense. "Now I must learn to play the mute."

In the beginning, Hollander's reading of tradition led him to cast the primal poet as a maker not a seer, as Adam not Orpheus. The tendency persists, if not always in a major key. With a breezy exuberance reminiscent of Auden, Hollander performs "Adam's Task" in the poem of that title:

> Thou, pambler; thou, rivarn; thou, greater
> Wherret, and thou, lesser one;
> Thou, sproal; thou, zant; thou, lily-eater.
> Naming's over. Day is done.
>
> (SE)

Hollander's debt to Auden, as "Ben Jonson's heir in our age," can scarcely be overestimated. However often he has lately turned to Stevens for poetic guidance, it was through his distinctive assimilation of Auden's influence that Hollander originally defined himself; his very ambivalence on the subject confirms its importance. Consider the ease with which "Under Aquarius," written in commemoration of Auden's sixty-fifth birthday, slips into the cadences of "In Praise of Limestone":

> Languid and unregimental,
> Hand in hand but, alas, thereby thus somehow in step,
> Young people drift in the square, the evening's readying early
> Still, and the quiet shade daubing the pavements with dim
> Colors of doubt, and of colder shadows awaiting their moment.
>
> (Tales Told of the Fathers, 1975)

Unfortunately omitted from *Spectral Emanations,* this fine poem argues a degree of poetic intimacy that has its threatening side, as Hollander notes by way of a typically rueful echo, a sober "alas." Auden's "band of rivals" climb "Arm in arm, but never, thank God, in step"; by following their "unregimental" example, however, Hollander's latecomers cannot but be "in step." As long ago as the time of "Upon Apthorp House," Hollander recognized the problem, likening *his* "W.H." to Shakespeare's:

> Take care, Old Enterprise! One tries
> The ancient models on for size
> And leaves them off when he can know
> They're more than something to outgrow.
> I've learned that time will not be tricked,
> So thanks, old habits I have kicked!
> And onelie begetters, please go pack,
> Old W.H., get off my back!
>
> (SE)

The Audenesque technique would seem to bely the manifest content of these lines. Like Yeats in "The Tower," Hollander feels he must bid his muse go pack, but he is careful to say *à demain* and not *adieu*; he can't quite kick the Auden habit—luckily for us, since Auden's influence has frequently given Hollander a needed shot in the arm. The rhythms of Auden's "Caliban to the Audience" are apparent in Hollander's prose sequence *In Place*; "Upon Apthorp House" itself has much the same relation to Marvell's "Upon Appleton House" that Auden's "Letter to Lord Byron" has to *Don Juan*. *Reflections on Espionage* is only the most dramatic example of an influence that in the end has proved more an inspiration than an inhibition. If that poem's machinery comes from *The Double Cross System* by John Masterman, its spirit is identifiably that of *The Orators* and other of Auden's early "spy" poems (e.g. "The Secret Agent"); from Auden, too, comes the conception of the poet as a double man, in need of a "cover" if only—only!— to make a living. Significantly, the death of Steampump—Auden's code-name in *Reflections on Espionage*—serves Hollander as his point of departure and as one of his poem's governing conditions:

> Steampump is gone. He died quietly in his
> Hotel room and his sleep. His cover people
> Attended to everything. What had to
> Be burned was burned. He taught me, as you surely
> Know, all that I know.

Well, not quite all. To the extent that, in deploying an Audenesque array of rhetorical strategems, Hollander has surrendered the initiative of meaning to his words themselves, he has certainly deviated from the insistent rationalism that characterized Auden after 1940. Still, in his pride of craft and artful rhetoric, Hollander has carried on a vital undertaking he is right to identify with Auden. And in converting an obsession—with, for example, echoes and allusions—into a system of tropes, he has enlarged the means at the literary artist's disposal.

II

Since Eliot, no poet besides Hollander has so relentlessly—almost systematically—woven quotations into the fabric of his original texts. One effect of such a procedure is to raise anew the question of what originality entails. "The fore-going generations beheld God and nature face to face; we, through their eyes," Emerson wrote. "Why should not we also enjoy an original relation to the universe?" Given the imitative nature of language, however, what would constitute literary originality? Adam's task having once been performed, is it not patently impossible to make an intelligible statement "in one's own words"? (Harry Mathews plays a fine trick on his students when he asks them to do just that.) Leave it to Hollander's Doctor Reinkopf, a man of pure mind, to pose the problem in Platonic terms (in *Powers of Thirteen*):

> *"Every soul is unique, and, thereby, original:*
> *It is only when it employs the body to make*
> *Something of something else, or utter something, that it*
> *Falls into the nature of being imitative."*

The testy Doctor insists on a rigid division between soul and body, dance and walk, poetry and prose, originality and imitation. But the poet knows better. Language does not live by denotation alone; where else do the material and spiritual realms intersect if not in the Word? With its surplus of meanings, language is as much an agent of creative imagination as it is an instrument of representation. Ambling along in measured footsteps, we can therefore count on "our soles and our wingtips" to circumvent the problem of "an original way of walking" or lift us beyond it, as Hollander demonstrates in these lines:

> *Walk* holds *talk* and *work* by their hands,
> Between—yet beyond—them both, perplexing the Doctor.
> The body's stride and trudge aside, our strolling involves
> Our soles and our wingtips equally beating against
> The pavements of the pure air and the clouded sidewalks;
> Whether gliding through the rainy town on errands of
> Light, or idling in some brightened mews at midnight, or
> Making the city's great *paseo* late on a fine
> Afternoon as shadows beckon to the lights of shops.

Like atoms converging in a magnetic field, the words bounce off one another, and their essences change in the process. *Talk* and *work* combine to yield *walk*; light errands split apart into "errands of / Light," a very different thing. To a pattern of hidden rhymes, the passage owes its music. "Stride" leads to "aside," "strolling" to "soles," "gliding" to "idling," "light" to "brightened" to "midnight." The reader is swept along—swept off his feet, one might say—in the melodious rush.

Like Eliot before him, Hollander would behold God and nature book to book, from a seat in a Borgesian library of Babel, *après le deluge* of cultural history. For Eliot's "visions and revisions," Hollander serves up "the future / Repast"; where *The Waste Land* splices together Marvell, Spenser, the Psalms, and Mrs. Porter, "Mount Blank" arranges an easy commerce between Shelley, Petrarch, *Exodus,* and the "ludicrous Snifflehorn." Hollander seems intent, Paul Zweig has observed, to "make it old." But he does so not out of a reactionary impulse, nor merely in order to make a virtue out of his necessarily "belated arrival," but in an effort to reclaim his original sources, originality being a condition of priority as much as of novelty. A true echo, Hollander points out, cannot but distort the sound that preceded it, and in the distortion is originality enough; to echo a past is to originate a future.

The way Hollander's poems illuminate one another and are illumined in turn by his critical writing ensures that separate treatment of any of his volumes will branch out eventually to touch upon the others. To take late things first, as echoes do, we might frame a discussion with *The Figure of Echo,* knowing that the many forms allusion can assume—from repetition to deliberate misquotation to erasure—all find a home in Hollander's verse. *The Figure of Echo* reads rather like a poem that happens to cloak itself in the language of critical discourse: just as Hollander's verse poems perform acts of interpretation, so his prose, defying easy categorization, has come to avail itself of the liberties of poetry.

The book begins with "Echo Acoustical." Under this heading, Hollander presents scientific explanations and mythic reverberations (thunder apprehended as an echo of lightning, for example), pausing to ponder some singular properties of the ineluctable modality of the audible. By nature, echo is a "trope of silence," Hollander argues. The thought underscores "Last Echo," one of the songs in the "Lyrical Interval" at the center of *Blue Wine.* Notice, in lines three and four, the characteristic play on an antecedent poem—in this instance "Ode on a Grecian Urn" with its "silence and slow time":

> Echo has the last word,
> But she loses the rest,
> Giving in to silence
> After too little time.
> And, after all, what is
> A last word, then? After
> All the truth has been told—
> No more than a cold rhyme.
>   (*BW*)

Hollander's esoterica is a delight, and the category of "Echo Acoustical" includes such gems as "echoes that would answer in Spanish what was cried out in French," "portable echo chambers," and "frozen echoes, or the voices of mariners flung up from shipboard in wintry northern seas, and released again in summer thawing" (FE). For textbook illustrations of these creative sorts of echo, we need only turn to Hollander's verse. Consider rhyme as a linguistic echo chamber in "The Old Guitar," whose music resounds "Wildly, like the roaring wind's melody, / Only an echo of its malady" (BW). Or listen to the trilingual, delayed-reaction echo in "Crocus Solus," where the poet adopts the transformational grammar Raymond Roussel put to use in Locus Solus. From "A sigh? No more" we travel to "vivace assai . . . ô Mort" and end with "A sign? O, more" (IP).

The second chapter of The Figure of Echo, "Echo Allegorical," contains among other speculations some that might trigger off a comparative discussion of James Merrill's "Syrinx" and John Ashbery's "Syringa," two highly distinctive renderings of mythic original song. "Syrinx" names the nymph who, pursued by Pan ("the great god Pain," in Merrill's poem), turned into a reed; Ashbery's poem has to do with the myth of Orpheus, but its title alone proposes a closer basis for comparison. A passage Hollander quotes from Francis Bacon moves me to put the issue on the agenda:

> The world itself can have no loves or any want (being content with itself) unless it be of *discourse*. Such is the nymph Echo, a thing not substantial but only a voice; or if it be more of the exact and delicate kind, *Syringa*,—when the words and voices are regulated and modulated by numbers, whether poetical or oratorical.
>
> (FE)

While he cites beneficent versions of Echo the goddess, Hollander's own poetry is manifestly Judaic in its conception of echo as "a secondary, or derivative, voice of the holy spirit" with "at best a contingent authority." It is worth keeping in mind that *bat kol*, meaning "daughter of a voice," is the Hebrew idiom for "echo." Hence the pathos of "Cohen on the Telephone" (SE), where we come across "Ben Cole, the son of your voice," who has changed his name from Cohen. "An assimilated echo," Hollander wryly notes.

"Echo Schematic," subject of the third chapter of The Figure of Echo, is exemplified in Rhyme's Reason—

Echo will have it that each line's last word
(ECHO:)   Erred.
Echo will chop down words like "fantasize"

(ECHO:)   *To size.*
Out of what stuff is Echo's wit then spun?
(ECHO:)   *Pun.*
Can English have a full, Italian echo?
(ECHO:)   *Ecco!*

—and, more complexly, in *Powers of Thirteen*:

That great, domed chamber, celebrated for its full choir
Of echoes: high among its shadowed vaults they cower
Until called out. What do echoes do when they reply?
Lie, lie, lie about what we cried out, about their own
Helplessness in the face of silence. What do they do
To the clear call that they make reverberate? *Berate,*
Berate it for its faults, its frangible syllables.

But only with "Echo Metaphorical" and "Echo Metonymic" do we reach the figure of speech that takes center stage in Hollander's poems. Simply put, it is a pun charged with meaning; the meaning derives from a subversive allusion to a prior text. The accents of Milton's Satan are clearly audible, *toujours déjà*, in both of the following:

to howl a loud howl like, "Down,
Be thou my Up."

(*SE*)

Despite the bleakness of most rural sights,
Choose Adirondack over Brooklyn Heights,
Better in solitude than fear to dwell,
To yawn in heaven, than explode in hell.

(*SE*)

In the hierarchy Hollander proposes in *The Figure of Echo,* a quotation that takes liberties with its source—an echo in the true sense—is superior in kind to a faithful citation. Echoes distort; and the manner and degree of distortion, its subtlety and profundity, form the basis for distinguishing a fruitful trope from a bad pun. The larger implications of this reasoning are significant. Robert Frost defined poetry as what gets lost in translation, but one could as easily argue that poetry *is* mistranslation; the Italian *traduttore, traditore* pun—"translating" likened to "traducing"—would seem to apply to poetry itself, or at least to the poems of our moment that, like Hollander's, bear a knowing relation to the influential past, approaching the world as though it were a text commanding interpretation—"a rod of text held out by / A god of meaning" (*BW*).

The most sophisticated form of mistranslation is Hollander's "Echo Metaleptic," also known as the trope of transumption. With his exposition of this arcane term and his delineation of its usage Hollander has done the critical community a considerable service. It is a fascinating trope. It proceeds, Hollander tells us, from "an interpretive or revisionary power which raises the echo even louder than the original text"—another way of saying that it signals, and authorizes, an act of appropriation; it eschews borrowing in favor of theft. By linguistic sleight of hand, the trope manages a complete transformation of the quoted material. Indeed, by substitution of a like-sounding word or by subtle erasure, "Echo Metaleptic" acts very much like an inspired typo. Hollander's canonical example is from Virgil's first eclogue: "Shall I, beholding what was my empire, marvel at a few ears of grain?"—where *ears* stands for *years*. Similarly, *swords* chips off into *words*, leaving us with "the clashed edges of two words that kill" in Stevens's "Le Monocle de Mon Oncle." Titles are notorious places for metaleptic reversals to lurk in. Hollander's "A Season in Hellas" makes the lyric that follows seem, precisely, pre-Rimbaldian; on the facing page of *Spectral Emanations*, "Mount Blank" supersedes Shelley's "Mont Blanc" with the universal blank of Emerson's "Nature."

It would be useful to compare Hollander on this score with Ashbery, whose brilliant pantoum "Variation on a Noel" leaves "Variation on a Novel" somewhere behind. Hollander's titles imply an effort to reconstitute and repossess the past by determined acts of will. Ashbery's thefts are equally deliberate but are predicated on the seemingly perverse wish to ignore the past even in the act of including it. Ashbery has mentioned that, writing a poem, he begins with the title rather than arriving at one as an afterthought. Twice in *Self-Portrait in a Convex Mirror* he begins with quotations: "As One Put Drunk into the Packet-Boat" is a line from Andrew Marvell's "Tom May's Death"; "As You Came from the Holy Land" comes from a poem attributed to Sir Walter Raleigh. By contrast, Hollander's sources are apt to conceal themselves out in the open, as it were; after all, if "Mount Blank" subverts its predecessor, it must depend for its effects on the reader's awareness of the original. Ashbery's modifications of tradition with individual talent would seem to rest on no such Eliotic assumption. His quotations paradoxically call little or no attention to their sources; they serve as openings, and their destination is unprecedented space. The quoted phrase is liberated from its initial context; the poet *presents* it, in several senses of the word. Yet, as Hollander writes in *The Figure of Echo*, "in order to under-

stand the title [of a poem], its relation to the work, and thereby something
about the work itself, the fragment of quoted material must be traced to its
source"—and yes, something about Ashbery's poems *does* impel the reader
to go back to the launching pad. It is as though the relation between Ashbery's "packet-boat" and Marvell's is meant "to be proposed but never
formulated," as Ashbery put it in another context; it must remain mysterious, a matter for the mirrors of speculation to reflect on.

III

I should like to conclude with some comments on *In Place* and *Powers
of Thirteen,* the former because, obscurely published, it has been unfortunately neglected; the latter because its brilliance is such as to warrant sending
out the appropriate early-warning signal loud and clear.

As prose poems, the works that constitute *In Place* are rather unusual.
A representative example, short enough to be quoted in full, goes by the
Stevensian title of "Figures of Speech. Figures of Thought. Figures of Earth
and Water."

> Once upon a time, the old, wild synecdoche of
>   landslides was frighteningly transumed when
>   a mountain—Mt. Black—rolled downward like
>   one of its own boulders, over the whole peaceless
>   land. In metonymy meanwhile, beyond the other
>   mountains, a mad sea was flowing somewhere,
>   like a river.
>
>   (*IP*)

The nearest thing to an antecedent form for this poem is Kafka's "On Parables." The world is apprehended in the one case as a rhetorical stratagem,
in the other as a parable with an enigmatic punchline.

As in Auden's "Caliban to the Audience," the dominant mode of *In
Place* seems to be late James made elegant; smooth if purely rhetorical transitions substitute for the master's hems, haws, and evasive patches of dialogue. I am struck by the presence of what Ashbery once called "the great
'as if.'" It makes appearances in a number of poems, though nowhere more
notably than in "The Old Pier-Glass." One could chart out "The Old Pier-
Glass" as a progression from "as if" to "more as if" to "what if" to "would
have had" to "would be": the conditionals surround an absence, as in a
frame:

It was as if, he thought, someone had censored
the whole of a well-meaning but naively
loquacious wartime letter, leaving about its
cut-out center only a frame to be sent on
nevertheless, with needless earnestness,
to its addressee.

(*IP*)

The phrase "so that" creates a similar effect in "Patches of Light / Like Shadows of Something." The pattern here leads from the suspended causality of the opening ("—So that we have, after all, to be grateful that our light lies broken in pieces") through a series of suppositions ("were we to have to live in the generality of it") and conditional statements ("Perhaps if everything were to be reconstituted along with it") to a very equivocal "as it is": "the very breaking-up of the radiance that might have forever remained a deep ground was what will always cause us to have embraced these discrete fragments—turning on and off, fading, ending in a border of darkness—as with the arms of our heart" (*IP*). Audacious though it is, this final simile must play second fiddle to the verbal pyrotechnics that precede it: the extraordinary juggling of tenses, the insistent "it," make us read the poem as the very epitome of a contingency clause.

The point, and it's a Jamesian point, is the construction of palpable metaphors out of airy nothings; the imagination is centered on the word. Grammar is generative, conjuring its own reality into being; reality is contingent on language, instead of the other way around. As though to dramatize the perceived disjunction between word and world, "The Old Pier-Glass" is a free-floating metaphor, where A = B but B is never identified. Something like this occurs at that moment in "The Beast in the Jungle" when James lets drop the idiomatic "sounding of their depths" and proceeds to renew the cliché: "It was as if these depths, constantly bridged over by a structure that was firm enough in spite of its lightness and of its occasional oscillation in the somewhat vertiginous air, invited on occasion, in the interest of their nerves, a dropping of the plummet and a measurement of the abyss." Out of nothing, something comes, and we can trace its shape even if we remain uncertain as to its meaning. "Patches of Light," meanwhile, presents itself as the consequence of some unknown cause, the "therefore" of an argument whose premises cannot be ascertained. Again I think of James's John Marcher, for whom May Bartram's face was "a reminder, yet not quite a remembrance": "It affected him as the sequel of something of which he had lost the beginning."

Like *Reflections on Espionage, In Place* seems to scatter clues liberally about, as though to facilitate decoding. These poems all concern aspects of writing; tropes are trumps. "The Way We Walk Now," which begins the sequence, is "about" the writing of prose poems; the vehicle is so apt— Valéry famously identified prose with walking, poetry with dancing—that the tenor need not be named straight out. In this way the poems assert their independence from a "key" even as they appear to lend the code-breaker a helping hand—and this is their final strength, an abstract lyricism:

> . . . But when true beauty does finally come
> crashing at us through the stretched paper
> of the picturesque, we can wonder how we had
> for so long been able to remain distracted
> from its absence.
>
> (IP)

That is the whole of "End of a Chapter," another sequel to a lost beginning.

Powers of Thirteen is a far more ambitious sequence, holding 169 poems, or thirteen squared; each contains thirteen lines, and each line contains thirteen syllables. In the manner of Harry Mathews's *Trial Impressions* (1977), numbers head the individual poems while for good measure italicized titles appear below them and to the right. The titles themselves convey a sense of the book's range of moods ("Taking It Easy," "Being Puzzled," "Speaking Plainly"), styles ("Literal Account," "Dreams and Jokes," "Promissory Note," "Eclogue"), and areas of inquiry ("Body and Soul," "An Apology for Poetry," "Public Landmarks," "Highway, 1949"). In these *sonnets manqués* or "maker's dozens," Hollander has framed an original mode of singing "in a world where forms are not given, where style is not canonical." Affording a maximum of variability within a tightly controlled order, the sequence achieves its most privileged moments not at the expense of poetic craft but precisely by its agency; the poems' form provides the author with both the means and the motive for metaphor. In "Letter," for example, every line begins with "M," the thirteenth (and middle) letter of the alphabet. What results is an explosion of alliterative association, a "Mess of amazing amusements"—pun on maze, pun on muse—and "Mid-forest musics." In the process the poem explores the nature of "the middle," which it comes to define as the place where "both ends meet." Goes without saying, perhaps, that "Letter" is located near the heart of the sequence and that "meet" both begins and ends the poem (*PT*).

The "you" to which most of *Powers of Thirteen* is addressed stands for any number of muses, from Calliope and Melpomene to "Laurie, Stella,

Delia, Celia, Bea and the others," from "the bemused / Daughters of memory" to language itself as the necessary medium for all musings. (At one point a working title for the sequence was "Taking You At Your Word.") Hollander has cheerfully appropriated Ashbery's habit of liberating the pronoun from a mixed point of reference. This "indeterminacy," far from nihilistic, generates a multiplicity of meanings, and that is its virtue. Again and again in *Powers of Thirteen* Hollander salutes "the power of 'might' that makes us write"—the conditionals of language that give poets their right of way. The book is, first and foremost, a celebration of linguistic possibility and verbal metamorphoses. As "a perpetual calendar," it marks occasions (May Day, the Fourth of July, Labor Day), meditates on the seasons, dwells on the theme of erotic love, studies public monuments, mixes memory and desire; in short, it performs many of the services of the traditional sonnet sequence, the poet having found a formula for subverting and thereby renewing that most venerable of extended forms. But, as Hollander has remarked, "unless poetry is parabolic about itself, it cannot be about anything else," and it is as a parable of its own making—a series of "quests for the nature of the quest"—that *Powers of Thirteen* establishes itself as Hollander's finest long work to date.

As usual with Hollander, the reader will need a scorecard to get the most out of the action. Hollander has appended two pages of notes to the sequence; there could as easily be five times as many. It pays, for example, to have in mind the famous first poem of Sidney's *Astrophel and Stella* ("Loving in truth, and fain in verse my love to show") when we read Hollander's "The Pretext" ("Lying in love and feigning far worse") or when we confront the poet's "truant pen" in "Your Command." Still, the esoteric mythmaking that made "Spectral Emanations" a difficult pleasure is absent here, and as a result the poetry is admirably accessible, with or without a gloss. From a subsequence of thirteen poems about the charms and perils of that magical integer, consider this meditation on names and numbers, beginnings and ends:

Just the right number of letters—half the alphabet;
Or the number of rows on this monument we both
Have to share in the building of. We start out each course
Now, of dressed stone, with something of me, ending where you
Handle the last block and leave something of you within
Or outside it. So we work and move toward a countdown,
Loving what we have done, what we have left to do. A
Long day's working makes us look up where we started from

> And slowly to read down to the end, down to a base,
> Not out, to some distant border, the terminal bland
> Destructions at their ends that lines of time undergo.
> Endings as of blocks of text, unlit by the late sun
> Really underlie our lives when all is said and done.
>
> (*PT*)

Italicized, the initial letters of the lines spell out their message for all to see, but the closing letters also form an acrostic: "The unnamed one." In its complexity, wit, and sheer ingenuity, the gesture is perfectly representative of the sleight-of-hand man in action.

HAROLD BLOOM

Preambles to What Was Possible

Preambles and Other Poems, Alvin Feinman's first and still his only volume, was published in 1964, when the poet was thirty-five. The poet and critic John Hollander, in a note written for his anthology of contemporary poetry, characterized his selections from Feinman as "perhaps the most difficult of those in this collection. Their difficulty is not that of allusion, nor of ellipsis, nor of problematical form, however, but the phenomenological difficulty of confronting the boundary of the visual and the truly visionary." To instance the three other really difficult but excellent poets of my generation, as examples of Hollander's kinds of difficulty, I would cite Geoffrey Hill for sustained indirection of allusiveness, John Ashbery for ellipsis, and A. R. Ammons for problematical form. Feinman presents the greatest difficulties of these four profoundly rewarding poets, difficulties not only for the reader, however energetic and generous, but clearly for the poet himself as well. Feinman's prime precursor is Crane, as Ashbery's is Stevens, and Ammons's (happily for him) the more remote Emerson, or a kind of merged Emerson-Whitman figure. Like Crane, Feinman begins with a volume of difficult yet frequently radiant lyrics, but unlike Crane he has not been able to go on to the larger form of internalized quest or visionary romance, and his inability (thus far) to continue appears to have doomed his remarkable volume to neglect.

From *The Ringers in the Tower.* © 1971 by The University of Chicago. The University of Chicago Press, 1971. Originally entitled "The Dialectic of Romantic Poetry in America."

The great poems in *Preambles and Other Poems* are the title-poem (this poet's longest, at eighty-four lines), "November Sunday Morning," "Pilgrim Heights," and the brief "Circumferences" that ends the volume. Only these will be considered here; all are in the line of descent from Emerson, and all mingle the two modes I have called Bacchus and Merlin. Here is "November Sunday Morning":

> And the light, a wakened heyday of air
> Tuned low and clear and wide,
> A radiance now that would emblaze
> And veil the most golden horn
> Or any entering of a sudden clearing
> To a standing, astonished, revealed . . .
>
> That the actual streets I loitered in
> Lay lit like fields, or narrow channels
> About to open to a burning river;
> All brick and window vivid and calm
> As though composed in a rigid water
> No random traffic would dispel . . .
>
> As now through the park, and across
> The chill nailed colors of the roofs,
> And on near trees stripped bare,
> Corrected in the scant remaining leaf
> To their severe essential elegance,
> Light is the all-exacting good,
>
> That dry, forever virile stream
> That wipes each thing to what it is,
> The whole, collage and stone, cleansed
> To its proper pastoral . . .
>   I sit
> And smoke, and linger out desire.

"Cleansed / To its proper pastoral," for here there is no boundary between the visual and the visionary, and the poet is naturalized again as shepherd of the Invisible. In the torments of his quest for an enabling act of the mind, Feinman arrives at only a handful (or fewer) of such privileged moments. "November Sunday Morning" is his only poem of a celebratory kind and all it celebrates is a certain cleansing light, but actually seen. And, vision seen, the poet rests quietly on heights, and lingers out desire. When he considers the radiance, he declares it as correction, that which cleanses each thing to what it is. Emerson might have marveled at so ascetic a privilege, but would have recognized this as Bacchic in his own sense, though reduced.

Stevens could begin only by reduction, to each variation upon the First Idea, each nothing that yet *was*. Feinman, as all his perceptive readers painfully realize, scarcely can bear to begin at all. This restricts his readers necessarily to those few who are prepared to tolerate his reluctance, for who can wish, even now, to be invited into so stark a theater of mind? Feinman's American ancestors, culminating in Crane, move toward the reader, in the large, vitalistic gestures of natural abundance, but Feinman's difficult art is the closest equivalent we have to Valéry and the even more painfully achieved middle phases of Rilke. I dwell on difficulty because there is no evading it in discussing *Preambles and Other Poems*. Their difficulty is their necessity, and in a subtle sense defines their dialectical stance as Bacchus or poetic possession and Merlin or Necessity itself. The central vision in the volume is of the mind, ceaselessly an *activity,* engaged in the suffering process of working apart all things that are joined by it:

> And so
> The mind in everything it joins
> And suffers to redeem apart
> Plays victim to its own intent
> ("Preambles")

> history

> At the close will cripple to these things:
> A body without eyes, a hand, the vacant
> Presence of unjoined, necessary things.
> ("Landscape, Sicily")

> And always the tips of the fingers of both her hands
> will pull or twist at a handkerchief
> like lovely deadly birds at a living thing
> trying to work apart something exquisitely,
> unreasonably joined.
> ("Relic")

> Only this presence destined
> As a weather from its source

> Toward broad or violent unleashings
> Fables of the suffered and the joined
> ("Three Elementary Prophecies")

I

> Who have called you upright, destiny, or wall,
> —How we exchange circumferences within
> The one footfall that bruises us asunder.
>   ("Circumferences")

This is the power of the mind over the universe of sense, not a power of renovation upon a universe of death (as in Wordsworth) but a tragedy of mind, victim to its own intent, which is to make by separations. Every joining of particulars in this poet's universe enforces a vacancy, every linkage indeed *vacates,* yet his sensibility finds exquisiteness only where we are bruised asunder. In Stevens, to "abstract" tends to dissociate, and probably Stevens should have used the latter word for his reductions to the First Idea. His immediate stimulus was Valéry, who had insisted "there are no names for those things amongst which one is completely alone," and who defined the characteristic of consciousness as "a process of perpetual exhaustion, of detachment without rest or exclusion from everything that comes before it, whatever that thing may be—an inexhaustible activity." No visionary poet could work within the limits of consciousness thus construed, and the visionary strain in Stevens became progressively more attenuated. Stevens had a mixed temperament, neither as wintry nor as Floridian as it sometimes appeared, and the poetics of Valéry were thus not wholly inimical to him. But Feinman's poetic temperament is Emersonian; like Crane, he is wholly a visionary, but afflicted (unlike Crane) with a critical consciousness in the mode of Valéry. He cannot create by dissociation, but only by joinings, like Whitman and Crane, joinings to which nevertheless he cannot give credence. His horror of the visual becomes, in the poems, a defense against madness, and still another hindrance to the fabling his gift requires.

Wordsworth, who in his wisdom feared the bodily eye as the most despotic of the senses, the one most likely to usurp the mind's mastery, has affected American poets (after the time of Bryant, when the influence was more direct) largely through the misprision of Transcendentalism. Thoreau is the major American instance of this misprision, since his *clinamen* from Wordsworth is the actual reversal of *The Prelude*'s warning, and apotheosizes the eye. Emerson, always more dialectical, vacillates in "Nature," where the eye that sees the radiance is the same eye that radiance employs to behold

us. Crane's furious synesthesia betrays an Emersonian uneasiness with pure
vision, yet Crane is tormented by particulars of light, and testifies frequently
to the eye's tyranny. Feinman, following Crane, is obsessed by light and by
sharp outline, self-consciously knowing the eye's threat to his poetry, but
unable to evade a terrible, continuous effort to merge with the God Ananke
in the form of "Light . . . the all-exacting good." "November Sunday Morning," a chilled epiphany, approximates the skeptical rapture of Shelley at
nearly his most intense, yet lacks the mellowness of Shelley's urbanity (or of
the Crane of the lovely "Sunday Morning Apples," a possible source of
Feinman's poem). It remains unique among this poet's work as the one
venture where the joined is accepted, and "each thing" is redeemed without
being pulled apart by the mind. "Wounded by apprehensions out of speech, /
I hold it up against a disk of light—," Crane says of the "stone of lust" in
"Possessions," a poem in *White Buildings* whose presence is felt in nearly
every poem in Feinman's book, in every hope of "all violences stayed and
sudden light." Strongest of these hopes is "Pilgrim Heights":

> Something, something, the heart here
> Misses, something it knows it needs
> Unable to bless—the wind passes;
> A swifter shadow sweeps the reeds,
> The heart a colder contrast brushes.
>
> So this fool, face-forward, belly
> Pressed among the rushes, plays out
> His pulse to the dune's long slant
> Down from blue to bluer element,
> The bold encompassing drink of air.
>
> And namelessness, a length compound
> Of want and oneness the shore's mumbling
> Distantly tells—something a wing's
> Dry pivot stresses, carved
> Through barrens of stillness and glare:
>
> The naked close of light in light,
> Light's spare embrace of blade and tremor
> Stealing the generous eye's plunder
> Like a breathing banished from the lung's
> Fever, lost in parenthetic air.
>
> Raiding these nude recesses, the hawk
> Resumes his yielding balance, his shadow

Swims the field, the sands beyond,
The narrow edges fed out to light,
To the sea's eternal licking monochrome.

The foolish hip, the elbow bruise
Upright from the dampening mat,
The twisted grasses turn, unthatch,
Light-headed blood renews its stammer—
Apart, below, the dazed eye catches

A darkened figure abruptly measured
Where folding breakers lay their whites;
The heart from its height starts downward,
Swum in that perfect pleasure
It knows it needs, unable to bless.

With only a few companions—Ashbery's "Soonest Mended," Ammons's "Saliences," Geoffrey Hill's "Annunciations" among them—this stands for me as one of the fully achieved and central poems by a poet of my generation. The miraculously subtle movement of the first stanza is a reduction or *epoché* on the "somewhat more loudly sweep the string" theme, here treated not as the advent of a greater subject but as the promise, altogether precarious, of a momentary end to an oxymoronic agony of near-solipsism. Agony, yet this is upon the heights, from which the heart at least must start downward, for life and poetry to go on. The poet's eye, dazed by its Bacchic intoxication with all the shore's particulars, yields its plunder first to a visionary light that might as well be a darkness to it, and then more fortunately to a sudden sense of otherness ("Apart, below . . . A darkened figure abruptly measured"). With this startling end to a perfect pleasure of solipsistic, Bacchic repletion, the poet's consciousness abandons a height "unable to bless" and descends "Where folding breakers lay their whites," to a scene where the ocean offers itself, obliquely indicating a new context where blessing is possible.

This ought to be the constant mode of *Preambles and Other Poems*, suggesting a way out of the impasse of blocked vision, of the world encountered in the Greenberg-Crane *Emblems of Conduct*. But Feinman, wherever his second and subsequent volumes may reach as vision, yields in most of his first volume to the Emersonian Necessity. Apart from "November Sunday Morning" and "Pilgrim Heights," he enters the realms of Merlin, most strikingly in his title-poem. "Preambles" is too long to give complete here, and is most inadequately represented by excerpts. Its title marks it as this poet's

bracketing of his quest, and necessarily it is a driving, dissociative composition, with the unenviable distinction of being the most genuinely difficult
poem of real coherence and value by an American poet of this century.
Though thoroughly justifiable, the difficulty is preamble to Feinman's failure
to make a canon of poems, to the slow waste of his genius. Though there
are parallel problems in consciousness in Valéry and Rilke, those poets fortunately were free of the peculiarly American malady of seeking to be Ananke, which in Feinman's case becomes the deplorable quest to write the last
possible poem, a work that takes the post-Romantic consciousness so far as
to make further advances in self-consciousness intolerable. More than any
poet, Feinman is the victim of what Wyndham Lewis called the Demon of
Progress in the Arts, which makes Feinman one of the most American of
poets.

"Preambles" is in three parts, each of seven quatrains. The first rejects
"All / Discursion fated and inept," everything in the poet's past scrutinies
that ended in irrelevance, which comes to not less than everything except for
a handful of particulars out of *the given*:

> I would cite
> Wind-twisted spaces, absence
> Listing to a broken wall . . .
>
> . . . such things
> As thwart beginnings, limit . . .
>
> . . . *Archai*
>
> Bruited through crumbling masteries
> To hang like swollen apples
> In the river, witnesses
> Stilled to their clotted truth.

The problem with poetry of this rare kind, a poetry of "whole meaning"
as Conrad Aiken termed "Preambles," is eloquently presented by Priscilla
Washburn Shaw in her commentary on Valéry's "Le Sylphe":

> For those readers who demand that metaphor be firmly anchored
> so that the links of comparison are readily visible and uni-direc-
> tional, an image like "ma tendre corbeille," and still more "la
> ceinture," is somewhat unsatisfactory, and even obscure. No ex-
> planation, or series of explanations, can totally satisfy if what is
> really desired is a tighter connection between image and referent,
> because it is just this which has deliberately been avoided. This

desire is present in even quite sophisticated readers, and it is
probably a fundamental aspect of our attempt to understand the
world intellectually and emotionally.

"Preambles" goes beyond Valéry by not only postponing or transposing
such attempts to understand, but abrogating them, thus moving to the limits
of the intelligible. Where Valéry beautifully restores our pleasure in particulars ("Les images sont nombreuses / a l'égal de mes regards"), the second
part of "Preambles," with strange serenity, surrenders to a process that ends
the private mind:

> To each defeat a signature
>
> The just reconnaissance
> That even fruit, each excellence
> Confirms its course   A leisure
> As of sap or blood arrested
>
> Only once and to the prime
> Its issue vivifies.

What is left "of every severed thing" completes the poem's third part:

> The *ecce* only, only hands
> Or hardnesses, the gleam a water
> Or a light, a paused thing
> Clothes in vacua killed
>
> To a limbless beauty   Take
> These torn possessives there
> Where you plead the radiant
> Of your truth's gloom   Own
>
> To your sleep, your waking
> The tread that is walked
> From the inner of its pace
> The play of a leaf to an earth.

I feel the immense distinction of this each time I read it, and am as
chilled by it as I am by the closing measures of Emerson's "Merlin" or the
splendid closing paragraphs of "Fate" where we are exhorted to build altars
to the Beautiful Necessity. Criticism has yet to do justice to Feinman's poetry,
particularly "Preambles," but that is because it comes at us asking more

than poetry can (or should) ask. The closing poem in Feinman's volume, "Circumferences," movingly presents the dilemma and the triumph (which are one) of his vision:

> Dawn under day, or dawning, lake, late edge,
> Assumptive pure periphery where one thrust prominence
> Now give me back my eyes, my stride almost
> A next abode, and source   O gathering, your smile
> Is softer and more slow than the guileless surf
> Drying forever at a farthest shore   I
> Who have called you upright, destiny, or wall,
> —How we exchange circumferences within
> The one footfall that bruises us asunder.

This knowing return to what Lacan terms the *Stade du miroir,* on the part of so rigorous a sensibility, so remorselessly advanced a consciousness, is more than yet another instance of the indestructibility of unconscious desire, more than a gently smiling acknowledgment of the equivocal role of primal narcissism in the forming of poetic vision, even at its purest. The poet, just at the point of dawn, studies his reflection in a lake, perhaps relents a little at his own stern questing, and ends his poetry's first phase by the one footfall that bruises him and his image asunder. The obliteration of the other is an exchange of circumferences, a realization of Emerson's wisdom in "Circles": "we seek with insatiable desire . . . to lose our sempiternal memory . . . in short to draw a new circle." But the history of Emerson's progeny—of Robinson, Crane, Feinman as representative poets, and of so many more—suggests that no new circles can be drawn in this great but darkening tradition.

CRUNK

The Work of Gary Snyder

Gary Snyder is an original man. He has written a poetry which is quite unusual and very different from most poetry written in the last years.

The poems take place "In the Woods and at Sea." In the woods and at sea, Mr. Snyder has been able to enjoy and praise the physical life. The movements of all physical things are not abstract or intellectualist, of course, and Mr. Snyder sees that all growing, physical things are in a sense like women, who have "a difficult dance to do, but not in mind."

Mr. Snyder's first book was published in 1959 by Cid Corman, called *Riprap* (Origin Press, 1959). In an appendix to the Grove Press anthology, Mr. Snyder made some remarks on *Riprap*:

> I've recently come to realize that the rhythms of my poems follow the rhythm of the physical work I'm doing and the life I'm leading at any given time—which makes the music in my head which creates the line. Conditioned by the poetic tradition of the English language and whatever feeling I have for the sound of poems I dig in other languages. *Riprap* is really a class of poems I wrote under the influence of the geology of the Sierra Nevada and the daily trail-crew work of picking up and placing granite stones in tight cobble patterns on hard slab. "What are you doing?" I asked Roy Marchbanks. "Rip-rapping," he said. His selection of natural rocks was perfect—. . . I tried writing poems of touch, simple,

From *The Sixties,* no. 6. © 1962 by The Sixties Press.

short words, with the complexity far beneath the surface texture.
In part the line was influenced by the five-and-seven-character
line Chinese poems I'd been reading, which work like sharp blows
on the mind.

The human voices and persons who sometimes rise in Mr. Snyder's
poems are always distinguished by this dignity. For example, in a poem in
Riprap called "Hay for the Horses," we see a man arrive at a barn with a
load of hay. Suddenly, at lunch time, his voice breaks out with his broodings:

Hay for the Horses

He had driven half the night
From far down San Joaquin
Through Mariposa, up the
Dangerous mountain roads,
And pulled in at eight a.m.
With his big truckload of hay
                          behind the barn.
With winch and ropes and hooks
We stacked the bales up clean
To splintery redwood rafters
High in the dark, flecks of alfalfa
Whirling through shingle-cracks of light,
Itch of haydust in the
                          sweaty shirt and shoes.
At lunchtime under Black oak
Out in the hot corral,
—The old mare nosing lunchpails,
Grasshoppers crackling in the weeds—
"I'm sixty-eight," he said,
"I first bucked hay when I was seventeen.
I thought, that day I started,
I sure would hate to do this all my life.
And dammit, that's just what
I've gone and done."

Snyder is not the man to make some complacent moralistic observation
on the driver's words. This sense of worth in the lives of all human beings
is not shared by very many recent American poets. But it recalls Whitman,
with whom Mr. Snyder has other powers in common. For example, there is

the presence of the poet himself as a living figure in nearly every poem. I mean here much more than the mere grammatical first person: I mean the pervading presence of the poet who simultaneously shares in the processes of life and reveals some of its meaning through his actions. Another power which Snyder shares with Whitman is his occasionally humorous awareness of himself in situations that challenge conventional pride. Give or take a few differences, Whitman might have written Mr. Snyder's poem "Cartagena":

> Rain and thunder beat down and flooded the streets—
> We danced with Indian girls in a bar,
>   water half-way to our knees,
> The youngest one slipped down her dress and danced bare to
>   the waist,
> The big negro deckhand made out with his girl on his lap in a
>   chair her dress over her eyes
> Coca-Cola and rum, and rainwater all over the floor.
> In the glittering light I got drunk and reeled through the
>   rooms,
> And cried, "Cartagena! swamp of unholy loves!"
> And wept for the Indian whores who were younger than me,
>   and I was eighteen,
> And splashed after the crew down the streets wearing sandals
>   bought at a stall
> And got back to the ship, dawn came,
>   We were far out at sea.

This poem, in its direct description of life in impolite society, might seem a Beat poem—up to a crucial point. Mr. Snyder's difference from the Beats (to which I shall return later) is apparent in a superior sensitivity. Like Whitman before him, he brings a sense of delicacy to bear upon his treatment of other people's lives. He also has a sense of privacy, even in the most raucous life, which appears in the several meditative poems in *Riprap*. The very first poem in the book is a short poem formed out of a moment in a forest look-out station. It is called "Mid-August at Sourdough Mountain Lookout":

> Down valley a smoke haze
> Three days heat, after five days rain
> Pitch glows on the fir-cones
> Across rocks and meadows
> Swarms of new flies.

> I cannot remember things I once read
> A few friends, but they are in cities.
> Drinking cold snow-water from a tin cup
> Looking down for miles
> Through high still air.

This poem ends, like the previous poem, with an image of utter clarity, as of clear water—a promise of spiritual depth.

The meditative power and the privacy that characterize this brief, beautiful poem are powers which Mr. Snyder displays throughout his work. It is important to mention them, because they imply the presence behind the work of a man who has thought deeply about the body and value of existence conscious of itself. In short, I think that Mr. Snyder is a poet who might be called devout, or religious in the most elementary sense. He regards life with a seriousness so profound that he is able to experience and express the inner life without resorting to the worn-out abstractions which so often nullify the public discussions of spiritual matters.

The poems cited are from his first volume, *Riprap*. It is a beautiful book, and one of the two or three finest books of poetry of the last ten years.

Riprap was a simple collection of occasional poems, but Snyder's next book, *Myths and Texts,* is more carefully organized. It was published by LeRoi Jones with the Eighth Street Bookstore in 1960 (Totem/Corinth Paperbook, New York).

Myths and Texts is arranged in three sections: "Logging," which describes Snyder's experience as a logger in Oregon, and also develops the theme of the destruction of the forests; "Hunting," which describes with great delicacy the lives of animals; and "Burning," which describes certain steps of spiritual life and labors of transformation from one level of life to another. The theme of the book as a whole is praise of physical life. There is a struggle to overcome what the poet calls the "ancient meaningless abstractions of the educated mind." "Get off my back, Confucius."

In the first section, Mr. Snyder is able to describe the violation of living creatures that takes place during a logging operation; he does so by leaping beyond the "meaningless abstractions." The following example is taken from "Poem #8":

> Each dawn is clear
> Cold air bites the throat.
> Thick frost on the pine bough
> Leaps from the tree

                    snapped by the diesel
          Drifts and glitters in the
                    horizontal sun.
          In the frozen grass
                    smoking boulders
                    ground by steel tracks.
          In the frozen grass
                    wild horses stand
                    beyond a row of pines.
          The D8 tears through piss-fir,
          Scrapes the seed-pine
                              chipmunks flee,
          A black ant carries an egg
          Aimlessly from the battered ground.
          Yellowjackets swarm and circle
          Above the crushed dead-log, their home.
          Pine oozes from barked
                    trees still standing,
          Mashed bushes make strange smells.

Although the poet seems most directly concerned, in this poem, with describing a process of destruction, it is interesting to note that his vision also includes a great number of living creatures, whose lives he watches carefully and tenderly. It is this very sense of detail in lives which, in the next group of poems, gathers into such intense focus as to see beyond the literal physical lives of the animals. That is, the group called "Hunting" moves beyond literal description into the beginnings of a spiritual evocativeness. At the end of the first poem in the section, the poet describes himself:

          I sit without thoughts by the log-road
          Hatching a new myth

and it is true. Snyder is always "hatching a new myth," in the sense that he is always seeking for a way to embody his celebration of physical life in some form that will reveal its religious meanings. He never refers to the tired terms of classical mythology. They do not even seem to occur to him. He does use myths, however, not by referring to them but by recreating them in his own poems. He has several poems dedicated to animals; and he refers to "deer" and "bear" as the northwest Indians do—not simply as single living creatures but also as spiritual forces. The result is a poetry of authentic strangeness,

where the spirituality of living creatures shines upon them in the darkness.
The following is a passage from "Poem #6":

> The others had all gone down
> From the blackberry brambles, but one girl
> Spilled her basket, and was picking up her
> Berries in the dark.
> A tall man stood in the shadow, took her arm,
> Led her to his home. He was a bear.
> In a house under the mountain
> She gave birth to sleek dark children
> With sharp teeth, and lived in the hollow
> Mountain many years.

It is in the third group of poems, "Burning," that Mr. Snyder more
frequently refers to the religious ideas of the Orient. What makes his religious
meditations and descriptions in "Burning" so strong is his ability to present
them in terms of the living plants and creatures which he has already described and celebrated in previous parts of his book. The following passages
taken from "Poem #6," "Poem #16," and "Poem #17" illustrate the tone
of the third section:

> "Forming the New Society
>   Within the shell of the Old"
> The motto in the Wobbly Hall
> Some old Finns and Swedes playing cards
> Fourth and Yesler in Seattle.
> O you modest, retiring, virtuous young ladies
>   pick the watercress, pluck the yarrow
> "Kwan kwan" goes the crane in the field,
>   I'll meet you tomorrow;
> A million workers dressed in black and buried,
> We make love in leafy shade.

> Earth! those beings living on your surface
> none of them disappearing, will all be transformed.
> When I have spoken to them
> when they have spoken to me, from that moment on,
> their words and their bodies which they

usually use to move about with, will all change.
I will not have heard them. Signed

( )

Coyote

Rain falls for centuries
Soaking the loose rocks in space
Sweet rain, the fire's out
The black snag glistens in the rain
And the last wisp of smoke floats up
Into the absolute cold
Into the spiral whorls of fire
The storms of the Milky Way . . .
The sun is but a morning star.

The theme of the praise of physical life present everywhere in the book dominates "Poem #16," "Hunting," which deals with a birth:

How rare to be born a human being!
Wash him off with cedar-bark and milkweed
            send the damned doctors home.
Baby, baby, noble baby
Noble-hearted baby.

All the virtues of humor, delicacy, respect for living creatures, human and animal, patience and silence, are to be found in *Myths and Texts,* and in a more generally coherent and disciplined form than in *Riprap*. It is best to conclude this brief introduction to the second book by allowing Mr. Snyder to speak for himself. His words are quoted in the Appendix to *The New American Poetry*:

Myths and Texts grew between 1952 and 1956. Its several rhythms are based on long days of quiet in look-out cabins; settling chokers for the Warm Springs Lumber Co. (looping cables on logs and hooking them to 'D' Caterpillars—dragging and rumbling through the brush); and the songs and dances of Great Basin Indian tribes I used to hang around. The title comes from the happy collections of Sapir, Boas, Swanton, and others made of American Indian folktales early in this century; it also means the two sources of human knowledge—symbols and sense-impressions. I tried to make my life as a hobo and worker, the questions of history and philosophy in my head, and the glimpses of the roots of religion I'd seen through meditation, peyote, and "secret frantic rituals" into one whole thing.

II

I have three ideas about Snyder's work as a whole that I want to bring up. First, his is essentially a Western imagination. His poems are powerfully located—sown, rooted—in the landscape of the far Western states. He is a Western writer just as, for example, Delmore Schwartz, Anthony Hecht, and Howard Moss are Eastern writers. This is the same distinction one would have made earlier between Theodore Dreiser and John P. Marquand; or between Sherwood Anderson and Lionel Trilling. These two sets of writers deal with different geographical landscapes but the distinction is deeper and subtler than that. They differ in what might be called the landscape of the imagination—which each in his way tries to discover and explore.

The Western writer feels a need to approach his characters and incidents with an imagination totally, if temporarily, freed from all concern with abstract ideas. The Eastern writer, such as Mr. Schwartz or Mr. Trilling, does not. Mr. Trilling, thoroughly aware of the existence of the west and the midwest and of the writers from these areas, still writes of them as a philosopher would write: his imagination, for better or for worse, is so saturated with abstract ideas that it would be difficult, if not impossible, for him to prevent their existence in the forefront of his mind. Existing there, they blot out many details of physical life. The poetry of Howard Moss, Anthony Hecht, and Delmore Schwartz is similarly saturated with abstract ideas.

Mark Twain is a Western writer: that is, his imagination is most powerfully moved when he is concerned with concrete details in the lives of nonintellectual people. Of course, he examines such lives with an intellect of great force and clarity. This is also true of early Hemingway. Similarly, Dreiser remains a Westerner even when he writes of New York or Boston. I think that one major sign of these writers' intellectual power is their ability to penetrate and explore the lives of people who are invisible to the academies—the "custodian" who comes in the afternoon and empties the professor's wastebasket; the timid young man who cleans out the rest rooms after ten o'clock at night; the frightened and ambitious textbook pitchman; the farmer who works in the field nearby; the idiot hired man. To force the fact of their mere existence into the consciousness of people whose whole lives are worries over social status is evidence of a strong intellect. With this power the grasp of the writers is permanently caught in sensuous details and imaginative images fresh in themselves. At any rate, the powerful mind that expresses its understanding of life in the forms of the imagination rather than in the forms of abstraction is the kind of American mind I have called Western. Most of its greatest representatives so far have been writers of fiction. One of the most interesting features of Gary Snyder's poetry is that in him we see this "western" imagination in a poet.

The point is worth examining further: it helps to identify Mr. Snyder's originality and it suggests a kind of American poetry that hasn't been very much explored—a kind of poetry which Mr. Snyder has been writing with freshness and dignity, which might be called a poetry of the Western imagination. The term itself doesn't matter much, except for the sake of convenience. It ought to suggest, however, certain features of poetry which are imaginative rather than rhetorical. In such poetry the forms of poems emerge from within the living growth of each particular poem and most definitely *not* in a set of conventions (such as the classical English iambic, with all its masterpieces of the past and its suffocating influence in the present). This new poetry is also marked by the presence of a powerful intelligence which does its thinking through the imagination itself, and not through repetition of the thoughts of established philosophical authorities or of classical myths which are degenerated through excessive or inaccurate use into obstructions rather than doorways to clear thought. Mr. Snyder does indeed embody certain myths in his poetry, but they are not classical myths, but "bear myths," and myths of the senses.

My second idea is that Mr. Snyder's poetry is very different from "Beat" poetry. Snyder has been associated primarily in magazines with the Black Mountain school and the Beats. His association with the latter (he is the hero of *Dharma Bums*) results from his friendship with Kerouac. Snyder's poetry is, however, immediately distinct both in imagination and in style from Beat work. A certain gentleness and care for civilization in Snyder is utterly absent in Ginsberg or Orlovsky, who are in favor, as they say, of "cat vommit." Ginsberg and Orlovsky make strong efforts to coarsen themselves, whereas Snyder does the very opposite. The Beat writers are opposed to civilization of all kinds: Snyder is not. Snyder's work everywhere reveals the grave mind of a man who is highly civilized and who, moreover, makes no pretense of denying his own intelligence.

Snyder's life is entirely different from the life of a Beat poet. Snyder took no part in the race for publicity among the Beats. Instead of merely talking about Zen, he went to Japan and entered a Buddhist monastery in Kyoto, where he still remains, learning Japanese, and undertaking serious study. The difference between his devotion to the Orient and the public exploitation of oriental religiosity by Jack Kerouac, among others, becomes immediately apparent. In order to read Chinese poets, Snyder learned ancient Chinese, a difficult language. He now makes his living translating from ancient Chinese and Japanese texts at a Zen institute in Kyoto, working in the institute in the afternoon and spending the morning at the monastery. His dedication to Chinese civilization is also shown in his translation of some ancient Chinese poems; here is his translation of a little poem by Po Chu-i:

> Tears soak her thin shawl
>   dreams won't come
> —In the dark night, from the front palace,
>   girls rehearsing songs.
> Still fresh and young,
>   already put down,
> She leans across the brazier
>   to wait the coming dawn.
>   (From "Floating World, 3")

My third idea is the reality of the oriental influence on Snyder. The influence of the orient on Snyder is interior: it is the desire to overcome vanity and ambition. This is an influence that is not necessarily available to collectors of oriental objects and books.

The great poets of Japan and, especially, of China, are almost invariably men who pride themselves on being men who devote their entire selves to the life of contemplation and imagination. In their poems they succeed in the struggle against vanity and the desire for power.

Another oriental influence concerns the method of construction of the poem. Chinese poems are formed out of images whose sensory force strikes the mind directly, not as an abstract substitute for an experience, but as an original experience in itself. Let me quote two short poems. The first is Chinese, and the second one of Mr. Snyder's:

> Sleeping a Spring Night in the
> Palace Annexe

The flowers hide palace walls sunk in the shadow,
Birds chatter on their way to roost,
The stars shine and twinkle into the ten thousand palace
        windows,
The nine terraces of heaven lie lulled in the added brightness of
        the moon.
Unable to sleep, I listen for the turning of the golden key in the
        lock.

Because of the wind I think I hear the jade ornaments tinkle.
Tomorrow morning I have to report to the throne,
So I keep wondering how much of the night has flown.
("Tu Fu," translated by Soame Jenyns)

Water

Pressure of sun on the rockslide
Whirled me in dizzy hop-and-step descent,
Pool of pebbles buzzed in a Juniper shadow,
Tiny tongue of a this-year rattlesnake flicked,
I leaped, laughing for little boulder-color coil—
Pounded by heat raced down the slabs to the creek
Deep tumbling under arching walls and stuck
Whole head and shoulders in the water:
Stretched full on cobble—ears roaring
Eyes open aching from the cold and faced a trout.

Mr. Snyder's poem, above, contains no external reference to China or to Chinese poetry. Somebody once said that the prose of the young Ernest Hemingway resembled clean pebbles shining side by side at the bottom of a clear stream-channel; and that is the way Mr. Snyder has let the images of his poem arrange themselves into lines. There is no forcing of the imagination into external and conventional rhetorical patterns, such as have ruptured a good many poems during recent years in America. And yet Mr. Snyder's poem is not formless. It is exquisitely formed from the inside. It follows the clear rhythm of the poet's run down the hill in the hot sun, turns suddenly when he plunges his head in the cold water, and comes to a delightful close with the poet, his skin alive with the chill, gazing under the surface, face to face with a fish.

I began by noting Mr. Snyder's conscious debt to Chinese poets, and ended by admiring his ability to convey the astonishment of a fish. The two points suggest the importance of Mr. Snyder's study of Chinese. He has bypassed its biographical and historical externals, such as might be flaunted by someone who wanted to impress his readers, and has learned how to form his imagination into poems according to a tradition which is great and vital, and which is wholly distinct from the tradition of British poetry, very great in itself but somewhat inhibiting to American imaginative experience.

It is distressing to have to say it again, but few people in American literary discussion seem to take seriously the fact that what Walt Whitman accurately called "British literature" is not the only tradition from which American writers can be permitted to learn anything. It is one thing, of course, for scholars and critics to make plump careers of writing articles on, say, Pasternak, Quasimodo, Joyce, Yeats, Tagore, and even Mao Tse-tung. But American poets, with a frequency that is dismal in proportion as it seems automatic—that is, conditioned—tend either to give up all hope of imaginative precision and delicacy altogether, as Ginsberg in his "Howl" or Freeman in his *Apollonian Poems,* or to regard all deviation from the iambic rhetoric of the British tradition as an absurdity when it fails or as a crime akin to parricide when it succeeds. Whitman patiently suggested the exploration of traditions beyond the British; but, as Hart Crane complained with terrible despair in one of his greatest letters, many people won't even read *Democratic Vistas.*

Perhaps the reading of such a work, endangering as it does the trite and completely false public image of Whitman which still persists in America despite the Beats' attempt to appropriate him, requires a courage which few men are willing to assume—a courage akin to Whitman's own. In any case, Gary Snyder has displayed a courage of similar kind, not in order to face Whitman's devastating and perhaps unsurpassed criticism of America's puritanical materialism; but in order to undertake one of the tasks of the imagination for which Whitman often felt poets in America should prove most capable: the exploration of living traditions which, shunning the British tradition, nonetheless display powers of poetry which equal and sometimes surpass that tradition; and to make this search for the purpose of claiming America itself—by which I mean literally our own lives and the people and places we live among day by day—for the imagination.

I have discussed the Chinese poets at some length in this essay because they mean so much to Mr. Snyder, and because they reveal in their own work the possibility of a further growth in American poetry which has scarcely been considered. My final impression of Mr. Snyder himself, however, does not depend on his debt to this or that writer.

What matters most to me is that Snyder has been able to live his daily life with the full power of his imagination awake to all the details of that life. A civilized and educated man, he is at his most sensitive and intelligent when he is writing about loggers, sailors, and animals. He has a poem which deals movingly with the moment when surveying the clutter of American life, he seems to decide to put off ambition and to be true to the imagination. The poem is called "Nooksack Valley." The poet has been sitting in a berry-picker's cabin, "at the end of a far trip north," and meditates on his American life so far, and on his possible future:

369 The Work of Gary Snyder

> a week and I go back
> Down 99, through towns, to San Francisco and Japan.
> All America south and east,
> Twenty-five years in it brought to a trip-stop
> Mind-point, where I turn
> Caught more on this land—rock tree and man,
> Awake, than ever before, yet ready to leave.
> damned memories,
> Whole wasted theories, failures and worse success,
> Schools, girls, deals, try to get in
> To make this poem a froth, a pity,
> A dead fiddle for lost good jobs.
> the cedar walls
> Smell of our farm-house, half built in '35.
> Clouds sink down the hills
> Coffee is hot again. The dog
> Turns and turns about, stops and sleeps.

In this poem, as in so many others, the poet meditates alone. His recording of solitude in his poems is another striking feature of his work, one which makes it rather unusual in recent American poetry. American poets in recent years have tended to be like other Americans in shunning any experience which has to be undertaken alone.

Mr. Snyder has courage and an air of faithful patience. He keeps his voice low, not out of timidity but out of strength.

LINDA GREGERSON

Negative Capability

It seems to me that we should rather be the flower than the bee.
JOHN KEATS to J. H. Reynolds, February 19, 1818

When Mark Strand reinvented the poem, he began by leaving out the world. The self he invented to star in the poems went on with the work of divestment: it jettisoned place, it jettisoned fellows, it jettisoned all distinguishing physical marks, save beauty alone. It was never impeded by personality. Nor was this radical renunciation to be confused with modesty, or asceticism. The self had designs on a readership, and a consummate gift for the musical phrase:

I give up my eyes which are glass eggs.
I give up my tongue.
I give up my mouth which is the constant dream of my tongue.
I give up my throat which is the sleeve of my voice.
I give up my heart which is a burning apple.
I give up my lungs which are trees that have never seen the moon.
I give up my smell which is that of a stone traveling through rain.
I give up my hands which are ten wishes.
I give up my arms which have wanted to leave me anyway.
I give up my legs which are lovers only at night.
I give up my buttocks which are the moons of childhood.
I give up my penis which whispers encouragement to my thighs.
I give up my clothes which are walls that blow in the wind
and I give up the ghost that lives in them.

From *Parnassus* 10, no. 1 (Fall 1981). © 1981 by the Poetry in Review Foundation.

I give up. I give up.
And you will have none of it because already I am beginning
again without anything.
("Giving Myself Up")

The poet's career has thrived on the honey of absence and, mid-career, Mark Strand has come forth with *Selected Poems.* The overview is both impressive and timely. Beneath a changing prosody, the central poetic strategies exhibit remarkable coherence. On the stage it had cleared, the self divided itself for dialogue: the *I* became an *I* and a *you,* an *I* and a mailman, an *I* and an engineer; the face appeared on both sides of a mirror, both sides of a picture window, both sides of the printed page. In 1978, with the simultaneous publication of *The Late Hour* and *The Monument,* the divided persona became a divided corpus. *The Monument,* a prose collage, is the logical extension of all that went before it: here the poet divests himself of even his poems. In *The Late Hour,* conversely, and surely as a consequence, the banished populations begin to reassemble: place names, personal names, the items of use and the trappings of memory resume some luster of their own. The habitual and strategic renunciation that characterized the earlier poems has been siphoned off into an extra-poetic territory. The new poems, those in the last third of *The Late Hour* and those that complete the present volume, have thus been freed for the work of restoration.

In the *Selected Poems,* the first polished surface held forth for regard is a series of ingenious couplets, the title poem of Strand's first book:

> Unmoved by what the wind does,
> The windows
> Are not rattled, nor do the various
> Areas
> Of the house make their usual racket—
> Creak at
> The joints, trusses and studs.
> ("Sleeping with One Eye Open")

This urbane series of feminine rhymes and triple rhymes and slant rhymes culminates in no less than a version of analyzed rhyme; the echo must multiply to complete its variations, and the couplet expands to become a final triplet:

> And I lie sleeping with one eye open,
> Hoping
> That nothing, nothing will happen.

Open, hoping, nothing, happen: the rhyme sequence constitutes, among
other things, a witty portrait of paranoia, wherein the most feared eventuality
is most devoutly invoked. The passive verbs or verbals (*unmoved, rattled*)
activate an echo of another sort. These words are the commonplaces of
psychological portraiture; context and tone suggest that we construe them
as such. But their grammatical subjects (*windows, areas*) argue for a purely
material interpretation. Thus two semantic frameworks are poised in sympathy and competition. Irony is hardly an adequate term for tactics of the
sort this poem deploys.

There are antecedents. Prosody, at least, has been refined to this particular double edge before, and Strand undoubtedly studied something of tone
from Donald Justice, whose perfect elegance is always perfectly double. Justice has polished a surface in order to aggravate the discrepancies between
manner and tone, has cultivated, in other words, the inherent ambiguity of
perfect manners. His powers of inflection are subtle in the extreme, and
nowhere so subtle as when he merges the cunning and the disingenuous, as
when, for example, he would have us encounter death in an end-stopped
couplet. A chasm opens beneath the studied naiveté in Justice's evocation of
a grandmother's funeral:

> I remember the soprano
> Fanning herself at the piano,
>
> And the preacher looming large
> Above me in his dark blue serge.
>
> My shoes brought in a smell of clay
> To mingle with the faint sachet
>
> Of flowers sweating in their vases.
> A stranger showed us to our places.
> ("First Death")

This poem is in fact a late one. Though Justice is the senior practitioner and
was for a year Strand's teacher, it rather behooves us to discuss affinity
between the two than to track down primogeniture. Strand quickly cleared
ground of his own, and made the reciprocities of influence one of his primary
themes. In later volumes, Justice and Strand entertain a sporadic dialogue in
which homage is sometimes difficult to distinguish from exorcism, a dialogue
subtle as journeymen who have learned one another's lessons well.

For a brief time, Strand's prosody assumed more flamboyance than
Justice's ever has, but the virtuosity was quickly toned down and channeled

in other directions. The surface complexities of Strand's first book afford considerable delight, though rhyme and meter and wordplay occasionally leave plain sense and syntax to fend somewhat for themselves. At times, humble connotation puts up a thin resistance to flashier denotation. Now and again, the poems exhibit imperfect tact, as any young poet who speaks too knowingly of "Old People on the Nursing Home Porch" is likely to exhibit imperfect tact. But the poet's informing preoccupations are already full-blown. When, in the same first volume, his poems emerge with the simpler surface we think of as characteristic, dislocation is still a central mode. The world and the self appear to exist ever more at each other's expense:

> In a field
> I am the absence
> of field.
> This is
> always the case.
> Wherever I am
> I am what is missing.
>
> When I walk
> I part the air
> and always
> the air moves in
> to fill the spaces
> where my body's been.
>
> We all have reasons
> for moving.
> I move
> to keep things whole.
> ("Keeping Things Whole")

This factoring of self and the world is manifestly a strategic withdrawal: it rather signals a consolidation of power than any sort of abdication. The *I* is now a catalyst for all the I is not.

Already in his first book, Strand began to employ the narrative or quasi-narrative formulas and the doubles that appear in so much of his subsequent work. I quote in full:

> A man has been standing
> in front of my house

for days. I peek at him
from the living room
window and at night,
unable to sleep,
I shine my flashlight
down on the lawn.
He is always there.

After a while
I open the front door
just a crack and order
him out of my yard.
He narrows his eyes
and moans. I slam
the door and dash back
to the kitchen, then up
to the bedroom, then down.

I weep like a schoolgirl
and make obscene gestures
through the window. I
write large suicide notes
and place them so he
can read them easily.
I destroy the living
room furniture to prove
I own nothing of value.

When he seems unmoved
I decide to dig a tunnel
to a neighboring yard.
I seal the basement off
from the upstairs with
a brick wall. I dig hard
and in no time the tunnel
is done. Leaving my pick
and shovel below,

I come out in front of a house
and stand there too tired to
move or even speak, hoping
someone will help me.

I feel I'm being watched
and sometimes I hear
a man's voice,
but nothing is done
and I have been waiting for days.
("The Tunnel")

End-rhyme, much muted, now hints at subterranean affinities. With the advertised suicide threat, Strand takes a shot at the confessional poets, whose methods he has always shunned, even inverted, but whose spectacle he has carefully studied. The use of obscenity as enticement requires no comment. The use of flight as a lure is as old as romance: Ariosto's Angelica and Spenser's Florimell had only to flee across the plain to engage all the knights for miles around in pursuit. Suspended flight may be more potent yet: it's the erotic lesson of a Grecian Urn, the perpetuation of desire by deferral.

Absence is power, and change, by a similar sleight, may clinch a static hold. "The Man in the Mirror," a somewhat later poem, plays absence in numerous keys. The poem is too long to quote in any substance, but its broadest moves are the departure and qualified reappearance of Narcissus in the glass. Both moves, the disappearance and the return, aggravate the bondage of his lover, because the image restored is manifestly decomposing, forecasting yet another and final departure:

You stood before me,
dreamlike and obscene,
your face lost
under layers of heavy skin,

your body sunk in a green
and wrinkled sea of clothing.

Mortality makes even reflection faithless. The face loves death more than it loves its former self. It is change, quite crudely, that enters the mirror and narrows the lovers' alliance to some parody of the immutable.

It will always be this way.
I stand here scared
that you will disappear,
scared that you will stay.

End-rhyme, we note, continues to serve. Here it seals the stanza with a stroke-like fate. Dreams of the double may always harbor a death wish of sorts, but they also harbor its opposite, the infatuating possibility of extending one's influence infinitely. Wherever I am, I am what is missing. I am, as Strand and Justice both have put it in separate poems, a horizon. The poet continues to mediate everything he has relinquished.

Strand's quasi-narratives suggest narrative sources: Borges, Kafka, and the parabolic or paradoxical structures they canonize. Strand's formats are based on many of the same commonplaces these other writers employ: the symbiosis of complementary characters, the transposition of matter and context, of dreamer and dreamed, of writer and written. His later verse fictions embrace with increasing frequency the postures and devices familiar from Beckett: narrative or dramatic interminability, the story that insists on its own telling and invents the one who tells it, the durability of voice amidst the longing for extinction, "the pain of revival and the bliss of decline." These phrases "From a Litany" appear in *Darker*, Strand's third book. In *The Story of Our Lives*, the echoes are more sustained:

> You want to wave but cannot raise your hand.
> You sit in a chair. You turn to the nightshade spreading
> a poisonous net around the house. You taste
> the honey of absence. It is the same wherever
> you are, the same if the voice rots before
> the body, or the body rots before the voice.
>
> ("In Celebration")

Strand borrows poetic shapeliness, then, from nonpoetic sources. He builds with three elementary figures: the circle that perpetuates motion; the Escher-like pattern that reverses foreground and background; and the asymptotic convergence of a line and a curve, Zeno's paradox maintaining decline and waylaying closure. The figures inevitably overlap.

The importance of Strand's narrative and dramatic models is structural, not thematic. This merits some insistence. When his critics use strategic affinities to account for affect and motive, when they intone not only *Borges, Kafka, Beckett,* but also *anguish, despair*—and they do—analogy has gone awry. It's not the sheer presence of wit that marks a different project, although the tenor and pervasiveness of Strand's wit provides a valuable antidote to solemn exegesis. But Borges and Beckett are witty too, and Kafka is some oracular equivalent; Beckett's more witty the closer he gets to the grave. No. It's Strand's pacing, his relative lassitude, that's the giveaway. The pallor behind Strand's narrative, the phlegm behind his very wit betray an occupation distinct from those of Beckett and Borges especially. Though he uses the formal vocabulary of a metaphysician, Strand's subject is not the problem of perception. Not Berkeley's subject. Not Descartes's. Neither the anguish of consciousness nor its rewards. His methods are those of a sensualist; his subject, the disposition and deployment of power: erotics, politics, and especially the erotics and politics of passivity. Ultimate power resides with one who is only acted upon, who only provokes. The poems are poems of seduction:

> A train runs over me.
> I feel sorry
> for the engineer
> who crouches down
> and whispers in my ear
> that he is innocent.
>
> He wipes my forehead,
> blows the ashes
> from my lips.
> My blood steams
> in the evening air,
> clouding his glasses.
>
> He whispers in my ear
> the details of his life—
> he has a wife
> and child he loves,
> he's always been
> an engineer.

And after an effort at separation:

> He rushes
> from the house,
> lifts the wreckage
> of my body in his arms
> and brings me back.
> I lie in bed.
>
> He puts his head
> down next to mine
> and tells me
> that I'll be all right.

> A pale light
> shines in his eyes.
> ("The Accident")

Luminous morbidity has had no comparable heyday since Lizzie Siddal first graced the pre-Raphaelite canvases. This is the exquisite transparence of Millais's Ophelia, languid unto death.

Certain versions of the accidental are chronically banished from Strand's poems: the accidental increments of material and social life, the detritus of fashion and wage labor and domestic arrangement, the shape of a chin, the lumps in the couch. But the syntax of accident chronically appears. Another way of putting this is to say that Strand suppresses the subjects of accident, the people and things that accident produces and leaves in its wake, in order to highlight the predicates of accident, the process itself. It is the shape of experience, not its contents, that interests him. In the system of his poems, events are wholly contingent or wholly fated, rather than caused or desired on a human scale. What happens happens for no reason or for the one reason (God, necessity, abstract pattern, the poet's whim), rather than for the intermediate reasons, the individual notations of human purpose. This is why the poems can be as shapely as they are, uncluttered by the merely anecdotal. In "The Accident," the speaker's imperturbability gives us our first clue that the anecdotal versions of cause and effect have been suspended, that the casual has supplanted the purposive. Even seduction works *through* the speaker, rather than at his explicit command. "The Accident" unearths the *casual* in *casualty*, the *causal* in both. Calamity provokes desire, enfeeblement arouses, contingency displaces will. Causality becomes diffuse or atmospheric. Compare these lines from "The Ghost Ship":

> Through the crowded street
> It floats,
>
> Its vague
> Tonnage like wind.
>
> .   .   .   .   .   .
>
> Slowly,
> Now by an ox,
>
> Now by a windmill,
> It moves.

Because both ox and windmill are potential sources of momentum, the sentence is almost drawn to "it is moved" instead of "it moves." But the poem does not require the passive voice to preserve the ship's passive locomotion. The power to move is the power of contagion. Thus we say that a thought or a lover can infect the will.

In "The Kite," the longed-for catatonia exerts an influence equally pervasive:

> It rises over the lake, the farms,
> The edge of the woods,
> And like a body without arms
> Or legs it swings
> Blind and blackening in the moonless air.

With no limbs to work its will, the kite proceeds by insinuation, blind and blackening. The three long stanzas of this poem are haunted by recurring elements: lake, farms, woods, rain, curtain, wings, wind. In each stanza, their relative pressures are differently disposed. Causality passes through altered configurations. The elusive notion of origin goes underground, like Hamlet's ghost.

In the first stanza, the kite appears to have some hold on the weather. As it rises,

> The wren, the vireo, the thrush
> Make way. The rush
> And flutter of wings
> Fall through the dark
> Like a mild rain.
> .   .   .   .
> An almost invisible
> Curtain of rain seems to come nearer.
> The muffled crack and drum
> Of distant thunder
> Blunders against our ears.

Of the line that runs from the kite to the weather, we know only that aural links and analogies predominate. The rain is never quite rain: it's a figure for sound, it's an immanent presence announced by sound.

In stanza two, the kite string is held by a man who seems to precipitate whole seasons:

> The wind cries in his lapels. Leaves fall
> As he moves by them.

In the final stanza, the elements of landscape resolve into the features
of a parlor. Outside the rain fell like a curtain, and here

> Inside the room
> The curtains fall like rain.

The poem is a hothouse where images bloom and cross-fertilize. The rem-
nants of end-rhyme now intimate some hidden course of generation:

> Darkness covers the flower-papered walls,
> The furniture and floors,
> Like a mild stain.
> The mirrors are emptied, the doors
> Quietly closed. The man, asleep
> In the heavy arms of a chair,
> Does not see us
> Out in the freezing air
> Of the dream he is having.

The kite rises, still a conductor, and the man begins to wake. The kite may
equal the dream or not; it certainly mediates the dream's authority. And
because parataxis is the mother tongue of dreams, equivalence and consequence are free to dissolve and reformulate. The panels of this poem are
angled for resonance, not for reflection. Strand's is not a lapidary art. He
relies not on taut juxtaposition but on the bland parataxis that loosens the
will at its hinges. His methods mature with a chronic humor, their own
slight fever. As the poet moves further away from his earliest poems, the
tension between line break and phrasing softens, enjambment nearly disap-
pears. The simplest of syntactical patterns simply repeat; the eddies and stills
of imagery even out. The poems encounter less and less resistance as they
move down the page, until their progress becomes as frictionless as that of
a kite or a ghost ship:

> We are reading the story of our lives
> which takes place in a room.
> The room looks out on a street.
> There is no one there,
> no sound of anything.
>   ("The Story of Our Lives")

"The Story of Our Lives" and "The Untelling," centerpieces of Strand's
fourth major collection, pursue the formal discoveries made in "The Kite."
Each poem contains a story which contains a poem which steadily dismantles

containment. As "The Story of Our Lives" proceeds, a man and a woman, side by side, consult the course of love in a book. Though love unfolds and doubles back, no point of origin or terminus appears, no point, that is, beyond which the mind might firmly declare itself to be outside the story:

> The book never discusses the causes of love.
> It claims confusion is a necessary good.
> It never explains. It only reveals.

In this way the book preserves the reasons for moving:

> It describes your dependence on desire,
> how the momentary disclosures
> of purpose make you afraid.

Books have promulgated desire before. When Paolo and Francesca, side by side, read the story of Lancelot and Guinevere, adulturous love renewed its kingdom: "A Gallehault was the book and he who wrote it; that day we read no farther in it" (*Inferno* V, 137–138). Gallehault served as a go-between for Lancelot and Guinevere. Boccaccio subtitled *The Decameron* "Prince Gallehault" and dedicated his book to *oziose donne*, idle ladies. The pattern for seduction is perfectly explicit, and perfectly vicarious. Strand's own poems mediate a vast inherited culture by appearing to build in a clearing. Their faithlessness is part of their pedigree, as faithlessness is the cement of love. Paolo and Francesca owed their fealty and their desire to Gianciotto, Lancelot and Guinevere to Arthur. The man and the woman on the couch must interpolate a breach of faith in order to perfect desire:

> I lean back and watch you read
> about the man across the street.
> . . . .
> You fell in love with him
> because you knew that he would never visit you,
> would never know you were waiting.
> Night after night you would say
> that he was like me.

Idle ladies are most apt to wander, so go-betweens play upon idleness. This explains why Strand's erotics should pass through languor to boredom at times. The man and the woman repeatedly fall asleep. The reader, left to stare at plainer and plainer walls, allows his thoughts to wander to Dante, Boccaccio, Borges, as the woman's thoughts wander to the man across the street. In the reader, Strand sows the seeds of the faithlessness that completes his hold. Mediation expands its inventory at every opportunity. Like a Greek messenger, the mailman in an early poem assumes the onus for news he bears:

> He falls to his knees.
> "Forgive me! Forgive me!" he pleads.
>
> I ask him inside.
> He wipes his eyes.
> His dark blue suit
> is like an inkstain
> on my crimson couch.
>
> ("The Mailman")

In "The Story of Our Lives,"

> the rugs become darker each time
> our shadows pass over them.

In calamity and in burlesque, in even its modest moments, the book's ambition is limitless: to own what passes through it, to be the portal the past must enter on its way to the future.

> *They sat beside each other on the couch.*
> *They were the copies, the tired phantoms*
> *of something they had been before.*
> *The attitudes they took were jaded.*
> *They stared into the book*
> *and were horrified by their innocence,*
> *their reluctance to give up.*
> *They sat beside each other on the couch.*
> *They were determined to accept the truth.*
> *Whatever it was they would accept it.*
> *The book would have to be written*
> *and would have to be read.*
> *They are the book and they are*
> *nothing else.*

The book engineers its own supersession. In "The Untelling," the story of the past is handed from a third-person frame to a first-person frame and back again, four full cycles in all. Each narrator figures as a character in the story his counterpart tells. The two are alternate versions of one another, separated in time, and each produces the other, as the child is father to the man. The points of view draw nearer in time and place as the poem proceeds: a man writes a poem in a room overlooking a lake; the child in the poem himself observes a scene from the opposite side of the lake; each revision begins somewhat earlier in the story, somewhat closer to the house, and finally in the room itself. The setting is vaguely Chekhovian, bucolic, elegiac; there's even the sound of a breaking string:

> He would never catch up
> with his past. His life
> was slowing down.
> It was going.
> He could feel it,
> could hear it in his speech.
> It sounded like nothing,
> yet he would pass it on.
> And his children would live in it
> and they would pass it on,
> and it would always sound
> like hope dying, like space opening,
> like a lawn, or a lake,
> or an afternoon.

The period in which the past occurs presumably approximates that of the poet's childhood, but the women wear dresses whose hems are made wet by the dew. Hemlines haven't touched the ground as a matter of course since a family longed to stop time in a cherry orchard:

> *I waited under the trees in front of the house,*
> *thinking of nothing, watching the sunlight wash*
> *over the roof. I heard nothing, felt*
> *nothing, even when she appeared in a long*
> *yellow dress, pointed white shoes, her hair*
> *drawn back in a tight bun; even when*
> *she took my hand and led me along the row*
> *of tall trees toward the lake where the rest had gathered.*
> . . . .
> *It seemed as if the wind drew the dark*
> *from the trees onto the grass. The adults stood*
> *together. They would never leave that shore.*
> *I watched the one in the yellow dress whose name*
> *I had begun to forget and who waited with*

the others and who stared at where I was
but could not see me. Already the full moon
had risen and dropped its white ashes on the lake.
And the woman and the others slowly began
to take off their clothes, and the mild rushes of wind
rinsed their skin, their pale bodies shone
briefly among the shadows until they lay
on the damp grass. And the children had all gone.
And that was all. And even then I felt
nothing. I knew that I would never see
the woman in the yellow dress again,
and that the scene by the lake would not be repeated,
and that that summer would be a place too distant
for me to find myself in again.

Her dress takes its color from the sunlight he watches before she appears, or gives the sunlight its place in his mind because she is about to appear. She guides him to the lake like a mother and leaves him like first love; he summons her to the place he holds for both. And even as he knew that he would never see her in yellow again, he sees her so in memory and in this poem. The forfeits of will and the footholds of longing are deeply equivocal:

His pursuit was a form of evasion:
the more he tried to uncover
the more there was to conceal
the less he understood.
If he kept it up,
he would lose everything.

According to the paradox of aging and generation, everything must be given up if everything is to be gained; growing up is rather like getting into heaven in that regard. That regard only, presumably. The adult blossoms on the corpse of the child he was. The child he makes, in imagination or in the flesh, his consolation for mortality, is also the agent of usurpation. In the end, he furthers his will not by testimony but by testament, by divestment, and thus the final lines of this poem:

He sat and began to write:

THE UNTELLING

To the Woman in the Yellow Dress

The dedication bequeaths the story to another, places it squarely in the hands of one who cannot but appear, and in her yellow dress at that. She as she was, she as she was to him. As Wills go, this one is quite a coup. In the courtship the poem enacts, the woman has played the role throughout of mediating third, the go-between for man and child. As long as man and child had to share the burden of narration, each could approach the other only by surrendering his own reality. The woman in the yellow dress is the agent in whom their stories overlap. By taking the story over, a matter she cannot refuse since her page is white, her part in the story is silence, she allows them to coexist at last in harmony, to assume their place in the fixed constellations.

The strategics of will and testament reveal absence in its other aspect, as a hedge against mortality. Poem after poem in Strand's corpus makes this clear: when absence cracks, mortality gets a foothold. This is the other side of "The Man in the Mirror." This is why, "When the Vacation Is Over for Good," we find we are dying. This is why "The Guardian" is invoked as he is: "Preserve my absence. I am alive." Divestment and renunciation are forms of preemptive suicide:

> I empty myself of the names of others. I empty my pockets.
> I empty my shoes and leave them beside the road.
> At night I turn back the clocks;
> I open the family album and look at myself as a boy.
>
> What good does it do? The hours have done their job.
> I say my own name. I say goodbye.
> The words follow each other downwind.
> I love my wife but send her away.
>
> My parents rise out of their thrones
> into the milky rooms of clouds. How can I sing?
> Time tells me what I am. I change and I am the same.
> I empty myself of my life and my life remains.
>
> ("The Remains")

Strand plays with the formulas of masochism and self-immolation, but the erotic and funerary aspects of divestment always come down to this: a solemn striptease and a wonderfully irreverent act of monument-building. The concurrence of these occupations incidentally clarifies the equivocal status of discards and the vicarious role of a readership. "I give up my tongue," says Strand on the page. "I have omitted to mention my wife or daughter." And by such ruses, he doesn't, he hasn't. Everything named is preserved. Everything abandoned to language is there to be taken up in another life, like the mummified food and playthings in a pharaoh's tomb. The reader is consigned to prurience. He watches the self enticing the self to love; he overhears, he oversees, and by such moves is taken on as permanent overseer, the custodian in whose care the monument resides.

The Monument itself absents itself from the Selected Poems. Its prose, however, is always and explicitly the prose of a poet, who comes to its pages empty-handed. As "The Untelling" was dedicated to the woman in the yellow dress, this volume is dedicated with sublime humor and manifest coerciveness "To the Translator of The Monument in the future." The honor conferred does not come free. (Strand has dedicated other poems to his most illustrious critics and to the illustrious editor through whom his finished poems pass first. The board of executors.) Again and again the supposed translator is reduced to the most abject dependence, his every insubordination secondguessed, his very speeches of protest written for him. "I live in you," The Monument says.

Epigraphs play a prominent role in the book. Passages from Thomas Browne, Unamuno, Nietzsche, Wordsworth, Borges, and Suetonius, to name but a few, are yoked into a single discourse. (We should write, says Petrarch, as the bees make sweetness, turning the various flowers into a single honey.) The poet claims the inherited past as his to bequeath and, by the way, rehearses the origins of epigraphic verse in wayside interments and epitaphs. Siste viator, The Monument reads. Stay, traveller. In Coleridge's epitaph, it's "Stop, Christian passer-by!"; on the seat in Wordsworth's yew-tree, "Nay, traveller! rest." As a legal will lays its hand on the living, as the Ancient Mariner waylays the wedding guest, The Monument stops the course of all who would continue outside its control. The Monument knows nothing indifferent; it knows only itself and its residue:

> Give us a blank wall that we might see ourselves more truly and
> more strange. Now give us the paper, the daily paper on which
> to write. Now give us the day, this day. Take it away. The space
> that is left is The Monument.
>
> (Section 45)

The Monument's "other voices" are more of the same:

> Sometimes when I wander in these woods whose prince I am, I
> hear a voice and I know that I am not alone.
>
> (Section 30)

The passage above appears in tandem with an epigraph derived from St. Mark: the poet is not above an aggrandizing pun on his own name, as long as it makes the issue clear. The Monument's final words, appropriately enough, were not its own until it commandeered them:

> To pass on, (O living! always living!) and leave the corpses behind.

Walt Whitman, now The Monument.

What The Monument leaves behind is matter for a changing poetic—sanction too, if a cover illustration may be so read. Assuredly, the picture of mortuary architecture that adorned *The Late Hour* when it first appeared cast something of a shadow: the hour was late as death approached. On the other hand, the monument was put farther behind with each new page one turned. From the back of the book, the poet regards us, still very much alive. Between its covers, the writing follows the course of one who has decided to return from the brink of the grave, to leave death to its own devices. The only poem whose absence I regret when I read the *Selected Poems* is "No Particular Day," in which the turning is first announced:

> Items of no
> particular day
> swarm down—
>
> moves of the mind
>
> . . . .
>
> that take us
> somewhere near
> and leave us
>
> combing the air
> for signs
> of change,
>
> signs the sky
> will break
> and shower down
>
> upon us
> particular
> ideas of light.

Sotto voce, the poet invokes what heretofore he has loudly banished. He has favored the generic for the authority it confers, furnishing his kingdom with everything in general and nothing in particular; but here he prepares to turn again to the accidents and givens that particularize experience.

In *Selected Poems,* "Exiles" becomes the fulcrum for change, the site on which the work of restoration commences. Its first section follows the plot more or less of Albee's *A Delicate Balance*: a certain "they" find life disappearing around them and run to "us" to be taken in. In the second section, they reverse their course, in what might be a prologue to the poet's later work:

> And on their way back
> they heard the footsteps
> and felt the warmth
> of the clothes they thought
> had been lifted from them.
> They ran by the boats at anchor,
> hulking in the bay,
> by the train waiting
> under the melting frost of stars.

This reunion with the world does not exactly end in a wash of optimism:

> They lay in their beds
> and the shadows of the giant trees
> brushed darkly against the walls.

It is, nonetheless, a reunion of moment, and here are the gifts that accrue: St. Margaret's Bay, the North West Arm, Mosher Island, Wedge Island, Hackett's Cove, Fox Point, Boutelier's wharf, Albert Hubley's shack, a furniture store, a black baby Austin, brants and Canada geese, a mother, a father, an uncle, a grandmother, and Winslow Homer's *Gulf Stream*. The change is enormous, this change that begins with the final third of *The Late Hour,* and it's not imparted by proper names alone. If the ravelings and auras of personal memory find quarter for once, this is not to suggest that the earlier poems had no sources in biography, or that the current poems never invent or lie. The *appearance* of personal history is what was not encouraged before and is very much encouraged now. When place names appear, as they occasionally do, in the earlier poems, they are poised on the scales of dislocation. As "The Last Bus" moves past Lota's park in Rio de Janeiro,

> The ghosts of bathers rise
>
> slowly out of the surf and turn
> high in the spray.

The image is designed to capture the material imagination but cannot be

solved in material terms. Far from being comfortably "placed" by setting, the reader encounters deliberate disorientation. So with distinguishing
items of clothing or social class. "Let us save the babies," an early persona
proposes,

> You shall wear mink
> and your hair shall be done.
> I shall wear tails.

To underscore a retreat to animal instinct, Strand has borrowed his perspective from the hoi polloi, who call such outfits "monkey suits." Since
"The Babies" is a Vietnam-era parable about the survival of the fittest generation, the playfulness is apt, but hardly a genre-painter's approach to circumstantial detail. So with memory. Heretofore, the memory Strand was
interested in was the memory he could engineer, the memory he could become. In recent poems, he grants some affection to the merely historical,
some credence to the merely found, and he diversifies the methods of pro-
voking recognition. No attentive reader will expect biography to "solve" a
good poem, or will underestimate Strand's loyalty to the methods and discoveries of fiction. But when the poet begins to grant the past and the reader
some license of their own, this loyalty is being reconstrued.

The final sections of *Selected Poems* include work as purely lyrical as
any Strand has written; the phrases are more extended, the mimetic strategies
far less guarded than any the poet has used before. One poem, based on an
ominous survey of the Thames in *Bleak House,* assembles a central sentence
of twenty-eight lines, whose eddyings and sweep reproduce the course of the
river itself. As to the elevation of the quotidian, one final example demands
our attention. The poem has provoked a fair amount of skepticism, even
among Strand's admirers, and may therefore be a useful test of his continuing
strength and perspective. The poem is named for the thing itself: "Pot
Roast."

> I gaze upon the roast,
> that is sliced and laid out
> on my plate
> and over it
> I spoon the juices
> of carrot and onion.
> And for once I do not regret
> the passage of time.

I sit by a window
that looks
on the soot-stained brick of buildings
and do not care that I see
no living thing—not a bird,
not a branch in bloom,
not a soul moving
in the rooms
behind the dark panes.
These days when there is little
to love or to praise
one could do worse
than yield
to the power of food.
So I bend

to inhale
the steam that rises
from my plate, and I think
of the first time
I tasted a roast
like this.
It was years ago
in Seabright,
Nova Scotia;

my mother leaned
over my dish and filled it
and when I finished
filled it again.
I remember the gravy,
its odor of garlic and celery,
and sopping it up
with pieces of bread.

And now
I taste it again.
The meat of memory.
The meat of no change.
I raise my fork
and I eat.

The senses that feed on well-being here are those most resistant to the embrace of language. The taste of a roast, the smell of an onion have the power to translate the speaker to another time precisely because they resist translation. The sensations of taste and smell withstand the dilution and obfuscation that readier equivalents inflict upon the process of sight. The reader, however, may understandably choke a bit upon Strand's version of the lime-flower tea and madeleine. As anecdote, the transporting powers of garlic and celery are credible, if uninspiring. In their figurative capacity, as revisionist versions of Proust, as the specific and composite key that unlocks the past, they cannot help being somewhat parodic: pot roast is about as close as a poet could get to generic food. Not mother's Christmas cardamon bread, not even Aunt Mabel's own barbeque sauce. Even a sympathetic reader might think at first that Strand has miscalculated tone: the language—"juice of carrot and onion"—gets awfully reverential at times; the poet might almost be eating the host. And, indeed, this disproportion is meant as a clue. Strand's closing lines are modeled on the closing lines of a Herbert poem, a poem about the final communion in heaven:

> You must sit down, sayes Love, and taste my meat:
> So I did sit and eat.
>
> ("Love III")

The meat is the meat of transubstantiation. Even without the detective work, we know something of this from the rhythms with which Strand's poem draws to a close: those rhythms argue that "meat of memory," "meat of no change" are in earnest. The earnestness reads like a callow mistake, until we find that the second helping is literally a double take. The past has been used up, as has the vision that Herbert believed in, as has the cultural nexus that fostered a sensibility like Proust's. And then the change: as when the bread is bread no more, the empty plate is filled again, and everything lost restored. The mother's shade enacts her blessing, and the agnostic has his sacrament too, the meat of memory to be savored like hope. And what of the humor?— the past recaptured in a pot roast, Jesus on a fork? Strand has accommodated radical disjunction before, purest burlesque and sobriety in a single poem, but never did disjunction entail a greater risk. What this poem has in mind, and brings to mind, precludes the somnambular voice that Strand so often used in the past to solve the problem of tone in a hybrid production. The title—"Pot Roast"—partakes of that poker-faced hilarity that alerted us to double meaning in earlier poems, but it's not reinforced by obvious gestures in kind. The poem relies on internal transformation, and accomplishes what it does by assuring that it will first be underestimated, even dismissed. In this manner the poem mimes its subject, and confesses to a diminished version of the myth it reenacts. History repeats, with some chagrin. To achieve his final proportion and tone, the poet has only the disposition of literary antecedents, the necessary and sufficient motives for parody, and the manifest subject of celebration.

Having channeled his most distinctive accomplishments into a poet's prose that sidesteps or cagily reroutes generic expectations, Strand is now experimenting with various reconstructions of the lyric voice. He's relaxed his censorship of quotidian detail; he's trying a gentler hand with the past and a lusher version of literary homage; he's practicing a less austere, more personalized and impure fable. Are the poems a dilution of the former enterprise? The poet himself has signaled a shifting of loyalties: "I'm really less interested in writing magazine verse or individual poems than in creating a literary spectacle . . . a little like *Barthes on Barthes* (*Missouri Review,* Summer 1981). But Strand has always enacted the spectacle he describes. If all writing distributes allegiance between an audience and a subject of regard, if all writing occupies a place on the spectrum that runs from the presentational to the contemplative or exegetical, Strand's characteristic work has steadfastly been of the former kind. The poems were rhetorical, which is to say they were designed to move an audience; the self was a rhetorical construct built in view of that audience; the argument was all ad hominem. Their beauty notwithstanding, the poems written since *The Monument* may prove to be something of a sideline. On the other hand, as a poem like "Pot Roast" should alert us, the play of presence and absence continues in all its vitality, even when, on first glance, presence seems to have become less problematic. The new bifurcation of voice, one part spoken by an altered lyric, one part by all that is left of the old, may signal the start of a dialogue we will all do well to attend to: the flower *and* the bee.

NATE MACKEY

The Changing Same: Black Music
in the Poetry of Amiri Baraka

Consistency is one of the last words anyone would use in characterizing
Baraka's thinking during the last two decades. Coming into his earliest
prominence as a member of the Beat/Black Mountain avant-garde of the
fifties and sixties, he wrote in 1959, still calling himself LeRoi Jones:

> For me, Lorca, Williams, Pound and Charles Olson have had the
> greatest influence. Eliot, earlier (rhetoric can be so lovely, for a
> time . . . but only remains so for the rhetorician). And there are
> so many young wizards around now doing great things that
> everybody calling himself poet can learn from . . . Whalen, Sny-
> der, McClure, O'Hara, Loewinsohn, Wieners, Creeley, Ginsberg
> &c. &c. &c.

Seven years later in an essay called "Poetry and Karma," having in the interim
abandoned Greenwich Village for Harlem and the "New American Poetry"
for the "Black Arts Movement," he writes of his earlier influences and
associates:

> White poetry is like white music (for the most part, and even
> taking into account those "imitations" I said, which are all as
> valid as W. C. Williams writing about Bunk Johnson's band).
> Hear the axles turn, the rust churned and repositioned. The death
> more subtly or more openly longed for. Creeley's black box,

From *Imamu Amiri Baraka: A Collection of Critical Essays.* © 1978 by Prentice-
Hall, Inc.

Olson's revivification of the dead, Ginsberg's screams at his own shadowy races or the creepier elements completely covered up with silver rubied garbage artifacts and paintings and manners and ideas, my god, they got a buncha ideas, and really horrible crap between them and anything meaningful. They probably belch without feeling.

Such openness not only to change but to about-faces of the most explosive kind is typical of his career, an openness he himself acknowledges in "The Liar":

> Though I am a man
> who is loud
> on the birth
> of his ways. Publicly redefining
> each change in my soul, as if I had predicted
> them,
>> and profited, biblically, even tho
>> their chanting weight,
>>> erased familiarity
>>> from my face.

Qualifications if not outright repudiations of earlier stances have thus come to be expected. *Black Magic Poetry,* the collection of poems written between 1961 and 1967, opens with "An Explanation of the Work" written in 1968 in which he more or less dismisses the work up to, say, 1965, calling "a cloud of abstraction and disjointedness, that was just whiteness."

His latest collection of poetry, *Hard Facts,* comprised of poems written between 1973 and 1975, announces yet another change of direction. At the height of his black nationalist phase, Baraka was fond of countering any mention of Marxist theory by insisting that socialism is contrary to the nature of whites and thus unattainable by them in any form other than intellectual abstraction, whereas black people, being by their very nature communistic (generous, nonexploitative, etc.), have no need of any such theories. Yet on the back cover of *Hard Facts* we find a portrait of Marx, Engels, Lenin, Stalin and Mao; and, in his introduction, Baraka explicitly disowns his earlier nationalist position:

> Earlier our own poems came from an enraptured patriotism that screamed against whites as the eternal enemies of Black people, as the sole cause of our disorder + oppression. The same subjective mystification led to mysticism, metaphysics, spookism,

&c., rather than dealing with reality, as well as an ultimately reactionary nationalism that served no interests but our newly emerging Black bureaucratic elite and petit bourgeois, so that they would have control over their Black market. This is not to say Black nationalism was not necessary, it was and is to the extent that we are still patriots, involved in the Black Liberation Movement, but we must also be revolutionaries who understand that our quest for our people's freedom can only be realized as the result of Socialist Revolution!

There are other changes. One notes another name change for example: the dropping of the Muslim title *Imamu* (meaning teacher), evidently bringing to an end his flirtation with Islamic religion. The poem "When We'll Worship Jesus" twice associates Allah with Christ, for several years now a villain in Baraka's work:

> jesus aint did nothin for us
> but kept us turned toward the
> sky (him and his boy allah
> too, need to be checkd
> out!)

In addition, two poems attack Kenneth Gibson, whom he helped get elected mayor of Newark not long ago. One thing, however, hasn't changed. Black music continues to be invoked—respectfully invoked—serving in *Hard Facts,* as in earlier work, as a harbinger of change:

> hung out with any and all thats bad and mad and wont be had.
>   In with
> all and all with in, out here stomping in the streets for the
>   trumpeting
> dynamic of the people themselves—new and renew—Our
>   Experience
> Nows the time, charley parker sd, Now's the time. Say do it, do
>   it, we gon
> do it.

In this essay I'll be talking about black music in its dual role of impulse (life-style or ethos as well as technique) and theme in Baraka's work, exploring its usefulness as a sort of focal point or thread pulling together disparate strands of Baraka's thought. His early attraction to Projectivist and Beat poetics, for instance, bespeaks an attitude or stance which he and other spokesmen for those poetics repeatedly called upon "jazz" to exemplify. Kerouac, Ginsberg, Creeley, McClure and others glowingly referred to bop improvisation as a technique from which poets could learn. Olson remarked in a letter to Cid Corman in the early fifties: "how does—or is there—an anology to (as i'd gather any of us do) to jazz?" Black music for Baraka, however, comes eventually to express the very spirit which leads to his repudiation of Olson and others—the black nationalist ferment of the middle and late sixties. This ferment in his particular case, I'm suggesting, is itself impelled by certain attitudes and impulses which also motivated his Beat/Projectivist writings and with which this repudiation is thus not entirely inconsistent. What he rejects is an alleged failure of the Beat and Black Mountain writers to live up to the extra-literary (especially political) implications of their poetics—implications they themselves often insist upon in their pursuit of a relevance wider than the merely aesthetic.

Olson's insistence that "the projective involves a stance towards reality outside a poem as well as a new stance towards the reality of the poem itself," Duncan's sense of the poetic as a process of "ensouling" and Spicer's assurances that "the objective universe can be affected by the poet" all attest to the importance of the notion of poetry as an agent of change and revelation to the poetic movement of which Baraka was—and remains—a part. The persistence of his celebration of black music has to do with the persistence of a "will to change" (to use Olson's phrase)—a will common to his Projectivist, black nationalist and Marxist periods—which the music invokes and exemplifies: "There is a daringly human quality to John Coltrane's music that makes itself felt, wherever he records. If you can hear, this music will make you think of a lot of weird and wonderful things. You might even become one of them."

II

Bankrupt utopia sez tell me
no utopias. I will not listen. (Except the raw wind
makes the hero's eyes close, and the tears that come
out are real.)

AMIRI BARAKA, "History As Process"

During the sixties assertions were often made to the effect that "jazz" groups provided glimpses into the future. What was meant by this was that black music—especially that of the sixties, with its heavy emphasis on individual freedom within a collectively improvised context—proposed a model social order, an ideal, even utopic balance between personal impulse and group demands. The musicians' exhiliration at contributing to evolving musical orders rather than conforming to an already existing one seemed to anticipate the freedom of some future communalist ethic. Bill Mathieu, in a review of Roscoe Mitchell's *Sound*, stresses a communalist impulse he hears in the music: "There is emerging the sense of the holy tribal family as the primal artistic source." In a review of Lester Bowie's *Numbers 1 & 2* he speaks of Bowie's music as an instance of a similar communalist experimentation, remarking at some length on a tuning-in process to which he applies the term *agreement*:

> In this music I hear the musicians making themselves fully known to each other. But the means are new. . . .
> In the old days, musicians used themes, rhythmic and harmonic inventions, expressive coloring, as the language of group play. These aspects are still present, but other work is done in other ways. The most important of these let us call *agreement*. The quality of agreement has always been a factor in making group music. Now, however, this aspect has become the illuminating aesthetic of contemporary music.

Baraka's writings on black music share with those of critics like Mathieu this tendency to discern inklings of an Edenic, open state or condition, though the terms of his particular sense of "agreement" are more insistently tribal or nationalistic—that is, black. The music's communalist impulse is understood by him in terms of the synonymy of blackness with collectivity. Accordingly, he interprets the interest in and experimentation with collective improvisation among the newer musicians as a return to the African ethic, a departure from which he takes the growth of the "jazz" solo to have been. Something like the observation that this openness proceeds from an agreement which exists *above* the music also gets made in terms of blackness (understood to be synonymous with spirituality as well). These notions of black communality clearly carry the weight of a wished-for release from egocentricity, from the solipsism so rhapsodically lamented in poems like "The Death of Nick Charles," *"An Agony. As Now."* or "A Guerrilla Handbook":

> Convinced
> of the man's image (since
> he will not look at substance
> other than his ego.

As this egocentrism is thought to be the issue of his white education, blackness represents a liberating concern for as well as openness to others. The
black-musician-as-saboteur's target thus becomes the Western cult of individualism, the music an assault upon the ego. "New Black Music," Baraka
writes in 1965, "is this: Find the self, then kill it."

As if in preparation for the coming communalist ethic, Baraka's poems
during the early sixties involve practices comparable to the surrealist *de-
réglèment de sens* as well as to the music's assault on the self. Like the
surrealists—the analogy is enhanced by the fact that Baraka, as did Breton,
Aragon and others, now espouses the Communist ideology—Baraka sought
in these poems a derangement of the ratiocinative ego. Like black surrealist
Aimé Césaire, moreover, he saw this derangement as a plunge into previously
repressed black ancestral strata. The sense of "a plunge into the depths" is
exactly what's evoked by Baraka's early poem "The Bridge," though the
poem relies on musical terminology rather than surrealist imagery. The title
refers to that portion of a "jazz" composition which leads the players back
to the main melody line, referred to by musicians as the tune's "head."
Baraka makes punning use of both terms, *bridge* and *head,* allowing his
having "forgotten" the latter to suggest an experience of ego-loss, his having
strayed beyond the former—"I can't see the bridge now, I've past / it"—to
suggest, again, a lostness which results in drowning, absorption into the
oceanic All. The poem in full:

> I have forgotten the head
> of where I am. Here at the bridge.2
> bars, down the street, seeming
> to wrap themselves around my fingers, the day,
> screams in me; pitiful like a little girl
> you sense will be dead before the winter
> is over.
> I can't see the bridge now, I've past
> it, its shadow, we drove through, headed out
> along the cold insensitive roads to what
> we wanted to call "ourselves."
> "How does the bridge go?" Even tho
> you find yourself in its length
> strung out along its breadth, waiting
> for the cold sun to tear out your eyes. Enamoured
> of its blues, spread out in the silk clubs of

this autumn tune. The changes are difficult, when
you hear them, & know they are all in you, the chords

of your disorder meddle with your would be disguises.
Sifting in, down, upon your head, with the sun & the insects.

(Late feeling) Way down till it barely, after that rush of
wind & odor reflected from hills you have forgotten the color
when you touch the water, & it closes, slowly, around your head.
The bridge will be behind you, that music you know, that place,
you feel when you look up to say, it is me, & I have forgotten,
all the things, you told me to love, to try to understand, the
bridge will stand, high up in the clouds & the light, & you,

(when you have let the song run out) will be sliding through
unmentionable black.

On a strictly musical level "The Bridge" evokes the tendency toward
deconstruction or defamiliarization among players of what was then—the
poem was written sometime between 1957 and 1961—beginning to be called
"the new thing." This tendency involved a departure from—even outright
abandonment of—bebop's reliance on the recurring chords referred to as
"the changes" of a particular piece. Rather than basing their improvisations
on the chord structure of the tune's head, the "new thingers" began to
venture into areas not so patly related to the harmonics of the piece being
played. To listeners accustomed to recurrent reminders of a tune's head in
the form of the soloist's confinement to the changes, the new music seemed
structureless and incoherent. These "nonchordal" excursions were often put
down as unmelodic ("Save the Popular Song") or as evidence of the musicians' confusion. The players were frequently said to sound *lost*. What Baraka does in "The Bridge" is make a poem of this charge—"I have forgotten
the head / of where I am"—making this "confusion" suggest a descent into
the black subconscious, into "unmentionable black." "The Bridge" is still,
however, a poem which *refers to* rather than *enacts* the sort of derangement
I've been talking about. We find in it very little of the "difficulty in focusing
on its controlling insights" M. L. Rosenthal sees as the characteristic defect
in Baraka's first two books of poems. The poem's "controlling" musical
conceit remains very much in view throughout.

Rosenthal, as have others, remarks on "the structural similarity of some
of its [*Preface to a Twenty Volume Suicide Note's*] pieces to jazz improvisation" and observes, "The spiraling, dreaming movement of associations,
spurts of energetic pursuit of melody and motifs, and driftings away of Jones's

poems seem very much an expression of a new way of looking at things, and of a highly contemporary aesthetic, of a very promising sort." He fails, however, to appreciate the connection between this "jazz" aesthetic and the "difficulty in focusing" he finds so disappointing. My own sense is that this difficulty is not so much a defect as a principled outgrowth of the African aesthetic underlying black music and Baraka's poetry. In *Blues People* Baraka quotes a passage from Ernest Borneman's "The Roots of Jazz" which is worth quoting again, a passage in which a description is offered of the African aesthetic in language and music:

> In language, the African tradition aims at circumlocution rather than at exact definition. The direct statement is considered crude and unimaginative; the veiling of all contents in ever-changing paraphrases is considered the criterion of intelligence and personality. In music, the same tendency towards obliquity and ellipsis is noticeable.

Baraka echoes Borneman when, in the course of his liner notes to Archie Shepp's *Four for Trane,* he applauds a certain "tendency towards obliquity" in the playing of altoist John Tchicai (whose solos he elsewhere describes as "metal poems"): "John Tchicai's solo on 'Rufus' comes back to me again. It slides away from the proposed."

Baraka's poems, especially those in *The Dead Lecturer,* likewise tend to slide away from the proposed, to refuse to commit themselves to any single meaning. The beginning of "The Measure of Memory (The Navigator)," for example, leads one to expect some sort of theodicy, but by the second line conceptualization has given way to a stream of images the relationship or relevance of which to the poem's opening assertion is nowhere made explicit:

> The presence of good
> is its answer (at the curb
> the dead white verb, horse
> breathing white steam
> in the air)
>   Leaving, into the clocks
> sad lovely lady fixed by words
> her man
> her rest
> her fingers
> her wooden house

> set against the rocks
> of our nation's
> enterprise.

The second stanza follows from—in the sense of being logically or thematically related to—the first only in that its image of disappearance echoes that
of "leaving" in the poem's sixth line:

> That we disappear
> to dance, and dance
> when we do,
> badly.

The third stanza follows from the second in that it continues to describe
what "we" do, but the discontinuity between it and the fourth stanza is not
only tolerated by Baraka but accentuated by the double line he inserts between them:

> And wield sentiment
> like flesh
> like the dumb man's voice
> like the cold environment
> of need. Or despair, a trumpet
> with poison mouthpiece, blind player,
> at the garden of least discernment; I
> stagger, and remember/my own terrible
> blankness and lies.
>
> ===================================
>
> The boat's prow angled at the sun
> Stiff foam and an invisible cargo
> of captains. I buy injury, and decide
> the nature of silence. Lines of speed
> decay in my voice.

The image of the boat in this final stanza recalls the word *navigator* in the
poem's title, but what does it or any of the poem's other images and assertions have to do with the proposition that "the presence of good/is its answer"? The connective is neither logic nor discourse, but the poet's voice.
Adhering to and putting into practice Olson's *dictum* that "in any given
poem always, always one perception must must must MOVE, INSTANTER, ON
ANOTHER," the poem has a mercurial, evanescent quality, as though it sought
to assassinate any expectations of traceable argument or logical flow. This

is exactly the quality Baraka praises in Shepp's "Rufus," going on in the liner notes to *Four for Trane* to speak of the music in terms more commonly applied to poems:

> "Rufus" makes its "changes" faster. *Changes* here meaning, as younger musicians use that word to mean "modulations," what I mean when I say *image*. They change very quickly. The mind, moving.
>
> (Baraka's italics)

The mind, moving. Poems like "The Measure of Memory (The Navigator)" seek to circumvent stasis, to be true to the essential mobility of the psyche. Their "tendency towards obliquity" is a gesture in the direction of totalization, toward an enlargement of the realm of that we take or will accept as being meaningful. "Poetry aims at difficult meanings," Baraka writes. "Meanings not already catered to. Poetry aims at reviving, say, a sense of meaning, or meaning's possibility and ubiquitousness."

This gesture toward totalization has to do with an anti-Western, antirationalist feeling, the West and its cult of rationality epitomizing a pursuit of order at the expense of the All. The West's exclusionary practices against nonwhite peoples are seen as one with its attempted suppression of the nonrational. The dreamish, arational quality of his poems is thus of a piece with Baraka's contempt for the confusion of rationality with rationalization ("Bankrupt utopia sez tell me / no utopias"). Hence his espousal of "insanity," the ultimate irrationality, in the form of a black dadaistic uprising in the poem "Black Dada Nihilismus" and in the essay "Philistinism and the Negro Writer."

At its worst Baraka's praise for the emotively expressive veers toward the anti-intellectualism—which, as usual, sounds a bit lame coming from an intellectual—of pieces like "New-Sense," in which he sets up an opposition between the expressive and the reflective. In its best aspects this anti-intellectualism is not so much a repudiation of thought as an effort to *re*think, to as it were *un*think the many perversions of thought—rationalization, "institutionalized dishonesty" and so forth—endemic to an unjust social order. The antireflective position, that is, having been arrived at by way of reflection, represents an instance of dialectical thinking, as in "Hegel":

> Either I am wrong
> or "he" is wrong. All right
> I am wrong, but give me someone
> to talk to.

An ongoing oscillation between these two impulses—or more exactly these alternate modes of a single impulse (toward totalization)—is what makes for the characteristic unrest of Baraka's thought. The unrest itself bespeaks a desire to transcend conditionality, the very desire with whose futility the poem "Jitterbugs" has to do:

> The imperfection of the world
> is a burden, if you know it, think
> about it, at all. Look up in the sky
> wishing you were free, placed so terribly
> in time, mind out among new stars, working
> propositions, and not this planet where you
> cant go anywhere without an awareness of the hurt
> the white man has put on the people. Any people. You
> cant escape, there's no where to go. They have made
> this star unsafe, and this age, primitive, though yr mind
> is somewhere else, your ass aint.

This repudiation, it perhaps bears repeating, comes of Baraka's own desire for some such transcendence, of the idealist, Hegelian, subtilizationist (call it what you will) impulse from which his poetry's obliquities derive.

The defamiliarization encountered in the poems, that is, betrays a sense of the world as not only determined or conditioned but *over*determined. This overdetermination is what their obliquities do battle with, seeking to expose, by circumventing, the partiality of common sense, of any consensually-constituted reality's necessary eclipse of unassimilable truths. The totalization at which they aim being outside their reach, they put in its place a vigilant sense of the patencies toward which consciousness tends as inescapably conditional, thus neverendingly susceptible to qualification. Baraka hears this spirit of interrogation and discontent in the most moving of black music, especially that of John Coltrane ("the heaviest spirit"). Of the version of Billy Eckstine's "I Want to Talk About You" on the *Coltrane Live at Birdland* album he writes:

> instead of the simplistic though touching note-for-note replay of the ballad's line, on this performance *each note is tested,* given a slight tremolo or emotional vibrato (note to chord to scale reference), which makes it seem as if *each one of the notes is given the possibility of "infinite" qualification.*
>
> (my italics)

A similar "testing" can be heard in most of Baraka's poems, giving them

that hesitant, stuttering quality suggestive of a discomfort with any pretense
of definitive statement. What this "testing" projects is a world of uncertain-
ties or of expanded possibilities, a world of shifting, unsettled boundaries in
which any gesture toward definition is unavoidably tentative, self-conscious
and subject to revision. This "uncertainty principle" often takes the rather
obvious form of a preponderance of questions, as in "The Clearing," where
repetitions of and variations upon the questions "Where are the beasts?",
"What bird makes that noise?", "Were you singing?" and "What song is
that?" occur throughout:

> Your voice down the hall. Are
> you singing? A shadow song
> we lock our movement
> in. Were you singing?
> down the hall. White plaster
> on the walls, our fingers
> leave their marks, on
> the dust, or tearing
> the wall away. Were you
> singing? What song
> was that?

Another characteristic use of repetition has much the same effect. While
not one of outright questions as in "The Clearing," the repetition of such
phrases as *or pain, the yes* and *flesh or soul* in *"An Agony. As Now."* suggests
a state of astonishment if not one of confusion. Each repetition being followed by a staccato burst of imaged evocation, the sense of a wrestling with
definition is given, of an obsessive anxiety toward the impossibility of any
settled sense of what these phrases mean:

> It can be pain. (As now, as all his
> flesh hurts me.) It can be that. Or
> pain. As when she ran from me into
> that forest.
> Or pain, the mind
> silver spiraled whirled against the
> sun, higher than even old men thought
> God would be. Or pain. And the other. The
> *yes.* (Inside his books, his fingers. They
> are withered yellow flowers and were never
> beautiful.) The yes. You will, lost soul, say

'beauty.' Beauty, practiced, as the tree. The
slow river. A white sun in its wet sentences.
Or, the cold men in their gale. Ecstasy. Flesh
or soul. The yes. (Their robes blown. Their bowls
empty. They chant at my heels, not at yours.) Flesh
or soul, as corrupt. Where the answer moves too quickly.
Where the God is a self, after all.)

Something of a treadmill or a stuttering effect results, the sense of someone
caught in a rut being heightened by the dead-ending options—the word *or*
occurs twelve times in the poem—created by posing the same word as an
alternative to itself ("Or pain. . . . Or pain. . . . Or pain"). This effect, as
I've already tried to suggest, is a very salient feature of the playing of those
black musicians Baraka most admires. (Listen, for example, to Sonny Rollins's "Green Dolphin Street," Coltrane's "Amen" or John Tchicai's "Everything Happens to Me.") In some poems, in fact, the use of repetition is
almost purely musical, in that sound seems to take precedence over sense:

> say day lay day may fay come some bum'll
> take break jake make fake lay day some bum'll
> say day came break snow mo whores red said they'd
> lay day in my in fay bed to make bread for jake
> limpin in the hall with quiverin stick.

Another statement Baraka has made about Coltrane can very fittingly be
applied to such gestures as these:

> One night he played the head of "Confirmation" over and over
> again, about twenty times, and that was his solo. It was as if he
> wanted to take that melody apart and play out each of its chords
> as a separate improvisational challenge. And while it was a mar-
> velous thing to hear and see, it was also more than a little fright-
> ening; *like watching a grown man learning to speak . . .* and I
> think that's just what was happening.
>
> (my italics)

III

Baraka's poetry (to borrow his own description of the new music) "began by calling itself 'free.'" "MY POETRY," he wrote in 1959, "is whatever
I think I am. . . . I CAN BE ANYTHING I CAN. . . . I *must* be completely free
to do just what I want, in the poem." This declaration of poetic freedom is
likewise "social," a "direct commentary on the scene it appears in." So

assertive an espousal of or aspiration toward poetic freedom implies the absence of any such freedom outside of poems. It may have been this absence Baraka had in mind in 1960 when he remarked, "I'm always aware, in anything I say, of the 'sociological configuration'—what it *means* sociologically. But it doesn't have anything to do with what I'm writing at the time." Though he seems to have at this point believed in poetry as an actual, albeit fleeting transcendence of material constraints, only a few years later he insists in "Green Lantern's Solo":

> Can you understand
> that nothing is free! Even the floating strangeness of the poet's
>   head
> the crafted visions of the intellect, *named, controlled,* beat and erected
> to work, and struggle under the heavy fingers of art.
>
> (Baraka's italics)

So, just as he's able to discern the "sociological configuration" from which the freedom-thrusts of black music derive, he's also aware of the contingencies his poems' obliquities seek to deflect. In fact, the poems become increasingly concerned with explicit statements regarding these contingencies, thus making for a certain tension between such directness and any attempts to "slide away from the proposed." Such attempts all but disappear, in fact, from the poems of the early seventies, poems such as those in *It's Nation Time* or, a bit more recently, a poem like "Afrikan Revolution":

> We are for world progress. Be conscious of your
> life! We need food. We need homes; good
> housing—not shacks. Let only people who want to
> live in roach gyms live in roach gyms
> We do not want to live with roaches. Let
> Nixon live with roaches if he wants to. He
> is closer to a roach. What is the difference
> between Nixon and a roach?
> Death to bad housing
> Death to no work
> We need work. We need education.

This contentment with the explicit (the sloganistic in fact), while inconsistent with "the denying or withholding of all signposts" so essential to the "jazz" aesthetic, is nonetheless consistent with and in fact articulates the "message" implied by—the "enraged sociologies" Baraka hears in—black music.

The poems in *Hard Facts* appear to signal an arrest of this trend toward utter directness, a return to the blend of the explicit with the oblique characteristic of *Black Magic Poetry*, a work in which one finds statements as outright as "President Johnson / is a mass murderer" or "The white man / at best / is corny," and images as indecipherable as "a black toe sewn in their throats." The poems in *Hard Facts*, while generously laced with an unambiguously Marxist line—"fight for the dictatorship until it is reality. The dictatorship of the proletariat, the / absolute control of the state by the working class"—nevertheless allow for the warp introduced by such lines as "In rag time, slanting / stick legs, with a pocket full of / toasted seaweed." Baraka appears to be attempting an accord between the conflicting claims of the accessible and the esoteric—for which also read the contingent and the indeterminate, the social and the spiritual, the Marxist and the Hegelian, ad nauseam—("the spiritual and free and soulful must mingle with the practical"). This is the synthesis, significantly, whose weight he envisions a future black music carrying, a music wherein all the dichotomies he's troubled by will have been rescued from conflict:

> But here is a theory stated just before. That what will come will be a *Unity Music*. The Black Music which is jazz and blues, religious and secular. Which is New Thing and Rhythm and Blues. The consciousness of social re-evaluation and rise, a social spiritualism. A mystical walk up to the street to a new neighborhood where all the risen live.
>
> (Baraka's italics)

(Except the raw wind makes the hero's eyes close, and the tears that come out are real.)

ROBERT B. STEPTO

"The Aching Prodigal":
Jay Wright's Dutiful Poet

This familiar music . . . demanded action.
RALPH ELLISON

I have been asked to provide a few words that might introduce Jay Wright
and his poetry to the general reader. This is an overwhelming task—so much
is there, so much is good—and it is a presumptuous one as well since I, too,
am the general reader. Perhaps I qualify for this work because I own copies
of the books and I have read them. Perhaps I should therefore begin by
saying something easy, such as, "Don't worry about biography, or about the
Anglo-American, Afro-American, and other transatlantic traditions; don't
worry about the history to be learned or the myths to be dispelled or the
language which is yours but which you do not speak, just read the poems—
let them introduce themselves." Jay Wright would, I think, approve of this
statement. But more must be said, all of it having to do with how one may
prepare one's self for reading a truly New World poet.

Think of New Mexico. Consider it not so much as a place of birth but
as a "dimension of history," a physical dimension of fact, a bead of the "map
of beads." There are towns with Anglo names like Hobbs, Gallup, and Farm-
ington; other towns are called Las Cruces, Los Alamos, Las Vegas. Albuquerque is on the Rio Grande, and so is Truth or Consequences. "New
Mexico assumed its present boundaries in 1863." (What else was going on
in 1863?) Forty-nine years later, it was admitted as a State to the Union. It

From *Callaloo* 6, no. 19 (Fall 1983). © 1984 by Robert B. Stepto.

had been a Territory; while a "dimension" of Mexico, a Province and a Department.

The people of New Mexico are, and have been for some time, brown, white, red, and black. One could rehearse a history of people-in-place sometimes living a "feast of the living," at other times killing or at least distrusting each other; a history which begins, from one view, when Spanish explorers first ventured North from Mexico in the 1530s. But there is an easier route to seeing what is at hand: consider the Santa Fe Railroad.

Santa Fe. Named that by whom? "Settled" by whom and who else? There was a massacre there in 1680; four hundred "settlers" were killed and Santa Fe was "recaptured"—by whom, for whom, for how long? Santa Fe is almost 400 years old; it is the second oldest city in the United States. One can go there today and live a kind of "feast of the living"—the hills are gorgeous, the haciendas win decorating awards, a college or two blithely teach western civilization, Anglos and Indians alike peddle craftwork of high quality, blue-corn tortillas are still available and still a manna from heaven. But one cannot get there easily by railroad.

Railroad. Built by whom? Stretched across whose land and when? And why? Who engineered, who conducted, who waited table and pointed out sights? Who observed from the observation car and saw what? Whose "noble image" graced the four-color posters and timetables that helped to fill the coffers? Who is the "we" in these lines?

> We'd learned that,
> when the snow was deep enough,
> we could show up by the tracks,
> looking ready and fit to work,
> and after the other men had been counted out,
> and sent trudging along the tracks,
> the foreman would sometimes turn to us.
> He always saved us for the last,
> even the giants, standing ready,
> with their uncommon eyes gripping him.

What New World rituals are enacted here? What grip—as force, as disease— claims all?

State, Territory, Province, Department; Brown, White, Black, Red. These are not terms but tongues: "tongues of the exiled dead" but also, as we must intuit, "tongues of the living." They are the keys of our "own cadences," of our own literacies; they are for those of us gripped in this geography the keys to the kingdom of this world ("el reino de este mundo").

They are also beads upon a very particular "secular rosary" fashioned for those who, like Wright's poet, may "come, black and bilingual, / to a passage of feeling" (from *The Homecoming Singer*) and sense that the journey must be undertaken again:

> Now I invoke my map of beads.
> I coil the spirit's veins about my wrists.
> I kneel at Ocumare to worry
>   the saint's bones,
> and rise on the walls of Cumaná.
> Poco a poco,
> I cut my six figures
> on another coast, in a western sunrise.
> In Carolina darkness, I push
> my jangada to the blessed water.
> I ask now:
> all the blessed means my journey needs,
> the moving past, the lingering shadow
> of my body's destination.

This is a useful passage for anyone being introduced to Wright's art because it is at once complicated and straightforward. Complication comes, I suppose, with the references. Denizens of this world that we are, we nonetheless have to be told (in notes Wright probably did not want to write) that Ocumare and Cumaná are in Venezuela, and that *jangada* is a Brazilian balsam wood raft. While the notes clear up something, they in no way clarify everything, for it is precisely at this point that the predictable—and in some measure, insidious—culturally-prescribed questions set in. Is this poet black? Is this poet Catholic? (If he is a black Catholic, why?) Why does this poet go to South America? Are Ocumare and Cumaná in *black* South America? (Somebody better check.) Does this black poet consider South America home, if so, why? Why is there some Spanish in those lines? (How many black people "around here" know Spanish?) What kind of reading led to these lines? What kind of living led to these lines? Is this a religious poem? Is this poem black?

I should hope that in constructing these hypothetical questions, and in suggesting here and there motivations for them, I have also presented the worst possible hypothetical scenario. But something tells me that I am touching, in Wright's words, less upon the "fantastic" than upon the "certainty of myth." One wants to say that complication, as it is represented by these questions, is merely the result of ignorance or, to shift to another plane, illiteracy. (How much Spanish must a New World citizen *know* in order to translate "poco a poco"?) But that will not do. What we must see as well is how the myths and rituals of American living, including some of the most meaningful ones, tether us. We travel but do not journey; we read but cannot translate; we are wise but usually only in terms of a local wisdom. We are, in short, the father in these lines:

> But he, with good reason,
> never read my poem,
> and I think he must have sat
> in his small living room,
> with the dying dog lying at his feet,
> drowsing under the television's hum,
> thinking how little I knew.

Perhaps we are right to think such thoughts. They are, after all, a currency with which we have purchased a survival. But we must begin to come to terms with how all such thinking sends our children away, and only occasionally makes of them poets (the making having so pitifully much to do with childhoods becoming undone). And even then, not all of these poets are like Wright's "aching prodigal," who dares to sing "without metaphor" of

> What it means to spring from the circle,
> and come back again.

Complication thus appears with the return, which stands at once for what is contemporary in our lives and post-modern in our literature. The return is a radical, contemporary act because it forces a new dimension of history in place; it is aesthetically post-modern because it is the nether side of the journey, the cloth unwoven (nightwork, starwork), the city left, the lid (or mantle) as colon between two worlds instead of a figure of one world or another. The return is a complication full of decision and, on a fully evoked ritualistic level, incision: we know how to send our children away, or at least how to watch them go, but can we imagine and suffer the "cut" of their new, "trembling" presence?

But to speak of the return is in some sense to leap ahead. The end is in the beginning in Wright's poetry (as elsewhere), but it is with journeys, not returns, that we usually begin. Journeys are as essential to Wright's art as are the returns, and it is they which provide the points of entry, as it were, to many poems. This is what is straightforward, what should be familiar.

An early poem, "The Baptism," begins this way:

> We had gone down to the river again,
> without much hope of finding it
> unmuddied.

"An Invitation to Madison County" has these first lines:

> I ride through Queens,
> out to International Airport,
> on my way to Jackson, Tougaloo, Mississippi.
> I take out a notebook,
> write 'my southern journal,' and the date.

The powerful final stanza of "The Death of an Unfamiliar Sister" [from *Soothsayers and Omens*] declares:

> Sister, I have walked to here,
> over this compassionate dust,
> to wait in this moving light
> for your last movement,
> the one movement
> that these others will not
> and cannot understand.

These lines from *Dimensions of History* seemingly rehearse those above:

> I strain to clasp my dust again,
> to make it mine,
> to understand the claims the living
> owe the dead.

Soon thereafter, we read,

> And so I start in search of that key,
> the ankh,
> that will unlock the act.

One image of what may then transpire is offered in the most recent book, *The Double Invention of Komo*:

> I forget my name;
> I forget my father's and mother's names.
> I am about to be born.
> I forget where I come from
> and where I am going.
> I cannot distinguish

right from left, front from rear.
Show me the way of my race
and of my fathers.

In the first three passages, the referents appear to "bare" a North American stamp—quite possibly a North *Afro*-American one as well: baptism and burial, Mississippi and New Mexico, past and present—all these converge "down by the river side." In contrast, the final three passages provide no familiar referents. The geography is utterly non-specific; the descent, insofar as the journey is of that nature, seems decidedly non-western; the image of the poet seeking and achieving the state of *tabula rasa* in order to *gain* the "way" of race and fathers alike unsettles and possibly offends more than one New World black culture. And yet, who presumes to declare that the final three passages depict foreign travel—or travail? Which "I" is the homeboy, which the alien, the *stranierò*? International Airport ("As I fly, I insist that nothing / may now turn to itself, alone, again") receives us all and disperses us upon our one-but-many journeys: Tougaloo and key; King and Komo; kin and cadence; river and dust. Albuquerque and Africa both require passports and preparation. In the North American South, the poet muses,

I wonder how long I'll have to listen
to make them feel I listen, wonder
what I can say that will say,
'It's all right. I don't understand,
a thing. Let me meet you here, in your home.
Teach me what you know,
for I think I'm coming home.'

In the midst of "The third phase of the coming out of Komo," he continues,

I have been trying to create a language
to return what you have lost,
and what you have abandoned,
a language to return you to yourself,
to return to you.

There is difference here. In both passages, the poet is an apprentice or initiate; however, in the second, more recent passage he is more mature and, one suspects, better traveled. His statement of vocation clearly tells us that while he has not yet mastered his craft, he has passed through listenership to that level of authorship achieved only when responsiveness prompts responsibility. But there is similarity as well. "Home" is imaged in both passages, and in both images it is a shared language not merely to be found but performed. Here, then, is a key matter for the general reader to understand: Wright's art is one which forces us to make the all-important distinction between poems which describe or simulate performative acts—consider, among North Afro-American forms, the sermonic poem and the blues poem—and those which *prepare* us for performative acts. Wright's poems close, often arrestingly; but full closure exists within the imagined act that is just beyond the "circumference" of written art and possibly of language itself.

In poetry, and perhaps in other art forms as well, to speak of home is to suggest how that art seeks its tradition. And so we must ask of Wright's art, who traveled this road before? Who also travels now?

Vera Kutzinski, in her essay-review of *The Double Invention of Komo,* assists us here when she declares, "Du Bois's weary traveler has indeed come a long way," and adds, "Even though Jay Wright may not exactly be another 'cowboy' in Ishmael Reed's 'Boat of Ra,' he certainly is a fellow *traveler,* another one of those uncanny presences that people and traverse Afro-America's post-modern landscape." To Du Bois and Reed, I would add, keeping in mind the landscape just cited, Jean Toomer. "I wonder how long I'll have to listen / to make them feel I listen" is not from *Cane* but worthy of it. Consider as well Robert Hayden. Some of Wright's best early poems—"Crispus Attucks" and "W. E. B. Du Bois at Harvard" to mention two—are distinctly Haydenesque. In intensity, control, and angle of vision, and perhaps in their "angle of ascent" as well, they complement the work of Hayden, the American poet I first think of when I come upon a Wrightian phrase such as "the master of the spear" or "The star I see awakens me."

However, as I have already suggested, Wright's art is neither American nor Afro-American in any familiar, provincial sense. The boundaries of the United States, even in this post-modern era of expansion (military and cultural), cannot contain Wright's poet's "fact of history," any more than the rhythmic structures of ballads and blues can fully define that poet's ancient cadences. In *Dimensions of History,* the "brothers" include Crispus Attucks and Frederick Douglass. However, the "strict black brothers" are Du Bois and Saint Augustine. That pairing in itself charts a larger, transatlantic geography and historical ritual ground. Albert Ayler, Dante, Goethe, Wilson Harris, and Wole Soyinka are among the artists most often cited either in Wright's poems or in his notes. They figure deeply in the poems, partly because they provide models (of vocation as well as craft) and myths. But they are also central because they collectively signify an even larger landscape, one which perhaps is *the* map of the fact for Wright's poetry precisely because it delineates the triangulating routes of new world black culture and consciousness while exploring a still larger world, an "enhanced world" as Wright has put it.

The tradition Wright's poetry seeks is thus a puzzle for most of us, chiefly because it does not readily align itself with any one culture or cosmology—it is not a homing pigeon sure of its cage or sure that the cup of water and that of seed promiscuously placed therein is worth the price of incarceration. This troubles us, especially we who teach literature, since we are in a sense the pigeon-keepers, the custodians of the fragile cages which are variously courses and pedagogies on the one hand, and literary histories cum cultural fences on the other. Our problem in great part is that deep down something tells us that we should throw away the cages—including even those with the "comparative literature" tags and other travel stickers—and Begin Again. But how? And where does one start? An "enhanced world" is hard enough to fathom; an "enhanced world literature" complete with a tradition seems virtually incomprehensible.

I suggest that we begin, as Jay Wright often has, with the counsel of Wilson Harris. In "Some Aspects of Myth and the Intuitive Imagination," he writes:

> With the fall of Pre-Columbian civilizations in America—and indeed with the sudden vulnerability of the ancient civilizations of China, India and Africa accompanying the circumnavigation and renewed penetration of the globe by European navigators and conquistadores—it would appear that a latent capacity, a latent restlessness, a sorrow, an anguish, an ecstasy as well, affected native craftsmen and a leap began to occur, the leap of the craftsman into the modern ambivalent artist. That leap was the beginnings of a community that brought Dürer into dialogue with the arts of Pre-Columbian America as it was to bring centuries later Picasso into dialogue with the masks of Africa.

This is useful; it offers both an idea of the modern and an image of the modern world community that is distinctly, as Frederick Turner would put it, "beyond geography." But we need something more, if for no reason other than to avoid the mistake of packing Wright, Soyinka, Harris, Walcott, Schwarz-Bart, Carpentier, and all such writers into world literature courses that remain as conceptually thin as they may be bibliographically new. Hence, Harris continues:

> That complex descent into the modern age is less than 500 years

old. It scarcely yet possesses criteria of evaluation though I would suggest such criteria must accept the deep fact that all images (or institutions or rituals) are partial, are ceaselessly unfinished in their openness to other partial images from apparently strange cultures within an unfathomable, and a dynamic, spirit of wholeness that sustains all our hopes of the regeneration of far-flung community in an interdependent world.

Statements of this kind effectively qualify the free-and-easy definitions of world literature that are some of our flimsiest constructions. This particular assertion has further value in that it yields a language with which we can describe Jay Wright's art and the "enhanced world" it letters.

Wright's poet is, in one of his guises, the new world craftsman impaled upon the cusp of the modern, and in another, that same craftsman extracted (most likely, self-extracted) from that horn and healed. In one instance, there is assault from pain and rupture, in the other, there is that of memory and perhaps, too, that of the astonishing thought that the healing process will never end. In either case, the poet is a dutiful, aching prodigal, whose images of home and of a lasting inner health strain to prompt the act that will make all of us whole.

JOHN HOLLANDER

Fabulous Traveler

Daryl Hine's beautiful and powerful new book opens on the wintry light
of a January morning, in a group of aphorisms touching on late beginnings,
cold, unpromising dawns, and metaphors of origination, but all full of
a rueful gratitude for what that light, thin and cold, "precious" and "elee-
mosynary," can yet give. But that light has a particular tinge to it: at the
end of "The Copper Beech" from *Minutes* of more than ten years earlier,
Hine invokes the tree—"Whose shade is not the green of contemplation /But
the imagination's rich metallic colour / Wherein, under libido, we live"—
eroticizing the light and air of the end of Stevens's "Esthétique du Mal" and
invoking the unstated words "believe," "love," and "leave," which share an
Indo-European base with "*libido,*" and help it reach out toward the etymologically unrelated "live." If for minor writers word-play is an evasion of
depth, a mere rippling of surface, for a true poet it is not, perhaps because
words are more than merely coins or counters for him. For Hine, words are
bodies, not so much in the way Milton reminded himself in *Areopagitica*
that texts are more like people than like things, but in the ways by which
they can embrace or hurt or overpower or protect each other. Poems which
are ordinarily tropes for acts of love become even more than that—the scene
of a figure of love at another level. This is one of the reasons why Daryl
Hine's prodigious wit, classical learning, and formal control never work like
neo-metaphysical, or *libertin,* or even scholastic conceptual machinery to

From *Canto* 3, no. 1 (1979), © 1979 by *Canto*; and from "Poetry in Review" in
Yale Review 73, no. 1 (Fall 1983), © 1983 by Yale University.

grind up passion into the stuff of joke. His devices, routines of moralization of landscape and meditative emblem-reading, his mythographies and rein-terpretations of themes and topoi which seem to flourish wherever he walks and turns his poetic eyes—all of these point beyond themselves and beyond, even, the points they purport to make.

For his control of learning and wit I can think of few poets alive that can approach him—the contractions of J. V. Cunningham, the exuberance of A. D. Hope are distant kin—and absolutely nobody of his age. Hine's access to a range of vocabularies is remarkable, and is always executed with a gentle ease, a *sprezzatura* marked by generosity rather than scorn. Thus, for example, this stanza from "Blight on Elm":

> Remember how we used to watch them change
> Their drip-dry garments spring and fall
> From green to brown and back again.
> This is how the suburbs lose their cool.
> By a coincidence never really strange
> The end in view is nearly natural,
> The beautiful laid level with the plain.

The punning between usage levels ("drip-dry" and "lose their cool"), the play with *plain* and *fancy* and *plane,* the radical revisionary enjambments which give discovered revised readings to "change" (intransitive becoming transitive) and "fall" (noun to verb)—to point these out is merely to identify the speaker's dialect. This is not poetry merely because of their presence. That mere presence makes such a passage splendid writing; but it is made poetry by what that writing is for and about: the parable of our very reading and comprehension of the effects. For instance, in these lines, the perception of a relation between catastrophe and its role in a natural cycle (possibly redemptive thereby, possibly not) is like a perception of enjambment. So, too, with the Tocquevilleian overtones of the leveling of beauty in democracy. The woods have continued to decay and fall from Virgil on, but unless there continues to be a renewal of signification in glimpses of the event, the ob-servation is only worthy of the nature column in the newspaper.

Again, in "Codex," Hine's meditation on his own notebook page reaches back in order to go truly forward. The rueful precision of his char-acterization of diary notations as "Private convictions on parole" makes a significant and parabolic use of the punned-upon relation between words and a given word (as upon beliefs and sentences, both declarative and for terms in jail). But the poem also points back to the important invention, in late classical times, of the codex, or paged book, to supplant the roll. For

Hine, the notebook is newly discovered in its opportunities for revisions and closures; the additional pun on coding provides those connections between the inscriptions of text and the enciphered messages of the rest of life. Thus the final stanza can complete, and close off, the meditation with another of those colloquial-traditional punning moves, provided by a found correspondence which itself makes the word-play moot:

> Distillation of a thought
> Secreted in the honeycomb
> Whose flowery images succumb
> To hyperbole, dry rot,
> Preserved upon the notebook page,
> A catchword and a calendar
> A habit and a hermitage . . .
> Close it like a closet door.

In truth the prison of book unto which we doom ourselves sometimes a prison is, and Hine's little misprision of that imprisonment cuts close to some of the most sophisticated points now being made by theorists of text about such questions.

I have chosen some of the less startling passages from *Daylight Saving* to show how even in aphoristic moments, ultimate questions of the highest seriousness are being raised. It is also the case that they exemplify Hine's brilliant vernacular, always in the employ of his questing attention. The poet as traveler has always been central in his work; as early as in the prodigiously promising *The Devil's Picture Book,* published when Hine was twenty-three, he had observed how Circe "shapes the moral traveller," and since then, as voyager and voyeur, he has traveled the literal globe and the troped sphere of language.

But this traveler is not Elizabeth Bishop's north-south voyager, and vastly different from the time traveler in Merrill, or Ashbery's metaphysical sidewalker. What he encounters and discovers, the places and scenes and ruins and visions he visits, the thoroughfares and byways he takes, the ways in which he loses his way—all of these occur in and about the mirrored world of language as well. The poet's voyeuristic gaze is as much riveted upon the verbal copulars as upon the mere physical instances of them. His own private revision of "Le Monocle de Mon Oncle" in another poem of love at near-forty ("My Optics") makes an itinerary of his relation to his own eyeglasses, which culminates in one of those remarkable, inevitably self-referential, moments of self-portraiture:

Often in the act of
Sex they are abandoned.
Balanced at the bedside
See our twin prescriptions
Gleam, a pair of glasses
Disaffected, empty,
Drained of speculation.
Touchingly myopic,
Lovers, twenty, forty,
Put their faith in contacts.
(Parenthetically
Feeling is believing.)

The imagination sees truly with the eyes' glasses off, and even the convex and concave parentheses (including the virtual ones, given the effect of the enjambment, around the word "parenthetically" itself) help to focus the mind's attention, allowing it to recognize the occasional intimacy of its otherwise distant handmaid, the sense of touch. That is why the revision of "seeing is believing" is not an empty joke. That is why the pun on the recently colloquial "contacts" for "contact-lenses" is not only appropriate, but self-glossing. For the average contemporary poet like X who does not make the visible a little hard to see, diction is a matter of style, and at most of tone. It is either that low and colloquial are sincere, direct, casual, bare, and authentic—or that they can be ruefully employed by the belated Poundian mentality to remind us how far things have fallen, how deeply the dialect of the tribe has been corrupted. But for the true poet, learned in the biology of language, the life of words is a figure for the life of human beings, and the dialectic of early and late uses is too serious a business to be reduced to the uses of mockery, of siding with the kids or the old people. For most writers of verse, this brutal and ridiculous "cloven fiction," as Blake called it, produces the stylistic factions of New and Old, Now and Then, and manifests itself as the groupies versus Lawrence Welk. The true poet is chained to the drivel of this sort of distinction by the sad necessities of literary kinship. But he or she will have no part of it; and Hine's mode of moving between the learned and the ordinary meanings of words is one of his principal means of transportation.

In the wonderful suite-poem, "Arrondissements," Hermes and Apollo accompany the wanderer through a Paris that lies both in and far beyond Baedeker's; like the brilliant "Vowel Movements" of his previous volume, *Resident Alien,* and the more overtly paradigmatic, alphabetically arrayed

"Linear A" in that same book, this district-by-district itinerary opens with
what is, in its local way, a statement of poetic theory:

A foreign city in a foreign language:
Errors you will find your way around
Less by misconstruction of an image
Idiomatic as the underground
Than by reference to the lost and found
Out-of-date semantic luggage
And archaic sentimental slang which
Used to mean so much. Beware of the sound,
Volumes of experience rebound,
Sense can take care of itself.

This mapping of place onto word is underlined and demonstrated by such
rubrics as the miniature independent plot of the rhymes—the kind that the
late W. K. Wimsatt taught readers to observe—that moves from *language* to
image to *luggage* to *slang which* (and thereby, "*slanguage*"), and will end,
in the rest of the stanza, in *baggage, dommage* and *youth from age* (the
poem instructs a younger companion). At one moment of waking, in the
Vl*ème*, the traveler observes how "Again today deciphers pornographic /
Night's incomprehensible design, / Every superstitious hieroglyphic / Reified
by an explicit sun" and we are reminded again of the sentimental nature of
all of the poet's journeying.

For in the world of this novelist, travel-writer, and preeminently elec-
trifying poet, Eros is in every place, in every topic. Like the graffiti which
the errant eye of the speaker in these poems everywhere encounters, the
signature of sex is inscribed on almost every available surface, even on the
walls of words and phrases—which for the unalienated resident, or the linguistic stay-at-home, remain otherwise blank. But it is only the nonreader
who is put off—or, in fact, on—by them: in such poems as "Atlantic and
Pacific," "Amor es Sueño," "Free Love," and others, the manifest erotic
meditation holds a torch up to the surrounding world. In emblematic inves-
tigations of a constellation ("Coma Berenices") and the TV screen ("Prime
Time") the quest for significance—that primary modern metaphor of erotic
questing—diverts the wanderer who is nonetheless impelled by the same
motion. In his beautiful sonnet to the great seventeenth-century Spaniard,
Luis de Gongora, a distant precursor, Hine maps his travels in the realms of
silver. The two initial lines, the reader may notice, conclude with the only
two rhyme-words in the poem, and they embrace the major metaphor of

language and world through which, and with which, this remarkable con-
quistador moves. The poem deserves quotation entire:

> To your language if not your native land,
> Which is a tongue when all is said
> That's done, perverse, gold, standard, and
> Curiously conservative, as dead
> As anything Amerigo invented,
> I pilgrim with my accents in my hand
> And your conceits unequalled in my head
> Through volumes of rock and canticles of sand.
> Like paradise, you are a promised land
> Aflow with ilk and money, brine and wed-
> lock, secrets that like circumstances stand
> Unalterable, maps to be misread.
> Were we translated here and now, instead
> Of reading we might understand.

Hine's virtuosity is such that it knows where to leave off, as well as
where to overwhelm. A rather important poem in *Daylight Saving* (relevant
to his whole oeuvre and, I suspect, to all of modern poetry) is his translation
of Callimachus's famous epigram attacking such Alexandrian contemporaries as Apollonius of Rhodes for their cyclic, or late secondary-epical poems.
Callimachus's poem connects erotic longing with writing and erotic loss with
the loss of originality: it is an early example of the echo-poem, in which an
echo mockingly deconstructs and undermines a pathetic utterance:

> Detesting the popular novel, I fail to derive any pleasure
>   From such a byway as this which the many frequent.
> Heartily loathing a flibbertigibbet love-object, I never
>   Drink from the tap; I despise what is common or mean.
> Yes, I admit you are handsome, Lysanias, terribly handsome:
>   Echo improves on the epithet "—and some one else's!"

The solution to the problem of translating Callimachus's "*kalos, naichi
kalos*"—the term for a beautiful athlete so common it is found on vases—
and the nasty echo which finds lurking in the almost "common or mean"
term the word "*allos*" ("other"—the "someone else") is brilliant, although
Hine plays it down by not italicizing "*and* someone else's," allowing the
echo-joke to rise up gently through the almost casual, but high, tone.

It would be perhaps too easy to make a case for Hine as our most
representative Alexandrian himself, but that would have little meaning unless

it were made clear that it was the Alexandrianism of our entire age, the condition sometimes misleadingly called "post-modern," that he exemplifies. A fine classical scholar and translator of the minor Homerica and of Theocritus, the author of seven books of verse and a most remarkable long poem called *In and Out,* as yet only privately published, his body of work is altogether impressive even at the age of forty-three. Certainly the major anglophone Canadian poet of his generation (only Jay Macpherson can at moments come up to his blend of skill and power), he has been a resident alien in Europe and, particularly, in this country for the past seventeen years. That he has not been highly enough acclaimed is, given the situation of literature in verse in this country today, unremarkable. For "the popular novel" in his Callimachus version we may read "the popularly novel" and the tired academicisms it stands for in American and British poetry. Hine does not write for idiots or illiterates, who increasingly have come to make up the audience and the judges of contemporary verse. A reviewer barely able to grasp the fact that something very complex may be going on in the rhetoric of these poems will only conclude that something is being put over on him or her, and on what poetry should be. And the notion that something very important may be being done *by means of what is going on* will be inaccessible to such a reviewer, with no sense of anything in literature but performance, signification being forbidden ground. It is a travesty of reportage merely to point out the operations of Hine's wit, the enormous success of his control of accentual-syllabic lines and rhyming, without indicating what they are doing to and for the vision of human life that this splendid body of poetry calls up. As for all important poets, form is not a matter of style—as it is for most polemicists of form—but of a reconstructed ground of language itself. It provides a vocal range, a set of givens as important for the poet as a theology. Even more, its very uses and occasions must continually provide parables and fables in themselves of that toward which poetry is always pointing.

In his "Vowel Movements," for example, the twelve-line stanzas are made to move through the domains of twelve different vowel sounds: in each stanza, the same vowel occurs on almost every stressed syllable throughout, so that each "region" of the poem is like a region or state or condition of language itself, another domain of experience. And it gets to the very guts of the notion of condition, of inner state: the poem's own dynamic, a peristaltic journey which takes the poet and the reader through the convolutions of its own bowel-vowels, is constantly being glossed along the way. Hine is too serious a writer not to allow his most masterful playing to raise ultimate questions, and "Vowel Movements" continually considers its own gestation,

not so much regarding its own beauty in a mirror, but looking through it
toward what lies beyond. In the /ay/ stanza, he can contemplate the false
versions of what he has himself striven to design:

> "Highly stylized" politely describes the bright eyesores
> Shining like diamonds or rhinestones in the night sky,
> Lifelike, provided life survives its vital cycle
> And the tireless indictment of time's diatribe,
> While mankind, sightless, frightened, like a child in twilight,
> Dies of the devices it was enlightened by.

Here, the final line, with its echo of the Shakespearean autumnal sonnet's
ending—"Consumed with that which it was nourished by"—that turns the
earlier heat into late light, ties up the metaphor of contrivance that it had
forced itself, by the very means of its own contrivances, to consider. The
scheme of assonantal domains, the figure, device, or pattern of such arrangement, becomes the basis for what is truly a *trope*, and the poem makes a
parable of its own devices.

It is this aspect of Hine's formal powers which the commentator must
confront, rather than their mere existence. Formal skill is, after all, a necessary but not a sufficient condition for poetic creation. One trouble with
an age like the present, in which one would be grateful even for more well-
written literary verse in the way of certain middle-aged British poets, is that
it makes even the empty pocket seem promising because it at least has no
hole in it. Daryl Hine is not to be praised for his learning, for his musical
and rhetorical skill, but for the mental travel on which they launch him.

Even if Hine's translation of all of the poetry of Theocritus were not in
itself a remarkable and distinguished book, the verse epilogue to it, in over
640 lines of beautifully modulated accentual English hexameters, would have
to be singled out as one of the more noteworthy poems of recent years.
Addressed to his third-century Alexandrian original, the verse essay touches
on most of the matters a reviewer of Hine's splendid version would want to
explore: the astonishing originality of Theocritus's bucolic pictures or
"idylls"; the fruitful subsequent history of the revisionary consequences of
these poems, their mythology, their kinds of allegorizing in the major fictional
mode we call Pastoral; the relations between complex, allusive, literary
Greek, moving in and out of several dialects, and modern literary English;
the theory of verse translation generally; literary eros; ancient and contemporary homosexuality; literary treatments of botanical fact, and much more.
Throughout, he speaks to the Greek poet with deep affection, as well as
with astonishingly broad and well-digested learning:

Gnomic and always ironic, your moral was seldom in earnest.
Nor were your morals. Your vices distinguish your virtue from Virgil's
Who, with a Latin solemnity followed your frivolous footsteps.

The masterful handling of the colloquial rhythms of modern American
speech and prose (by no means the same) in the hexameter framework is
made even more masterful by the display of skill at what Samuel Johnson
called "representative versification," as in the last line quoted above, where
Virgil's "Latin solemnity" has already been established by the close of the
preceding line, with its "virtue from Virgil's" rhythmic-semantic phrase, and
its momentary fiction that the two words are etymologically, and therefore
essentially, connected, infecting each with the touch of the other.

The translations themselves are remarkable for the way in which the
learning and the skill seem to surrender their domains to the empire of the
ear, the total poetic sound always allowing the reader to understand that a
good deal has been going on in the original which is at least being represented
in the English. The outdoor symphony of the *locus amoenus,* as described
by Simichidas, a persona for Theocritus himself, in Idyll VII, the famous
account of the Harvest Home, is full of the later resonances of this topos in
subsequent poetry, from Virgil to Walt Whitman and beyond:

> Over our heads many poplars and loftily towering elm trees
> Soughed as they stirred in the breezes, while nearby the
>   numinous water
> Laughed as it flowed from the caves of the nymphs with a
>   metrical chatter,
> Whilst all about in the shadowy branches the smoky cicadas
> Worked at their chirruping—they had their labour cut out for
>   them! Far off
> Out of the thick-set brambles the tree-frog croaked in a
>   whisper:
> Linnets and larks were intoning their tunes, and the wood-dove
>   made moan.
> Busy and buzzing, the bees hovered over the musical waters.

The Keats here in the "making moan," and the interpretive "musical waters"
for the *pidax* or "spring" of the Greek (such springs and fountains having
long been established as tropes of poetic eloquence) are entirely appropriate
for so allusive and resonant a text to begin with, and the last line is at once
more allusive and more accurate than the Tennysonian "And o'er the foun-

tain hung the gilded bee" of Charles Stuart Calverley's 1860s version of this idyll.

Idyll VI, with its poetical contest between Daphnis and Damoetas, is splendid; so is the couplet-for-couplet bout of the mime in V, the great prototype of what jazz musicians called a "cutting session." In the epithalamium for Helen, Idyll XVIII, where Dryden (one of Hine's few truly poetical predecessors in translating Theocritus into English) must let his style have its way:

> With Pallas in the loom she may contend,
> But none, ah none can animate the lyre
> And the mute strings with vocal souls inspire!
> Whether the learn'd Minerva be her theme,
> Or chaste Diana bathing in the stream;
> None can record their heavenly praise so well
> As Helen, in whose eyes ten thousand Cupids dwell.

Hine gives us something that will always be less dated, as well as more deeply neo-classical:

> Nobody cuts from her patterned, elaborate loom such a close-knit
> Web as she weaves with her shuttle between the immovable uprights.
> No one has such understanding of playing the lyre as she does,
> Singing in honour of Artemis, also of buxom Athena,
> No one like Helen whose glances are pregnant with every desire.

The spell which the girl Simaetha works with her jinxing conjuring wheel to bring her lover back to her in II has a famous problematic refrain, and Hine does wonderfully with it:

> First of all barley is burnt on the fire—will you sprinkle it thickly,
> Thestylis? Idiot, where have your wandering wits taken wing to?
> Must I be made an amusement of even by you, dirty creature?
> Scatter the barley and say, "I am scattering Delphis' bones now."
> *Magical whirligig, fetch to my house my unfaithful beloved.*

Hine's previous translation of the Homeric hymns, while most impressive, had an Alexandrian cast to it. But Theocritus is clearly his poet, and he shows us how much he is our poet as well. It is not so much that he has had to contend with a tradition of translation (as the translator of Homer or Virgil must do), for aside from the splendid 1588 version of six of the idylls by an anonymous Elizabethan, Dryden's really fine version of Idyll XXVII, and some momentary felicities of Calverley and Leigh Hunt, he is the first poet of importance to attempt a version both learned and imaginatively potent. In an age in which versifiers translate into lame free verse poems from languages which they do not know how to read, employing prose cribs which they turn into unsounding cut-up prose, this book set amazingly high standards.

Hine has no doubt suffered a want of attention that he might have attained without his own want of vulgarity, crudity, and the knowledge of what poetry is, but such attention is given by that majority of whom Frost observed that they would rather vote than think. His astonishing *In and Out* (—of the Roman Church, as well as the old in and out of sex), with its intertwined chronicles of sexual and religious vocations and conversions, might, if commercially published, momentarily gain him a "gay" constituency, but it would be a readership as trivial for his poetry as one which seized on that wonderful book-length narrative because it is written in blank anapestic trimeter—as if either "theme" (or "area of interest") or "form" were in itself any more central than the unwritten-upon lines of a notebook: they may be blue, or gray, widely or narrowly spaced, and so forth. But it is what is written on and between and, ultimately, by means, and by way of, them which matters. Poems may have subjects as well as objects, but it is what they make of them that provides what they are about. Literalists cannot perceive this, but literalists—the morticians of poetry—never could, whether they author or consume the sweet, empty light verse of the Hallmark greeting card, or the scarcely less empty dark verse—the almost universal modes of bad American *vers libre*—which help extend the power of the unvanquished goddess Dulness everywhere. There are very few poets as good as Daryl Hine, and almost none like him. At the end of even a minor visit to some amusing *banlieu* one is moved to hail this remarkable guide, a walking university, with the *"in lumine tuo videbimus lumen"* of one's former standing university, "in thy radiance we see light," or with the blunter *"lux et veritas"* of his present one. In any event, a more than ironic point of light against Dulness's universal darkness. It will not go out.

Biographical Notes

ROBERT PENN WARREN

Robert Penn Warren was born in Todd County, Kentucky, on April 24, 1905. His birthplace furnishes the background of his novel *Night Rider* (1938). At sixteen he entered Vanderbilt University, where he studied under Donald Davidson and John Crowe Ransom. His first poetry appeared in *Fugitive*, a college publication. From 1925 to 1927 he taught at the University of California while working on his master's degree. After one year at Yale on a fellowship he went to Oxford as a Rhodes Scholar.

He received his B.Litt. from Oxford and returned to the United States, where he taught at Southwestern College, Vanderbilt, and then at Louisiana State University. While at Louisiana he was managing editor with Cleanth Brooks of the *Southern Review*. In 1930 he married Emma Brescia.

In 1935, Warren published *XXXVI Poems*, followed by a critical work, *Understanding Poetry*, written with Cleanth Brooks. Warren received a Guggenheim Award in 1940, published *Eleven Poems on the Same Theme* in 1942, and wrote *At Heaven's Gate*, which appeared in 1943. A year later, he published *Selected Poems, 1923–1943*.

Warren's best known work of fiction, *All the King's Men*, was published in 1946, winning him the Pulitzer Prize for literature in 1947. The motion picture version of the novel was named best film of 1949 by the Academy of Motion Picture Arts and Sciences. *Blackberry Winter*, a novella, appeared that same year. *The Circus in the Attic and Other Stories* appeared in 1948, and *World Enough and Time* was published in 1950. *Brother to Dragons*, a long dramatic poem, appeared in 1953 (a new version was published in 1979). *Band of Angels*, a novel, appeared in 1955, and *Segregation* appeared in 1956.

His works to date include *Promises: Poems 1954–1956* (1957); *Selected Essays* (1958); *The Cave* (1958); *You, Emperors and Others: Poems 1957–1960* (1960); *The Legacy of the Civil War* (1961); *Wilderness: A Tale of the Civil War* (1961); *Flood: A Romance of Our Time* (1964); *Who Speaks for the Negro?* (1965); *Selected Poems New and Old, 1923–1966* (1966); *Incarnations* (1968); *Audubon: A Vision* (1969); *Homage to Theodore Dreiser* (1971); *Meet Me in the Green Glen* (1971); *Or Else-Poem/Poems 1968–1974* (1975); *Democracy and Poetry* (1975); *Selected Poems: 1923–1975* (1976); *A Place to Come To* (1977); *Now and Then: Poems, 1976–1978* (1978); *Being Here: Poems, 1978–1979* (1980); *Rumor Verified: Poems*

(1981); and *Chief Joseph of the Nez Perce* (1983). A fourth *Selected Poems* appeared in 1985.

Warren taught at the University of Minnesota from 1942 to 1950, and then went to Yale as a visiting professor. The following year he joined the faculty of the Yale Drama School as a professor of playwriting. In 1950 he divorced Emma Brescia and married Eleanor Clark in 1952. They have two children: Gabriel, a sculptor, and Rosanna, a poet. Warren became Professor of English in 1961, and taught at Yale until his retirement in 1973.

Among his many prizes and awards are the Shelley Prize, 1942; the National Book Award for poetry, 1958; the Pulitzer Prize for poetry, 1958 and 1979; the Bollingen Prize, 1967; and a MacArthur Prize Fellowship, 1981. In 1986 he was appointed the first Poet Laureate of the United States. He now lives in Fairfield, Connecticut.

ROBERT FITZGERALD

Robert Fitzgerald was born in Geneva, New York, on October 12, 1910. He spent his childhood in Springfield, Illinois. His mother died before he was three, and he lived with his grandmother while his father practiced law. He attended the Choate School for a year and entered Harvard in 1929. In 1931, he sent his first poems to *Poetry,* and was awarded the Midland Authors prize for that year. He studied philosophy and classical languages at Trinity College, Cambridge, for one year, and received his B.A. from Harvard in 1933. T. S. Eliot was Norton lecturer at Harvard that year and accepted two of Fitzgerald's poems for the *Criterion.* Fitzgerald gave up his plan to go to law school and instead pursued a literary career while working as a reporter for the *New York Herald Tribune,* staying there until 1935. In the space of one year Fitzgerald put together his first volume of poetry, *Poems,* and with Dudley Fitts translated Euripides' *Alcestis*; both were published in 1935. In 1936, *Time* offered him a job and he worked in various departments there until 1940. He again took one year off and translated Sophocles' *Oedipus at Colonus* and worked on *A Wreath for the Sea,* which appeared in 1943.

From 1946 to 1953 Fitzgerald taught courses at Sarah Lawrence College. He also taught at Princeton from 1950 to 1952. In 1957 he took a professorship at Notre Dame; he moved to the University of Washington in 1961. In 1964 he taught at Mount Holyoke College, and in 1965 he settled at Harvard as Boylston Professor of Rhetoric.

Fitzgerald's early translations of classical Greek literature include Sophocles' *Antigone* (1939 with Fitts) and *Oedipus Rex* (1949 with Fitts). But Fitzgerald's outstanding skill as a translator of ancient Greek and Latin is best demonstrated in his verse translations of the epics of Homer and Virgil. His version of Homer's *Odyssey* won the 1961 Bollingen Award for Translation of Poetry, and his version of the *Iliad* earned him the Landon Award and the Ingram Merrill Literary Award. His *Aeneid* is considered by many to have been his masterpiece.

These translations of Greek verse reflect Fitzgerald's poetic abilities in English. His published poetry includes *In the Rose of Time* (1956) and *Spring Shade* (1972).

Fitzgerald died on January 16, 1985, in Hamden, Connecticut, after a long illness.

ELIZABETH BISHOP

Elizabeth Bishop was born in Worcester, Massachusetts, on February 8, 1911, to parents of Canadian descent. When Bishop was eight months old, her father died. When she was four, her mother had a psychological collapse and was institutionalized. She was raised thenceforth by her maternal grandparents in Nova Scotia. She attended the Walnut Hill School in Natick, and received her B.A. in 1934 from Vassar College where her classmates included Mary McCarthy, Eleanor Clark, and Muriel Rukeyser. While at Vassar, Bishop began a lifelong friendship with Marianne Moore, whose poetry influenced her own work.

After college she traveled in Brittany and Paris for nearly a year, and then in North Africa and Spain. In 1937 she made her first visit to Key West and immediately became attracted to the keys. She had begun to publish her poems in *Poetry*, *Partisan Review*, and other periodicals. After another brief trip in Europe, she bought an old house in Key West and lived there for several years. She continued to write poetry inspired by and occasioned by her travels. Although she wrote with less frequency during the war years, Bishop published enough poems to create a first volume entitled *North & South*, which she brought out in 1946. A year later she received a Guggenheim fellowship.

In the following years Bishop won prizes from Bryn Mawr and the American Academy of Arts and Letters, so that in 1951 she was able to use her prize money to travel in South America and through the Strait of Magellan. Illness kept her in Brazil for some time, and when she recovered, she decided to stay there. For the next twenty-three years she lived with her friend Lota Constenat de Macedo Soares in Rio de Janeiro and Ouro Preto, Brazil.

North & South—A Cold Spring appeared in 1955 and won the Pulitzer Prize, a Partisan Review Fellowship, and an Amy Lowell Traveling Fellowship. *Questions of Travel* was published in 1965, and *Complete Poems* followed in 1969, winning a National Book Award. In the fall of 1970 Bishop began a yearly one-semester teaching appointment at Harvard, and upon the death of Lota Soares, moved to Boston. With the publication of *Geography III* in 1976 came the Neustadt International Prize for Literature. Bishop died in 1979, and *The Complete Poems: 1927–1979*, was published posthumously.

GWENDOLYN BROOKS

Gwendolyn Brooks was born on June 7, 1917, in Topeka, Kansas. She grew up on the South Side of Chicago, however, where she lives today. Strongly encouraged by her parents, she wrote poetry throughout her childhood, and at sixteen published her first poem in *The Defender*. She met her husband, aspiring writer Henry Blakely, at an NAACP Youth Council meeting, and they were married in 1939. Their son, Henry Jr., was born in 1940, and their daughter, Nora, in 1953.

Brooks's first book, *A Street in Bronzeville,* was published in 1945, and she received a grant from the National Institute of Arts and Letters, *Mademoiselle*'s Merit Award, and a Guggenheim Fellowship. With the publication of *Annie Allen* in 1949, Gwendolyn Brooks became the first black woman to win a Pulitzer Prize for poetry.

Maud Martha appeared in 1953, followed by *Bean Eaters* in 1960, *Selected Poems* in 1963, *In the Mecca* in 1968, and *The World of Gwendolyn Brooks* in 1971.

Brooks taught at various colleges in Illinois in the 1960s and in 1968 was named Poet Laureate of Illinois. Late in the 1960s, she became active in the Black Arts Movement; along with other black poets, she began to organize "neighborhood cultural events"—art exhibits, music festivals, and poetry readings—in Chicago's black neighborhoods. She also began to publish her books with presses owned and operated by blacks. *Riot* (1969), *Family Pictures* (1970), *Aloneness* (1971), a children's book, and *Beckonings* (1975) were all published with the Broadside Press. Brooks was awarded her first honorary degree in 1970 from Northwestern University, and it has been followed by more than forty such degrees. She has received two Guggenheim Fellowships since 1970 and the Shelley Award from the Poetry Society of America. She continues to publish with black presses: *Primer for Blacks* (1980) and *To Disembark* (1981) were published by the Third World Press.

ROBERT DUNCAN

Robert Duncan was born in Oakland, California, on January 7, 1919. His mother died soon after he was born, and he was adopted by orthodox Theosophists, who chose him on the basis of his astrological configuration. His adoptive family raised him in Bakersfield, within a world of Theosophical principles, correspondences, and tales that form the background of much of his poetry. His grandmother was a member of a Hermetic order much like Yeats's Order of the Golden Dawn. He began writing poetry in high school, with encouragement from an inspired and inspiring teacher, Edna Keough. He published his first poems in school magazines under the name Robert Edward Symmes, but changed his name back to Duncan in 1942.

He attended Berkeley from 1936 to 1938 and then left for New York, where he fell in with the Anaïs Nin circle that included Kenneth Patchen and George Barker. He published "The Homosexual in Society" in 1944 and returned to San Francisco in 1945. The following year he moved to Berkeley and associated with a small group of poets sponsored by Kenneth Rexroth. He attended Berkeley again from 1948 to 1950. Duncan began what soon became a very close relationship with the artist Jess Collins (known simply as Jess), and in "The Song of the Borderguard" he revealed the new spirit this relationship gave him.

Duncan's early poems can be found in the volumes *The Years As Catches, First Poems 1939–46; The First Decade: Selected Poems 1940–1950;* and *Derivations, Selected Poems 1950–56.* In 1952 he joined the circle of poets and writers at *Origin,* and this led to his association with the *Black Mountain Review* and a regular correspondence with Charles Olson. Duncan's play *Medea* was performed at Black Mountain College before the institution closed in 1956, and was later published as *Medea at Kolchis* (1965).

In 1957 Olson began a series of lectures entitled "The Special View of History" on Whitehead and process philosophy, which strongly stimulated Duncan and other *Origin* poets, as well as Beat arrivals from the road who heard them. Duncan published *Letters* in 1958 and *The Opening of the Field,* considered to be one of his most important books, in 1960. His development after this point can be charted in the volumes *Roots and Branches* (1964), *Of the War: Passages 22–27* (1966), *Bending the Bow* (1967), *Tribunals* (1970), and *A Seventeenth Century Suite* (1973). A second volume entitled *The Years As Catches* appeared in 1977.

MAY SWENSON

May Swenson was born in Logan, Utah, in 1919, to Swedish Mormon parents. She graduated from Utah State Agricultural College with a B.A. in English, and went to work as a reporter for various newspapers in and around Logan. She then went to New York, where she worked as a secretary and then as an editor for New Directions Press. Her first poems were published by the *Saturday Review of Literature*; appearances in *The Nation, Poetry, The Hudson Review, Partisan Review*, and *Contact* followed. Her first book, *Another Animal: Poems*, was published in 1949. *A Cage of Spines* appeared in 1958, and she won an Amy Lowell Traveling Fellowship in 1961. *To Mix with Time* (1963) followed this journey, and in 1965 Swenson became the poet in residence at Purdue University. *Poems to Solve* was published in 1966, *Half Sun, Half Sleep* in 1967; *Iconographs* and *More Poems to Solve* appeared in 1970. Her most acclaimed book, *New and Selected Things Taking Place*, was published in 1978 and nominated for the National Book Award in 1979. Swenson also won a ten-thousand-dollar fellowship from the Academy of American Poets in 1979.

RICHARD WILBUR

Richard Wilbur was born in New York on March 1, 1921. His father, a portrait artist, moved the family to North Caldwell, New Jersey, where Richard and his brother Lawrence grew up. He attended Amherst College, where he contributed stories and poems to the student magazine *Touchstone*. He graduated in 1942, married Charlotte Hayes Ward, and then enlisted and served in the 36th (Texas) Division, first in Italy at Monte Cassino, then at Anzio, and finally along the Siegfried line in Germany. He wrote a great deal of poetry during this period, and after returning home, he did graduate work at Harvard, receiving his A.M. in 1947. That same year, he published his first volume of poetry, *The Beautiful Changes and Other Poems*. He spent the next three years as a member of the Society of Fellows at Harvard, ostensibly at work on two scholarly works—one on the concept of the dandy, and another on Poe—neither of which he ever completed.

With the publication in 1950 of his next volume of poetry, *Ceremony and Other Changes,* Wilbur was appointed Assistant Professor of English at Harvard, where he remained until 1954. In 1952–53, while on a Guggenheim fellowship, Wilbur began his career as a translator with an English version of Molière's *Le Misanthrope*. In 1954 Wilbur was appointed to an associate professorship at Wellesley College. In 1956 he published his third and most honored volume of poetry, *Things of This World*. The volume brought him the Edna St. Vincent Millay Memorial Award, the National Book Award, and a Pulitzer Prize. Also that year, in collaboration with

John LaTouche, Wilbur wrote the lyrics for Leonard Bernstein's New York production of Voltaire's *Candide*.

His poetic career continued with the publication of *Advice to a Prophet and Other Poems* (1961); *The Poems of Richard Wilbur* (1963); *Walking to Sleep, New Poems and Translations* (1969); *The Mind-Reader* (1977); and *Seven Poems* (1981). His translation of Molière's *Tartuffe* (1963) was produced at Lincoln Center in 1964, and made him corecipient of the Bollingen Poetry Translation Prize. He has also translated Molière's *The School for Wives* (1972), and *The Learned Ladies* (1973). Wilbur moved to Smith College in 1977 as writer-in-residence, and now lives in Cummington, Massachusetts.

ANTHONY HECHT

Anthony Hecht was born in New York on January 16, 1923. He received his bachelor's degree from Bard College in 1944, just in time to serve with the army for three years—first in Europe, then in Japan. Upon his return, he took a series of teaching jobs across the Midwest, in New England, and in New York. At Kenyon College he studied with and was influenced by the poet and critic John Crowe Ransom. Hecht's first poems appeared in the *Kenyon Review*, which Ransom edited.

In 1954 Hecht published his first book of poetry, *Summoning of Stones*. His next book, *The Hard Hours* (1967), contains some of his best-known poems. *Millions of Strange Shadows* includes translations of Voltaire's "Poem upon the Lisbon Disaster," of a chorus from Aeschylus' *Seven against Thebes*, and of some poems by the exiled Russian poet Josef Brodsky, now writing in America.

In 1978, "The Venetian Vespers," a poem of over 1,000 lines, was published in *Poetry*. The poem supplied the title to a collection of new poems published in 1979. Hecht currently teaches at the University of Rochester.

JAMES DICKEY

James Dickey was born in Atlanta, Georgia, on February 2, 1923. He attended Clemson College in South Carolina in 1942, and then Vanderbilt University, where he studied under Monroe K. Spears. He served in the Army Air Force during World War II and again in the Air Force during the Korean War. In 1948 he married Maxine Syerson, who died in 1976; in 1976 he married Deborah Dodson. Dickey taught at Rice University and the University of Florida. He was poet-in-residence at Reed College from 1962–64, San Fernando State College from 1964–66, and the University of Wisconsin at Madison in 1966. Since 1969 he has been Professor of English and writer-in-residence at the University of South Carolina, Columbia.

As a writer and as an individual Dickey is agonistic and intense: he held records in track at Vanderbilt, flew fighter-bombers in Korea, and worked in advertising for six years. He can play bluegrass on both the 6- and 12-string guitar, and he is an accomplished bow hunter. Dickey lectures, teaches, and even acts: he played the redneck sheriff in the film version of his novel, *Deliverance*.

Dickey's first collection of poetry was *Into the Stone*, which appeared in *Poets of Today VII* (1960), edited by John Hall Wheelock. *Drowning with Others* was published in 1962, and *Helmets* appeared in 1964. *Buckdancer's Choice* (1965) won him the 1966 National Book Award. *Self Interviews*, an autobiographical work, appeared in 1970. His 1970 novel, *Deliverance*, won him a wide audience.

Dickey's books include *The Eye Beaters, Victory, Madness, Buckhead and Mercy* (1970); *Jericho: The South Beheld* (1974); *The Zodiac* (1976); *God's Images* (1977); and *The Strength of the Fields* (1979). Among his recent volumes are *The Eagle's Mile* (1981); *Falling, May Day Sermon and Other Poems* (1982); *The Early Motion: "Drowning with Others" and "Helmets"* (1982); *Night Hurdling* (1983); *False Youth: Four Seasons* (1983); *For a Time and Place* (1983); and *The Central Motion: Poems 1968–1979* (1983).

DENISE LEVERTOV

Denise Levertov was born in Ilford, Essex, England, on October 24, 1923. Her mother was Welsh; her father was a Russian Jew who converted to Christianity, became an Anglican minister, and took on the strenuous task of trying to unify Christianity and Judaism.

Levertov began writing poetry as a child, and at twelve had the audacity to send a sample of her poetry to T. S. Eliot. He responded, advising her to continue writing. "Listening to Distant Guns" was published in *Poetry Quarterly* in 1940, and thereafter her work was frequently accepted by British literary magazines. Her first book, *The Double Image*, was published in late 1946.

While traveling in Switzerland after the war, Levertov met the American writer Mitchell Goodman and married him. They moved to the United States in 1948, when she was pregnant with their son, Nikolai Gregory. She became a citizen of the United States in 1955, and her first American book, *Here and Now*, was published in 1957 by City Lights Press. Other volumes followed quickly: *Overland to the Islands* appeared in 1958, and *With Eyes at the Back of Our Heads*, a collection that won the Bess Hopkin Prize from *Poetry* in 1960. In 1962, Levertov received a Guggenheim Fellowship; in the early 1960s she was poetry editor of *The Nation*. From 1964 to 1966 she was an associate scholar at the Radcliffe Institute for Independent Studies in Boston, and in 1965 she received a medal from the American Institute of Arts and Letters and, with Muriel Rukeyser and other poets, established an activist group called Writers and Artists Protest against the War in Vietnam. *Sorrow Dance*, published in 1967, reflects this activism and the death of Levertov's sister, Olga. Other books written during the war years, *To Stay Alive* and *The Freeing of the Dust*, are also strongly marked by these experiences of war and protest.

Divorced in the mid-1970s, Levertov has taught in various colleges and universities, published two more books of poetry, *Life in the Forest* (1978) and *The Collected Earlier Poems: 1940–1960* (1979), and has published *Light up the Cave* (1981), a collection of prose, reviews, and essays.

KENNETH KOCH

Kenneth Koch was born in Cincinnati, Ohio, on February 27, 1925. He served in the Pacific during World War II, and on his return he entered Harvard where he studied under Delmore Schwartz and became friends with John Ashbery. He graduated in 1948 and went on to Columbia, receiving an M.A. in 1953 and a Ph.D. in 1959. He has been on the Columbia faculty since 1959, and has directed a poetry workshop at the New School for Social Research since 1958. He married Janice Elwood in 1954.

Poems, Koch's first book, was published in 1953, and contains six poems and a short play. During the fifties, Koch became a part of the New York poetry and art scene that included such fellow writers as John Ashbery and Frank O'Hara, and painters such as Jane Freilicher and Larry Rivers. Koch's playful poetry has often been accompanied by equally playful illustrations by Rivers. Ko, or A Season on Earth appeared in 1959, followed by Permanently in 1960. Thank You and Other Poems (1962) collected some of his best early poetry in one volume. The Pleasures of Peace and Other Poems appeared in 1969, and includes "Some South American Poets," a set of translations of nonexistent poems by imaginary authors. The Art of Love appeared in 1975. The Duplications, a 3,600-line Disneyesque digression into nearly everything, appeared in 1977. Koch's recent work includes The Burning Mystery of Anna (1979) and Days and Nights (1982).

A. R. AMMONS

Archie Randolph Ammons was born in Whiteville, North Carolina, on February 18, 1926. He attended Wake Forest College and received his B.S. in 1949. He then studied at Berkeley from 1951 to 1952. Ammons published his first book of poetry, Ommateum, with Doxology, in 1955. His second volume, Expressions of Sea Level, appeared eight years later in 1963. In a burst of inspiration just before the publication of this second book, Ammons kept a journal in the form of a long poem on a roll of adding machine tape from December 6, 1963, to January 10, 1964, entitled Tape for the Turn of the Year.

Following the publication of Expressions of Sea Level came Corson's Inlet: A Book of Poems (1965), Northfield Poems (1966), Uplands (1970), and Briefings: Poems Small and Easy (1971). Ammons's Collected Poems 1951–1971 came out in 1972 and one year later Ammons received the National Book Award for Poetry.

Sphere: The Form of a Motion appeared in 1974 and was nominated for the National Book Award. Ammons received the Bollingen Prize in Poetry for that year. Diversifications appeared in 1975, followed by The Snow Poems (1976), A Coast of Trees (1981), Worldly Hopes (1982), and Lake Effect Country (1983).

JAMES MERRILL

James Merrill was born in New York, New York, on March 3, 1926. He received his B.A. from Amherst College in 1947. His father, Charles Edward Merrill, was a famous financier and one of the original partners of the financial empire now known as Merrill Lynch Pierce Fenner & Smith.

Merrill first published his poetry privately in 1942. The first book to appear publicly was The Black Swan and Other Poems (1946). First Poems was published in 1951. The Country of a Thousand Years of Peace and Other Poems was first published in 1959 and revised in 1970. *Water Street* was published in 1962. Merrill published an experimental novel, *The (Diblos) Notebook,* in 1965, and followed that with *The Fire Screen* (1966).

The appreciation of Merrill's poetry over the past twenty years has led to several notable awards: *Nights and Days* (1966) won the National Book Award for Poetry; *Braving the Elements* (1972) earned Merrill the Bollingen Prize; *Divine Comedies* (1976) won the Pulitzer Prize; and finally, *Mirabell: Books of Number,* published in 1978 but composed entirely in the summer of 1976, also won a National Book Award. His recent books include *Scripts for the Pageant* (1980), *From the First Nine: Poems* (1982), and *The Changing Light at Sandover* (1982).

ALLEN GINSBERG

Allen Ginsberg was born in Newark, New Jersey, on June 3, 1926. He received his A.B. from Columbia University in 1948. His father taught high-school English for forty years and published three volumes of poems. Throughout Ginsberg's childhood, his mother, Naomi Wolf, suffered paranoiac delusions of persecution.

In the years prior to the appearance of the well-known volume *Howl and Other Poems,* in 1956, Ginsberg associated with Neal Cassady, Jack Kerouac, William Carlos Williams, William Burroughs, and Gregory Corso. He left New York, spent some time in the Yucatan, and ended up in San Francisco, where he came into contact with Kenneth Rexroth, Gary Snyder, Robert Duncan, and Lawrence Ferlinghetti. When it appeared, *Howl* was negatively reviewed by some, but Richard Eberhart in the *New York Times Book Review* gave one of the first positive reactions to the book. Ferlinghetti, who published the book, was charged with disseminating "indecent writings." The judge eventually decided in favor of Ginsberg's free expression.

Empty Mirror: Early Poems appeared in 1961, followed by the disturbing volume, *Kaddish and Other Poems, 1958–60.* The volume includes those poems he read to the Group for the Advancement of Psychiatry, a reading that led to his introduction to LSD by Timothy Leary. Ginsberg's next volume, *Reality Sandwiches* (1963), collects other poems from the period 1953–60.

In search of other spiritual paths, Ginsberg consulted with Martin Buber in Israel and with Hindu holy men in India, and in July of 1963 went through a spiritual transformation that he recorded in "The Change." In 1967, Ginsberg visited Ezra Pound in Italy shortly before his death.

Ginsberg became the leading poetic voice, or Yawp, of the Beat movement. He has also been an innovator of alternatives in other genres. Ginsberg's creative incarnations have taken varied forms: beatnik, prophet, guru, activist, philosopher, gadfly, mystic. In 1967 he joined in a "Gathering of the Tribes for a Human Be-In," and participated in a symposium entitled "Dialectics of Liberation" with Paul Goodman, Stokely Carmichael, and Herbert Marcuse. In the fall of that year he directed the exorcism of the Pentagon by the Yippies, and in 1968 helped the Yippies in their plans to stage a Be-In at the Democratic National Convention in Chicago. In 1974, he cofounded the Jack Kerouac School of Disembodied Poetics as part of the Naropa Institute, a Buddhist University in Boulder, Colorado, founded by the Kagu Buddhist master Trungpa.

During the seventies Ginsberg journeyed deeper into Oriental religion. In his acceptance speech for the National Book Award in 1974, he declared that "there is no longer any hope for the salvation of America." His published work during the sixties and early seventies can be charted in *Planet News, 1961–1967* (1968), *The Fall of America* (1972), and *Mind Breaths: Poems 1972–1977* (1978).

Ginsberg's more recent published works include *Poems All Over the Place: Mostly Seventies* (1978), *Plutonian Ode: Poems 1977-1980* (1982). He published his *Collected Poems* in 1986 and lived and wrote in lower Manhattan until his death in 1997.

GALWAY KINNELL

Galway Kinnell was born on February 1, 1927, in Providence, Rhode Island. Kinnell received an A.B. from Princeton University in 1948, and a master's degree from the University of Rochester in 1949. He has been a visiting professor at several American colleges and universities, and has taught English in Hawaii, Nice, and Teheran.

Kinnell's first volume of poetry, *What a Kingdom It Was,* appeared in 1960. His next several volumes include: *Flower Herding on Mount Monadnock* (1964), *Body Rags* (1968), *Poems of Night* (1968), *The Hen Flower* (1969), *First Poems, 1946–54* (1970), and *The Shoes of Wandering* (1971).

Kinnell achieved major recognition with his publication of *The Book of Nightmares* (1971) and *The Avenue Bearing the Initial of Christ into the New World: Poems 1946–1964* (1974). His recent volumes include *Mortal Acts, Mortal Words* (1980), *How the Alligator Missed Breakfast* (1982), *Selected Poems* (1982), and *The Past* (1986). Kinnell, who received the National Book Award in 1983, has also translated a number of works by French authors, including *The Poems of François Villon* (1965). He lives in Sheffield, Vermont.

JOHN ASHBERY

John Ashbery was born in Rochester, New York, on July 28, 1927. He grew up on a fruit farm in Sodus, near Rochester. From Deerfield Academy he entered Harvard and received his B.A. in 1949. He received an M.A. from Columbia in 1951. In 1953, a small volume of Ashbery's poetry was privately printed by the Tibor de Nagy Gallery, entitled *Turandot and Other Poems.*

In 1955 Ashbery submitted a manuscript to the Yale Younger Poets competition. The manuscript was rejected by a preliminary reader before it could even be read by the judge, W. H. Auden. Auden himself felt that none of the manuscripts he had seen that year were worthy of publication, but when he heard of an Ashbery manuscript that had been cut out, he asked to see it and subsequently selected it. *Some Trees* was published in 1956 as Volume 52 of the Yale Series of Younger Poets. This was followed by *The Tennis Court Oath* (1962), *Rivers and Mountains* (1966), *Selected Poems* (1967), *Three Madrigals* (1968), *Sunrise in Suburbia* (1968), *A Nest of Ninnies* (1969), *The Double Dream of Spring* (1970), *The New Spirit* (1970), *Three Poems* (1972), *The Vermont Notebook* (1975), *Self-Portrait in a Convex Mirror* (1977), *Houseboat Days* (1977), *As We Know* (1979), and *Shadow Train* (1981). *A*

Wave appeared in 1984, and *Selected Poems* in 1985, the year that Ashbery won a MacArthur Prize Fellowship.

W. S. MERWIN

William Stanley Merwin was born in New York, New York, on September 30, 1927. He grew up in Union City, New Jersey, and in Scranton, Pennsylvania. He received his A.B. in English from Princeton University in 1947, and went to Europe for three years. Merwin published his first book of poetry, *A Mask for Janus*, in 1952. Since then he has produced an impressive body of work, and has earned ongoing recognition from critics. His volumes of poetry include *The Dancing Bears* (1954), *Green with Beasts* (1956), *The Drunk in the Furnace* (1960), *The Moving Target* (1963), *The Lice* (1967), *The Carrier of Ladders* (1970), *The Miner's Pale Children* (1970), *Asian Figures* (1973), *Writings to an Unfinished Accompaniment* (1973), *The Compass Flower* (1977), and *Finding the Islands* (1982).

JAMES WRIGHT

James Arlington Wright was born on December 13, 1927, in the steel mill town of Martin's Ferry, Ohio. After his army service in Japan during World War II, Wright attended Kenyon College. Upon graduation in 1952 he received the Robert Frost Poetry Prize; he spent the following year in Vienna on a Fulbright scholarship, studying the work of Theodor Storm. After returning to the United States, Wright entered the University of Washington in Seattle and studied under Theodore Roethke. He received an M.A. in 1954 and a Ph.D. in 1959. He taught at the University of Minnesota from 1957 to 1963, and at Macalester College from 1963 to 1965. From 1966 until his death in 1980 he taught at Hunter College in New York City.

The Green Wall, Wright's first published book of poetry, appeared in 1957 as Volume 53 of the Yale Series of Younger Poets. The volumes that followed include *Saint Judas* (1959); *The Lion's Tail and Eyes: Poems Written Out of Laziness and Silence* (1962); a collection of poems by Wright, Robert Bly, and William Duffy, *The Branch Will Not Break* (1963); *Shall We Gather at the River* (1968); *Collected Poems* (1971) for which he was awarded the Pulitzer Prize in 1972; *Two Citizens* (1973); *Moments of the Italian Summer* (1976); and *To a Blossoming Pear Tree* (1977). Wright died on March 25, 1980.

IRVING FELDMAN

Irving Mordechai Feldman was born on September 22, 1928, in Brooklyn, New York. He received his B.S. in 1950 from the City College of New York, and received an M.A. from Columbia University in 1953. He taught English in Puerto Rico from 1954 to 1956, at the University of Lyons for one year, and then at Kenyon College from 1958 to 1964. Since 1964 he has been Professor of English at the State University of New York at Buffalo. His published poetry includes *Works and Days and Other Poems* (1961), *The Pripet Marshes and Other Poems* (1965), *Magic Papers and Other Poems* (1970), *Lost Originals* (1972), *Leaping Clear* (1976), *New and Selected Poems* (1979), and *Teach Me Dear Sister* (1983).

ADRIENNE RICH

Adrienne Rich was born in Baltimore, Maryland, on May 16, 1929. She wrote poetry throughout her childhood, and when she graduated from Radcliffe College in 1951 her first book, *A Change of World,* was published in the Yale Series of Younger Poets. The following year she received a Guggenheim Fellowship and traveled in Europe. When she returned in 1953, she married Alfred H. Conrad, a professor at Harvard. Their first son, David, was born in 1955, the same year that *Diamond Cutters and Other Poems* appeared. Two other sons were born, Paul, in 1957, and Jacob, in 1959. In 1960, Rich won the National Institute of Arts and Letters Award for Poetry, and was the Phi Beta Kappa poet at William and Mary College. The following year she received another Guggenheim Fellowship and took her family to live in the Netherlands. The year 1962 brought her a Bollingen Foundation Grant for the translation of Dutch poetry, and the next year an Amy Lowell Traveling Fellowship.

Snapshots of a Daughter-in-Law (1963) won The Bess Hopkin Prize from *Poetry.* In 1965 Rich was the Phi Beta Kappa poet at Swarthmore College; the following year *Necessities of Life* was published and nominated for the National Book Award. In 1966, Rich was the Phi Beta Kappa poet at Harvard, and from 1966 through 1968 she taught, variously, at Swarthmore, Columbia, and in the Open Admission and SEEK programs at the City College of New York. *Selected Poems* was published in England in 1967, and *Leaflets* appeared in 1969.

In 1970 her husband died. Rich remained in New York City with her sons, continuing to teach and write with an increasingly feminist focus. *The Will to Change* was published in 1971, winning the Shelley Award of the Poetry Society of America, and *Diving into the Wreck* appeared in 1973. She accepted the National Book Award for *Diving,* along with the other nominees, Audre Lorde and Alice Walker, "in the name of all the women whose voices have gone . . . unheard." Her *Poems: Selected and New* appeared in 1974, followed by a historical work, *Of Woman Born: Motherhood as Experience and Institution,* in 1976. Her most recent works have included *The Dream of a Common Language* (1978), *A Wild Patience Has Taken Me This Far* (1981), and *Sources* (1983).

ROBERT PACK

Robert Pack was born on May 19, 1929, in New York, New York. He received his B.A. from Dartmouth College in 1951 and an M.A. from Columbia University in 1953. He has taught at Barnard College and is currently Professor of English at Middlebury College.

Pack's first volume of poetry, *The Irony of Joy,* appeared in 1955. This was followed by *A Stranger's Privilege* (1959), *The Forgotten Secret* (1959), *Then What Did You Do?* (1961), *Guarded by Women* (1963), *Selected Poems* (1964), *How to Catch a Crocodile* (1964), *Home from the Cemetery* (1969), *Nothing But Light*

(1972), *Keeping Watch* (1976), *Waking to My Name: New and Selected Poems* (1980). Pack now lives in Vermont.

JOHN HOLLANDER

John Hollander was born on October 28, 1929, in New York, New York. He received his A.B. and M.A. degrees from Columbia University in 1950 and 1952 and a Ph.D. from Indiana University in 1959. Hollander is a member of the Society of Fellows at Harvard University and has taught at Connecticut College and Hunter College.

Hollander's first volume of poetry, *A Crackling of Thorns*, was chosen by W. H. Auden to be Volume 54 of the Yale Series of Younger Poets in 1958. His books published since then include *A Beach Vision* (1962), *Movie-Going and Other Poems* (1962), *Various Owls* (1963), *Visions from the Ramble* (1965), *The Quest for the Gole* (1966), *Philomel* (1968), *Types of Shape* (1969), *The Night Mirror: Poems* (1971), *The Immense Parade on Supererogation Day and What Happened to It* (1972), *Selected Poems* (1972), *Town and Country Matters: Erotica and Satirica* (1972), *The Head of the Bed* (1974), *Tales Told of the Fathers* (1975), *Reflections on Espionage, The Question of Cupcake* (1976), *Spectral Emanations: New and Selected Poems* (1978), *Blue Wine and Other Poems* (1979), and *Powers of Thirteen* (1983).

Hollander is a critic and an authority on versification. His books of criticism include *Vision and Resonance* (1975); *Rhyme's Reason: A Guide to English Verse* (1981), which explains poetic forms through use of those forms; and *The Figure of Echo: A Mode of Allusion in Milton and After* (1981). Hollander has a special interest in music and art, which figure strongly in his poetry. He is also the inventor, with Anthony Hecht, of the double dactyl. Entitled *Jiggery-Pokery: A Compendium of Double-Dactyls,* their study appeared in 1983.

Hollander is currently Professor of English at Yale University and lives in Woodbridge, Connecticut.

ALVIN FEINMAN

Alvin Feinman was born in New York, New York, on November 21, 1929. He attended Brooklyn College and Yale Graduate School, and then taught philosophy at Yale for several years before leaving to live a contemplative life in New York City.

After the publication of his only book, *Preambles and Other Poems,* in 1964, Feinman began to teach literature at Bennington College, where he currently teaches. Though never widely read, Feinman's difficult and subtle poems enjoy an appreciation by an elite group of poets and critics.

GARY SNYDER

Gary Snyder was born on May 8, 1930, in San Francisco, California. He received a B.A. from Reed College in anthropology and literature in 1951. He began graduate work at the University of Indiana and then moved to Berkeley, where he studied Oriental languages. From 1956 to 1968 Snyder studied Zen Buddhism in Japan. He has also occupied himself at various times as a logger, fire-lookout, Forest Service trail-crew worker, and seaman. He has two children by his third wife, Japanese-born Masa Uehara. Snyder has been identified with the poets of the Beat generation, and appeared in Jack Kerouac's novel *The Dharma Bums* (1960) disguised as Japhy Ryder.

Snyder's first book, *Riprap,* appeared in 1959. His volumes since then include *Myths and Texts* (1960); *Riprap and Cold Mountain Poems* (1965); *Six Sections from Mountains and Rivers without End* (1965); *A Range of Poems* (1966); *Three Worlds, Three Realms, Six Roads* (1966); *The Back Country* (1967); *The Blue Sky* (1969); *Earth House Hold* (1970); *Regarding Wave* (1970); *Manzanita* (1972); *The Fudo Trilogy* (1973); *Turtle Island* (1974), which won the Pulitzer Prize in 1974; *Myths and Texts* (1978); and *Axe Handles* (1983).

Snyder now lives in a loose backwoods community and practices the neo-neolithic lifestyle that he advocates, teaching and speaking a few months each year.

MARK STRAND

Mark Strand was born on Prince Edward Island, Canada, on April 11, 1934. He received his B.A. from Antioch College in 1957. He attended Yale University for two years, and received a B.F.A. degree in 1959. He received an M.A. from the University of Iowa in 1962, and worked as an instructor in the English department there for three years. Strand teaches at the University of Utah in Salt Lake City.

Strand's first book of poetry, *Sleeping with One Eye Open* (1964), received little attention. But the volumes that have since appeared have taken up some of the themes foreshadowed in this first book and have been well-received. These include *Reasons for Moving: Poems* (1968); *Darker: Poems* (1970); *The Story of Our Lives* (1973); *The Sergeantville Notebook* (1973); *Elegy for My Father* (1973); *The Late Hour* (1978); *The Monument* (1978); *Selected Poems* (1980); and *The Planet of Lost Things* (1982).

AMIRI BARAKA

Amiri Baraka was born Everett LeRoi Jones on October 7, 1934, in Newark, New Jersey. He attended Rutgers University but transferred to Howard University and graduated in 1954 with a B.A. in English. He enlisted in the Air Force and served as a gunner and aerial climatographer with the Strategic Air Command stationed in Puerto Rico until January 1957.

In 1957 Jones moved to New York City and pursued a range of activities that included writing jazz criticism, studying philosophy at Columbia, and taking classes at the New School for Social Research. He founded and functioned as editor for the small magazine *Yugen* and the Totem Press in New York. His marriage in 1958 to Hettie Roberta Cohen, a cofounder of *Yugen,* ended in divorce in 1965. Jones's poetry earned increasing attention toward the end of the 1950s. He taught a poetry class at the New School for Social Research from 1961 until 1964. His first published volume, *Preface to a Twenty Volume Suicide Note,* appeared in 1961 to wide acclaim.

It was followed by *Blues People, Negro Music in White America* (1963); *The Dead Lecturer* (1964); and *The System of Dante's Hell* (1965).

In the early 1960s Jones became more and more concerned with the theater and with social issues. He took teaching positions at SUNY Buffalo and at Columbia. Two of his plays were produced for the first time in 1964: *Dutchman*, which received the Obie Award for best Off-Broadway play; and *The Slave*, which won second prize at the Dakar International Art Festival in 1966. In 1964, he founded and directed the Black Arts Repertory Theatre in Harlem. In 1965 he divorced his white wife and moved to Harlem. In 1967 he married Sylvia Robinson, who in 1968 took the name Bibi Amina Baraka when Jones adopted his African Bantuized Muslim name, Imamu Amiri Baraka. He has since dropped the title Imamu.

By this time Jones had become a militant spokesman for the black American community. His poetry had correspondingly moved from being overtly linked to the Projectivist and Beat poets to being outwardly "blacker" in character. The volumes of this later period include *Black Art* (1966); *Tales* (1969); *The Baptism and the Toilet* (1967); *Black Music* (1967); *Arm Yourself, or Harm Yourself! A One Act Play* (1967); *Black Magic: Collected Poetry, 1961–1967* (1969); *Slave Ship* (1969); *Four Black Revolutionary Plays: All Praises to the Black Man* (1969); *A Black Value System* (1970); *Jello* (1970); *Raise Race Rays Raze: Essays since 1965* (1971); *Spirit Reach* (1972); *African Revolution: A Poem* (1973); *The Motion of History and Other Plays* (1978); *Selected Poetry of Amiri Baraka/LeRoi Jones* (1979); and *Selected Plays and Prose of Amiri Baraka/LeRoi Jones* (1979).

JAY WRIGHT

Jay Wright was born on May 25, 1935, in Albuquerque, New Mexico. He attended the University of New Mexico and transferred to Berkeley, where he earned his B.A. He also received an M.A. from Rutgers. Wright is known as both a poet and playwright. His books include *Death as History* (1967); *The Homecoming Singer* (1971); *Soothsayers and Omens* (1976); and *The Double Invention of Komo* (1980). Various poems and plays by Wright have appeared in literary magazines and in anthologies and journals devoted to black literature. Jay Wright lives in rural Vermont.

DARYL HINE

William Daryl Hine was born on February 24, 1936, in Burnaby, British Columbia, Canada. He attended McGill University in Montreal from 1954 to 1958, and received an M.A. and Ph.D. from the University of Chicago in 1965 and 1967, respectively. He then taught English for two years at the University of Chicago.

Hine's first volume of poetry, *Five Poems*, appeared in 1954. His second published volume, *The Carnal and the Crane* (1957), earned him major recognition as a poet. His later books include *The Devil's Picture Book* (1960); *Heroics: Five Poems* (1961); *The Wooden Horse* (1965); *The Death of Seneca, a Play* (1968); *Minutes: Poems* (1968); *The Homeric Hymns and The Battle of the Frogs and the Mice* (1972), a volume of translations; *Resident Alien* (1975); *In and Out: A Confessional Poem* (1975); *Daylight Saving* (1978); *Selected Poems* (1980); *Theocritus: Idylls and Epigrams* (1983), translations; and *Academic Festival Overtures* (1986). Hine now lives in Evanston, Illinois.

Contributors

HAROLD BLOOM, Sterling Professor of the Humanities at Yale University, is the author of *The Anxiety of Influence, Poetry and Repression,* and many other volumes of literary criticism. His forthcoming study, *Freud: Transference and Authority,* attempts a full-scale reading of all of Freud's major writings. A MacArthur Prize Fellow, he is general editor of five series of literary criticism published by Chelsea House.

DAVID BROMWICH is Associate Professor of English at Princeton University. He is the author of *Hazlitt: The Mind of the Critic,* and of many essays on contemporary poetry.

JOHN HOLLANDER is Professor of English at Yale University. His criticism includes *The Untuning of the Sky, Vision and Resonance,* and *The Figure of an Echo.* His poetry is most readily available in his *Spectral Emanations: New and Selected Poems.*

GARY SMITH teaches English at Southern Illinois University, Carbondale.

DENISE LEVERTOV is a poet and critic. Her books include *With Eyes at the Back of Our Heads; The Collected Earlier Poems, 1940–1960;* and *Light Up the Cave.*

RICHARD HOWARD—poet, translator, and critic—is best known for his books of poems, *Untitled Subjects* and *Findings,* for his translation of Baudelaire, and for his capacious commentary on contemporary American poetry, *Alone with America.*

ROBERT B. SHAW is Professor of English at Mount Holyoke College. He is the author of *The Call of God: The Theme of Vocation in the Poetry of Donne and Herbert.* His volumes of poetry include *In Witness, Three of a Kind,* and *Comforting the Wilderness.*

ASHLEY BROWN is one of the founders of *Shenandoah,* and teaches at the University of South Carolina. He has edited several collections of criticism, and is preparing a collection of his own essays for publication.

DIANA (SURMAN) COLLECOTT teaches English and American literature at the University of Durham.

J. D. McCLATCHY is a poet and critic. His books include *Anne Sexton: The Artist and Her Critics* (1978), *Scenes from Another Life: Poems* (1981), and *Stars Principal* (1986). He is currently teaching in the Creative Writing Program at Princeton University.

DIANE MIDDLEBROOK is Professor of English at Stanford University. She is the author of *Worlds into Words: Understanding Modern Poems.*

CHARLES MOLESWORTH is Professor of English at Queens College of the City University of New York. He is the author of *Common Elegies,* and contributes often to *Poetry, Salmagundi,* and *The Nation.*

ALFRED CORN is, together with Douglas Crase, a leading member of the poetic generation following that of Ashbery and James Merrill. His books include *All Roads at Once* and *A Call in the Midst of the Crowd.*

HELEN VENDLER is Professor of English at Boston University and at Harvard. Her books include studies of George Herbert and of Keats.

PAUL MARIANI, a poet and critic, is Professor of English at the University of Massachusetts at Amherst. He is the author of *Crossing Cocytus and Other Poems* and *William Carlos Williams: A New World Naked.*

DAVID LEHMAN, poet and critic, has edited *Beyond Amazement,* a book of critical essays on John Ashbery.

CRUNK is the pseudonym of Robert Bly, a poet and essayist. His books include *The Light around the Body, Leaping Poetry: An Idea and Translation,* and *This Tree Will Be Here for a Thousand Years.*

LINDA GREGERSON is the author of *Fire in the Conservatory.*

NATE MACKEY teaches literature at the University of California, Santa Cruz.

ROBERT B. STEPTO teaches English and Afro-American Studies at Yale University. He has written *Behind the Veil,* and is coeditor of *Chant of Saints,* an anthology of Afro-American literature.

Bibliography

Altieri, Charles. *Enlarging the Temple: New Directions in American Poetry during the 60s.* Lewisburg, Pa.: Bucknell University Press, 1978.

Berke, Roberta Elzey. *Bounds Out of Bounds: A Compass for Recent American Poetry.* New York: Oxford University Press, 1981.

Boyers, Robert, ed. *Contemporary Poetry in America: Essays and Interviews.* New York: Schocken Books, 1974.

Breslin, James E. B. *From Modern to Contemporary: American Poetry, 1945–1965.* Chicago: The University of Chicago Press, 1984.

Carroll, Paul. *The Poem in Its Skin.* Chicago: Follett Publishing Company, 1968.

Charters, Samuel Barclay. *Some Poems/Poets: Studies in American Underground Poetry since 1945.* Berkeley: OYEZ Press, 1971.

Dickey, James. *Babel to Byzantium: Poets and Poetry Now.* New York: Farrar, Straus and Giroux, 1968.

Fredman, S. *Poet's Prose: Crisis in American Verse.* New York: Oxford University Press, 1983.

Howard, Richard. *Alone with America: Essays on the Art of Poetry in the United States since 1950.* New York: Atheneum, 1969.

Kalstone, David. *Five Temperaments: Elizabeth Bishop, Robert Lowell, James Merrill, Adrienne Rich, John Ashbery.* New York: Oxford University Press, 1977.

Kherdian, David. *Six San Francisco Poets.* Fresno, Calif.: The Giligia Press, 1969.

Kostelanetz, Richard, ed. *The Avant-Garde Tradition in American Literature.* Buffalo, N.Y.: Prometheus Books, 1982.

———. "Introduction." In *Possibilities of Poetry: An Anthology of Contemporaries,* edited by Richard Kostelanetz. New York: Dell Publishing Company, 1970.

Kuzma, Greg, ed. *A Book of Rereadings in Recent American Poetry.* Lincoln, Nebr.: Pebble and Best Cellar Press, 1979.

Lieberman, Laurence. *Unassigned Frequencies: American Poetry in Review, 1961–1977.* Urbana: University of Illinois Press, 1977.

Mariani, Paul. *A Usable Past: Essays on Modern and Contemporary Poetry.* Amherst: University of Massachusetts Press, 1984.

Mazzaro, Jerome, comp. *Modern American Poetry: Essays in Criticism.* New York: Donald McKay Company, 1970.

———. *Postmodern American Poetry.* Urbana: University of Illinois Press, 1980.

451

McClure, Michael. *Scratching the Beat Surface.* San Francisco: North Point Press, 1982.

Mills, Ralph J. *Cry of the Human: Essays on Contemporary American Poetry.* Urbana: University of Illinois Press, 1975.

Molesworth, Charles. *The Fierce Embrace: A Study of Contemporary American Poetry.* Columbia: University of Missouri Press, 1979.

————. *Gary Snyder's Vision: Poetry and the Real Work.* Columbia: University of Missouri Press, 1983.

Nelson, Cary. *Our Last First Poets: Vision and History in Contemporary American Poetry.* Urbana: University of Illinois Press, 1981.

Nemerov, Howard. *Reflexions on Poetry and Poetics.* New Brunswick, N.J.: Rutgers University Press, 1972.

Peters, Robert. *The Great American Poetry Bake-off, First Series.* Metuchen, N.J.: Scarecrow Press, 1979.

————. *The Great American Poetry Bake-off, Second Series.* Metuchen, N.J.: Scarecrow Press, 1979.

————. *The Peters Black and Blue Guide to Current Literary Journals, First Series.* Silver Spring, Md.: Beach and Company, Publishers, 1983.

————. *The Peters Black and Blue Guide to Current Literary Journals, Second Series.* Silver Spring, Md.: Beach and Company, Publishers, 1985.

Pinsky, Robert. *The Situation of Poetry: Contemporary Poetry and Its Traditions.* Princeton: Princeton University Press, 1976.

Rexroth, Kenneth. *American Poetry in the Twentieth Century.* New York: Herder and Herder, 1971.

Stepanchev, Stephen. *American Poetry since 1945.* New York: Harper and Row, 1965.

Vendler, Helen. *Part of Nature, Part of Us: Modern American Poets.* Cambridge: Harvard University Press, 1980.

Williams, Jonathan. *Elegies and Celebrations.* Highlands, N.C.: Jargon Society, 1962.

ROBERT PENN WARREN

Bedient, Calvin. "Greatness and Robert Penn Warren." *The Sewanee Review* 89 (1981): 332–46.

————. *In the Heart's Last Kingdom.* Cambridge: Harvard University Press, 1984.

Beebe, Maurice, and L. A. Field, eds. *Robert Penn Warren's* All the King's Men: *A Critical Handbook.* Belmont, Calif.: Wadsworth Publishing Co., 1966.

Beiner, Robert. "The Required Past: *World Enough and Time.*" *Modern Fiction Studies* 6 (1960): 55–64.

Bohner, Charles H. *Robert Penn Warren.* New York: Twayne Publishers, 1964.

Callander, Marilyn Berg. "Robert Penn Warren's *Chief Joseph of the Nez Perce*: A Story of Deep Delight." *The Southern Literary Journal* 16, no. 2 (1982): 24–33.

Chambers, Robert H., ed. *Twentieth Century Interpretations of* All the King's Men: *A Collection of Critical Essays.* Englewood Cliffs, N.J.: Prentice-Hall, 1977.

Clements, A. L. "Theme and Reality in *At Heaven's Gate* and *All the King's Men.*" *Criticism* 5, no. 1 (1963): 27–44.

Core, George. "In the Heart's Ambiguity: Robert Penn Warren as Poet." *The Mississippi Quarterly: The Journal of Southern Culture* 22 (1969): 313–26.
Davison, Richard Allan. "Robert Penn Warren's 'Dialectical Configuration' and *The Cave.*" *CLA Journal* 10 (1967): 349–57.
Edgar, Walter B., ed. *A Southern Renascence Man: Views of Robert Penn Warren.* Baton Rouge and London: Louisiana State University Press, 1984.
Fiedler, Leslie A. "Three Notes of Robert Penn Warren," In *No! In Thunder: Essays on Myth and Literature.* Boston: Beacon Press, 1960.
Gray, Richard. *The Literature of Memory.* Baltimore: The Johns Hopkins University Press, 1977.
———. *Robert Penn Warren: A Collection of Critical Essays.* Englewood Cliffs, N.J.: Prentice-Hall, 1980.
Grimshaw, James A., Jr. *Robert Penn Warren: A Descriptive Bibliography 1917–1978.* Charlottesville: University Press of Virginia, 1982.
———. "Robert Penn Warren's *Annus Mirabilis.*" *The Southern Review* n.s. 10 (1974): 504–16.
———, ed. *Robert Penn Warren's* Brother to Dragons: *A Discussion.* Baton Rouge and London: Louisiana State University Press, 1983.
Guttenberg, Barnett. *Web of Being.* Nashville: Vanderbilt University Press, 1975.
Justus, James H. *The Achievement of Robert Penn Warren.* Baton Rouge and London: Louisiana State University Press, 1981.
Kaplan, Charles. "Jack Burden: Modern Ishmael." *College English* 22 (1960): 19–24.
King, Richard H. *A Southern Renascence: The Cultural Awakening of the American South, 1930–55.* New York and Oxford: Oxford University Press, 1980.
Law, Richard G. "*Brother to Dragons*: The Fact of Violence vs. The Possibility of Love." *American Literature* 49 (1978): 560–79.
Lieberman, Laurence. "The Glacier's Offspring: A Reading of Robert Penn Warren's New Poetry." *The American Poetry Review* 10, no. 2 (1981): 6–8.
Longley, John L., Jr. *Robert Penn Warren.* Austin, Tex.: Steck-Vaughn, 1969.
———, ed. *Robert Penn Warren: A Collection of Critical Essays.* New York: New York University Press, 1965.
Moore, John Rees. "Robert Penn Warren: You Must Go Home Again." *The Southern Review* n.s. 4 (1968): 320–32.
Moore, L. Hugh, Jr. *Robert Penn Warren and History: The "Big Myth We Live."* The Hague: Mouton and Co., 1970.
Rotella, Guy. "Evil, Goodness and Grace in Warren's *Audubon: A Vision.*" *Notre Dame English Journal* 11 (1978): 15–32.
———. " 'One Flesh': Robert Penn Warren's *Incarnations.*" *Renascence* 31 (1978): 25–42.
Shepherd, Allen. "Robert Penn Warren as a Philosophical Novelist." *Western Humanities Review* 24 (1970): 157–68.
Snipes, Katherine. *Robert Penn Warren.* New York: Frederick Ungar Publishing Co., 1983.
Spiegelman, Willard. "The Poetic Achievement of Robert Penn Warren." *Southwest Review* 62 (1977): vi–vii, 411–15.

Strandberg, Victor. *The Poetic Vision of Robert Penn Warren.* Lexington: The University Press of Kentucky, 1977.

Tjanos, William. "The Poetry of Robert Penn Warren: The Art to Transfigure." *The Southern Literary Journal* 9, no. 1 (1976): 3–12.

Walker, Marshall. *Robert Penn Warren: A Vision Earned.* Glasgow: Robert MacLehose and Co., 1979; in the U.S. by Barnes and Noble Import Division of Harper and Row.

Wilcox, Earl J. "'A Cause for Laughter, A Thing for Tears': Humor in *All the King's Men.*" *The Southern Literary Journal* 12, no. 1 (1979): 27–35.

ROBERT FITZGERALD

Benet, William Rose. Review of *Wreath for the Sea. Saturday Review of Literature* 27 (29 Apr. 1944): 24.

Brinnin, J. M. Review of *In the Rose of Time: Poems. Yale Review* 46 (1957): 455–56.

Morse, Samuel French. Review of *In the Rose of Time: Poems. The New York Times* (17 Feb. 1957): 5.

Scott, W. T. Review of *Wreath for the Sea. Poetry* 64 (1944): 111–14.

Williamson, Alan. Review of *Spring Shade: Poems. Poetry* 119 (1972): 298–99.

ELIZABETH BISHOP

Alvarez, A. "Imagism and Poetesses." *The Kenyon Review* 19 (1957): 321–29.

Ashbery, John. "The Complete Poems." *The New York Times Book Review* 118 (1 June 1969): 8.

Bloom, Harold. "Books Considered." *The New Republic* 176 (5 Feb. 1977): 29.

———. "The Necessity of Misreading." *The Georgia Review* 29 (1975): 267–88.

Bogan, Louise. "On 'North and South.'" *The New Yorker* 22 (5 Oct. 1946): 121.

Booth, Philip. "The Poet as Voyager." *The Christian Science Monitor* 58 (6 Jan. 1966): 10.

Bromwich, David. "The Retreat from Romanticism." *Times Literary Supplement* (8 July 1977): 831.

———. "Verse Chronical." *The Hudson Review* 30 (1977): 279–92.

Brown, Ashley. "Elizabeth Bishop." In *Dictionary of Literary Biography.* Detroit: Gayle Research, 1980.

———. "Elizabeth Bishop in Brazil." *The Southern Review* 13 (1977): 688–704.

Davison, Peter. "The Gilt Edge of Reputation." *The Atlantic Monthly* 217 (Jan. 1966): 82–85.

Dodsworth, Martin. "The Human Note." *The Listener* 78 (30 Nov. 1967): 720.

Ehrenpreis, Irvin. "Loitering between Dream and Experience." *The Times Literary Supplement* (18 Jan. 1968): 61.

———. "Viewpoint." *The Times Literary Supplement* (8 Feb. 1974): 132.

Estess, Sybil P. "The Delicate Art of Map Making." *The Southern Review* 13 (1977): 705–27.

———. "Shelters for 'What Is Within': Meditation and Epiphany in the Poetry of Elizabeth Bishop." *Modern Poetry Studies* 8 (1977): 50–60.

Fowlie, Wallace. "Poetry of Silence." *Commonweal* 65 (15 Feb. 1957): 514–16.

Frankenberg, Lloyd. "Meaning in Modern Poetry." *Saturday Review* 29 (23 March 1946): 5.

———. *Pleasure Dome.* Boston: Houghton Mifflin, 1949.

Garrigue, Jean. "Elizabeth Bishop's School." *The New Leader* 48 (6 Dec. 1965): 22.

Gibbs, Barbara. "A Just Vision." *Poetry* 69 (1947): 228–31.

Goldensohn, Lorrie. "Elizabeth Bishop's Originality." *The American Poetry Review* 7, no. 2 (1978): 18–22.

Hamilton, Ian. "Women's-Eye Views." *The Observer* (31 Dec. 1967): 20.

Hollander, John. "Questions of Geography." *Parnassus* 5 (1977): 359–66.

Jarrell, Randall. "Fifty Years of American Poetry." In *Third Book of Criticism.* New York: Farrar, Straus and Giroux, 1969.

———. *Poetry and the Age.* New York: Farrar, Straus and Giroux, 1969.

Kalstone, David. "All Eye." *Partisan Review* 37 (1970): 310–15.

———. "Conjuring with Nature: Some Twentieth-Century Readings of Pastoral." In *Twentieth Century Literature in Retrospect,* edited by Reuben Brower. Cambridge: Harvard University Press, 1971.

Liebowitz, Herbert. "The Elegant Maps of Elizabeth Bishop." *The New York Times Book Review* 126 (6 Feb. 1977): 7.

Lowell, Robert. "For Elizabeth Bishop 1–4." In *History.* New York: Farrar, Straus and Giroux, 1973.

Mazzoco, Robert. "A Poet of Landscape." *The New York Review of Books* 9 (12 Oct. 1967): 4.

McNally, Nancy L. "Elizabeth Bishop: The Discipline of Description." *Twentieth Century Literature* 11 (1966): 189–201.

Merrill, James. "Elizabeth Bishop, 1911–1979." *The New York Review of Books* 26 (6 Dec. 1979): 6.

Moore, Marianne. "Archaically New." In *Trial Balances,* edited by Ann Winslow. New York: Macmillan, 1935.

———. "A Modest Expert." *The Nation* 163 (28 Sept. 1946): 354.

Moss, Howard. "All Praise." *The Kenyon Review* 28 (1966): 255–62.

Nemerov, Howard. "The Poems of Elizabeth Bishop." *Poetry* 87 (1955): 179–182.

Perloff, Marjorie. "The Course of a Particular." *Modern Poetry Studies* 8 (1977): 177–92.

Pinsky, Robert. "Elizabeth Bishop, 1911–1979." *The New Republic* 181 (10 Nov. 1979): 32.

———. "The Idiom of a Self: Elizabeth Bishop and Wordsworth." *The American Poetry Review* 9, no. 1 (1980): 6–8.

Rizza, Peggy. "Another Side of This Life: Women as Poets." In *American Poetry since 1960: Some Critical Perspectives,* edited by Robert B. Shaw. London: Carcanet, 1973.

Schwartz, Lloyd. "One Art: The Poetry of Elizabeth Bishop, 1971–1976." *Ploughshares* 3, nos. 3/4 (1977): 30–52.

Schwartz, Lloyd, and Sybil P. Estess, eds. *Elizabeth Bishop and Her Art.* Ann Arbor: University of Michigan Press, 1983.

Shore, Jane. "Elizabeth Bishop: The Art of Changing Your Mind." *Ploughshares* 5, no. 1 (1979): 178–91.

Smith, William Jay. "Geographical Questions: The Recent Poetry of Elizabeth Bishop." *Hollins Critic* 14, no. 1 (1977): 1–11.

Spiegelman, Willard. "Elizabeth Bishop's 'Natural Heroism.'" *The Centennial Review* 22 (1978): 28–44.

———. "Landscape and Knowledge: The Poetry of Elizabeth Bishop." *Modern Poetry Studies* 6 (1975): 203–24.

Wilbur, Richard. "Elizabeth Bishop: A Memorial Tribute." *Ploughshares* 6, no. 2 (1980): 10–14.

Williams, Oscar. "North but South." *The New Republic* 115 (21 Oct. 1946): 525.

GWENDOLYN BROOKS

Furman, Marva Riley. "Gwendolyn Brooks: The 'Unconditioned' Poet." *CLA Journal* 17 (1973): 1–10.

Hansell, William H. "Aestheticism vs. Political Militancy in Gwendolyn Brooks' 'The Chicago Picasso' and 'The Wall.'" *CLA Journal* 17 (1973): 11–15.

Hudson, Clenora F. "Racial Themes in the Poetry of Gwendolyn Brooks." *CLA Journal* 17 (1973): 16–20.

Hull, Gloria T. "A Note on the Poetic Technique of Gwendolyn Brooks." *CLA Journal* 19 (1975): 280–85.

Miller, R. Baxter. "'Does Man Love Art?': The Humanistic Aesthetic of Gwendolyn Brooks." In *Black American Literature and Humanism*, edited by R. Baxter Miller. Lexington: The University Press of Kentucky, 1981.

Smith, Gary. "The Black Protest Sonnet." *American Poetry* 2, no. 1 (1984): 2–12.

Spillers, Hortense J. "'An Order of Constancy': Notes on Brooks and the Feminine." *The Centennial Review* 29 (1985): 223–48.

Stetson, Erlene. "*Songs after Sunset* (1935–1936): The Unpublished Poetry of Gwendolyn Elizabeth Brooks." *CLA Journal* 24 (1980): 87–96.

Werner, Craig. "Gwendolyn Brooks: Tradition in Black and White." *Minority Voices* 1, no. 2 (1977): 27–38.

ROBERT DUNCAN

Bertholf, Robert J. "Shelley, Stevens and Robert Duncan: The Poetry of Approximations." In *Artful Thunder: Versions of the Romantic Tradition in American Literature in Honor of Howard P. Vincent*, edited by Robert J. DeMott and Sanford E. Morovitz, 269–99. Kent, Ohio: Kent State University, 1975.

Bertholf, R. J., and Ian W. Reid, eds. *Scales of the Marvelous*. New York: New Directions, 1979.

Creeley, Robert. "A Light, a Glory, a Fair Luminous Cloud." In *A Quick Graph: Collected Notes & Essays*, edited by Donald Allen, 195–97. San Francisco: Four Seasons, 1970.

Donoghue, Denis. Review of *Derivations: Selected Poems 1950–1956*. *The New York Review of Books* (7 May 1970): 35.

Olson, Charles. "Against Wisdom as Such." In *Human Universe and Other Essays,*
edited by Donald Allen, 188–202. New York: Grove, 1967.
Sorrentino, Gilbert. Review of *Derivations: Selected Poems 1950–1956. Poetry* 116
(1970): 110.

MAY SWENSON

Smith, Dave. "Perpetual Worlds Taking Place." *Poetry* 135 (1980): 291–96.
Stanford, Anne. "May Swenson: The Art of Perceiving." *The Southern Review* 5
(1969): 58–75.
Stepanchev, Stephen. "May Swenson." In *American Poetry since 1945.* New York:
Harper and Row, 1965.

RICHARD WILBUR

Cummins, Paul F. *Richard Wilbur: A Critical Essay.* Grand Rapids, Mich.:
William R. Eerdmans, 1971.
Dickey, James. "The Death and the Keys of the Censor." *The Sewanee Review* 79
(1961): 318–22.
———. "The Stillness at the Center of the Target." *The Sewanee Review* 70 (1962):
484–503.
Feverty, Frederick E. "The Poetry of Richard Wilbur." *Tri-Quarterly* 2, no. 1 (1959):
26–30.
Hill, Donald. *Richard Wilbur.* New York: Twayne Publishers, 1967.
Salinger, Wendy, ed. *Richard Wilbur's World.* Ann Arbor: University of Michigan
Press, 1983.

ANTHONY HECHT

Booth, Phillip. Review of *The Hard Hours. The Christian Science Monitor* (1 Feb.
1968): 9.
Carruth, Hayden. Review of *The Hard Hours. Poetry* 112 (1968): 424.
Howard, Richard. Review of *Millions of Strange Shadows. Poetry* 130 (1977): 103.
Lieberman, Laurence. Review of *The Hard Hours. Yale Review* 57 (1968): 601–3.
Meredith, William. Review of *The Hard Hours. New York Times Book Review*
(17 Dec. 1964): 17.
Simpson, Louis. Review of *The Hard Hours. Harper's Magazine* (Aug. 1968): 74.
Thompson, John. Review of *The Hard Hours. The New York Review of Books*
(1 Aug. 1968): 35.

JAMES DICKEY

Bly, Robert. "The Work of James Dickey." *The Sixties,* no. 7 (1964): 41–57.
Bowers, Neal. *James Dickey: The Poet as Pitchman.* Columbia: University of Missouri Press, 1985.

Calhoun, R. J., ed. *James Dickey: The Expansive Imagination; A Collection of Critical Essays*. Delano, Fla.: Everett/Edwards, 1973.

Glancy, Eileen. *James Dickey: The Critic as Poet; An Annotated Bibliography with an Introductory Essay*. Troy, N.Y.: Whitson Publishing Company, 1971.

Lieberman, Laurence. *The Achievement of James Dickey: A Comprehensive Selection with a Critical Introduction*. Glenview, Ill.: Scott, Foresman, 1968.

Silverstein, Norman. "On James Dickey." *Salmagundi* 22/23 (1973): 258–68.

DENISE LEVERTOV

Carruth, Hayden. "Four New Books." *Poetry* 93 (1958): 107–16.

———. "An Informal Epic." *Poetry* 105 (1965): 259–61.

Costello, Bonnie. "Flooded with Otherness." *Parnassus* 8 (1979): 198–212.

Creeley, Robert. *"Here and Now." New Mexico Quarterly* 27 (1957): 125–27.

Hartman, Geoffrey. "Les Belles Dames Sans Merci." *The Kenyon Review* 22 (1960): 691–92.

Mills, Ralph, Jr. "Denise Levertov: Poetry of the Immediate." *Tri-Quarterly* 4, no. 2 (1962): 31–37.

Ostriker, Alicia. "In Mind: The Divided Self and Women's Poetry." *Midwest Quarterly* 24, no. 4 (1983): 351–65.

Pack, Robert. "To Each Man His Own Muse." *Saturday Review* (8 Dec. 1962): 26–29.

Rexroth, Kenneth. "Levertov and the Young Poets." *The New Leader* (9 July 1962): 21–22.

Sautter, Diane. "Tacit and Explicit Tulips." *Pre/Text: Interdisciplinary Journal of Rhetoric* 1, nos. 1/2 (1982): 45–59.

Stepanchev, Stephen. *American Poetry since 1945*. New York: Harper and Row, 1965.

Wright, James. "Gravity and Incantation." *The Minnesota Review* 2 (1962): 424–27.

KENNETH KOCH

Dupee, F. W. "Kenneth Koch's Poetry." In *King of the Cats*. New York: Farrar, Straus and Giroux, 1965.

Gunn, Thom. Review of *Ko; or, a Season on Earth*. *Yale Review* 49 (1960): 592–98.

O'Hara, Frank. "Another Word on Kenneth Koch." *Poetry* 85 (1955): 349–51.

———. "On and On about Kenneth Koch: A Counter-Rebuttal." In *Standing Still and Walking in New York,* edited by Donald Allen, 62–63. Bolinas, Calif.: Grey Fox Press, 1975.

Rexroth, Kenneth. Review of *Ko; or, a Season on Earth*. *The Nation* (12 Mar. 1960): 233.

Spender, Stephen. Review of *A Change: Plays, Films, and Other Dramatic Works*. *The New York Review of Books* (20 Sept. 1973): 8.

Whittemore, Reed. Review of *The Pleasures of Peace, and Other Poems. The New Republic* (2 Aug. 1969): 23.

A. R. AMMONS

Bedient, Calvin. "Sphere." *The New York Times Book Review* (22 Dec. 1974): 12–13.
Bloom, Harold. "Emerson and Ammons: A Coda." *Diacritics* 3 (Winter 1973): 45–56.
————. "In the Shadow of Shadows: For Now." In *The Map of Misreading*, 198–203. New York: Oxford University Press, 1975.
Davie, Donald. "Cards of Identity." *The New York Review of Books* (6 Mar. 1975): 10–11.
Diacritics 3, no. 4 (1973). Special A. R. Ammons issue.
Fishman, Charles. "A. R. Ammons: The One Place to Dwell." *Hollins Critic* 19, no. 5 (1982): 2–11.
Hartman, Geoffrey H. "Collected Poems 1951–1971." *The New York Times Book Review* (19 Nov. 1972): 39–40.
Hollander, John. "Briefings." *The New York Times Book Review* (9 May 1971): 5–20.
Howard, Richard. "A New Beginning." *The Nation* (18 Jan. 1971): 90–92.
Jacobson, Josephine. "The Talk of the Giants." *Diacritics* 3 (Winter 1973): 34–39.
Kalstone, David. "Uplands." *The New York Times Book Review* (9 May 1971): 5–20.
Lehman, David. "Perplexities Embraced." *The Times Literary Supplement* (25 May 1984): 523.
Perloff, Marjorie. "Tangled Versions of the Truth: Ammons and Ashbery at 50." *The American Poetry Review* 7, no. 5 (1978): 5–11.
Rosenfeld, Alvin. "A. R. Ammons: The Poems of a Solitary." *The American Poetry Review* 5, no. 4 (1976): 40–41.
Wilson, Matthew. "Homecoming in A. R. Ammons's Tape for the Turn of the Year." *Contemporary Poetry* 4, no. 2 (1981): 60–76.
Zweig, Paul. "The Raw and the Cooked." *Partisan Review* 41 (1974): 608–12.

JAMES MERRILL

Berger, Charles, and David Lehman. *James Merrill: Essays in Criticism*. Ithaca: Cornell University Press, 1982.
Bishop, Jonathan. *Who Is Who*. Ithaca: Glad Day Press, 1975.
Brown, Ashley. "An Interview with James Merrill." *Shenandoah* 19, no. 4 (1968): 3–15.
Dickey, James. "James Merrill." In *Babel to Byzantium*. New York: Farrar, Straus and Giroux, 1968.
Donoghue, Denis. "Waiting for the End." *The New York Review of Books* (6 May 1971): 27–31.

Ehrenpreis, Irvin. "Otherworldly Goods." *The New York Review of Books* (22 Jan. 1981): 47–51.

Harmon, William. "The Metaphors and Metamorphoses of M." *Parnassus* 8 (1980): 29–41.

Kennedy, X. J. "Translations from the American." *The Atlantic Monthly* (Mar. 1973): 101–3.

Labrie, Ross. "James Merrill at Home: An Interview." *Arizona Quarterly* 38 (1982): 19–36.

McClatchy, J. D. "The Art of Poetry, 31: James Merrill." *The Paris Review* 24, no. 4 (1982): 184–219.

Moffett, Judith. "Sound without Sense: Willful Obscurity in Poetry." *New England Review and Bread Loaf Quarterly* 3 (1980): 294–312.

———. "What Is Truth?" *The American Poetry Review* 8, no. 5 (1979): 12–16.

Nemerov, Howard. "The Careful Poets and the Reckless Ones." *The Sewanee Review* 60 (1952): 318–29.

Parisi, Joseph. "Ghostwriting." *Poetry* 135 (1979): 161–73.

Sheehan, Donald. "An Interview with James Merrill." *Contemporary Literature* 9 (1968): 1–14.

Sloss, Henry. "James Merrill's 'Book of Ephraim.'" *Shenandoah* 27, no. 4 (1976): 63–91, and 28, no. 1 (1976): 82–110.

Spender, Stephen. "Can Poetry Be Reviewed?" *The New York Review of Books* (20 Sept. 1973): 8–14.

Vendler, Helen. "James Merrill's Myth: An Interview." *The New York Review of Books* (3 May 1979): 12–13.

White, Edmund. "The Inverted Type: Homosexuality as a Theme in James Merrill's Poetry." In *Literary Visions of Homosexuality*, edited by Stuart Kellog. New York: Haworth, 1983.

———. "On James Merrill." *The American Poetry Review* 8, no. 5 (1979): 9–11.

ALLEN GINSBERG

Bloom, Harold. "On Ginsberg's *Kaddish*." In *The Ringers in the Tower: Studies in the Romantic Tradition*. Chicago: The University of Chicago Press, 1971.

Breslin, James. "Allen Ginsberg: The Origins of 'Howl' and 'Kaddish.'" *The Iowa Review* 8 (Spring 1977): 82–108.

Hyde, Lewis, ed. *On the Poetry of Allen Ginsberg*. Ann Arbor: University of Michigan Press, 1984.

Kramer, Jane. *Allen Ginsberg in America*. New York: Vintage Books, 1968.

Merrill, Thomas F. *Allen Ginsberg*. New York: Twayne Publishers, 1969.

Mottram, Eric. *The Wild Good and the Heart Ultimately: Ginsberg's Art of Persuasion*. London: Spanner Books, 1982.

Simpson, Louis. *A Revolution in Taste*, 45–82. New York: Macmillan, 1978.

GALWAY KINNELL

Benedikt, Michael. "The Apotheosis of Darkness vs. Bardic Privilege." *Poetry* 121 (1972): 105–11.

Bloom, Harold. Review of *Mortal Acts, Mortal Words*. *The New York Times Book Review* (22 June 1980): 13.

Bogan, Louise. Review of *What a Kingdom It Was*. *The New Yorker* 37 (1 Apr. 1961): 130.

Davie, Donald. "Slogging for the Absolute." *Parnassus* 3 (1974): 9–22.

Dickstein, Morris. Review of *Selected Poems*. *The New York Times Book Review* (19 Sept. 1982): 12.

Pack, Robert. Review of *Flower Herding on Mount Monadnock*. *Saturday Review* 47 (14 Nov. 1964): 60.

Rosenthal, M. L. Review of *The Book of Nightmares*. *The New York Times Book Review* (21 Nov. 1971): 77.

Shaw, Robert B. Review of *Mortal Acts, Mortal Words*. *The Nation* 231 (8 Nov. 1980): 476.

JOHN ASHBERY

Auden, W. H. "Foreword." In *Some Trees* by John Ashbery. New Haven: Yale University Press, 1956.

Bloom, Harold. "John Ashbery: The Charity of the Hard Moments." In *Figures of Capable Imagination*. New York: Seabury Press, 1976.

———. "Measuring the Canon: John Ashbery's 'Wet Casements' and 'Tapestry.'" In *Agon*. New York: Oxford University Press, 1982.

Boyers, Robert. "A Quest without an Object." *The Times Literary Supplement* (1 Sept. 1978): 962–63.

Breslin, Paul. "Warpless and Woofless Subtleties." *Poetry* 137 (1980): 42–52.

Cott, Jonathan. "The New American Poetry." In *The New American Arts*, edited by Richard Kostelanetz. New York: Horizon Press, 1965.

Di Piero, W. S. "John Ashbery: The Romantic as Problem Solver." *The American Poetry Review* 2, no. 4 (1973): 39–41.

Donadio, Stephen. "Some Younger Poets in America." In *Modern Occasions*, edited by Philip Rahv. New York: Farrar, Straus and Giroux, 1966.

Ehrenpreis, Irvin. "Boysenberry Sherbet." *The New York Review of Books* (16 Oct. 1975): 3–4.

Erwin, John W. "The Reader Is the Medium: Ashbery and Ammons Ensphered." *Contemporary Literature* 21 (1980): 588–609.

Evans, Cynthia. "John Ashbery: 'A Moment Out of the Dream.'" *The American Poetry Review* 8, no. 4 (1979): 33–36.

Howard, Richard. "Sortes Virgilianae." *Poetry* 117 (1970): 50–53.

Jackson, Richard. "Writing as Transgression: Ashbery's Archaeology of the Moment: A Review Essay." *Southern Humanities Review* 12 (1978): 279–84.

Keller, Lynn. "'Thinkers without Final Thoughts': John Ashbery's Evolving Debt to Wallace Stevens." *ELH* 49 (1982): 235–61.

Kermani, David K. *John Ashbery: A Comprehensive Bibliography*. New York and London: Garland Press, 1976.

Kostelanetz, Richard. "How to Be a Difficult Poet." *The New York Times Magazine* (23 May 1976): 8–33.

Lehman, David. *Beyond Amazement: New Essays on John Ashbery.* Ithaca: Cornell University Press, 1980.

Lieberman, Laurence. "Unassigned Frequencies: Whispers Out of Time." *The American Poetry Review* 6, no. 2 (1977): 4–18.

Middleton, Christopher. "Language Woof-Side Up." *The New York Times Book Review* (17 June 1984): 8.

Molesworth, Charles. " 'This Leaving-Out Business': The Poetry of John Ashbery." *Salmagundi* nos. 38–39 (1977): 20–41.

Moramarco, Fred. "John Ashbery and Frank O'Hara: The Painterly Poets." *Journal of Modern Literature* 5 (1976): 436–62.

O'Hara, Frank. "Rare Modern." *Poetry* 89 (1957): 307–16.

Perloff, Marjorie. *The Poetics of Indeterminacy.* Princeton: Princeton University Press, 1981.

———. " 'Transparent Selves': The Poetry of John Ashbery and Frank O'Hara." *Yearbook of English Studies* 8 (1978): 171–96.

Shattuck, Roger. "Poet in the Wings." *The New York Review of Books* (23 Mar. 1978): 38–40.

Shetley, Vernon. "Language on a Very Plain Level." *Poetry* 140 (1982): 236–41.

Simon, John. "More Brass than Enduring." *The Hudson Review* 15 (1962): 455–68.

Spurr, David. "John Ashbery's Poetry of Language." *The Centennial Review* 25 (1981): 150–61.

W. S. MERWIN

Cassity, Turner. "Dresden Milkmaids: The Pitfalls of Tradition." *Parnassus* 5 (1976): 295–305.

Crunk. [Robert Bly] "The Work of W. S. Merwin." *The Sixties,* no. 4: 32–43.

Davis, Cheri. *W. S. Merwin: Criticism and Interpretation.* Boston: Twayne, 1981.

Nelson, Cary. "W. S. Merwin's Deconstructive Career." In *Our Last First Poets.* Chicago: University of Illinois Press, 1981.

JAMES WRIGHT

Butscher, Edward. "The Rise and Fall of James Wright." *The Georgia Review* 28 (1974): 257–68.

Crunk. [Robert Bly] "The Work of James Wright." *The Sixties,* no. 8: 53–78.

Deutsch, Babette. Review of *Collected Poems. The New Republic* 165 (17 July 1971): 27.

Lacey, Paul A. "That Scarred Truth of Wretchedness." In *The Inner War,* 57–81. Philadelphia: Fortress Press, 1972.

Mills, Ralph, Jr. "James Wright's Poetry: Introductory Notes." *Chicago Review* 17 (1964): 128–43.

Molesworth, Charles. "On James Wright." *Salmagundi* 1 (1973): 222–33.

Stitt, Peter. "James Wright: The Garden and the Grime." *The Kenyon Review* 4 (1984): 76–91.

IRVING FELDMAN

Dickey, James. Review of *Works and Days, and Other Poems. The New York Times Book Review* (24 Dec. 1961): 4.

Dugan, Alan. Review of *Works and Days, and Other Poems. Poetry* 100 (1962): 311–14.

Flint, R. W. Review of *Lost Originals: Poems. The New York Times Book Review* (25 Feb. 1973): 41.

Fussell, Paul. Review of *The Pripet Marshes, and Other Poems. Saturday Review* 48 (3 July 1965): 32.

Molesworth, Charles. Review of *New and Selected Poems. The New York Times Book Review* (9 Mar. 1980): 8.

Pritchard, W. F. Review of *New and Selected Poems. Poetry* 136 (1980): 298–99.

Sorrentino, Gilbert. Review of *Leaping Clear, and Other Poems. The New York Times Book Review* (19 Sept. 1976): 8.

Thompson, John. Review of *Leaping Clear, and Other Poems. The New York Review of Books* 23 (Oct. 1976): 33.

ADRIENNE RICH

Altieri, Charles. "Self-Reflection as Action." In *Self and Sensibility in Contemporary American Poetry,* 165–90. Cambridge: Cambridge University Press, 1984.

Atwood, Margaret. "Adrienne Rich: *Poems, Selected and New.*" In *Second Words.* Toronto: House of Anansi Ltd., 1982.

Gelpi, Barbara Charlesworth and Albert Gelpi, eds. *Adrienne Rich's Poetry.* New York: W. W. Norton and Company, 1975.

Howard, Richard. "Adrienne Rich." In *Alone with America,* 493–516. New York: Atheneum, 1980.

Hudgins, Andrew. " 'The Burn Has Settled In': A Reading of Adrienne Rich's *Diving into the Wreck.*" *Texas Review/Southwest Review* 2, no. 1 (1981): 49–65.

Kalstone, David. *Five Temperaments: Elizabeth Bishop, Robert Lowell, James Merrill, Adrienne Rich, John Ashbery.* New York: Oxford University Press, 1977.

McDaniel, Judith. *Reconstituting the World: The Poetry and Vision of Adrienne Rich.* Argyle, N. Y.: Spinsters Ink, 1978.

Vivley, Sherry Lute. "Adrienne Rich's Contemporary Metaphysical Conceit." *Notes on Contemporary Literature* 12, no. 3 (1982): 6–8.

ROBERT PACK

Engels, John. Review of *Guarded by Women. Poetry* 102 (1963): 403–4.

Kennedy, X. J. Review of *Home from the Cemetery. The Nation* 210 (30 Mar. 1970): 378.

Kermode, Frank. Review of *A Stranger's Privilege. Spectator* (6 Mar. 1959): 333.

Sullivan, Nancy. Review of *Home from the Cemetery. Poetry* 116 (1970): 123–25.

JOHN HOLLANDER

Bloom, Harold. *The Head of the Bed*. Boston: David Godine, 1964.
————. Review of *Spectral Emanations: New and Selected Poems*. *The New Republic* 179 (9 Sept. 1978): 42.
Carruth, Hayden. Review of *Crackling of Thorns*. *Poetry* 93 (1958): 107–9.
Flint, R. W. Review of *Spectral Emanations: New and Selected Poems*. *The New York Times Book Review* (28 May 1978): 4.
Gunn, Thom. Review of *Crackling of Thorns*. *Spectator* (8 Aug. 1958): 200.
Guttman, Allen. "Irving Feldman, John Hollander, Harvey Shapiro." In *The Jewish Writer in America*. New York: Oxford University Press, 1971.
Martz, L. L. Review of *Reflections on Espionage: The Question of Cupcake*. *Yale Review* 66 (1976): 114–19.
Pritchard, W. F. Review of *Blue Wine and Other Poems*. *Poetry* 136 (1980): 299–302.
Shapiro, Harvey. Review of *Crackling of Thorns*. *The New York Times Book Review* (7 Sept. 1958): 10.
Wood, Michael. Review of *Spectral Emanations: New and Selected Poems*. *The New York Review of Books* 28 (27 July 1978): 27.

ALVIN FEINMAN

Hartman, Geoffrey H. *Beyond Formalism: Literary Essays 1958–1970*. New Haven and London: Yale University Press, 1968.
Hollander, John. *The Poems of Our Moment*. New York: Pegasus Press, 1968.
Martz, Louis L. Review of *Preambles and Other Poems*. *Yale Review* 54 (1965): 611–13.
Spector, R. D. Review of *Preambles and Other Poems*. *Saturday Review* (13 Feb. 1965): 48.
Strickhausen, Harry. Review of *Preambles and Other Poems*. *Poetry* 107 (1965): 183–85.

GARY SNYDER

McCord, Howard. *Some Notes to Gary Snyder's Myths and Texts*. Berkeley, Calif.: Sand Dollar Press, 1971.
McLean, William Scott, ed. *The Real Work: Interviews and Talks 1968–1979; Gary Snyder*. New York: New Directions, 1980.
Molesworth, Charles. *Gary Snyder's Vision: Poetry and the Real Work*. Columbia: University of Missouri Press, 1983.
Paul, Sherman. *Repossessing and Renewing: Essays in the Green American Tradition*. Baton Rouge: Louisiana State University Press, 1976.
Steubing, Bob. *Gary Snyder*. Boston: Twayne Publishers, 1976.
Williamson, Alan. *Introspection and Contemporary Poetry*. Cambridge: Harvard University Press, 1984.

MARK STRAND

Bloom, Harold. "Dark and Radiant Peripheries: Mark Strand and A. R. Ammons." *The Southern Review,* n.s. 8 (1972): 133–41.

——. Review of *The Late Hour. The New Republic* 179 (29 July 1978): 29.

——. Review of *The Monument. The New Republic* 179 (29 July 1978): 29.

Crenner, James. "Mark Strand: Darker." *Seneca Review* 2 (April 1971): 87–97.

Ehrenpreis, Irvin. Review of *Selected Poems. The New York Review of Books* 28 (8 Oct. 1981): 45.

Lieberman, Laurence. Review of *Reasons for Moving. Yale Review* 58 (1968): 147–49.

AMIRI BARAKA

Dace, Letitia. *LeRoi Jones (Imamu Amiri Baraka): A Checklist of Works by and about Him.* London: Nether Press, 1971.

Dennison, George. "The Demagogy of LeRoi Jones." *Commentary* (Feb. 1965): 67–70.

Jacobus, Lee A. "Imamu Amiri Baraka: The Quest for Moral Order." In *Modern Black Poets,* edited by Donald B. Gibson. Englewood Cliffs, N.J.: Prentice-Hall, 1973.

Taylor, Clyde. "Baraka as Poet." In *Modern Black Poets,* edited by Donald B. Gibson. Englewood Cliffs, N.J.: Prentice-Hall, 1973.

JAY WRIGHT

Callaloo 6, no. 3 (1983). Special Jay Wright issue.

Hollander, John. Review of *The Double Invention of Ko. The Times Literary Supplement* (30 Jan. 1981): 115.

Pinckney, Darryl. "You're in the Army Now." *Parnassus* 9 (1981): 306–14.

DARYL HINE

Bennett, Joseph. Review of *The Wooden Horse. The New York Times Book Review* (4 Sept. 1966): 4.

Bewley, Marcus. Review of *The Wooden Horse. The New York Review of Books* 6 (31 Mar. 1966): 20.

Hoffman, Daniel. Review of *Minutes. The New York Times Book Review* (24 Nov. 1968): 59.

Rawley, J. M. Review of *Selected Poems. National Review* 33 (29 May 1981): 621.

Skelton, Robin. Review of *The Wooden Horse. Poetry* 109 (1966): 57–58.

Stevens, Peter. Review of *The Wooden Horse. Canadian Forum* 43 (Apr. 1966): 307.

Acknowledgments

"Introduction" [originally entitled "American Poetic Schools and Techniques (Contemporary)."] by Harold Bloom and David Bromwich from *Princeton Encyclopedia of Poetry and Poetics* edited by Alex Preminger, © 1974 by Princeton University Press. Reprinted by permission.

"Modes and Ranges of a Long Dawn" by John Hollander, © 1986 by John Hollander. Published for the first time in this volume. Printed by permission.

"The Poetry of Robert Fitzgerald" by Harold Bloom, © 1986 by Harold Bloom. Published for the first time in this volume. Printed by permission.

"Elizabeth Bishop's Dream-Houses" by David Bromwich from *Raritan* 4, no. 1 (Summer 1984), © 1984 by *Raritan*. Reprinted by permission.

"*A Street in Bronzeville,* The Harlem Renaissance and the Mythologies of Black Women" (originally entitled "Gwendolyn Brooks's *A Street in Bronzeville,* The Harlem Renaissance and the Mythologies of Black Women") by Gary Smith from *MELUS* 10, no. 3 (Fall 1983), © 1983 by the University of Cincinnati. Reprinted by permission.

"A Memoir and a Critical Tribute" (originally entitled "Some Duncan Letters—A Memoir and a Critical Tribute") by Denise Levertov from *Insight,* edited by R. J. Berthoff, © 1979 by New Directions Publishing Corp. Reprinted by permission.

"'Turned Back to the Wild by Love'" (originally entitled "May Swenson: 'Turned Back to the Wild by Love'") by Richard Howard from *Alone with America* by Richard Howard, © 1980 by Richard Howard. Reprinted by permission of the author.

"Richard Wilbur's World" by Robert B. Shaw from *Parnassus* 5, no. 2 (Spring 1977), © 1977 by the Poetry in Review Foundation. Reprinted by permission.

"The Poetry of Anthony Hecht" by Ashley Brown from *Ploughshares* 4, no. 3 (1978), edited by Dewitt Henry, © 1978 by Ploughshares, Inc. Reprinted by permission.

"From 'The Other' through *The Early Motion*" (originally entitled "James Dickey: From 'The Other' through *The Early Motion*") by Harold Bloom from *The*

Southern Review (Winter 1985), © 1984 by Louisiana State University. Reprinted by permission.

"Inside and Outside in the Poetry of Denise Levertov" by Diana (Surman) Collecott from *Critical Quarterly* 22, no. 1 (Spring 1980), © 1980 by Manchester University Press. Reprinted by permission of the author.

"Kenneth Koch" (originally entitled "Poetry in Review") by John Hollander from *Yale Review* 74, no. 4 (Summer 1985), © 1985 by Yale University; and from *Partisan Review* 27, no. 2 (Spring 1960), © 1960 by Partisan Review (originally entitled "Ko, or a Season on Earth by Kenneth Koch"). Reprinted by permission.

" 'When You Consider the Radiance' " (originally entitled "A. R. Ammons: 'When You Consider the Radiance' ") by Harold Bloom from *The Ringers in the Tower* by Harold Bloom, © 1971 by the University of Chicago. Reprinted by permission of The University of Chicago Press.

"Lost Paradises" by J. D. McClatchy from *Parnassus* 5, no. 2 (Spring 1977), © 1977 by the Poetry in Review Foundation. Reprinted by permission.

"Bound Each to Each" by Diane Middlebrook from *Parnassus* 2, no. 2 (Spring 1974), © 1974 by the Poetry in Review Foundation. Reprinted by permission.

" 'The Rank Flavor of Blood' " (originally entitled " 'The Rank Flavor of Blood': The Poetry of Galway Kinnell") by Charles Molesworth from *The Fierce Embrace* by Charles Molesworth, © 1979 by the Curators of the University of Missouri. Reprinted by permission of the University of Missouri.

"A Magma of Interiors" by Alfred Corn from *Parnassus* 4, no. 1 (Fall 1975), © 1976 by the Poetry in Review Foundation. Reprinted by permission.

"The New Transcendentalism: The Visionary Strain in Merwin" (originally entitled "The New Transcendentalism: The Visionary Strain in Merwin, Ashbery, and Ammons") by Harold Bloom from *Figures of Capable Imagination* by Harold Bloom, © 1976 by Harold Bloom. Reprinted by permission of Seabury Press.

" 'The Body Wakes to Burial' " (originally entitled "James Wright: 'The Body Wakes to Burial' ") by Richard Howard from *Alone with America* by Richard Howard, © 1980 by Richard Howard. Reprinted by permission of Atheneum and the author.

" 'Who Will Call These Things His Own?' " (originally entitled "Irving Feldman: 'Who Will Call These Things His Own?' ") by Richard Howard from *Alone with America* by Richard Howard, © 1980 by Richard Howard. Reprinted by permission of Atheneum and the author.

"Ghostlier Demarcations, Keener Sounds" by Helen Vendler from *Parnassus* 2, no. 1 (Fall 1973), © 1973 by the Poetry in Review Foundation. Reprinted by permission.

"Robert Pack" by Paul Mariani from *A Usable Past: Essays on Modern and Contemporary Poetry* by Paul Mariani, © 1984 by the University of Massachusetts Press. Amherst: University of Massachusetts Press, 1984. Reprinted by permission.

"The Sound and Sense of the Sleight-of-Hand Man" by David Lehman from *Parnassus* 12, no. 1 (Fall/Winter 1984), © 1985 by the Poetry in Review Foundation. Reprinted by permission.

"Preambles to What Was Possible" (originally entitled "The Dialectic of Romantic Poetry in America") by Harold Bloom from *The Ringers in the Tower* by Harold Bloom, © 1971 by The University of Chicago. Reprinted by permission of The University of Chicago Press.

"The Work of Gary Snyder" by Crunk from *The Sixties,* no. 6, © 1962 by The Sixties Press. Reprinted by permission.

"Negative Capability" by Linda Gregerson from *Parnassus* 10, no. 1 (Fall 1981), © 1981 by the Poetry in Review Foundation. Reprinted by permission.

"The Changing Same: Black Music in the Poetry of Amiri Baraka" by Nate Mackey from *Imamu Amiri Baraka: A Collection of Critical Essays,* edited by Kimberly Benston, © 1978 by Prentice-Hall, Inc. Reprinted by permission.

" 'The Aching Prodigal': Jay Wright's Dutiful Poet" by Robert B. Stepto from *Callaloo* 6, no. 19 (Fall 1983), © 1984 by Robert B. Stepto. Reprinted by permission.

"Fabulous Traveler" by John Hollander from *Canto* 3, no. 1 (1979), © 1979 by *Canto*; and from "Poetry in Review" in *Yale Review* 73, no. 1 (Fall 1983), © 1983 by Yale University. Reprinted by permission of *Canto* and Yale University.

Index

"Abnegation" (Rich), 298–99
"Accident, The" (Strand), 378–79
"Adam's Task" (Hollander), 335
Advent 1966 (Levertov), 80, 81
"Advice to a Prophet" (Wilbur), 107
"Afrikan Revolution" (Baraka), 408
"After Dark" (Rich), 298
"After Returning from Camden Harbor" (Pack), 310–12
"After the Judgment" (Feldman), 272
"Alarm, The" (Wright), 256, 257–58
"All That Time" (Swenson), 99
All the King's Men (Warren), 9
Alone with America (Howard), 113
"Alyscamps at Arles, The" (Swenson), 97
Ammons, A. R., ix, xi, 3, 6, 165–98, 245, 347
"An Agony. As Now" (Baraka), 399, 406–7
Annie Allen (Brooks), 44, 56
Another Animal (Swenson), 87, 88
"Another Animal" (Swenson), 89
"Another Night in the Ruins" (Kinnell), 230
"Apologia pro Vita Sua" (Ammons), 193–94
"Apprehensions" (Hecht), 125
"Approaching Prayer" (Dickey), 137–38, 139
"A. R. Ammons Discusses the Lacaria Trullisata" (Bly), 178–79
Ariosto, Ludovico, 157, 160, 161

"Armadillo, The" (Bishop), 34–35
Arnold, Matthew, 121, 217
"Arrondissements" (Hine), 424–25
"Art and Unhappiness" (Pack), 309
"Artist, The" (Koch), 158–59
Art of Love, The (Koch), 163–64
"Art of Love, The" (Koch), 163–64
Ashbery, John, ix, x, xi, 2, 3, 6, 199, 235–44, 339, 341–42, 345, 347
"As One Put Drunk into the Packet Boat" (Ashbery), 241, 341
"As You Came from the Holy Land" (Ashbery), 341
At Heaven's Gate (Warren), 9
"Attention" (Ammons), 196
"at the hairdresser's" (Brooks), 55
"At Thomas Hardy's Birthplace, 1953" (Wright), 256
Auden, W. H., 3, 24, 116, 117, 125, 126, 199, 202, 207, 223, 334, 335–36, 342
"August 19, Pad 19" (Swenson), 98
"Autumn Sequence" (Rich), 295
"Avenue Bearing the Initial of Christ into the World" (Kinnell), 222

"Babies, The" (Strand), 390
Bacon, Francis, 339
"Ballad of a Sweet Dream of Peace" (Warren), 10
Ballad of Billie Potts, The (Warren), 10
"Ballad of Chocolate Mabbie, The" (Brooks), 50

"Ballad of Pearl May Lee" (Brooks), 50–51

Ballad of the Brown Girl, The (Cullen), 50–51

"Baptism, The" (Wright), 414–15

Baraka, Amiri (LeRoi Jones), ix, 360, 395–409

"battle, the" (Brooks), 55

Bean Eaters, The (Brooks), 56

"Bear, The" (Kinnell), 226, 227, 230, 232

"Bearded Oaks" (Warren), 11

Beat Poets, 5, 359, 365, 368, 395, 397–98

Beautiful Changes, The (Wilbur), 103

Beckett, Samuel, 377

Beckonings (Brooks), 56

Beddoes, Thomas, 71, 76

"Behold the Lilies of the Field" (Hecht), 120

"Bending the Bow" (Duncan), 60, 69

Berryman, John, ix, 1, 2, 4

"Bessie" (Brown), 53–54

Bible, x, 216, 316

"Birth" (Feldman), 273

"Birthday Poem, A" (Hecht), 125

Bishop, Elizabeth, ix, x, xi, 1, 5, 27–42, 96, 316

"Black Dada Nihilismus" (Baraka), 404

Black Magic Party (Baraka), 396, 409

Black Mountain School, 4, 144, 149, 365, 395, 398

Blake, William, 86, 138, 139, 169, 186, 213–14, 215, 216, 222

"Blake's Songs of Innocence and Experience Tuned by Allen Ginsberg" (Ginsberg), 214

"Blight on Elm" (Hine), 422

Bloom, Harold, ix, 1–8, 19–25, 127–42, 165–98, 205, 245–50, 313, 320, 332–34, 347–55

Blues People (Baraka), 402

"Blue Wine" (Hollander), 330, 334

Blue Wine and Other Poems (Hollander), 327, 328, 331, 338, 339, 341

Bly, Robert, xxi, 5, 178–79, 225, 232, 260

Body Rags (Kinnell), 223, 226–31, 233, 234

"Book of Ephraim, The" (Merrill), 114, 200–9

Book of Nightmares, The (Kinnell), 226, 229, 231–34

Book of Resemblances, A (Duncan), 63

Borges, Jorge Luis, 377, 382

Borneman, Ernest, 402

Borregard, Ebbe, 71

"Boston Nativity, The" (Lowell), 121

Bowers, Edgar, 113–14

Branch Will Not Break, The (Wright), 254, 258, 259–60

Braving the Elements (Merrill), 200

"Brazil, January 1, 1502" (Bishop), 36–38

"Bridge, The" (Baraka), 400–402

Briefings (Ammons), 169, 183, 184, 188, 192, 195–98

Bromwich, David, x, 1–8, 27–42

Brooks, Gwendolyn, xi, 43–56

"Brotherhood in Pain" (Warren), 14–16

Brother to Dragons (Warren), 10, 12–13

Brown, Ashley, xi, 113–26

Brown, Sterling, 48, 51, 53–54

Browning, Robert, x, 3, 20, 189, 324

"Burning" (Snyder), 360, 362

"Burning Oneself Out" (Rich), 285–86

Byron, George Gordon, Lord, 161, 169

Cage of Spines, A (Swenson), 90, 91

Callimachus, 426–27

Calverley, Charles Stuart, 429–30

Cantos (Pound), 4, 63

Caroling Dusk (Cullen), 47

Carrier of Ladders, The (Merwin), 247–48, 249

"Cartagena" (Snyder), 359

"Cascadilla Falls" (Ammons), 194–95

Cassady, Neal, 218–19

"Centaur, The" (Swenson), 90–91, 96

"Center" (Ammons), 195–96
Ceremony (Wilbur), 104
Césaire, Aimé, 400
Change of World, A (Rich), 281–85
Char, René, 252
"Children of Darkness" (Wilbur), 109–10
"Chimes for Yahya" (Merrill), 209
"Christmas is Coming" (Hecht), 118–19
"Circumferences" (Feinman), 348, 350, 355
"Circus, The" (Koch), 163
"City Limits, The" (Ammons), 168, 169, 198
Clampitt, Amy, ix
"Clearing, The" (Baraka), 406
"Clouds" (Levertov), 74
"Clown and Destiny" (Feldman), 276–77
Cocteau, Jean, 72
"Codex" (Hine), 422–23
"Cohen on the Telephone" (Hollander), 339
Coleridge, Samuel Taylor, 134, 148, 179
Collecott, Diana, 143–55
"Collected Poems" (Koch), 159
Collected Poems (Wright), 263
Collins, William, 128, 134
Color (Cullen), 44, 49
Coltrane, John, 398, 405, 407
"Comedian as the Letter C, The" (Stevens), 36, 319
"Condition Botanique, La" (Hecht), 116, 117
"Copper Beech, The" (Hine), 421
Corman, Cid, 62, 357, 398
Corn, Alfred, ix, xi, 235–44
Corsons Inlet (Ammons), 169
"Corsons Inlet" (Ammons), 177, 179–86
"Cost, The" (Hecht), 123
"Cottage Street, 1953" (Wilbur), 108–9
Crackling of Thorns, A (Hollander), 328

Crane, Hart, x, 2, 22, 128, 134, 183, 213, 224, 245, 347, 350–51
Crase, Douglas, ix
Creeley, Robert, ix, 4, 62, 65, 144, 149, 222, 395
"Crispus Attucks" (Wright), 417
"Crocus Solus" (Hollander), 328, 339
Crunk, xii, 357–69
"Crusoe in England" (Bishop), 33–34, 41
Cullen, Countee, 44, 46, 47, 49, 50
cummings, e. e., 1, 44
Cunningham, J. V., 1, 422

Dante Alighieri, 77, 201, 207, 382
Darker (Strand), 377
"date, the" (Brooks), 54–55
Davie, Donald, 3, 333
Daylight Saving (Hine), 423, 426
"Days and Nights" (Koch), 164
Dead Lecturer, The (Baraka), 402
"Death of an Unfamiliar Sister, The" (Wright), 415
"Death of a Toad, The" (Wilbur), 107
Deren, Maya, 202, 209
Derivations (Duncan), 63
Devil's Picture Book, The (Hine), 423
Diamond Cutters, The (Rich), 290–93, 307
(Diblos) Notebook, The (Merrill), 204
"Dichtung und Wahrheit" (Hecht), 124
Dickey, James, ix, xi, 3, 127–42, 183, 245
Dickinson, Emily, x, 1, 2, 28, 38, 57, 86, 89, 105, 109, 111, 132, 183, 192
Dimensions of History (Wright), 415, 417
Divine Comedies (Merrill), 200–212
Divine Horsemen (Deren), 209
Diving into the Wreck (Rich), 285–90, 298, 303–6
"Diving into the Wreck" (Rich), 286–87
"Divisions upon a Ground" (Hecht), 116

Donne, John, 328
Doolittle, Hilda (H. D.), 62, 63, 143
Double Dream of Spring, The (Ashbery), 2, 236
Double Image, The (Levertov), 58, 59, 60
Double Invention of Komo, The (Wright), 415–17
"Dover Beach" (Arnold), 121
"Dover Bitch, The" (Hecht), 121
"Dream, The" (Hecht), 119–20
"Drinking from a Helmet" (Dickey), 137, 139–41
Drowning With Others (Dickey), 127, 135
"Drowning With Others" (Dickey), 132–34
Dryden, John, 430
du Bellay, Joachim, 119–20, 121, 125
Du Bois, W. E. B., 417
"Dudley Fitts" (Fitzgerald), 21, 23
Dunbar, Paul Laurence, 43, 44, 49
Duncan, Robert, ix, xi, 1, 4, 5, 58–83, 145, 398
Duplications, The (Koch), 160
"Dying" (Feldman), 272–73

Early Motion, The (Dickey), 136, 139
"Earth Psalm" (Levertov), 59
"East River" (Swenson), 93–94
Eberhart, Richard, 1, 222
Eliot, T. S., x, 1, 2, 3, 4, 12, 44, 45, 46, 48, 57, 71, 105, 150, 152, 153, 217, 248, 293, 327, 336, 337, 395
Emerson, Ralph Waldo, x, 1, 2, 3, 6, 8, 127, 128, 129, 136, 138, 148, 149, 165, 167, 168, 169–71, 172, 173, 177–78, 179, 186, 192, 245–46, 247, 249, 332, 336, 341, 348, 349, 350–51, 355
"End of a Chapter" (Hollander), 344
"End of March, The" (Bishop), 31
"end of the day, the" (Brooks), 54
Erikson, Erik, 213, 215

Esthétique du Mal (Stevens), 116–17, 119
"Evening in the Country" (Ashbery), x
"Evolution" (Swenson), 87–88, 97
"Exchange, The" (Swenson), 97
"Exile" (Hecht), 124
"Explorers, The" (Rich), 291
Expressions of Sea Level (Ammons), 171
"Eye, The" (Wilbur), 109
"Ezra" (Ammons), 166–67, 175–76

Faces in a Single Tree (Pack), 323–24
"Fall Comes in Back-Country Vermont" (Warren), 14
"Falling" (Dickey), 137, 138
Fall of America, The (Ginsberg), 213, 216–19
Family Pictures (Brooks), 56
"Feast of Stephen, The" (Hecht), 123–24
Feinman, Alvin, x, xii, 6, 127, 347–55
Feldman, Irving, ix, xi, 269–80
Figure of Echo, The (Hollander), 327, 330, 334, 338–42
"Filling Station" (Bishop), 36
"Firebombing, The" (Dickey), 138
"First Snow in Alsace" (Wilbur), 107
"Fish, The" (Bishop), 41
Fitts, Dudley, 19, 21
Fitzgerald, Robert, ix, xi, 19–25, 122
"Floating World, 3" (Po Chu-i), 366
Flood (Warren), 9
Flower Herding on Mount Monadnock (Kinnell), 223–26
"Flower Herding on Mount Monadnock" (Kinnell), 225–26
"For Now" (Merwin), 247
"For Robert Frost" (Kinnell), 223–24
"For the Conjunction of Two Planets" (Rich), 284–85
"For the Felling of a Tree in Harvard Yard" (Rich), 282–83
"Forties Flick" (Ashbery), 239–40
"Fountains of Aix" (Swenson), 96–97
"Fresh Air" (Koch), 163

Freud, Sigmund, 66, 128, 129, 134, 315, 316
"From a Litany" (Strand), 377
"From a Survivor" (Rich), 286
"Frontispiece" (Swenson), 92
Frost, Robert, x, 1, 2, 6, 30, 57, 92, 109, 153, 168, 247, 256–57, 309, 310, 315, 323, 324
Frye, Northrop, 128, 137

"Gardens of the Villa d'Este, The" (Hecht), 117, 118
Gates of Wrath, The (Ginsberg), 213–15, 216, 218, 219
Geography III (Bishop), 36
"Ghost of a Chance" (Rich), 294
"Ghost Ship, The" (Strand), 379—80
Ginsberg, Allen, ix, xi, 3–4, 153, 213–19, 222, 330, 365, 368, 396
"Giving Myself Up" (Strand), 372
"Gnome, The" (Feldman), 274
Goodman, Mitchell, 57, 62, 81, 144
"Grace" (Wilbur), 106
"Gravelly Run" (Ammons), 173
"Green: An Epistle" (Hecht), 125
"Green Lantern's Solo" (Baraka), 408
Green Wall, The (Wright), 253
Gregerson, Linda, xii, 371–93
Guarded by Women (Pack), 316
"Guardian, The" (Strand), 386
"Guerrilla Handbook, A" (Baraka), 399–400
"Guide" (Ammons), 173–74, 186, 187

"Hairy" (Swenson), 93
Half Sun Half Sleep (Swenson), 97–101
Hard Facts (Baraka), 396–97, 408–9
Hard Hours, The (Hecht), 115, 116, 118, 119–20, 121, 123
Hardy, Thomas, 11, 255–56, 309
"Harlem Dancer, The" (McKay), 49–50
Harlem Renaissance, 43–56
Harlem Shadows (McKay), 47, 48
"Harlem Shadows" (McKay), 53
Harris, Wilson, 418–19

Hawthorne, Nathaniel, 333
Hayden, Robert, 417
"Hay for the Horses" (Snyder), 358
H. D. (Hilda Doolittle), 62, 63, 143
"H. D. Book, The" (Duncan), 63
"Head of the Bed, The" (Hollander), 332
Hearne, Vicki, ix
Heavenly City, Earthly City (Duncan), 58, 60, 63
"Heavenly City, Earthly City" (Duncan), 60–61
"Heaven of Animals, The" (Dickey), 135
Hecht, Anthony, ix, xi, 3, 6, 113–26, 364
"Hegel" (Baraka), 404–5
"Helicon" (Hollander), 330
Helmets (Dickey), xi, 136–37
Here and Now (Levertov), 146
Hine, Daryl, ix, xii, 421–31
"History as Process" (Baraka), 398
Hollander, John, ix, xi, xii, 3, 6, 9–17, 157–64, 327–46, 347, 421–31
Homecoming Singer, The (Wright), 413
Home from the Cemetery (Pack), 315, 317, 319
Homer, 19, 427
Hope, A. D., 422
Hopkins, Gerard Manley, 105, 106, 147, 313
Howard, Richard, ix, xi, 3, 85–101, 113, 118, 121, 125, 134, 136, 169, 251–67, 269–80, 333
"Howl" (Ginsberg), 5, 222, 368
"How We Are Spared" (Merwin), 247
Hughes, Langston, 43, 44–45, 47, 49, 54
Hughes, Ted, 318
"Hunting" (Snyder), 360, 361
"Hymn" (Ammons), 171–72, 184, 196
"Hymn IV" (Ammons), 196–97

"If Anything Will Level with You Water Will" (Ammons), 192
"Images for Godard" (Rich), 301

"Imaginary Iceberg, The" (Bishop), 35–36
In and Out (Hine), 427, 431
"In Bed" (Koch), 159
Incarnations (Warren), 16
"In Celebration" (Strand), 377
Indian Journals (Ginsberg), 216, 217
"Inheritance" (Pack), 324–25
"In Limbo" (Wilbur), 108
In Place (Hollander), 327, 336, 339, 342–44
"Interpretation of Dreams, The" (Koch), 163
In the Mecca (Brooks), 56
"In the Mountain Tent" (Dickey), 135–36
"In the Woods and at Sea" (Snyder), 357
Into the Stone (Dickey), 127, 128
"Invitation to Madison County, An" (Wright), 415
Irony of Joy, The (Pack), 316
"It Out-Herods Herod. Pray You, Avoid It" (Hecht), 123
It's Nation Time (Baraka), 408

Jackson, Davis, 201, 202
Jakobson, Roman, 151–52
James, Henry, 129, 152, 343
"Janet Walking" (Ransom), 115
Jarrell, Randall, ix, 1, 2, 3, 107, 110, 222, 316
Jeffers, Robinson, 1, 60, 245
"Jeremiah" (Pack), 321
"Jitterbugs" (Baraka), 405
Johnson, Carol, 120
Johnson, James Weldon, 43–44, 45
Johnson, Samuel, 24, 107, 139
Jones, LeRoi. See Baraka, Amiri
Jonson, Ben, 331–32, 334, 335
"Joy" (Levertov), 154–55
"Juggler" (Wilbur), 106–7
Jung, Carl, 204–5, 211
Justice, Donald, 373, 377

Kafka, Franz, 342, 377
"Kansas City to St. Louis" (Ginsberg), 218–19
Keats, John, xii, 2, 33, 76–77, 128, 148, 153, 309, 310, 371
"Keeping Things Whole" (Strand), 374
Keeping Watch (Pack), 321
Kerouac, Jack, 365
Kinnell, Galway, xi, 3, 6, 222–34
"Kiss, The" (Pack), 313–15
"kitchenette building" (Brooks), 46
"Kite, The" (Strand), 380
Ko, or a Season on Earth (Koch), 160–63
Koch, Kenneth, ix, xi, 5, 157–64
Kora in Hell (Williams), 152
"Kursaal at Interlaken, The" (Rich), 283–84
Kutzinski, Vera, 417

"Lag, The" (Rich), 293
Lamentations (Hollander), 329–30
Landor, Walter Savage, xi, 19–20, 23, 25
"Landscape, Sicily" (Feinman), 349
"Landscape of the Star" (Rich), 290, 291
"Laser" (Ammons), 192–93
"Last Bus, The" (Strand), 389–90
"Last Will and Testament of Art Evergreen, The" (Pack), 312, 318–19
"Late August on the Lido" (Hollander), 328
"Late Autumn Daybreak, A" (Wright), 262–63
Late Hour, The (Strand), 372, 388, 389
Lawrence, D. H., 34, 137, 138
"Leaf, The" (Warren), 16
Leaflets (Rich), 298–99
Lehman, David, xii, 327–46
"Lemuel's Blessing" (Merwin), 247
"Letter" (Hollander), 344
Levertov, Denise, xi, 5, 57–83, 143–55
"Liar, The" (Baraka), 396
Lice, The (Merwin), 2, 247
"Liebestodt" (Levertov), 61

"Life at War" (Levertov), 83
"Lightning, The" (Swenson), 100
"Like This Together" (Rich), 298
"Linear A" (Hine), 424–25
"Lines" (Ammons), 181–82
"Lithuanian Dance Band" (Ashbery), 236–37, 241–42
Locke, Alaine, 47
"Logging" (Snyder), 360–61
Longfellow, Henry Wadsworth, 2, 248
"Looking at a Mountain-Range While Listening to a Mozart Piano Concerto" (Pack), 322–23
"Looking Over the Acreage" (Ammons), 197
Lorca, Federico Garcia, 395
"Lost in Translation" (Merrill), 209, 210
Lost Originals (Feldman), 279–80
"Love Calls Us to the Things of This World" (Wilbur), 107–8
"Love Lies Sleeping" (Bishop), 41–42
Lowell, Robert, ix, 1, 2, 3, 4, 33, 105, 115, 121, 199, 293
Lowry, Malcolm, 128
"Lucifer in the Train" (Rich), 290
"Lull, The" (Hecht), 125–26
"Lunch" (Koch), 159–60
Lycidas (Dickey), 134
"Lycidas" (Feldman), 280

McClatchy, J. D., xi, 199–212
McKay, Claude, 46–48, 49, 53
Mackey, Nate, xii, 395–409
MacLeish, Archibald, 248
"Mad Young Aristocrat on Beach" (Warren), 14
Magic Papers (Feldman), 278
"Mailman, The" (Strand), 383
Mallarmé, Stéphane, 85
"Man in the Mirror, The" (Strand), 376–77, 386
"Man-Moth, The" (Bishop), 31–33
"Manuelzinho" (Bishop), 36
Man with the Blue Guitar, The (Stevens), 57, 169, 185
"Märchenbilder" (Ashbery), 237

Mariani, Paul, xi, 309–25
Maritain, Jacques, 143
"Marriage in the Sixties, A" (Rich), 293
Marvell, Andrew, 11, 117, 331, 336, 341, 342
"Masseur de Ma Soeur, Le" (Hecht), 116
Mathews, Harry, 337, 344
Mathieu, Bill, 399
"Mathilde in Normandy" (Rich), 283
"May Day Sermon" (Dickey), 136, 137
"Measure of Memory, The" (Baraka), 402–4
Medieval Scenes (Duncan), 60
Melville, Herman, 2, 10, 183, 223
Meredith, William, 222
Merrill, James, ix, x, xi, 3, 6, 113, 114, 117, 199–212, 339
Merwin, W. S., x, xi, 2, 3, 6, 245–50
"Message Hidden in an Empty Wine Bottle that I Threw into a Gully of Maple Trees One Night at an Indecent Hour, A" (Wright), 258–59
"Metaphysical" (Fitzgerald), 23, 24–25
"Mid-August at Sourdough Mountain Lookout" (Snyder), 359–60
"Middle-Aged, The" (Rich), 290, 292, 295, 304
Middlebrook, Diane, xi, 213–19
"Milkweed" (Wright), 260–61
Miller, Joseph Hillis, 150
Miller, Perry, 180
Millions of Strange Shadows (Hecht), 115, 121, 123
Milton, John, x, 2, 6, 161, 216, 340
"Miltonic Sonnet" (Wilbur), 107
Mind-Reader, The (Wilbur), 103, 108
"Mind-Reader, The" (Wilbur), 111
Minutes (Hine), 421
Molesworth, Charles, xi, 221–34
"Moment" (Ammons), 176
"Monocle de Mon Oncle, Le" (Stevens), 116, 341, 423
Monument, The (Strand), 372, 387–88, 393
"Monument, The" (Bishop), 28–31, 33

Moore, Marianne, 1, 5, 34, 62, 109, 143, 150
"More Light! More Light!" (Hecht), 120
Moss, Howard, 3, 90, 364
"mother, the" (Brooks), 46
"Mother of the Blues" (Brown), 51–52
"Mount Blank" (Hollander), 328, 338, 341
Moving Target, The (Merwin), 2, 246, 247
Muir, Edwin, 105, 107
Mushroom Hunter's Field Guide, The (Bly), 179
"My Olson Elegy" (Feldman), 280
"My Optics" (Hine), 423–24
Myths and Texts (Snyder), 360–64

Nash, Ogden, 162
Necessities of Life (Rich), 295–98
"Necessities of Life" (Rich), 295–97
Nemerov, Howard, 222, 316
New British Poets, The (Rexroth), 58
New Negro, The (Locke), 47
"New-Sense" (Baraka), 404
News from the Cabin (Swenson), 93, 94
"New York" (Hollander), 331, 332
"Nightingale, The" (Hecht), 113
"Night in the Forest" (Kinnell), 227, 232
Night Mirror, The (Hollander), 333
Nights and Days (Merrill), 200
"Ninth of Ab, The" (Hollander), 329, 330
"Ninth of July, The" (Hollander), 329
"Ninth Symphony of Beethoven Understood at Last as a Sexual Message, The" (Rich), 285
"Nooksack Valley" (Snyder), 368–69
"No Particular Day" (Strand), 388
North & South (Bishop), 35, 36
"Northern Pike" (Wright), 261–62
"Note on the Imagination" (Levertov), 75
Nothing But Light (Pack), 319

"November Sunday Morning" (Feinman), 348–49, 351, 352
Now and Then (Warren), 17
"Now Full of Silences" (Pack), 320

"obituary for a living lady" (Brooks), 54
"Offset" (Ammons), 194
O'Hara, Frank, 5–6
"Old Guitar, The" (Hollander), 339
"old marrieds" (Brooks), 48–49
"Old Pier-Glass, The" (Hollander), 342–43
Olson, Charles, 1, 4, 62, 144, 145, 150, 222, 395–96, 398, 403
Ommateum, with Doxology (Ammons), 165–67, 169, 171, 172, 175, 184, 193, 198
"Once Removed" (Hecht), 115
"One Art" (Bishop), 35
"One Thing That Can Save America, The" (Ashbery), x
"On the Calendar" (Hollander), 330–31
"On the Eyes of an S.S. Officer" (Wilbur), 107
"On the Marginal Way" (Wilbur), 107
"On the Skeleton of a Hound" (Wright), 259
Or Else (Warren), 17
"Original Sin" (Warren), 10
Orlovsky, Peter, 365
"Other, The" (Dickey), 127, 128–32, 133, 142
"Out of my Head" (Swenson), 96
"Over Denver Again" (Ginsberg), 219
"Overland to the Islands" (Levertov), 145–46, 155
"Over 2,000 Illustrations and a Complete Concordance" (Bishop), 38–41

Pack, Robert, xi, 309–25
"Parade of Painters" (Swenson), 92–93

"Patches of Light/Like Shadows of Something" (Hollander), 343
Pater, Walter, 20, 312
Paul, Sherman, 168
Perelman, S. J., 160
"Periphery" (Ammons), 191–92
Perse, St.-John, 62
"Peter" (Wilbur), 109
"Philistinism and the Negro Writer" (Baraka), 404
"Photograph of an Unmade Bed, The" (Rich), 301
"Piazza di Spagna, Early Morning" (Wilbur), 106
"Pictures in a Gallery" (Hollander), 328
"Pilgrim Heights" (Feinman), 348, 351–52
"Place of Pain in the Universe, The" (Hecht), 119
"Planetarium" (Rich), 302
Plath, Sylvia, 4, 108–9, 291, 293
"Pleasures" (Levertov), 149
Po Chu-i, 366
Poe, Edgar Allan, 2, 75, 111
"Poem, The" (Kinnell), 226, 227–29
"Poem Is a Walk, A" (Ammons), 179
"Poetics of the Physical World, The" (Kinnell), 224, 225
Poetry, 58, 60, 125, 143
"Poetry, Personality, and Death" (Kinnell), 229, 231
"Poetry and Happiness" (Wilbur), 111
"Poetry and Karma" (Baraka), 395–96
"Poetry's Debt to Poetry" (Wilbur), 111
Pope, Alexander, 199, 327
"Porcupine, The" (Kinnell), 226, 227, 229–30
"Portraits" (Fitzgerald), 21–23
"Pot Roast" (Strand), 390–93
Pound, Ezra, x, 1, 2, 4, 5, 6, 57, 62, 71, 76, 143, 165, 221, 222, 245, 248, 395
Powers of Thirteen (Hollander), 327, 334, 337, 342, 344–46

"Prayer in My Sickness, A" (Wright), 255
"Prayer to My Father While Putting My Son to Bed" (Pack), 320
"Preambles" (Feinman), 348, 349, 352–55
Preambles and Other Poems (Feinman), 347–55
Preface to a Twenty Volume Suicide Note (Baraka), 401–2
"Pretext, The" (Hollander), 345
"Primary Ground, A" (Rich), 289
Pripet Marshes and Other Poems, The (Feldman), 274–78
"Projective Verse" (Olson), 62, 145, 150, 222
"Prologue" (Feldman), 274–75
Promises (Warren), 10, 14
Proust, Marcel, 392
"Psalm" (Merwin), 248
Puella (Dickey), 129

"Queen of the Blues, The" (Brooks), 51–53
"Question" (Swenson), 90
Questions of Travel (Bishop), 36

Raleigh, Sir Walter, 341
Ransom, John Crowe, 1, 104, 114, 115, 272
"Rape" (Rich), 287–88
"Red-Tailed Hawk and Pyre of Youth" (Warren), 137
Reed, Ishmael, 417
Reflections on Espionage (Hollander), 331, 336, 344
"Reflective" (Ammons), 188
"Relic" (Feinman), 349
"Remains, The" (Strand), 386–87
Resident Alien (Hine), 424
Responses (Wilbur), 111–12
"Return: An Elegy, The" (Warren), 12
Rexroth, Kenneth, 58, 144
"R. F., His Hand Against A Tree" (Swenson), 92

Rhyme's Reason (Hollander), 327, 330, 332, 334, 339
Rich, Adrienne, ix, xi, 281–307
Rilke, Rainer Maria, 66, 146, 148, 211, 349, 353
Rimbaud, Arthur, 161
"Ring, The" (Pack), 321–22
Riot (Brooks), 56
Riprap (Snyder), 357–60
"Rites and Ceremonies" (Hecht), 119–20
"River That is East, The" (Kinnell), 224
Robinson, Edward Arlington, 1, 2, 247, 256, 309, 355
Roethke, Theodore, 1, 2, 3, 128, 134, 137, 138, 168, 222, 224, 225, 245, 316, 318
Rollins, Sonny, 407
"Roofwalker, The" (Rich), 294
"Roosters" (Bishop), 27, 34
Rosenthal, M. L., 401–2
Rossetti, William Michael, 57
Roussel, Raymond, 339
"route of evanescence, A" (Dickinson), 109
Rukeyser, Muriel, 58
"Running" (Wilbur), 106

"Sadie and Maude" (Brooks), 54
Saint Judas (Wright), 255, 256
"Saliences" (Ammons), 177, 179, 184–89
"Samuel Sewall" (Hecht), 116
Sandburg, Carl, 2, 57
Sarraute, Nathalie, 237
"Satanic Form" (Swenson), 88, 98
"Save the Popular Song" (Baraka), 401
"Scales, The" (Koch), 163
"School Lesson Based on Word of Tragic Death of Entire Gillum Family" (Warren), 14
Schuyler, James, 5, 6
Schwartz, Delmore, 1, 364
"Scurry" (Swenson), 93

Sea and the Mirror, The (Auden), 117, 207
"Season in Hellas, A" (Hollander), 328, 341
Selected Poems (Ammons), 171
Selected Poems (Ashbery), x
Selected Poems (Strand), 372–93
Selected Poems, 1950–1982 (Koch), 157
Self-Portrait in a Convex Mirror (Ashbery), 235–44, 341
"Self-Portrait in a Convex Mirror" (Ashbery), 242–44
Seven Against Thebes (Aeschylus), 123
Sexton, Anne, 4
Shakespeare, William, x, 4, 11, 76, 125, 209, 257, 328, 335, 428
Shall We Gather at the River (Wright), 253, 259–60
Shapiro, Karl, 222
Shaw, Priscilla Washburn, 353–54
Shaw, Robert B., xi, 103–112
Shelley, Percy Bysshe, 31, 76, 129, 170, 213, 214, 216, 338, 341, 351
"Shooting Script" (Rich), 302–3
Sidney, Sir Philip, 345
Simpson, Louis, 6
"Six Million, The" (Feldman), 275–76
"Sketch, A" (Wilbur), 109
"Slave Quarters" (Dickey), 138
"Sleeping with One Eye Open" (Strand), 372–73
Smart, Christopher, 128, 216, 247, 248
Smith, Gary, xi, 43–56
Snapshots of a Daughter-in-Law (Rich), 293–94
Snodgrass, W. D., 4
"Snow" (Rich), 301
"Snow Log" (Ammons), 189–90
Snyder, Gary, ix, xii, 3, 357–69
"Solstitium Saeculare" (Fitzgerald), 23–24
"Somebody's Life" (Hecht), 123
"Some Notes on Organic Form" (Levertov), 72, 146–47
Something in Common (Hughes), 44
"Song" (Feldman), 277

"Song of Praise, A" (Cullen), 49
"Songs for the Air" (Hecht), 115
"Soonest Mended" (Ashbery), x, 239
Soothsayers and Omens (Wright), 415
Sophocles, 121, 122
Sorrow Dance, The (Levertov), 154
"Souls Lake" (Fitzgerald), 20–21
"South Beach" (Pack), 316–17
Southern, Terry, 162
Southern Road (Brown), 48
Spectral Emanations (Hollander), 327,
    328, 329–35, 339, 340
"Spectral Emanations" (Hollander),
    332, 333, 334, 345
"Speech for the Repeal of the Mac-
    Carran Act" (Wilbur), 107
Spenser, Edmund, 2, 10
Spring and All (Williams), 14
Spring Shade (Fitzgerald), 19
"Stanzas Written at Night in Radio
    City" (Ginsberg), 214
Stein, Gertrude, 62, 63
Stepto, Robert B., xii, 411–19
Stevens, Wallace, x, 1, 2, 8, 9, 30, 36,
    57, 75, 116–17, 128, 134, 142,
    146, 153, 160, 165, 168, 169,
    182, 189, 203–4, 239, 245, 247,
    252, 296, 309, 315, 319, 321,
    341, 342, 350, 421
"Stoic, The" (Bowers), 114
"Stone, The" (Pack), 318
Storm, Theodor, 255, 258
Story of Our Lives, The (Strand), 377
"Story of Our Lives, The" (Strand),
    381–83
Strand, Mark, xii, 3, 6, 371–93
Stranger's Privilege, A (Pack), 316
Street in Bronzeville, A (Brooks), 43–
    56
"Structure of Rime XXI" (Duncan), 74
"Study of History" (Rich), 300–301
Summer Session 1968 (Ammons), 194
Summoning of Stones, A (Hecht), 115–
    19
"Sundays of Satin-Legs Smith"
    (Brooks), 46
"Supple" (Swenson), 94

"Swan Dive" (Hecht), 123
Swenson, May, ix, xi, 85–101

Tale of Time (Warren), 14
Tales Told of the Fathers (Hollander),
    335
Tape for the Turn of the Year (Am-
    mons), 179, 189
"Tapestry" (Ashbery), x
Tate, Allen, 2, 4, 115–16, 119, 126
Taylor, Edward, 4
Tchicai, John, 402, 407
"Tenderness toward Existence" (Kin-
    nell), 234
Tennyson, Alfred, Lord, x, 2, 20
"Teresa" (Wilbur), 109
Thank You (Koch), 163
Theocritus, 427, 428–31
Things of This World (Wilbur), 107
Thomas, Dylan, 134, 144
Thoreau, Henry David, 2, 149, 153–
    54, 155, 170–71, 179, 180–81,
    217, 350
"Three Elementary Prophecies" (Fein-
    man), 349–50
Three Poems (Ashbery), 2, 236, 240
"Three Prompters from the Wings"
    (Hecht), 122
Thurley, Geoffrey, 150–51
To a Blossoming Pear Tree (Wright),
    264–67
"To a Soldier Killed in Germany"
    (Hecht), 115
"To Confirm a Thing" (Swenson), 89
"Today I Was So Happy I Made This
    Poem" (Wright), 260
"To Death" (Levertov), 59, 60
"Tomb of Stuart Merrill, The" (Ash-
    bery), 239
To Mix with Time (Swenson), 94–97
Toomer, Jean, 417
"To the Family of a Friend on His
    Death" (Pack), 316
"Tourist and the Town, The" (Rich),
    290
Trakl, Georg, 260

Trilling, Lionel, 272, 364
"Truth, The" (Swenson), 99
"Trying to Talk with a Man" (Rich),
  289–90
Tu Fu, 366–67
"Tunnel, The" (Strand), 374–76
Twain, Mark, 364
Two Citizens (Wright), 263–64, 265
"Two Songs" (Rich), 299
Types of Shape (Hollander), 330

"Uncle Speaks in the Drawing Room,
  The" (Rich), 282
"Under Aquarius" (Hollander), 335
Understanding Poetry (Brooks and War-
  ren), 9
"Unsaid Word, An" (Rich), 283
"Unsounded" (Rich), 283
"Untelling, The" (Strand), 381, 383–
  86, 387
"Upland" (Ammons), 190–91
Uplands (Ammons), 169, 183, 184,
  188, 191–95
"Upon the Apthorp House" (Hol-
  lander), 332, 334, 335–36

"Valentine, A" (Hecht), 115
Valéry, Paul, 86, 211, 239, 349, 350,
  353–54
Vendler, Helen, xi, 201, 281–307, 333
"Venetian Vespers, The" (Hecht), 114
"Venice Poem, The" (Duncan), 70
"Verse for Urania" (Merrill), 209, 211–
  12
"Vertigo" (Rich), 284
"Villa Adriana" (Rich), 290, 291
Virgil, xi, 19, 20, 24, 169, 341, 429
Vision and Resonance (Hollander),
  331–32
Visions from the Ramble (Hollander),
  329, 333
"Vow, A" (Ginsberg), 216–17
"Vow, The" (Hecht), 121, 122
"Vowel Movements" (Hine), 424–25,
  427–28

"Voyage in the Blue" (Ashbery), 241

Waking to My Name (Pack), 309, 315,
  322, 325
"Walking to Sleep" (Wilbur), 111
Warren, Robert Penn, ix, x, xi, 1, 9–
  17, 137
"Water" (Snyder), 367
Water Street (Merrill), 199–200
"Way Through, The" (Levertov), 67
"Way to the River, The" (Merwin),
  246–47
"Way We Walk Now, The" (Hol-
  lander), 344
Weary Blues (Hughes), 44
"W. E. B. Du Bois at Harvard"
  (Wright), 417
"Welcoming Poem for the Birth of My
  Son" (Pack), 317
"Wet Casements" (Ashbery), x
Wheelwright, John Brooks, 21–22
"when I die" (Brooks), 55
"When Sue Wears Red" (Hughes), 49
"When the Vacation Is Over for Good"
  (Strand), 386
"When We'll Worship Jesus" (Baraka),
  397
Whitman, Walt, x, xi, 1, 2–3, 5, 57,
  140, 141–42, 144, 150, 153, 160,
  165–66, 167, 168, 169, 186, 189,
  214, 216, 218, 222, 358–59, 368
Wilbur, Richard, xi, 1, 3, 103–12, 144,
  248, 315, 316
"Wild Sky, The" (Rich), 290
"Will, The" (Merrill), 204
Williams, William Carlos, x, 1, 2, 4–5,
  6, 14, 57, 58, 61, 62, 63, 67, 71,
  143, 144, 145, 146, 147, 150,
  151, 152–55, 213, 245, 286, 321,
  395
Will to Change, The (Rich), 299–303
Wimsatt, W. K., 425
"With Janice" (Koch), 164
Wordsworth, William, x, 2, 3, 16, 41,
  169, 179, 180, 189, 215, 216,
  310, 315, 324, 350

Works and Days and Other Poems
    (Feldman), 270–74, 275, 277, 278
World Enough and Time (Warren), 9
World Order (Duncan), 82
Wright, James, ix, xi, 3, 5, 6, 225,
    251–67
Wright, Jay, xii, 411–19
"Writer, The" (Wilbur), 108

"Yánnina" (Merrill), 209, 210

Yeats, William Butler, 16, 104, 122,
    123, 129, 137, 138, 142, 201,
    209, 213, 214, 316, 333
"Young Prostitute" (Hughes), 54
"Your Command" (Hollander), 345

"Ziz, The" (Hollander), 330
Zodiac, The (Dickey), 134, 137, 138
Zukofsky, Louis, 62, 63, 143–44